D1713745

Donated to

SAINT PAUL PUBLIC LIBRARY

BETWEEN EAST AND WEST
Finland in International Politics, 1944-1947

THE NORDIC SERIES   Volume 13

ADVISORY BOARD

BETWEEN EAST AND WEST

Finland in International Politics, 1944-1947

Tuomo Polvinen

EDITED AND TRANSLATED BY
D. G. Kirby and Peter Herring

University of Minnesota Press • Minneapolis

Published by the University of Minnesota Press,
2037 University Avenue Southeast, Minneapolis, MN 55414
Published simultaneously in Canada
by Fitzhenry & Whiteside Limited, Markham.
Printed in the United States of America.
Jacket photograph and book design by Gwen M. Willems.

The University of Minnesota Press appreciates assistance
from the Ministry for Foreign Affairs of Finland for this
English-language edition.

Library of Congress Cataloging-in-Publication Data

Polvinen, Tuomo.
    Between East and West.
    (The Nordic series ; v. 13)
    Abridged translation of: Suomi kansainvälisessä
politiikassa.
    Bibliography: p.
    Includes index.
    1. World War, 1939-1945 — Diplomatic history.
2. Finland — Foreign relations — 1917-1945.   3. Finland —
Foreign relations — 1945-   .   4. Finland — Politics
and government — 1917-1945.   5. Finland — Politics and
government — 1945-   .   I. Kirby, D. G.   II. Herring,
Peter.   III. Title.   IV. Series.
D754.F5P6513   1986   940.53'224897   85-20863
ISBN 0-8166-1459-8

Contents

Preface

The original Finnish version of my study of Finland in international politics, 1941-47, first appeared in three volumes between 1979 and 1981. The present translation covers more or less the latter half of the period, between the summer of 1944 and the autumn of 1947.

It has not been my intention primarily to write a history of the foreign policy of Finland in these years. Such a study would require far more on the internal background — economic life, public opinion, and political parties, for example. The problems of a small country cannot be considered in isolation; they have to be seen in a broader context, as a part of the pattern of international politics. My main task has therefore been to try to explain how the victors in World War II regarded the Finnish problem and what sort of solutions they deemed appropriate and best suited to their own interests. The attitude of the Great Powers toward the Finnish economy, and the question of war reparations in particular, has recently been the subject of a detailed study by Hannu Heikkilä. The main emphasis of my book is upon the political and military side. If it succeeds in presenting to an international readership a general picture of the settlement of one of the less crucial issues in the aftermath of World War II, then it will have served its purpose.

I wish to thank David Kirby and Peter Herring and my publishers, University of Minnesota Press and Werner Söderström, for working together in harmony to produce this English-language version. I would also like to thank the staffs of the archives and libraries mentioned in the Bibliography for their kind assistance. Transcripts of Crown copyright records in the Public Record Office appear by permission of the Controller of Her Majesty's Stationery Office.

T. P.

Foreword
D. G. Kirby

In the bitterly cold winter of 1939-40, the peoples of the Western nations looked on in sympathetic admiration as the Finnish Army fought, in atrocious conditions and against overwhelming odds, to preserve Finland's independence against the assaults of the Red Army. The British and French governments saw the conflict as an opportunity, on the pretext of intervention on Finland's behalf, to drive a wedge between the signatories of the Nazi-Soviet Pact and to deprive Germany of vital Swedish iron ore supplies. The plans for intervention were, however, to be overtaken by events. Finland was forced to conclude a peace treaty in Moscow on 13 March 1940. Less than a month later, alarmed by Allied activities in northern waters, Germany invaded Denmark and Norway. By the end of the summer of 1940, German armies had triumphed in the west and the Soviet Union had incorporated the three Baltic republics. The Phoney War was over; as armed struggle spread across the globe, the fate of Finland ceased to be an issue of great moment in the Allied countries. In the summer of 1941, the Finns were to find themselves on the side of Germany in a second war with the Soviet Union; by the end of the year, the British government had been persuaded by its new ally to declare war on Finland.

The growing anxiety of the Finnish leaders as it became clear that their once all-powerful cobelligerent was losing the war: the attempts of these men to extricate Finland before it was too late: and the final tumultuous crisis of the summer of 1944, when Finland did manage to break the link, only to be plunged into the uncertainties of concluding peace: this is the core of the first part of Professor Polvinen's widely acclaimed study. I have summarized it briefly here as a prelude to the story of how Finland fared in the increasingly stormy weather of the post-Yalta period.

In the gray winter months of 1944-45 — with high-ranking Russian officers lodged in the starkly functional building of the Hotel Torni in the center of Helsinki, supervising the carrying out of the terms of an armistice which seemed to many to presage the final elimination of Finland's national independence, and with little prospect of immediate aid from the Western nations to start the back-breaking task of reconstruction — the future looked grim. But if Finland had suffered defeat (and the presence of the Allied Control Commission was a permanent reminder of this fact), the country had avoided occupation. Here is a crucial difference between Finland and the other former satellite countries. In Bulgaria, Rumania, and Hungary, the old authoritarian regimes collapsed. In Finland, continuity was preserved, and the Finns themselves were able to make the necessary adjustments without recourse to violence or radical revision of the constitutional and political framework. It was the subtleties of the Finnish constitution which enabled Marshal Mannerheim to assume the presidency in August 1944 and to free his country from the binding alliance with Germany which his predecessor had been compelled to conclude in a personal capacity in June. The Finns were to have recourse to their constitution in future years when pressed by another authoritarian regime.

In his annual report for the year 1948, the British minister to Helsinki endorsed the comment made by his predecessor at the end of 1946: there was never any doubt that Paasikivi was not only the best man for the presidency, but very nearly ideally suited to it. Juho Kusti Paasikivi was a scion of the preindependence generation of Finnish nationalists who had preached the necessity of coming to terms with the geopolitical reality of Russia. He first served in government in 1908-09, and he was prime minister for five months in 1918. In the interwar years, he had been one of the few Finnish politicians to advocate a more accommodating approach to the Soviet Union. In the atmosphere of strident russophobia which befogged Finnish political life, his was a voice in the wilderness. Highly critical of the wartime policy of successive governments, and regarded by many as dangerously ''soft'' toward the Soviet Union, he was nevertheless entrusted with important diplomatic missions in 1939 and 1944. In the bitter days of defeat, he was to emerge as the only man of sufficient stature and determination to lead his country into the uncertainties of the postwar world. Like Winston Churchill, whom in many respects he resembled, his greatest moment was to come in the twilight of his life, at the time of greatest national need.

In the gathering gloom of the Cold War, the settlement of Finland's fate shines out as one of the few successes of the peacemakers. True, the peace which was finally concluded owed a lot to Finland's willingness to accept the terms imposed by the victors and to make the best of them: but by their willingness to break with the past and to forge durable good relations with the Soviet Union — the alpha and omega of Paasikivi's policy — the Finns have managed to secure a prosperity and an acknowledged status in the world which few could have foreseen in the nervous years of 1944-47. Professor Polvinen's study offers a rather different — and to British and American readers, perhaps a novel — perspective of the "shattered peace" and the polarized world with which we have had to live since 1945. His account of the painful and often hazardous path to peace for a defeated small nation is cast within the growing tensions of the Great Powers; but it is enlivened by his consummate ability to draw our attention to the foibles and human failings of the protagonists. Bathos and even elements of farce are intermingled with the solemnity of high occasions and moments of great tension. Professor Polvinen has woven these disparate elements together into a highly readable narrative. If this translation has succeeded in capturing some of the flavor of the original Finnish text, the following pages should provide an entertaining and instructive introduction to one of the most momentous periods of recent history and an explanation of Finland's present position in the world — not "finlandized," as some would maintain, but as a fully independent sovereign state whose foreign policy, forged in the harsh realities of war and defeat, is deemed by the Finnish people themselves as entirely consonant with national interests.

BETWEEN EAST AND WEST
Finland in International Politics,
1944-1947

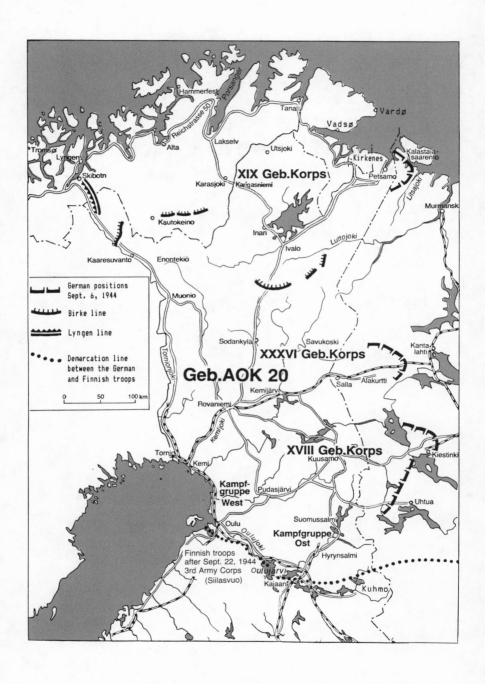

Hammerfest
Porsanger
Reichstrasse 50
Tanafi
Vardø
Vadsø
Alta
Lakselv
Utsjoki
Kirkenes
Tromsø
Lyngen
Kalastaja-saarento
Skibotn
XIX Geb.Korps
Petsamo
Karasjoki
Karigasniemi
Litsajoki
Murmansk
Kautokeino
Inari
Luttojoki
Ivalo
Kaaresuvanto
Enontekiö
Muonio
German positions
Sept. 6, 1944

Birke line

Lyngen line

Demarcation line
between the German
and Finnish troops

0   50   100 km

Sodankylä
Savukoski
Kanta-lahti
XXXVI Geb.Korps
Geb.AOK 20
Kemijärvi
Salla
Alakurtti
Rovaniemi
Tornionjoki
XVIII Geb.Korps
Torni
Kuusamo
Kiestinki
Kemi
Kemijoki
Kampf-
gruppe
West
Pudasjärvi
Uhtua
Oulu
Oulujoki
Suomussalmi
Kampfgruppe
Ost
Hyrynsalmi
Finnish troops
after Sept. 22, 1944
3rd Army Corps
(Siilasvuo)
Oulujärvi
Kajaani
Kuhmo

ARCTIC OCEAN

NORWAY

1940   '39

Petsamo
Pechenga

Murmansk

Jäniskoski

1944

KOLA

PENINSULA

1939

SWEDEN

Rovaniemi

Tornio

WHITE
SEA

Oulu

Belomorsk

GULF OF BOTHNIA

Kajaani

SOVIET

OSTROBOTHNIA

KARELIA

Murmansk Railway

FINLAND

Karhumäki

1940   1939
1944

Pori   Tampere

Mikkeli   Lake
           Saimaa

Petroskoi
Petrozavodsk

LAKE
ONEGA

OLONETS

Karelian
Isthmus

Saimaa canal

LAKE
LADOGA

Svir River

Turku

Vuoksi
R.

Åland Islands

Karjaa   Helsinki

Viipuri
Vyborg

Porkkala GULF   Suursaari
Hanko   OF FINLAND
                          Koivisto
                          Island

Leningrad

Naissaar   Tytärsaari

USSR

BALTIC
SEA

Tallinn

ESTONIAN   SSR

.... Finnish – Soviet border
               in 1939
–·–·–·– borders in 1940
–+–+– border of area ceded
       to Soviet in 1944 (1947)
–·–·–+ present borders

0   km   100

Introduction
Finland in 1944

In common with the other states that emerged from the ruins of the eastern European empires in the aftermath of World War I, Finland was swept into the conflict that engulfed the continent some twenty years later. Unlike these states, however, its part in the war and ultimate fate were rather different. In the winter of 1939-40, Finland fought its own war with the Soviet Union. Bereft of allies, the Finns put up a stubborn resistance before being worn down by the superior forces of the Red Army. By the terms of the Peace of Moscow (12 March 1940), Finland was compelled to cede one-ninth of its territory to the Soviet Union; but the republic survived with its independence and institutions intact. After an uneasy interim peace, Finland once more entered into hostilities with her eastern neighbor, this time as a cobelligerent of Germany. By the end of 1941, it had regained the lost territories and Finnish troops had penetrated deep into Soviet Karelia, where they were to remain for the next two and a half years.

The so-called Continuation War imposed severe strains upon the meager resources of a small country. As the tide of war turned after Stalingrad, the Finnish war leadership began to cast around for a way to detach the country from the German war machine and to conclude peace with the Soviet Union. In this final phase of war, the attitudes of the Western powers were to be of increasing importance, although the scope for Western intervention on Finland's behalf was limited by virtue of the Grand Alliance against Hitler's Germany, with whom Finland was still associated.

By 1944, the policy of the Western powers toward Finland had become firmly established. In December 1941, Britain had declared war on Finland at the request of the Soviet Union. The underlying principle of British policy was that the problem of a small northern state should not be allowed to upset relations with the Soviet Union, a Great Power seen as essential to the winning of the war against Germany. A strict policy of nonintervention in the Soviet-Finnish conflict was considered the best means to this end. Any initiative launched by the British to bring about a separate peace for Finland might arouse suspicions in the Kremlin about Britain's intentions. As Britain had no vital interests at stake in the region, it was thought more expedient to let Moscow and Helsinki settle their differences between themselves. Propaganda was nonetheless employed in an effort to sway Finnish public opinion towards a relaxation of the war effort and to bring the Finns to the point of turning directly to Moscow in search of a separate peace.

The situation was more complicated for the United States, which had not declared war on Finland. American public opinion was well disposed towards Finland, a circumstance that President Roosevelt's opponents on the home front sought to turn to their advantage. American voters took seriously the official war aims reflected in the phraseology of the Atlantic Charter—a fact of which Roosevelt was compelled to take note in his policy. If Finland could be weaned away from Berlin, the ideological character of the war would be greatly simplified and Finland might be steered toward a separate peace with the Soviet Union on terms acceptable to American public opinion—such, in broad terms, would be an ideal solution. Furthermore, the maintenance of diplomatic relations with Finland could be justified as a means of counterbalancing the political, military, and economic pressure applied by Germany to Finland. Washington also sought to undermine the war policy of the Finnish government by breaking up the solidarity of Finnish public opinion. The threat of retribution by Germany, should Finland try to leave the war, was considered a problem with which the Finns themselves would have to cope. As early as autumn 1941, Randolph Higgs, who was in charge of the Finnish desk at the State Department, expressed the view that the occupation of Finland by Germany would benefit the Allies because German forces would thus be tied up as in Yugoslavia. Wary of the possible reaction of the American public, however, Washington had to tread a cautious path in this respect.

In March 1943, an American offer of mediation to secure a separate peace for Finland failed because, in Washington's view, the two sides were too far apart. The Finns held fast to the frontiers of the pre-Winter War period; the Russians demanded those of the Peace of Moscow. For the Americans to exert pressure on Finland to accept Stalin's terms was considered unthinkable in view of public opinion in the United States, whereas to show dissatisfaction with the offer made by the Eastern ally was considered too risky for Soviet-American relations. In these circumstances, the United States found it necessary to withdraw the offer of mediation and to follow the same policy of nonintervention that London had adopted after December 1941. Diplomatic relations were not completely severed, however. Indirectly, recognizing the Finnish claim to be fighting a separate war, the Americans tried to ''supervise'' the Finnish government through the representatives of the United States in Helsinki to ensure that the Finns did not make too many concessions to the Germans. Active mediation for peace was not, however, to be taken up again by the Americans.

At the summit conference of the Big Three at Teheran in November-December 1943, Marshal Stalin was at pains to stress that an independent Finland remained one of the Soviet Union's war aims. Churchill and Roosevelt expressed their approval of the peace terms proposed by the Soviet Union for Finland, though the British prime minister doubted the ability of Finland to pay the war reparations demanded. Having expected the Soviet Union to demand unconditional surrender, Churchill and Roosevelt were agreeably surprised by Stalin's readiness to negotiate with Finland. Through their press and radio, and diplomatic channels in the case of the United States, the Western powers sought to induce the Finns to start discussions.

In December 1943, William Averell Harriman, the American ambassador in Moscow, received instructions from Washington to avoid bringing up the question of Finland because, as the instructions noted, "our status as an Ally of the Soviet Union makes our position in the matter somewhat delicate." The initiative in mediation for peace should be left to the Swedes, who, in the eyes of the State Department, "have a . . . vital interest in getting Finland out of the war as soon as possible."

In spring 1944, a new effort to secure peace betweeen Finland and the Soviet Union got under way in Stockholm. Before publishing the terms communicated to Finnish emissary J. K. Paasikivi in Stockholm during February 1944, the Soviet Union let its allies know the main points. Roosevelt directed Harriman to notify Soviet Foreign Minister V. M. Molotov that Washington appreciated the information received. Because the United States was not at war with Finland, it did not wish to comment on the terms but would be grateful for information about progress in the peace talks. This in fact occurred, with the State Department receiving verbatim reports of Moscow's correspondence with Helsinki throughout spring 1944.

The United States continued to refrain from active intervention during these talks. Harriman, inspired by a remark made by the Swedish chargé d'affaires in Moscow that the Finns regarded war reparations as the main impediment to approval of the peace terms in Finland, suggested that the United States might consider taking steps to help overcome this obstacle; but the suggestion met with no response from Washington.

The Western powers had also to take into account the possibility that Finland would refuse to accept the terms offered. In the opinion of the State Department, this would be grist to the mill of German propaganda and would also weaken the chances of detaching other small powers from the side of Nazi Germany. In addition, American inaction might create an unfavorable image in the neutral and occupied countries of Europe. Hugh S. Cumming, chief of the State Department's Division of Northern European Affairs, believed that the United States was faced with three main options: breaking off diplomatic relations with Finland; a mutual closing of the legations in Helsinki and Washington without a formal breach of relations; or a reduction of staff in the Finnish legation, bringing personnel strength in Washington down to the already reduced American representation in Helsinki. The issue of American-Finnish relations was not to be so swiftly resolved, though some pressure was brought to bear on the Finnish government and the legation in Washington.

In Finland, meanwhile, the terms presented by the Soviet Union were felt to be excessively heavy and were suspected as the thin edge of the wedge, leading to the final destruction of the country's independence. The West offered no guarantees. The belief in a German victory had long since vanished. In these circumstances, the Finns relied on delaying tactics in the hope that the expected landing in the West would act as a counterbalance to Soviet influence on the continent of Europe. President Risto Ryti and Foreign Minister Henrik Ramsay believed it might even be possible to stand aside until the collapse of Germany brought about a final settlement. Finland might then hope to take advantage of the circumstances of a general European peace.

The peace talks finally broke down in April 1944. U.S. Secretary of State Cordell Hull noted that neither side seemed willing to continue negotiations at this stage and that the point had been reached that would seem to favor the rupture of diplomatic relations between the United States and Finland. Such a step would weaken the position of the Finnish government at home and abroad, and it would certainly be viewed favorably in the Soviet Union. At this time, the Allies were planning a joint declaration to the small nations fighting on the German side, urging them to change their allegiance to avoid worse consequences. For this reason, the United States decided for the time being to relinquish the idea of separate measures affecting Finland. As the joint declaration failed to achieve its aim, however, the sands of time were beginning to run out for American-Finnish relations by June 1944.

Matters were more straightforward for the British government, since Britain was formally at war with Finland. Although the British believed it would be regrettable if the peace talks broke down over the question of war reparations, the terms presented by the Soviet Union were supported by His Majesty's Government. In spring 1944, the possibility of questions being asked in the House of Commons by members anxious to ensure a just peace guaranteeing Finland's independence compelled the government to contemplate an appeal to the Soviet Union to agree to a final settlement of the reparations payment as part of the general peace settlement. The breakdown of negotiations in the second half of April 1944, however, allowed the government to abandon this idea. No discussion of the Finnish peace issue ensued in Parliament.

In June 1944, the Soviet Union launched a full-scale offensive in the Karelian

Isthmus, driving the Finnish army back beyond the frontier of 1939. In London and Washington, observers believed the Finnish army to be on the verge of collapse. The Foreign Office noted that it was more important than ever for Britain to steer clear of the Finnish question. Talk of the preservation of Finland's independence might only encourage the Finns to hope for disagreements among the Allies: an "understanding" British attitude would merely increase the Finns' will to resist and might affront the Soviet Union. In these circumstances, American notions of a joint declaration by the three Great Powers, urging Finland to abandon the struggle, met with no response either from the Soviet Union or Britain.

The State Department now acted upon the question of relations with Finland. Of the three options outlined earlier that year by Cumming, the third was chosen: the Finnish minister to Washington and three officials at the legation were asked to leave the country. This action satisfied the Soviet Union and Britain, where it was felt that Finnish resistance had been strengthened by the belief that the United States would finally rescue Finland from its plight. This judgment was accurate because Washington's action, although not amounting to a final rupture of diplomatic relations, was seen in Helsinki as tantamount to "hitting a man when he's down."

Events were now reaching a climax. The Finnish government interpreted the Soviet reply to their offer of negotiations as a demand for unconditional surrender, which was not considered acceptable. In desperation, the Finns had to turn to Germany for help in warding off the Soviet attack. The Germans in turn exacted a heavy price for their assistance. On 26 June 1944, President Ryti handed German Foreign Minister Joachim von Ribbentrop a letter, addressed personally to Hitler and not countersigned, in which the president bound Finland not to make a separate peace. Unaccustomed to the ways of democracy, the Germans did not realize that the Finnish parliament's freedom of action had thus been preserved and that the president's personal agreement could be annulled later by his resignation from office.

Paying no attention to these constitutional niceties, the American chargé d'affaires in Helsinki considered that the last flickering hopes of Finnish freedom of action had been extinguished and that the moment for breaking off diplomatic relations had dawned. Cordell Hull agreed; on his recommendation, President Roosevelt decided to break off relations on the morning of 29 June—a decision officially put into effect by the State Department the next day. War was not declared on Finland, however. The policy long followed by Britain was now adopted by the United States. The Ribbentrop agreement permitted the United States to proceed without misgivings to a breach of relations, which at one stroke freed it from the troublesome burden of the Finnish question while removing the fear of a serious reaction from the American public.

PART I
Finland Leaves the War

1 Ceasefire (September 1944)

As Finland gradually began to edge toward the conclusion of a separate peace with the Soviet Union in the summer of 1944, the attitude of the Western powers toward the conflict remained unchanged. Both Britain and the United States saw the Soviet Union as primarily responsible for resolving the issue; for domestic reasons, however, Washington wanted the preservation of Finland's independence as Stalin had promised at Teheran. The Western powers had no wish to become involved in the details of the peace terms, such as the frontier question and the matter of reparations—even though it was acknowledged that these would pose problems for the Finns—because such involvement might affect their relations with the Soviet Union. For the time being, the Western powers preferred to leave Finland and the Soviet Union to settle these problems between themselves.

For the political leadership of the United States, the best solution would be a modus vivendi arrived at by both sides: the Soviet Union refraining from using its military strength to interfere in Finland's internal affairs, and Finland adopting a friendly policy towards the Soviet Union without becoming communist. "Such development would provide the basis, for the first time, to destroy the mutual mistrust between Finland and the Soviet Union which has heretofore blighted their relations with each other and would be conducive to participation by the two countries in the world peace organization to which we aspire." Forced bolshevization, on the other hand, would create a permanent hotbed of unrest in northern Europe. Finland's eventual participation in some sort of Nordic cooperation scheme within the framework of a world organization was acceptable in principle to the United States on condition that the Soviet Union agreed. Such a move should not be allowed to clash with general American economic policy. This reservation was clearly an indication of the desire of the American government, which favored an open-door policy, to prevent the formation of closed market zones after the war. In the short term, American policy was to continue putting pressure on Finland to conclude a separate peace with the Soviet Union. The Americans did not believe, however, that they could make promises of economic aid to Finland should peace be concluded. The United States would play no part in the drafting of the details of the armistice agreement, now or at any future date, but would welcome any information on this matter from its allies.[1]

The general outlines of British policy were presented to the War Cabinet on 9 August 1944 in a memorandum prepared by Sir Anthony Eden, the British foreign secretary. Eden surmised that Moscow would have two choices in its postwar foreign policy. First, to cope with the monumental task of reconstruction and to concentrate once more on the process of directing the planned economy, the Soviet Union might seek cooperation with the Western powers and possibly China, either within the framework of the United Nations or (if that organization failed to get off the ground) without it. Eden thought that this was the most likely possibility, provided the Kremlin was convinced of the Allies' intention of keeping Germany weak and did not begin to suspect that Britain and the United States were seeking to create a union of European states around a resurgent Germany.

As a second possibility, the Soviet Union might try to take advantage of its military gains during the war by continuing to expand and by trying, with the aid of the extreme left, to provoke an open conflict with the forces of imperialism. Eden did not attach much credence to this alternative. In the immediate postwar years, the Soviet Union would be particularly interested in Western economic aid and cooperation. The "negative" line of action might still have influential protagonists in the Kremlin, but Stalin personally belonged to the ranks of those who favored peaceful cooperation!

In its future relations with Russia, Eden suggested that Britain would have to observe a punctiliously correct, open, and businesslike course, without deviating in the slightest from its own ideological position. Insofar as the Soviet Union showed a desire to respect Britain's vital strategic interests, His Majesty's Government had no cause to oppose the wishes of the Soviet government provided they were reasonable and did not conflict with British interests. In this wide-ranging memorandum, Eden also paid attention to Scandinavia. There he could not foresee any incompatibility between British and Soviet interests. It was to be expected that Moscow would support left-wing parties in Norway, Denmark, and Sweden, but the communists' chances of success in these countries had to be regarded as extremely limited. There were no signs of any Soviet designs for territorial expansion in this area; on the contrary, Stalin had offered bases in Denmark and Norway to Britain in the Moscow talks in December 1941. Finland, on the other hand, belonged to the Soviet security zone. "Although we shall no doubt hope that Finland will be left some real degree of at least cultural and commercial independence and a parliamentary regime, Russian influence will in any event be predominant in Finland and we shall not be able, nor would it serve any important British interests, to contest that influence.''[2]

Of the states still fighting on the German side in 1944, the first to be drawn to the negotiating table was Rumania. The major offensive launched by Soviet troops on the river Pruth on 20 August 1944 had developed into a massive breakthrough, with the Russians rapidly advancing into the heart of the country. All measures of resistance having been rendered ineffective, the circle of officers and politicians associated with King Michael staged a coup on 23 August 1944, arresting the dictator Antonescu. The new government of General Sanatescu immediately sought a ceasefire, which the Soviet Union accepted. On 25 August 1944, Moscow agreed that the Germans should have until 15 September to withdraw from Rumania.[3] Hitler's attempt to overthrow the new government led to an open conflict between the former allies, and Rumania now changed sides immediately. Since no armistice terms had been agreed upon beforehand by the Soviet Union and the Western powers, negotiations with the Rumanian delegation in Moscow did not produce a decision until 12 September. According to the terms of the armistice agreement signed on that date, Rumania was to deploy at least twelve divisions (in fact, Rumania's contribution in the end turned out to be considerably greater than this minimum figure) in the war against Germany and Hungary. Operations would be conducted under the command of the Soviet military leadership. In addition, the Allied (i.e., Russian) troops were to be allowed unrestricted access to Rumanian territory to conduct operations against the Axis powers. Bessarabia and northern Bukovina were to be transferred to the Soviet Union in accordance with the terms of the 1940 agreement, but Rumania was to receive Hungarian Transylvania in compensation. The Soviet Union was to be paid an indemnity of $300 million in goods (petroleum products, grain, lumber, ships, etc).

In accordance with the principles adopted at the Moscow conference of foreign ministers in 1943, the Soviet Union, as the country that had borne the main burden of the war against Rumania, saw itself as having the right in the first instance to determine the terms of the armistice. The Soviet representatives on the Allied Control Commission, which was to be set up to ensure the execution of these terms, was to have the final powers of decision, in the same manner as the Western powers had maintained overriding powers of direction in Italy. The chairman of the Control Commission was Marshal Rodion Malinovsky, who signed the armistice agreement with Rumania on behalf of the Allies on 12 September. Although there was some concern in American circles that Rumania would come under the ''unlimited economic and political control of the Soviet Union,'' Harriman's instructions did not allow the American ambassador any scope for vigorous opposition. The preservation of good relations with the Soviet Union was still the overriding priority. Bearing in mind American public opinion, the Roosevelt administration sought to avoid getting involved in the confused affairs of the Balkans, where the United States had no major interests at stake.

The delay in signing the armistice agreement was caused in the first instance by the British, who were far more anxious than their American allies to play a part in the shaping of the future of the Balkans after the war. To prevent the Rumanian economy from sliding into a state of dependence upon the Soviet Union, the British sought to lower the costs of indemnification. Similarly, they wished to increase their power on the Control Commission. These efforts were in vain. His Majesty's Government now tried another tack. Since Moscow held fast to the principle that the members of the Control Commission could only contact Rumanian officials through the Soviet chairman, the British demanded the right to appoint a special political representative in Bucharest to maintain relations directly with the Rumanian government. This did not, of course, presuppose the restoration of official diplomatic relations. Molotov agreed to this proposal on the grounds that the Soviet Union had been offered a similar opportunity to send its representative to Italy. Objections were also not raised to the sending of an American political representative to Bucharest. Broadly speaking, therefore, the terms of the armistice agreement signed with Rumania on 12 September corresponded in all essentials to the aims laid down by the Russians.[4]

The crucial decision regarding Finland was made on the evening of 24 August 1944. It was reached at a meeting on board the train of the commander in chief and new president of the republic, Marshal Gustaf Mannerheim. Mannerheim had been elected president by the Finnish parliament when Ryti resigned the office at the beginning of August, after the Russian advance had been halted. Prime Minister Antti Hackzell; Minister of Defense Gen. Rudolf Walden; the leader of the Social Democratic Party and former minister, Väinö Tanner; and Georg Gripenberg, the Finnish minister in Stockholm, were also present at the meeting. Germany was continuing to deliver goods and provisions to Finland, so there was something to be gained by allowing the fateful decision to be postponed as long as possible. Nevertheless, those present at the meeting were unanimously of the opinion that Finland could no longer drag its feet. On 17 August, Marshal Mannerheim had bluntly informed Field Marshal Keitel that Finland intended to seek its own salvation and that the promise made by his predecessor President Risto Ryti, binding Finland to an undertaking not to seek a separate peace, was no longer valid. Fearful of what Hitler might do, the Finns had bided their time: but from Berlin there was no discernible reaction. Events in the Balkans appeared to be developing at a rapid pace. The Finnish parliament, recently returned from the summer recess, was also displaying signs of unrest. Prime Minister Hackzell pressed the case for a speedy decision by mentioning the possible danger of a Soviet air attack on Helsinki as a means of softening up the Finns. This might well result in the fall of the government, which would be blamed for unnecessary procrastination, and the formation of a new cabinet that would be prepared to make even greater concessions than the previous one.

After a formal cabinet meeting on the following day, 25 August, Gripenberg flew back to Stockholm with a letter signed by Foreign Minister Carl Enckell and addressed to Aleksandra Kollontay, Soviet minister to Sweden and a longtime friend of Finland. The letter proposed that negotiations be started in Moscow. The Soviet minister was to be informed verbally that President Mannerheim had told Field Marshal Keitel that he did not consider himself bound by the promise made to the German government by his predecessor.[5] Before making its decision, the Finnish government had ensured that Sweden would be willing to help Finland with food and raw materials in the period following a ceasefire.

That same evening, with the help of the Swedish Foreign Ministry, Gripenberg was able to meet Kollontay and to present her with his message. The reply from Moscow came four days later, on 29 August. Finland was to break off relations with Germany immediately and publicly and to demand the withdrawal of German troops from Finnish territory by 15 September at the latest. If Germany did not withdraw its troops from Finland within the stipulated period, they were to be disarmed and handed over to the Allies as prisoners of war. Fulfillment of these preliminary terms by the Finnish government was an essential precondition for any negotiations in Moscow. The French version of the text handed over by Kollontay to Gripenberg contained a fault in the translation, which had the *Allies* assuming responsibility for disarming the Germans and treating them as prisoners of war. This was only cleared up the following day when the Finns received the Russian text telegraphed from Moscow to the Soviet legation in Stockholm.[6] The ambassadors of the Western powers in Moscow were informed of the Soviet reply to Gripenberg's message by Molotov on 26 August. The British voiced their approval, in accordance with their established position, whereas the United States refrained from comment. Molotov promised to go into the details of the actual armistice at a later stage.[7]

In Helsinki, however, the mood was hesitant. Taking a leap into the dark by breaking off relations with Germany without knowing anything of the terms that the Soviet Union was contemplating seemed a difficult thing to do. Even the preliminary terms had proved to be unclear, as already indicated. If the Germans did not leave voluntarily within two weeks, Finland would be faced with a new war involving casualties and material losses. As it had in Rumania, would the Soviet Union demand freedom to operate in Finland as a condition of assistance, with all the far-reaching consequences that entailed? Mannerheim, anxious to share the burden of responsibility with his predecessor and leading figures in the previous government, invited Risto Ryti, Edwin Linkomies, Henrik Ramsay, Väinö Tanner, Antti Hackzell, and Carl Enckell to his residence on the evening of 30 August to discuss the Soviet Union's preliminary conditions. Erik Heinrichs, chief of general staff, also attended. In spite of their misgivings, those present decided unanimously to recommend a positive answer to Moscow. The course of the war indicated that there was no other way out. As Britain and the United States had ipso facto approved the offer (Kollontay had already passed on this information), hopes of any fundamental changes seemed unrealistic. Kollontay had stressed the danger of delay. She believed that the Finns ought to come forward and make their own proposals and show that they were genuinely seeking peace. It was also pointed out at the evening meeting at the presidential residence that the general mood of the populace during the summer months had turned decisively towards peace and that the threat of countermeasures by the Germans had receded. In Mannerheim's view, the period stipulated by the Soviet Union would suffice for the German troops in southern Finland to be withdrawn, though it was too short a period within which to deal with the troops in Lapland.[8]

On the following day, Kollontay clarified the preliminary terms at the request of the Finns and on the basis of information received from Moscow. The public breach of relations with Germany was essential for the Russians as an indication that the Finns were in earnest about the withdrawal of German troops. As the form of words in the preliminary proposal of terms indicated, there was no need to inform the Germans *who* was to disarm them. Finland and the Soviet Union could work out the practical details later. Kollontay had informed Erik Boheman, secretary-general of the Swedish Foreign Ministry, that "it is Moscow's understanding that the Finns cannot disarm the German troops in Lapland in any event, and this is not demanded. On the contrary, she had assured [Boheman] that Moscow was ready to come to some agreement on how these troops were to be disarmed." The presentation of the ultimatum to the Germans, and its publication, would suffice as a fulfillment of the preliminary terms. It was not intended that the Finnish delegation would be allowed to go to Moscow only after the German troops operating in Finland had been disarmed.[9]

Kollontay's information was an encouragement for the Finnish government. On the question of the German troops in Lapland, the Soviet minister—afraid that the peace negotiations might break down—may have given the Finns a rather generous interpretation of her government's demands. On the basis of Gripenberg's telegram of 31 August, which contained the details of Kollontay's talks with Boheman, the Finnish Foreign Ministry now seemed to believe that the Soviet Union would not insist upon Finland disarming General Rendulic's troops stationed in Lapland.[10] To her diplomatic colleagues in Stockholm, Kollontay voiced her grave anxiety about the slowness of the Finns, which the Kremlin might intercept as a sign of lack of good will.[11]

Moscow had clearly learned a lesson from the experiences of the previous spring, when negotiations with Finland had collapsed. This time, the Finns were to be made to commit themselves decisively to peace. The breach of relations with Berlin and the evacuation of German troops from at least the greater part of the country would render a return to a policy of continuing the war a practical impossibility. From the Finnish point of view, the situation was eased by the absence of any demand for surrender and by the fact that the period within which the Germans were to leave Finland extended to the middle of September: in spring, the Russians had demanded immediate measures to intern German troops.[12]

The president now set course according to the information emanating from the Swedish capital. Lt. Gen. Oscar Enckell received instructions to travel to Stockholm to propose to the Soviet representatives there an extension of the deadline. When Boheman refused point-blank to act as intermediary, this venture was abandoned because it would clearly be interpreted in Moscow as a delaying tactic. Kollontay and her subordinates were, moreover, not even empowered to negotiate on such matters. Instead, Mannerheim addressed himself directly to Stalin that very same day (1 September) by telegram "in order to be able to confirm that Finland truly was capable of fulfilling that which she promised." Finland could take care of the voluntary evacuation or the internment of German troops located south of the line from Oulujoki through Oulujärvi to Sotkamo. It could also defend this line from attacks from the north or by sea. This necessitated the release of enough troops to carry out these tasks, however, and for this reason hostilities on the Finnish-Soviet front would have to be brought to a conclusion as soon as possible—Mannerheim suggested 0800 hours on 3 September. The withdrawal of Finnish troops to the frontier established by the Peace of Moscow in 1940 could in that event commence on 6 September, while to avoid incidents Soviet units should begin their advance two days later. Thereafter Mannerheim could guarantee that his troops would have withdrawn behind the 1940 frontier line by 20 September. Providing these proposals were acceptable, Mannerheim thought Finland capable of meeting the preliminary terms demanded by Moscow.[13]

In his telegram, Mannerheim appears to have excluded (at least for the time being) any possibility of a Finnish offensive in Lapland. Gripenberg had, however, given the Soviet legation to understand that the Finns would take part in the disarming operations against the Germans in Lapland, though they wanted first to reach agreement with the Soviet military leaders in Moscow over coordination of operations and assistance for this task. This information was relayed to Moscow by Kollontay. But in later discussions with the Soviet minister, Gripenberg denied that he had given any such understanding. He had not added anything to the views expressed by Mannerheim in his telegram. This "correction" was not reported to Moscow by Kollontay and Vladimir Semyonov, the counsellor at the Soviet legation, because they believed that the Kremlin would in consequence refuse to receive the Finnish peace delegation. Helsinki had announced, to be sure, that Finnish resources were insufficient to disarm the Germans in Lapland; but this did not mean that Finland would not in any way participate in this operation stipulated in the preliminary terms. The *extent* of Finnish participation, on the other hand, could be discussed in Moscow, as Kollontay and Semyonov had already indicated on 2 September.[14] On the basis of the evidence now available, it is impossible to say what these differences of interpretation signify. If Gripenberg's claim is valid, it is likely that Kollontay, who feared a breakdown in the peace talks, prepared her report in the light of what she estimated were the prevalent anticipations in Moscow. Since the conversation between Gripenberg and Semyonov was conducted through an interpreter, the possibility of a faulty interpretation or misunderstanding cannot entirely be ruled out. In any event, the seeds for a subsequent clash of views had been sown.

It is also important to note that the Finnish president was prepared at this stage, before the commencement of actual negotiations, to evacuate Karelia as far as the frontiers of 1940. Behind the ceasefire proposal lay a desire to improve the atmosphere in which negotiations would be conducted, as well as a natural wish to bring an end to the bloodshed as soon as possible and to ensure that the expected withdrawal of troops would take place in maximum favorable circumstances. In addition, according to Heinrichs, Mannerheim was troubled by the thought that any delay in securing a ceasefire might bring about a Soviet offensive against Finnish forces at the same time as they were preparing to fight the Germans. In a simultaneous war against two major powers, the resources of a small state were simply not enough. Heinrichs admits that Mannerheim's suspicions of Soviet intentions were groundless, which does not alter the fact that this was the way many people were thinking at the time.[15]

Mannerheim now acted swiftly. Before the Soviet reply had time to reach Finland, parliament was called into secret session on the evening of 2 September and Prime Minister Hackzell announced the opening of discussions with the Soviet Union and the decision to sue for peace. The Social Democrats, the Swedish People's Party, and the Liberals proclaimed their acceptance of the decision and appealed to the other parties to join in unanimous approval of the government's action. The chairmen of the Agrarian and conservative Coalition Party groups were, however, compelled to announce that their members were divided in their views. Of the Agrarian parliamentary group, only five members approved the government's measures. In the final vote, the government won the day by 108 to 45 votes. Many M.P.s had not managed to make it to the hastily convened session, some stayed away for tactical reasons, and one abstained.[16]

Immediately after the session of parliament, the prime minister broadcast news of the decision to the nation. The former prime minister Edwin Linkomies, recalled: "I spoke with Hackzell for a moment in the Speakers' room in the parliament building, just before he went to broadcast his message. He seemed extremely tired and kept on arranging the sheets of the manuscript of his speech, which had somehow become muddled up."[17] In fact, one important detail was left out of the speech—that Finland was to break off relations with Germany immediately. This was naturally seized upon by the Soviet Union as an indication that Finland was again playing for time, and Hackzell's carelessness was seen as a deliberate ploy. Matters were not improved when Foreign Minister Carl Enckell forgot to inform the Soviet Union officially, via Stockholm, of his announcement of a breach of relations to the German minister in Helsinki that evening. With President and Commander in Chief Mannerheim in his headquarters in Mikkeli for most of the time, the political leadership of the country in Helsinki was in the hands of old men (Hackzell, Walden, Enckell) who were worn out by considerable physical and mental stress and rapidly reaching the limits of their endurance in new and demanding circumstances.[18]

Kollontay reached her own conclusions from Hackzell's speech. Around midnight that same evening she telephoned Boheman, shedding tears of joy "because Finland is now saved."[19] The secretary-general told Gripenberg that anyone overhearing the telephone conversation would quite easily have suspected Boheman of being "a Soviet agent," so lavish were Kollontay's thanks for his activities as an intermediary. On the following day, 3 September, the reply to Mannerheim's proposals was received from Moscow. Counsellor Semyonov, having received the message, rang Boheman, who had already gone to bed, asking him to arrange without delay a meeting with Gripenberg in the secretary-general's apartment on Strandvägen. Hastily donning his dressing gown, Boheman rushed down the staircase to open the door for his visitors. Gripenberg having just arrived, the doorknob slipped from the grasp of the half-awake secretary-general and the outer door slammed shut, leaving the two men outside on the steps. Telephone calls from a nearby kiosk failed to rouse Boheman's soundly sleeping Danish housekeeper. For a moment it seemed as if the ceasefire would have to be negotiated by a pyjama-clad intermediary on a park bench in Strandvägen. A few seconds before Semyonov arrived, however, a couple of other residents in the same house turned up and let the men in.[20]

Semyonov now announced that the Soviet government remained absolutely committed to its preliminary terms; the Finnish government was to declare publicly that it had broken off relations with Germany and had demanded the withdrawal of German troops from Finnish territory by 15 September at the latest. All German troops who remained after the deadline were to be disarmed and handed over as prisoners of war to the Allies. If these terms were met, the Soviet Union was ready to offer armed assistance to enable the task to be carried out. If Helsinki issued the aforementioned declaration, Moscow was prepared to cease military activities on the Finnish front at 0800 hours on 4 September. All other questions could be discussed at the armistice negotiations.[21] The "other questions" of Semyonov's message included the withdrawal of Finnish troops behind the 1940 frontier, as proposed by Mannerheim. This measure would have to wait until the negotiations: considerably more time was thus gained for the evacuation of Karelia.

The ceasefire, on the other hand, was rapidly becoming a pressing matter. There was only a few hours left before the time proposed by the Soviet Union for the guns to fall silent. Boheman, Gripenberg, and Semyonov drafted a proposed communiqué there and then in the secretary-general's apartment that was to be immediately published by the Finnish government:

> The government of Finland has broken off relations with Germany and has demanded the withdrawal of German troops from Finland by 15 September at the latest. In the event of German troops not having been evacuated by the deadline date, they will be disarmed and handed over as prisoners of war to the Allies.

Gripenberg tried in vain to reach Enckell by telephone from Boheman's apartment to relay the text of the communiqué to Helsinki. Only after he had returned to the legation after midnight did he finally manage to get in touch with the foreign minister, who promised to take action straight away. Enckell dictated the communiqué to the Finnish News Agency (STT) for dispatch to the press and radio and got in touch with army headquarters. After the chief of general staff had made sure that the news would reach all units in time, the army received the order of the commander in chief to cease fire that morning (4 September) at 0800 hours. At 2:30 a.m. Gripenberg reported on these measures to Semyonov, who promised immediately to relay to Moscow the news that the preliminary terms had now been met. In all probability, time was too short to inform Soviet front-line troops. This might explain why they failed to observe the ceasefire, much to the consternation of contemporaries, until one day later than the Finns, on the morning of 5 September 1944. When Finnish front-line troops, surprised by the continuation of hostilities, got in touch with the commander of the Karelian front, Gen. K. A. Meretskov, who was ignorant of the ceasefire agreement, he telephoned headquarters in Moscow and was told that the Finns had not yet accepted the Soviet Union's preliminary terms. Not until 5 September did the order come for a ceasefire.[22] In the absence of sources, it remains an open question whether or not this action was meant to underscore a military victory or as a punishment for Hackzell's supposed "delaying tactics."

The difference of opinion over the question of disarming the German troops had, however, taken root. To avoid further loss of life and material destruction, the Finns sought as far as possible to settle the matter peacefully without plunging the country once more into war. Suspicious of Soviet intentions, they were likewise unwilling to allow Russian troops into Finland to take care of the matter. On the other hand, Moscow had explicitly let it be known that the Russians expected the Finns to play an active part in disarming German troops in Lapland. It remained to be seen how long the patience of the Kremlin would last.

But preliminary terms had been met and the road to Moscow opened. Prime Minister Hackzell was deputed to head the Finnish delegation to the talks, with Minister of Defense Rudolf Walden, Chief of General Staff Heinrichs, and Lt. Gen. Oscar Enckell as members of the delegation, together with the head of chancery at the Finnish Foreign Ministry, P. J. Hynninen; Legation Counsellor Johan Nykopp; and Erik Castrén and Berndt Grönblom as expert advisors. The secretary of the delegation was to be Georg Enckell. The selection of three generals for the delegation stemmed partly from the emphasis placed on the importance of military expertise by Kollontay and Semyonov. They would be needed in Moscow to discuss the practical details of the disarming of the troops in Lapland. Mannerheim also thought that "officers may be better able to understand one another than politicians in different camps." [23] The delegation crossed the front line at Juustila on the morning of 7 September 1944 and arrived in Moscow that same day. There now began a long period of waiting.

2 The Moscow Negotiations

On 5 September 1944, the British ambassador to Moscow, Sir Archibald Clark Kerr, was obliged to observe somewhat sourly to Foreign Minister V. M. Molotov that His Majesty's Government had still not received any information of the terms of the armistice to be offered to Finland. Molotov admitted that this had now become a pressing matter. The Soviet government was at present engaged in preparing the articles of the armistice and had found this a suitable occasion to use the draft agreement with Rumania as a model.[1]

One day later, as the Finnish delegation was preparing itself for departure from Helsinki railway station, Molotov gave the British and American ambassadors in Moscow a draft of the *peace terms* to be offered to Finland. Later that evening, both men were once more invited to meet Molotov to be given further details. Harriman declared, however, that he would attend only as an observer.[2]

Why was the Soviet Union prepared to make an exception of Finland and go for a final peace at such an early stage? The full answer to this question can only be provided when the original Soviet sources are revealed, of course: but the dangers of erroneous conclusions are minimized if we bear in mind the efforts of the Kremlin—evident from at least 1943 and the conference of foreign ministers in Moscow—to confine the Finnish question as far as possible to the two countries concerned and to exclude all others. Molotov's reluctance to inform the Allies in good time of Russian intentions towards Finland, although the preparation of the terms might only just have started, was probably part of this same line of thought. The moment was right for the Kremlin: the United States seemed unwilling to interfere, and Britain was unlikely to influence the essential features of any treaty with Finland because it lacked the strength and desire to do so. Who could say what the situation would be after the war, when the Western capitalist powers might well adopt an anti-Soviet line once more and try to interfere in the arrangement of Soviet-Finnish relations in a manner unfavorable to Moscow? Seen from this point of view, it was better to settle the matter once and for all by concluding a peace treaty with Finland. The treaty would also show all skeptics that the Soviet Union harbored no further intentions towards Finland.

In addition to the British and American ambassadors, Molotov had also invited the members of the Soviet peace delegation to the briefing session on the evening of 6 September. The People's commissar for foreign affairs was accompanied by his deputies, V. G. Dekanosov and M. M. Litvinov. The armed forces were represented by Marshal K. E. Voroshilov; the commander of the Baltic Fleet, Adm. V. F. Tributs; and the head of the operations section on the general staff, Gen. S. M. Shtemenko. General Zhdanov, the future chairman of the Allied Control Commission in Helsinki, was not present.[3]

In its essentials the draft treaty contained virtually the same terms as those presented to the Finns in the spring of 1944, including those relating to the frontiers of 1940. The demand made in the preliminary terms for the disarming of all German troops remaining in Finland after 15 September 1944 and their surrender to the Allies as prisoners of war was likewise repeated. If necessary, the Soviet Union would offer armed assistance for this task. Finnish troops were to withdraw beyond the 1940 frontiers in the order stipulated in a protocol to be attached to the treaty.

What was new was the demand for the lease of a naval base at Porkkala. Molotov explained that this had been worked into the draft treaty at the request of Soviet naval and army officials. Marshal Voroshilov emphasized that the security of Leningrad necessitated a base, a "new Gibraltar" on both sides of the Gulf of Finland. Porkkala would be a more satisfactory arrangement for the Finns than Hanko, which the Russians had occupied after the Winter War and the treaty of Moscow, because they would not be losing an important commercial port. Molotov rejected Clark Kerr's contention that the leased zone would affect communications by cutting across a vital railway line. The military would need sufficient space, and the Finns could easily build new communication lines around the zone. When the ambassador went on to ask if it did not seem a little unpleasant to place themselves within the range of Finnish artillery at Helsinki, the whole Soviet delegation joined Molotov in rejecting such an idea. A situation in which Finns and Russians would see fit to fire on one another was no longer to be contemplated. Molotov was at pains to point out to the representatives of the Western powers that the idea was simply to bottle up the Gulf of Finland. The lack of a similiar clause in the terms presented in the spring was passed over in silence by the Soviet foreign minister.

Having now broken off relations with Germany, Finland was to do the same with the "satellite" states. The airfields in southern and southwest Finland, with their facilities, were to be made available for use to the Allied (Soviet) military command as bases for the Soviet Air Force to conduct assaults on German troops in Estonia and the German navy operating in the Baltic. Petsamo would be transferred to the Soviet Union in accordance with the terms proposed in the spring. A new feature was that Finland was to bear the cost of compensation to the Anglo-Canadian Mond Nickel Company, which owned mines in the area. Molotov made a point of drawing Clark Kerr's attention to the fact that the sum total of the actual war indemnities had been lowered, in response to the earlier request of the British government, from $600 million to $300 million. The British ambassador, however, refrained from taking up this point. The basis on which the pricing of the war indemnity goods was to rest was for the time being not determined.

The other clauses of the draft treaty—which dealt with matters such as the punishment of war criminals, the banning of fascist or pro-Hitler organizations and propaganda, and numerous economic particulars—followed for the most part the pattern of the Rumanian treaty. An Allied Control Commission was also to be set up in Finland. Its task would be to supervise the carrying out of the peace terms until the end of the war against Germany. Clark Kerr pointed out that the draft made no mention of any recognition of the United Nations, nor of the relationship of this treaty to others of a more general nature. The British ambassador also believed that Finland should be obliged to break off relations with Japan, as Rumania had had to do. On this issue, Molotov was in agreement; since the Soviet Union was not at war with Japan, however, it had avoided taking up the matter.[4]

Replying to Harriman, Molotov said that the Soviet Union did not intend to exchange diplomatic representatives with Finland before the cessation of the war with Germany. "I inferred from this that political representatives of other governments of the United Nations would not be welcome, although the establishment of consulates would, I assume, be permitted." Harriman now wanted to hear the views of his government on the Soviet peace proposals for Finland, especially on the questions of future American representation in Helsinki and the Petsamo compensation settlement. The ambassador also sought instructions as to whether he should act as an observer to the negotiations with the Finnish delegation.[5]

Harriman received his instructions the next day. The State Department did not wish the ambassador to be present at the negotiations, and he was to refrain from comment on the terms laid down by Moscow in his dealings with both sides. On the other hand, Washington wished to be kept informed about the course of the negotiations. The question of American representation in Helsinki would be decided at a later stage according to circumstances. The State Department nevertheless hoped that the door would remain open for the setting up of an American consulate in Helsinki, should it prove necessary. With regard to Petsamo, the United States had no direct interests; the question of compensation to be paid by Finland to the owners of property there was thus essentially one for the British.[6]

The American ambassador was reluctant to accept the passivity of his government. The placing of the burden of compensation to the Mond Nickel Company upon the Finns, whose ability to pay was uncertain, was a serious precedent. Clark Kerr had expressed his opposition to the proposal to his American colleague. It seemed likely that the British—aware that they were not strong enough to force the Soviet Union to change its position—would appeal to the United States for assistance, and the Americans should be prepared for such an eventuality.

> I believe also that the Department should give consideration to the general
> position in which we will find ourselves in regard to the Finnish armistice
> and preliminary peace when finally concluded if they include any terms
> which are not in accord with our basic principles. The question is how far
> it will be interpreted that we have acquiesced if we make no comment or
> reservation before the documents are signed.

Harriman also confessed that, occupied with other pressing matters, he had not had an opportunity to study the terms in more detail or to consider all possible implications.[7] No response came from Washington. With the approach of the presidential elections in November 1944, there was reason for special caution in American policy towards the Soviet Union. The United States had to avoid any steps that might annoy its Eastern ally or weaken the American electorate's belief in the phraseology of the Atlantic Charter as the foundation of a future postwar world order.[8]

As an involved party, the British government could not get away so easily from the Finnish problem, and the Soviet terms were subjected to detailed scrutiny at the Foreign Office. The head of the Northern Department, Christopher Warner, could not conceal his irritation with the situation that had now arisen. Frequent requests for information on the terms of the armistice to be proposed to Finland after the spring of 1944 had met with the response that the matter was not pressing. "Now, when the Finnish delegation was actually on its way to Moscow, M. Molotov presents as very urgent a draft which immensely complicates matters by trying to combine an armistice with a peace treaty."[9]

In Warner's opinion, the British government should officially inform the Soviet Union that it regarded the conclusion of a final peace treaty at the present moment as a sheer impossibility. Many of the Moscow proposals that concerned (for example) the ceasefire, the disarming of the Germans, and the surrender of airfields were by their very nature temporary; as such, they were better suited to an armistice, not as clauses of a final peace treaty. Nevertheless, the draft did contain a number of basic points, though Clark Kerr had rightly referred to missing features, such as the return to normal relations and the question of postwar organization in general, that could not be left out of the peace treaty. Furthermore, it had to be borne in mind that many of these general provisions would have to be the same in each and every peace treaty that the Allies would have to conclude with their present enemies, including Germany. There was thus good reason to think carefully about them beforehand, and Washington's opinion should at the very least be consulted. To conclude a peace treaty, His Majesty's Government would have to submit the matter to Parliament, whereas this was not necessarily the case with an armistice agreement. For these reasons, Clark Kerr was to ask Moscow to send a new draft to London, one that outlined the terms of an *armistice* with Finland.

Nevertheless, as Warner observed, it might be in British and Soviet interests to establish agreement at this stage on certain points that appertained to the normal processes of concluding a peace treaty. Finnish, British, and world opinion would be calmed psychologically if the articles dealing with frontier and territorial questions were immediately declared to be definitive, as the Soviet Union obviously wanted. Warner thus believed that there were fears in Finland and the Western countries of *renewed* territorial demands from the Soviet Union at some later stage. Warner's chain of thought could indeed be seen as cutting across a basic British principle, which was that territorial questions could only be settled after the war. Adherence to this general principle would in this instance, however, stir up vigorous protests in Moscow. His Majesty's Government had already accepted the Soviet Union's territorial claims presented in the spring of 1944 (with the exception of the Porkkala base, which arose in the September negotiations) as reasonable and had officially given its approval. The Finns were undoubtedly resigned to the loss of territory. Warner took the view that this matter could be classed as a special case, affecting (of the Allies) only the Soviet Union and perhaps Norway, which might thus justify a more permanent arrangement than a normal armistice.

Warner thought that the fact that the Soviet Union had not demanded free access for its troops to Finnish territory, as it had done in the case of Rumania, was a very positive sign, though he acknowledged that military assistance in driving out the Germans might lead at least partially to the same thing. Clear time limits had also been placed upon the use of Finnish airfields. It was important, in Warner's opinion, that the conditions did not include any blanket clause that might afford an opportunity to present new demands. On the negative side was the matter of Petsamo and the question of compensation for the nickel interests being left to the Finns. This was to be resisted. Warner was not very happy either about the demand for a naval base at Porkkala. An urgent inquiry from the Foreign Office to the chiefs of staff had revealed, however, that this demand was not thought to impinge in any serious manner upon the interests of His Majesty's Government. For the Russians, the sealing of the Gulf of Finland had become a vital security issue as a result of the experiences of the recent past. If the British raised objections, this would create "the worst possible impression" in Moscow. On this matter, therefore, it would be best not to raise objections.

In conclusion, Warner declared that the Soviet draft peace treaty was impossible to accept. Instead, an armistice should be concluded with Finland. Nevertheless, certain articles of a permanent nature could be detached from the draft, such as those restoring the Peace of Moscow's main provisions, the surrender of the Petsamo area to the Soviet Union, the return of Hanko to Finland, the cession of Porkkala to the Soviet Union, and the restoration of the 1940 Åland agreement. These could form a brief, separate preliminary peace treaty that would be signed at the same time as the armistice. This solution would mean a compromise between a definitive peace and a simple armistice. Only when this issue had been settled could Britain enter into detailed discussions of the different articles of the peace treaty. If Molotov were disinclined to go along with this, he was to be told firmly that consideration of the terms of the armistice would take time. This would, of course, be even more the case when it came to the definitive peace treaty. His Majesty's Government had been urging the Soviet Union to send its draft treaty for several weeks, but to no avail. Eden approved Warner's proposals and the corresponding instructions were sent to Clark Kerr in Moscow.[10]

From the Russian point of view, matters were now taking an unfavorable turn. Any delay would, in the last resort, be of benefit only to Hitler. The deadline for the withdrawal of German troops from Finland was gradually approaching, and the Allies had not yet started to discuss the terms of the armistice. The Finnish delegation, which had already arrived in Moscow, was obliged to while away the tension-filled hours by seeing the sights of the city.

The deadlock was soon broken. On 9 September, Molotov informed Clark Kerr that the Soviet government had dropped its draft peace treaty. Its articles would be divided into two parts, as the British desired: an armistice treaty and a preliminary peace treaty. To the latter would be transferred, in addition to the articles already mentioned by the British, those dealing with reparations, the restoration of Allied property in Finland, the banning of fascist organizations, and the punishment of war criminals. Everything else would feature in the armistice treaty. Referring to the approaching deadline, Molotov stressed the pressing urgency of the matter: he expressed a wish to begin discussions of the terms with Clark Kerr the following day. "He was as usual deaf to my reminders that if there had been delay in ejection (of the Germans), it had been on the Soviet side. All he did was to put on an old-fashioned face."[11]

Its initial demands having been met, the Foreign Office could now send Clark Kerr its observations regarding the details of the conditions. Attention was concentrated in the first instance upon the Petsamo question. The placing of the burden of compensation on the shoulders of the party that was *ceding* the territory would make a "most regrettable impression" on world opinion. Moreover, the transfer of the territory from one state to another was not in itself the real reason for the problem that had arisen. The real reason was to be found in the laws of the Soviet Union, which prohibited the mining company from continuing its operations in the usual manner in the new circumstances—within the Soviet Union. It was a general principle that a state that acquired additional territory at the same time assumed all the obligations that were entailed. This had been the case with Germany and Alsace-Lorraine in 1871, for example. Behind all this appealing to public opinion and juridical principles, the British were probably worried that Finland, obliged to pay an indemnity of $300 million to the Soviet Union, would not have anything left with which to pay the Anglo-Canadian nickel company.

Although the total sum of the indemnity had been reduced from the $600 million mentioned in the spring, Britain was still dissatisfied. Because the matter was tied to the decision concerning Rumania (the armistice with Rumania was signed on 12 September 1944), the Foreign Office was, however, unable to give Clark Kerr any detailed instructions. Nevertheless, it was important that the British members of the Control Commission be given the right to maintain direct contact with the Finnish government. If this were not feasible, a special political representative would be sent to Helsinki, as to Bucharest, to maintain these contacts. The clause relating to the disarming of German troops was to be broadened to include mention of the internment of citizens of other enemy countries. The Soviet proposal that the Finnish text of the treaty be elevated to equal authentic status with the Russian and English texts was unacceptable. It would give rise to a dangerous precedent, since German clearly could not be accepted as having a corresponding status in the prevailing circumstances.[12]

For his part, Clark Kerr earnestly cautioned his government not to become involved in the reparations question. It had not been thought appropriate to suggest any fixed sum during the discussions in the spring of 1944. Such an attempt now would rest on even more shaky foundations. It was better not to enter into a fight that the British were unlikely to win and that would cause unnecessary bitterness.[13] The British government followed the line recommended by the ambassador in signing the armistice with Rumania on 12 September, and it let the matter rest with regard to Finland as well.

Moscow showed itself prepared to be flexible on other questions of detail raised by the British and in his telegram of 11 September Clark Kerr was able to confirm that agreement with the Soviet Union was near. The only exception was the Petsamo compensation issue, which had reached complete deadlock. Molotov was not even prepared to acknowledge the British arguments, preferring to refer to the enormous suffering that Finland had visited upon the Soviet Union. The people's commissar for foreign affairs wanted to hand over the terms (excluding the question of compensation for Petsamo) to the Finnish delegation the following day so that it would have something to chew over. This the British government was not prepared to accept, though the Foreign Office was aware of the possibility that it might well have to beat a retreat on the matter.[14]

The next day, after negotiations over the armistice with Rumania had ended Deputy People's Commissar for Foreign Affairs Dekanosov asked Clark Kerr to remain behind for a moment. The British ambassador was now told that the Soviet Union agreed to compensate the Anglo-Canadian nickel company out of the reparation payments received from Finland. The sum to be paid would not exceed $20 million, and it would be paid only when the Soviet Union had started to receive indemnity payments from Finland. This should not be construed in the future as a precedent that might be injurious to the Soviet Union. The deadlock had now been broken, and Clark Kerr recommended that his government accept the offer. The Kremlin had begun to acknowledge its responsibilities in the desired manner, "and . . . it is no concern of ours whence they draw the sum wherewith to meet it." After discussions with the Treasury and the Canadian government, the Foreign Office gave its consent in principle. The solution was made easier by Moscow's willingness to pay the compensation in dollars and not (for example) in timber products, which the Canadians did not need. On the evening of 13 September, Clark Kerr was authorized to agree to the draft treaty being presented to the Finns. The part dealing with the compensation to the Mond Nickel Company was to be left out, and a separate Anglo-Soviet protocol was to be drafted later to embrace the offer made by Dekanosov. Molotov agreed to this the following day.[15]

Agreement had now been reached in principle, but there was yet another surprise in store for the British. Just before the terms were laid before the Finnish delegation on the evening of 14 September, Molotov summoned Clark Kerr and told him that the Soviet Union wished to give up the idea of signing two separate treaties—the preliminary peace treaty and the armistice. To simplify the procedure, the articles of both treaties would be combined into one document that would be called an armistice agreement. It would be signed in the name of the Soviet Union and the United Kingdom, as representing all the countries at war with Finland, by General Zhdanov. Clark Kerr naturally had no objections to this procedure, which had been followed in the case of Rumania.[16]

What caused this change of mind on the part of the Kremlin? One clue might lie in the fact that the preliminary peace treaty would have been signed by *all* the states at war with Finland, including the British dominions, which had already authorized their representatives in Moscow to undertake this task.[17]

As these discussions were taking place, serious differences had appeared between the Western powers and the Soviet Union at the Dumbarton Oaks conference, which was planning the future United Nations organization and the structure of its membership. Moscow demanded the admission of full rights of membership for the sixteen republics of the Soviet Union. Behind this demand lay a suspicion that the Latin American countries might to some extent be tied to the United States or the British dominions to the United Kingdom. The Soviet Union thus sought in some way to compensate for this eventuality, but the Western powers strongly rejected the proposal. This Great Power conflict now cast its shadow over the treaty about to be made with Finland. Molotov told Clark Kerr that if representatives of the dominions turned up to sign the preliminary peace treaty with Finland, representatives of the western republics of the Soviet Union would be present to perform the same function. The British were naturally not disposed to accept this and a new delay seemed inevitable.[18] The entire problem could instead be resolved, in the Rumanian manner, by one armistice agreement signed by General Zhdanov on behalf of the victors. The two parties having reached this agreement in the afternoon of 14 September, the Finnish delegation was summoned from their headquarters in the Hotel Savoy.

The period of enforced waiting had got on the nerves of the delegates. They had tried on several occasions, through the good offices of the Swedish legation in Moscow, to get the negotiations started; they had even appealed to Kollontay to help them in this endeavor.[19] However, when Hackzell paid a courtesy visit to Molotov on 8 September, he was told that the negotiations would be delayed. Discussions with the Rumanians had first to be brought to a conclusion, in addition to which the Soviet Union would have to reach agreement with its Allies on the terms to be presented to Finland. Molotov also said that Leningrad officials and the population of that area had pressed for the occupation of Finland as the only solution. The Soviet government had to look at things on a broader perspective and would commence negotiations in spite of this pressure, however understandable it might be.[20]

Having digested this news, Hackzell told Swedish Minister Söderblom that he believed Finland would avoid occupation with the probable exception of certain areas in the north, where military operations might require it. With this in mind, the Finnish government contemplated the evacuation of the population of northern Finland. British involvement in the negotiations was seen by Hackzell as an encouraging sign.[21] But the constant strain proved too much for the prime minister, who was already in poor health. On the evening of 14 September, after the summons to the negotiating table had been received, he suffered an apoplectic stroke from which he never recovered.[22]

Within a few hours of Hackzell's sudden stroke, the delegations assembled for their first session in the Spiridonovka, the rooms of the Commissariat for Foreign Affairs. After handing the terms of the armistice over to General Walden, the temporary head of the Finnish delegation, Molotov spoke of the preliminary terms already presented to Finland. Pressed by the people's commissar to give an account of the measures that the Finns had taken to start disarming the Germans, Walden was unable to answer.[23] The Finns could still claim that the deadline did not expire until the following day. The delegation did not have precise details of German troop movements. Moreover, the preliminary terms had only spoken of disarming the Germans and had not specified who was to do it. This matter would have to be discussed in more detail in Moscow. Molotov now began to get annoyed. If the Finnish minister of defense and the chief of general staff did not know about the German troops operating on the territory of their country, then who did? The Germans were highly unlikely to disarm themselves. The Soviet Union was ready to discuss what assistance might be necessary with the Finns in Moscow, but this did not justify them dragging their heels over the execution of the measures specified in the preliminary terms.

The opening shots of the discussions did not bode well for the overall atmosphere of the talks. The secretary of the Finnish delegation thought that Walden had been "unsure and imprecise" when trying to rebuff Molotov's fierce attacks. Clark Kerr's impression was also not a positive one. He could not make out whether the Finns' "helplessness" was genuine or pretended. "Molotov showed most surprising patience and in the confusion of conversation which followed seemed to me to treat Mr. Walden as a good-natured nurse would treat a very backward child." [24] Walden's tactics may have had some bearing on the fact that Mannerheim, suspicious of Soviet intentions, was not keen on concentrating the main strength of the Finnish army in the north against the Germans. The Finns wished to push the Germans out by means of peaceful negotiations. As the evacuation of the 20th Mountain Army with all its equipment would take several weeks, even if there were no technical hitches, the Finns now tried to gain time to avoid for as long as possible the eruption of a new and costly war. In the absence of the relevant sources, it must remain an open question how far the reports of Kollontay, a committed advocate of peace, may have given the Kremlin too rosy a picture of the Finns' preparedness for an offensive. [25]

With the arrival of Foreign Minister Enckell in Moscow on 16 September and his assumption of leadership of the delegation, the Finns' grip on the discussions improved. The battle of Suursaari (where a German assault on a strategically located island in the Gulf of Finland was repulsed on 15 September) could be presented as concrete evidence of the breach between Helsinki and Berlin. The Germans in southern Finland had withdrawn entirely. But in spite of the explanations offered by Carl Enckell, Oscar Enckell, and Erik Heinrichs, the Finns were unable to produce any evidence of setting about the task of disarming the Mountain Army in Lapland. On the contrary, Molotov thought, they seemed to be doing their best to help the Germans withdraw, instead of attacking them. Molotov's language became ever more threatening, and it was hardly relieved by British accusations that he had dallied over sending the terms to London and thereby delayed operations in Lapland. To give more weight to his words, the commissar informed the peace delegation on 17 September that Soviet troops had crossed the frontier in two places—Suomussalmi and Kuusamo—because the Finns had not fulfilled the preliminary conditions. The situation was at its worst on the last full day of negotiations, 18 September, when Molotov read out an announcement issued by the German news agency, Transocean. This claimed that the Germans were at that moment successfully engaged in the withdrawal of troops and equipment from Lapland. The operation had gone off smoothly "as a result . . . of well-organized collaboration between German troops and the Finnish authorities." Molotov had been given a useful piece of evidence to fuel his suspicions, though the Finns tried their best to explain that the Germans were trying in their own interests to sabotage the Soviet-Finnish talks.[26]

Why did Molotov place such importance on the Finnish contribution to the disarming of the Germans? Clearly, the Soviet Union was not especially keen on sacrificing its own troops for the job because these were needed in more important places. But surely this was not the only reason. The matter of prestige in the clash with the British over the delay in settling the terms still hovered in the background. On the other hand, the *Waffenbrüderschaft* between Finland and Germany had to be smashed once and for all. The decision in the spring of 1944 to continue the war side by side with Germany must not be allowed to recur. Heinrichs also noted a kind of "pedagogical" aspect to the negotiations: the Finns had to learn the hard way the consequences of joining forces with the enemies of the Soviet Union and allowing them to dispose of the territory of the republic for their own use. From the point of view of future good relations, it was also important for the Finns themselves to take care of the tidying-up operations in their own territory.[27]

Of the actual armistice negotiations, there is little to be said.[28] The articles were gone through at a rapid pace, with Molotov seeing them as "minimal demands" and the British ambassador contenting himself with the role of a passive observer. The frontier question Molotov regarded as finally settled. Enckell's suggestion that Porkkala might be exchanged for Hanko was deemed unacceptable for military reasons. Mannerheim had authorized the delegation to offer a naval base on Åland or territory in Lapland in place of the Porkkala base, but Enckell—having noted the determination of the Russians to seal the Gulf of Finland between Naissaar and Porkkala—did not even raise this possibility. Molotov had gone into detail about the Porkkala base being essential for the security of Leningrad, and he would hardly have been likely to accept substitute offers. The Finns also had to take care not to irritate the Swedes. Having discovered through a member of the Finnish delegation (Berndt Grönblom) that they had been given authority to offer a naval base on Åland as an alternative to Porkkala, the Hansson government reacted furiously, barely concealing its apprehension and anger at the Finns' "disloyalty." Even though the matter was not raised in Moscow, Helsinki was obliged to pacify the Swedes.[29]

With the exception of technical details and a few alterations of words, the concessions made to the Finnish delegation were limited to the extension of the period of payment of reparations from five to six years, as in the case of Rumania, and the prolongation of the period reserved for demobilization from two to two and a half months. Heinrichs's plea for greater flexibility was not accepted. On this issue, the Soviet Union harbored justifiable suspicions that the Finns were pursuing a delaying tactic and were reluctant to take on the Germans. When Enckell wondered if the Mond Nickel Company might not present the Finns with a bill for compensation for its Petsamo nickel mines, Molotov, faintly amused, replied that there was no need to worry on that score. "Anyway, we will come to terms with Great Britain on this matter. Isn't it so, Mr. Kerr?" "Undoubtedly," was the equally discreet reply.[30]

On this last day of negotiations (18 September), The Finnish delegation discussed among themselves what might be done at the last moment to soften the terms. They considered having President Mannerheim come to Moscow to negotiate personally with Marshal Stalin. But the idea was not even put to their Soviet counterparts. When he received Enckell that same afternoon, Molotov adopted a very tough line; "inflamed by his own words," he accused the Finnish government of being "bloody and criminal." It is possible that the communiqué issued by the Transocean news agency that day had influenced Molotov. He declared that the terms of the armistice were to be signed without delay. Otherwise, the delegation might as well go home and the consequence would be the occupation of the entire country, for which preparations had already been made.[31] The Enckell delegation saw no other course open but to sign the armistice agreement, a responsibility that they took upon themselves around midday on 19 September 1944. The authorization to act in the name of Parliament, granted that morning, did not arrive until after the treaty had been signed.[32]

The reaction of the Finnish political leadership was pessimistic. President Mannerheim and acting Prime Minister von Born believed that the bolshevization of Finland could hardly be avoided. Similar sentiments were present in the military leadership.[33] The Swedish legation in Helsinki reported that there was a sense of disappointment amongst the members of the peace opposition, those who had argued for a separate peace with the Soviet Union for almost two years. In spite of everything, they had hoped for "something better."[34] In Stockholm, Gripenberg was already prepared to describe the situation with the words "Finis Finlandiae."[35] In the force of his reaction, he was exceeded only by Secretary-General Boheman, who described the terms of the armistice to American minister Herschel Johnson as "criminal."

> I have never seen him more depressed. As the Department knows, his background on Finnish-Soviet relations is extensive. . . . He said that he had never received a greater shock or disillusionment than he had when he really understood what these terms mean.

Boheman was particularly alarmed by the order attached to Article 5 according to which the Finnish government undertook to stop the postal correspondence of the diplomatic representatives and consuls in Finland, as well as all en clair or coded radio, telegraph, and telephone messages to the outside world, until the expulsion of the German troops had been finally carried out. In Boheman's opinion, this was a bad sign. The terms had obviously been planned so as to allow the Russians an extremely flexible freedom of maneuver, not only militarily but also in regard to the internal administration of the country. The terms placed the Russians in a position where they could do what they wanted while the outside world remained in complete ignorance. Boheman emphasized to the British minister that the Porkkala base would mean the end of Finland's independence: the country would become a protectorate of the Soviet Union. The same could be said of the terms as a whole. Boheman declared that he regretted ever having acted as intermediary, pushing Finland into peace negotiations that had proved to be so disastrous. "He evidently has the matter greatly on his conscience."[36]

In London, the situation was regarded with more dispassionate concern. Eden believed that Boheman's fears were exaggerated. "It is true that the area at Porkkala-Ud is larger than the Hangö leased area and that it runs to within 10 miles of Helsinki. But Helsinki would be just as much under a permanent threat from Russian bombers were there no lease at Porkkala-Ud." In spite of their relative severity, the terms were tolerable. As an example, Eden pointed to the halving of the reparations bill to $300 million, thanks to the British, and the extension of the period of payment. Taken as a whole, the treaty did not, in Sir Anthony's view, imply in any way the end of Finland as an independent nation.[37]

3 The War in Lapland

In September 1944, the German 20th Mountain Army in Lapland, under the command of Gen. Lothar Rendulic, comprised three corps—nine divisions in all. The *XIX Geb. Korps* (commanded by Gen. Ferdinand Jodl) operated on the Arctic Ocean front around Kalastajasaarento and Litsajoki. The *XXXVI Geb. Korps* (commanded by Gen. Emil Vogel) was stationed as it had been since 1941 on the so-called Verman line east of Salla, on both sides of the railway line leading to Kantalahti. The *XVIII Geb. Korps* (commanded by Gen. Friedrich Hochbaum) was farther south, around Kiestinki and Uhtua. In addition, the Mountain Army was supported by several air bases in different parts of Lapland, a complete air surveillance network, antiaircraft units, and troops assigned to guard duties.

Rendulic's divisions were still up to full strength; battle hardened, they had settled down relatively well to conditions in Lapland over the years. Uncharacteristically, Hitler was not exaggerating when he told Rendulic, appointed successor to General Dietl in June 1944: "In the Mountain Army you are taking charge of the best army which I have at my disposal. It consists almost entirely of mountain troops. They are thoroughly hardened and trained in battle. You will find a lot of your countrymen [Austrians] up there."[1] In southern Finland, on the other hand, with the exception of the 303rd Assault Gun Brigade stationed in the Karelian Isthmus, the Germans had only a few small naval and Luftwaffe units and an insignificant number of support units.

Contingency plans in the event of Finland's withdrawal from the war had been talked about in the High Command of the Armed Forces (OKW) and at the headquarters of the 20th Mountain Army in Rovaniemi since the autumn of 1943.[2] From the German point of view, the most worrying source of danger lay on the open right flank of the Mountain Army. The *Führerweisung 50* issued in

September 1943 formed the basis of the operational plan *Birke*, completed on 8 April 1944. The intention was to withdraw the two southernmost army corps to prepare positions around Ivalo and Kaaresuvanto to protect the Petsamo nickel mines. The *XXXVI* and *XVIII Geb. Korps* would move from the Kantalahti, Kiestinki, and Uhtua fronts towards Rovaniemi. The former would then continue its march along the Arctic Ocean road northwards to Ivalo, while the latter would march northwest along the Rovaniemi-Skibotn road to the level of Kaaresuvanto. This disengagement would be protected by the watercourse of the Oulu River. Kuusamo and Rovaniemi would be secured and held until the withdrawal was complete. As there were no railways in northern Lapland, and motorized transport was not fully reliable because of a lack of vehicles and the shortage of fuel, the major part of the route—which at its longest stretch was more than one thousand kilometers—would have to be covered on foot. The preparations indicated in this plan (fortification works, the movement of supplies, transport arrangements, etc.) were carried out during the summer of 1944.[3]

The Mountain Army command did not believe the Russians would stay behind the frontier if Finland concluded a ceasefire. Militarily, it would have been an act of "unforgivable gullibility" to have placed any trust in such an eventuality. In the German calculations, the gravest threat lay in a Soviet penetration of the Oulu and Tornio areas. This would mean more than an open southern flank and the cutting off of the Mountain Army from the harbors of the Gulf of Bothnia: the OKW and the Germans in Rovaniemi also paid serious attention to the possibility that Sweden, either voluntarily or under pressure (as had occurred in 1941, when the Germans brought pressure to bear on the Swedish government to allow transit of German troops across Swedish territory), might grant the Russians right of transit through Swedish territory from Tornio to Narvik. This would cut off the Mountain Army from the harbors of southern Norway, leaving it completely encircled.[4]

What the Finns intended to do was a source of constant anxiety for Rendulic during the summer of 1944. Would they open up the southern flank of the Mountain Army to the Russians, and would they also join in a Russian offensive? Mannerheim, at any rate, was not disposed to let Rendulic see his cards. Meeting the marshal for the last time on 2 September 1944 just before the final breach of relations, General Rendulic took refuge in a barely concealed threat. If the Finns and Germans were to fire on one another, he declared, the result would be losses of up to 90 percent on both sides because "the best soldiers in Europe" would be shooting at one another.[5]

A few hours later that same day, Mannerheim informed Rendulic of the letter to Hitler breaking off relations, which ended: "I hope that, even though you cannot accept the step which I have taken, you will feel the same way as I and all the Finnish people do, and try to act in a manner which will allow the dismantling of hitherto existing relations without unnecessary friction.'' The letter was sent the same night by telex to Hitler's headquarters.[6]

Hitler's reaction seemed at first to meet the Finns' hopes. The Germans were no longer strong enough to take effective countermeasures. Moreover, if the terms laid down by Moscow proved to be impossible, the Finns might still decide to follow the example of spring 1944 and continue fighting by the side of Germany. At his situation review session (*Lagebesprechung*) on 3 September, the führer decided that relations with Finland were to be maintained "within the framework of cordial mutual understanding" (*im Rahmen gütlichen Einvernehmens*). It was decided to abandon *Tanne West*, the plan to occupy the Åland Islands, because of lack of manpower: the 416th Division, which had been assigned to this task, could not be relieved of occupation duties in Denmark. The German war leadership feared that the British might seek to take advantage of the situation by invading Denmark and securing an entry into the Baltic. This might well be decisive for the whole war. In addition, there was good reason to avoid provoking an ever more hostile Sweden, whose iron ore and ball bearings were vitally important for Germany. As regards *Tanne Ost*, the seizure of Suursaari, which was to be carried out under the auspices of the navy, Admiral Dönitz confirmed that he did not have enough trained troops for the assault. The führer thus decided to postpone the operation for the present. Operation *Birke* was to be set in motion, though Hitler's directives of 5 September ordered that the Finns were not to be told of the Germans' intention to take up defensive positions within the territory of the republic, on the Kaaresuvanto-Ivalo line. On the contrary, they were to be led to believe that the withdrawal would continue right into Norway. The pullback outlined in *Birke* began on the evening of 6 September.[7]

At the time, the Germans tried to recruit volunteer units in Finland who might continue the fight alongside their former comrades in arms. Something of this sort had been discussed by Hitler and Dietl in June 1944. One idea was to revive the old World War I *Jägerbataillon 27*, in which Finnish volunteers had served in the Imperial German army. According to directives approved by Hitler, public propaganda was to be avoided. Pro-German Finns were to be persuaded by word of mouth to go northwards to join up with the Mountain Army. Because of the perilous supply situation only soldiers in fighting condition and pro-German politicians would be accepted. Women and children would not be taken in. *Heeresgruppe Nord* in Estonia was also interested in Finnish volunteers, whom Himmler was keen to attract to his SS forces as well. General Erfurth, the German liaison officer at the Finnish general headquarters, who was about to leave Helsinki, thought the whole idea was wishful thinking. For the time being at least, such schemes had not the slightest chance of success.[8] The same view was held by the German minister to Helsinki, Wipert von Blücher, whom Ribbentrop urged to organize a pro-German resistance movement in Finland. The minister was obliged to inform Berlin that the Finnish people and army to all intents and purposes stood solidly behind Mannerheim. Partisan activities backed by Germany would only be feasible in the event of Russian occupation of the country and acts of violence against the population. Until this occurred, there was no point in talking about partisans. Quite a different matter, in von Blücher's opinion, was the intelligence service in operation after the breach of relations, which the Gestapo had already taken care to set up.[9]

The aim of the Finnish leadership, it need hardly be said, was to make sure as many German troops as possible left the territory of the republic peacefully by 15 September. The country was war weary and its resources badly depleted. There was thus a desire to avoid further casualties and material destruction as far as possible. On the other hand, government officials did not wish to endanger the prospects of peace. When they heard, to their great relief, that the Mountain Army had begun voluntarily to withdraw, Mannerheim and Heinrichs assured Erfurth that they were ready to assist and hasten the withdrawal of their former comrades in arms across the frontier in whatever way possible.[10] The evacuation of the small numbers of troops, personnel, and equipment in southern Finland was relatively easy to arrange. On 6 September, the 303rd Assault Gun Brigade was put on board ships in Helsinki harbor bound for Denmark. The German legation, headed by Minister von Blücher, got on board an express train for Turku on 10 September to travel via Sweden to Germany. Three days later, General Erfurth and his staff left Helsinki by sea for Germany.[11] Southern Finland was cleared of Germans by 14 September 1944.

The situation in the north was quite different. From the beginning, it seemed unlikely that the Mountain Army with all its troops and equipment would be able to withdraw in the short period allowed. On 6 September, a delegation headed by I. Kopola, the sectional head of the Ministry of Supply, arrived in Rovaniemi to negotiate the purchase for the Finnish government of materials, buildings, and fixtures that the Germans might wish to leave behind. Two days later, agreement had been reached. The Germans sold about 20,000 tons of coal, some machines, and their building supplies depot in Tornio. They also handed over to the Finnish state all their buildings, stores, and depots south of the Oulu line.

The only significant exception in southern Finland was the airfield at Pori, which Rendulic believed must be destroyed. If Soviet planes were allowed to operate from Pori, German sea communications in the Gulf of Bothnia would be placed in jeopardy and might even be severed completely. As a result of the talks in Rovaniemi, the Finns succeeded in obtaining useful machinery and supplies for the work of reconstruction, even though most of these later had to be handed over to the Russians as German war booty. The Germans for their part got rid of buildings and materials of little use to them, which in all likelihood they would have had to destroy in view of their inadequate transport capacity.[12] After the Suursaari episode, however, the Germans lost some 13,000 tons of sea transport when the Finnish ships assisting them steamed in midjourney into Finnish or Swedish ports.

Even before the ceasefire reached with the Soviet Union came into force, Mannerheim gave the order on 3 September for the 6th Division to be withdrawn from the Karelian Isthmus and sent by train to Kajaani, with the 15th Brigade moving to Oulu. The "Pennanen Detachment" that had been supporting the German troops in the Petsamo area was withdrawn from the front and stationed in Kemi to protect the Karihaara industrial area.[13] Rendulic for his part detached units from the *XXXVI* and *XVIII Geb. Korps* that were to form two reinforced, motorized regiments. These combat units, *Kampfgruppe West* and *Kampfgruppe Ost*, were located at Oulu and Hyrynsalmi to protect the southern flank of the Mountain Army.

There was thus a growing tension between the two former cobelligerents as both sides prepared and concentrated their forces against each other. Confusion over the point of overlap between German and Finnish troops at Kontokki, in East Karelia, strengthened the belief of German headquarters in Rovaniemi that the Finnish army command intended to allow the Russians to get at the German flank. At the same time, the evacuation of the civilian population from Lapland was in full swing. In addition to this, Finnish army headquarters announced to Rendulic that the local railways would be at the Germans' disposal for the evacuation of men and matériel to the harbors at the head of the Gulf of Bothnia only until 14 September. Rendulic, angry and mistrustful of Finnish intentions, saw this as a stab in the back for his army. Before his departure, Erfurth had also told the Finns that the evacuation of the Mountain Army could not possibly be completed by the 14th and that permission to use the railways would have to be sought for a further period. As Erfurth was about to leave the country, some new contact between Rovaniemi and the Finnish GHQ in Mikkeli was essential. The OKW now took it upon itself to interfere, with Jodl attempting to calm down Rendulic, warning him not to take any rash actions. The general had to bear in mind that "the Russians, in the end, have more powerful means of persuasion than we have."[14] On the other hand, the evacuation of the population of Lapland was possible only with the consent of the Germans, a fact of which Rendulic was well aware.

The Finnish GHQ now deemed it best to open up direct contact with the Mountain Army command; on 11 September, Mannerheim sent Lt.Col. U. S. Haahti to Rovaniemi to discuss the German withdrawal with Rendulic. This special envoy was to try to smooth out differences and, by negotiation, to avoid as much bloodshed and loss of property as possible. The right to use the railways would have to be played off against the evacuation of the civilian population. German fears of a Soviet attack on their southern flank via Finnish territory were to be allayed. It was to be pointed out to Rendulic that the purpose of the 6th Division and the 15th Brigade now concentrated on the demarcation line was not to put pressure on the Germans, but rather to follow their withdrawal movements in order to avoid as far as possible the necessity of evacuating civilians and to prevent the area from becoming a battlefield. The deadline for the German withdrawal from south of the Oulujoki-Oulujärvi demarcation line was to be 2400 hours on 14 September. If possible, Haahti was to secure Oulu and the crossing points on the Oulu river by negotiation.[15]

The first round of talks took place in Rovaniemi between 11 and 13 September. In addition to Lieutenant Colonel Haahti, the head of the local Finnish liaison staff—Col. Oiva Willamo—also attended some of the talks. On the German side, the participants were General Rendulic, Major General Hölter, his chief of staff, and occasionally Lieutenant Colonel Übelhack, head of the operational section. The principal negotiators were Haahti and Hölter. Agreement was reached over the withdrawal of German units northwards across the Oulujoki-Oulujärvi-Kuhmo watercourse. After a lengthy period of haggling, the Germans agreed to the occupation of Oulu by Finnish troops from 0000 hours on 15 September. Haahti was able to inform Mikkeli on 12 September: "Oulu saved."[16]

In accordance with the agreement concerning the demarcation line, Oulu harbor would be closed to the Germans after 14 September. With regard to the railways still on the German side, the two parties reached a compromise solution along the lines of Haahti's instructions. The Germans would allow the evacuation of the civilian population and the Finns promised in return "unofficially" to transport sixty freight cars of German matériel daily along the stretch of track between Rovaniemi and the coast until 29 September. A proposal by the Germans for the Mountain Army to take charge of traffic between Salla and Rovaniemi after 15 September was referred by Haahti to GHQ. The reply was to the effect that outsiders must be given the impression that the Finns would no longer have any dealings with the Germans after 14 September: but in practice, they had to be ready to make "sensible compromises." Thus, Haahti announced that all rolling stock on the Salla line would be brought back to Rovaniemi by 14 September. The Finns would not put up any resistance if the Germans "forcibly" seized it the next night. This was on condition, however, that the Mountain Army assisted the transport of evacuees from Kemijärvi westwards and guaranteed that Finnish railway personnel would be allowed to get away. A solution satisfactory to both sides had thus been reached. The Finns could continue to evacuate the populace, and the Germans would be allowed to transport valuable matériel and equipment to Kemi, Tornio, and Rovaniemi even after 14 September.[17]

The most difficult part of the negotiations concerned the question of what the Germans intended to destroy. On 5 September, Hitler had ordered the destruction of all immovable property in German possession, both in southern and northern

Finland, as the withdrawal took place. The Mountain Army had not yet carried out the order, however: Rendulic defended his inactivity to the OKW by referring to public opinion in Finland. Acts of destruction would in all likelihood prompt the Finns to hinder the evacuation of supplies vital to the Mountain Army. The talks in Rovaniemi confirmed what had already become evident during the earlier discussions between Kopola and the Germans; in spite of Hitler's general directives, the Germans would withdraw from southern Finland without resorting to widespread destruction, with the exception of the Pori airfield. Haahti now sought to persuade them to act in the same way in northern Finland. Hölter rejected this appeal on strategic grounds, because then the command of the Mountain Army would be giving the enemy an opportunity to penetrate the army's rear. Nevertheless, Haahti was left with the impression that the Germans might give up the idea of destroying dwellings and buildings, although they regarded the blowing up of bridges as vital for their own operations.[18] At this stage, the talks in Rovaniemi had reached the critical deadline as 15 September dawned. The southernmost German force, *XVIII Geb. Korps*, had already pulled out of East Karelia across the 1940 Finnish frontier, while *XXXVI Geb. Korps* was fighting a retreat in the face of fierce pressure in the area of Salla.

The first serious setback to the "unofficial" collaboration between Finland and Germany was the clash on Suursaari. The German naval liaison officer stationed on the island reported on a couple of occasions to the OKM at the beginning of September that the Finnish garrison would not put up any resistance should the Germans stage a landing. Admiral Dönitz now shifted from his earlier, rather pessimistic assessment of the situation and decided to go ahead with *Tanne Ost* in an effort to seal off the Gulf of Finland. Hitler approved the plan on 13 September. The operation, launched on the night of 14-15 September, soon revealed the inaccuracy of the information about the Finnish attitude. The garrison put up a stiff resistance, and the poorly prepared landing—which was staged with inadequate forces — was beaten back with heavy losses to the Germans within a few hours. In his memoirs, Mannerheim noted that the Germans "by their foolish attempt eased our position at a time when Finland was forced to resort to arms to drive them out of the country."[19]

In fact, however, matters had not yet reached that stage. Finnish vessels sailing in the Baltic were given orders to put in at Finnish or Swedish ports without delay. The consequences for the transportation of German war matériel has already been mentioned. On the morning of the 15th, Haahti received from Mannerheim a demand addressed to Rendulic whereby, "in order to avoid new incidents and to minimize the threat of a demand for transit for Soviet troops," the Mountain Army should withdraw its units out of the entire coastal zone of the Gulf of Bothnia and, in the east, out of the zone to the south of Suomussalmi. Haahti was also told to demand precise times for the evacuation of these areas.[20] At this stage, it will be remembered, Molotov had the previous evening in

Moscow demanded concrete measures against the Germans in northern Finland at the first session of the armistice talks.

Rendulic suspected that the Finnish army command was acting as a stalking-horse for the Russians, who were striving to reach Tornio and on to Narvik; at first, he refused point-blank to give up the Bothnian coast—at least for the time being. Haahti's mention of the pressure being brought to bear in Moscow merely increased Rendulic's suspicions, though he did stress that the Germans did not intend to stay in Finland, but would withdraw gradually northwards. Preparation of a summary timetable for the withdrawal was feasible, and as a "sign of goodwill" toward Mannerheim, the areas to the south of Suomussalmi would be evacuated immediately. Having received this reply, Haahti set off for Mikkeli on the evening of the 15th to present a personal account.

At headquarters on the 16th, Mannerheim declared Rendulic's reply to be satisfactory; Haahti received orders to return to Rovaniemi to continue the negotiations. Quartermaster-General A. F. Airo ordered Haahti to report continually on the German plans for withdrawal, and he added: "Let's make this into the sort of autumn maneuvers we used to have in peacetime. You report daily to Nihtilä [head of the operational section at GHQ] how far the Germans will withdraw for the next couple of days, and we'll give the Finnish troops here the corresponding assault objectives." Airo accepted the fact that the Germans were going to destroy bridges behind them, seeing this as advantageous in the end to the Finns because it would afford them an explanation for the slowness of their advance. Haahti was also to tell the distrustful Germans that the Finns would not immediately repair bridges. Road bridges would be repaired to take supply vehicles, but not armored vehicles. This last hint was relevant, since the Germans knew that the Finns had recently moved the Lagus armored division northwards, partly to the coastal area. Ostrobothnia, with its terrain broken by one river after another, was truly ideal for such a withdrawal.[21]

News of the talks in Moscow caused Mannerheim to change his position. General Tuompo noted in his diary on 18 September: "The Marshal . . . set off for Helsinki yesterday at 1300 hours. Before departure he had another fierce set-to with Airo. The Marshal wanted our troops . . . to march to Kemi and Tornio. Airo thought this impossible, because it would lead to open war with the Germans."[22] In other words, while the quartermaster-general sought to prolong the "autumn maneuvers" for as long as possible, the commander in chief was ready to attack the Germans, having won the time necessary to bring troops up into position with the aid of the maneuvers and having evacuated the population of northern Finland before the fighting began. According to Haahti's notes, Mannerheim was worried about the course of the armistice negotiations. The Finns in Moscow had to have some genuine evidence of action against the Germans or else Soviet troops would in all probability intervene directly.[23]

Haahti returned to Rovaniemi on the evening of 17 September. The next day,

Rendulic accepted the proposals of the Finnish GHQ. Such an arrangement suited the Germans as well, since it would avoid unnecessary bloodshed, would protect the delicate southern flank, and would gain time for the evacuation transports and marches envisaged in Operation *Birke*. Haahti was informed of the lines to which the Finnish troops could advance on the 19th and 20th of that month. The same procedure was followed on the following days. The "autumn maneuvers" had got under way and the Finnish troops began their "offensive" on 19 September, following at one day's distance the retreating Germans. Haahti also made sure that Rendulic was informed that, if Finland was compelled to declare war on Germany because of Soviet pressure, he (Haahti) would have to be interned by the Germans and would in that case still be able to continue directing the maneuvers.[24] This was not needed, however.

Everything went according to plan to the last days of September, with the "front" moving slowly northwards without any bloodshed and the Finns able to show the whole time that they were "taking possession" of the terrain. The evacuation of the civilian population of Lapland was completed by 23 September. Some 71,000 people with their domestic animals and personal belongings had been moved south of the Oulu river, and 56,000 were moved to Sweden, after agreement had been reached between the Finnish and Swedish governments.[25] As a result of the "autumn maneuvers," many of the parishes of Oulu province did not have to be evacuated at all. The destruction carried out by the Germans was largely confined for the time being to lines of communication, and the local inhabitants were usually warned in advance so as to avoid casualties. The one exception was at Hyrynsalmi, where a case of arson, evidently as the result of an arbitrary decision by the local commander, prompted General Rendulic to warn against deliberate provocation. For the same reason, Rendulic abandoned plans to destroy the industrial complex at Karihaara in Kemi, even though he feared it could later be used by the Russians, because any such attempt would have led to armed conflict with the Pennanen Detachment stationed there.[26]

On 26 September, Rendulic reported to the OKW that his troops were on good terms with the Finnish army, and he begged Berlin not to spoil the relationship with its excessive propaganda aimed at the Finnish military and political leadership. Rendulic also opposed the idea of setting up an active unit of the *Sicherheitsdienst* in Lapland, because that might be seen as a sign of hostility in Helsinki.[27] He also issued a stern order to his troops on the 26th, forbidding the destruction of Finnish dwellings and other civilian buildings. "Indiscipline will be dealt with severely (*Gegen Disziplinlosigkeiten ist scharf einzuschreiten*)."[28]

The culminating point in this collaborative venture was probably Rendulic's hint to Haahti that, if really pressed, a small German detachment might allow itself to be interned so that the Finns could claim "positive results" to Moscow.[29] On the other hand, the Soviet media had already seized upon the Finns' inactivity, which was seen—with good reason—as deliberate.[30] This was indeed the heart of the matter. How long would Moscow be satisfied with vague announcements of the repossession of certain areas of territory? Returning to Mikkeli from Rovaniemi, Haahti himself observed in his farewell remarks to Hölter: "We certainly can't keep this up for much longer, but I think I can promise that when we are forced to change our tactics, we'll let you know." Rendulic knew that although the Finns did not want to fight the Germans, they were determined to make peace and would thus accept the demands made by the Soviet Union.[31] Looked at as a whole, it can be said that the Finns, by their "autumn maneuvers," did delay the outbreak of hostilities and thereby prevent an excessive shedding of blood and loss of property. On the other hand, however, they ran a serious risk of upsetting the Soviet Union, with whom they had concluded an armistice.

How was the situation viewed now, on the other side of the frontier? Military operations against the Finns having ceased, the commander of the Karelian front, Gen. K. A. Meretskov, was now preparing for a large scale flanking movement to surround the German Mountain Army. To the disappointment of the general, who viewed the situation simply from a military point of view, Stalin did not accept his plan, since the expulsion of the Germans from Lapland was the duty of the Finns.[32] The instructions received by Meretskov did not leave any room for interpretation. "Headquarters demands that you observe its orders punctiliously and warns you once more, that if you do not carry out headquarters' instructions, and try to advance, you will be relieved of your duties as commander of the front."

The troops on the Karelian front were to be moved instead to support the forces concentrated around Litsajoki and Kalastajasaarento, to drive back Ferdinand Jodl's *XIX Geb. Korps* and to take the Petsamo area. The offensive in this area commenced on 7 October 1944. The Soviet Union thus had prepared plans for northern Finland, though Stalin curbed Meretskov's freedom of operation. The intelligence section on the Karelian front was alert, however, and on the basis of its reports Meretskov's staff had a pretty clear idea that the Finns were not engaging the enemy and that the Germans were being permitted to withdraw peacefully from Salla and Rovaniemi. They had to be given a push, and for this reason Gen. G. K. Kozlov of the 19th Army, advancing from Kantalahti, wanted to strike a swift blow westwards to capture Rovaniemi. Stalin's headquarters would not agree to this, however. Kozlov's proposal would have meant that Soviet troops would have driven a wedge *between* the Germans and the Finns. The burden of the fighting would thus have fallen to the Russian troops, with the Finns standing idly by, which was not in the spirit of the armistice agreement. Pursuit of the retreating Germans was to cease at the frontier, and the bulk of the troops were to be transferred to the north.[33]

The Soviet leadership had other ways of speeding up Finnish operations and of tying the Germans down in the south while Meretskov prepared his offensive against Petsamo. After the first officers of the Control Commission arrived

in Finland (General Zhdanov did not arrive until 5 October), a delegation drawn
from among them traveled on 23 September to headquarters in Mikkeli. The
operational section informed them of military operations against the Germans
and of troop locations and fortified places on the eastern frontier. The suspicious
Finnish officers supposed that the Commission's interest in these matters was
linked to plans for occupation.[34]

The Control Commission could not be kept in the dark for long, however.
Headquarters was ordered to prepare by 27 September a written operational plan
for the internment of the Germans in northern Finland. The basic idea of the
plan was to make sure of the Oulu-Kajaani watercourse, with its crossing points,
for a future offensive. The objective of the offensive was to inflict losses on the
Germans and capture the major centers of population (Tornio, Kemi, and
Rovaniemi) and to prevent their destruction. At the same time, the Germans
were to be pushed into unfavorable terrain and interned in central and northern
Lapland with the onset of winter.[35] Finnish troops in the north were to be
reinforced and united under the command of Lt. Gen. Hj. Siilasvuo. This 3rd
Army Corps was given the task of interning the German forces in Lapland.
Siilasvuo took charge of their front on 27 September. The evacuation of the
civilian population of Lapland came to an end at this time, which meant that
the one major obstacle to military operations was now out of the way.

There were indications that the Control Commission was tightening its grip
even before it responded to this operational plan. Fearing that they might lose
their freedom of action, the Finns, on Siilasvuo's orders, began in some places
to push ahead of the timetable agreed upon with the Germans from 28 September.
In some instances, this led to armed clashes. On 29 September, for example, a
day before the agreed timetable, the Finns moved into the strategically important
crossroad village of Pudasjärvi. On the following day, General Rendulic handed
over a note to Colonel Willamo (Colonel Haahti had already left Rovaniemi and
returned to Mikkeli) protesting against these incidents. For the time being, he
was willing to interpret them as the result of misunderstandings by on-the-spot
Finnish officers, the significance of which he did not wish to exaggerate. *If*,
however (Rendulic added), the breaking of agreements already made began to
look like part of a systematic Finnish policy, the consequence could only be the
outbreak of open hostilities between the former comrades in arms.[36]

The general's suspicions proved correct. Attaching his main priorities to the
course of foreign policy, Mannerheim had won the day at GHQ for his policy
of engaging in active military operations against the Germans. The government
also stressed the importance of swift and decisive action. "By the express command of the Marshal of Finland, the advance is to be pressed vigorously and
flanking movements will be mounted to take prisoners, and to destroy or capture
equipment."[37] At the end of September, plans were prepared in Siilasvuo's
headquarters for further military operations. To root out the Germans entrenched

along the rivers of Ostrobothnia, a landing was to be staged in their rear at Tornio (according to the original plan, Kemi). This was due to commence on 30 September, but a storm at sea caused the operation to be postponed for a day. Colonel Nihtilä's efforts to salvage the last remnants of the Haahti-Hölter agreement by having the landing called off were unsuccessful.[38]

In the meantime, the Control Commission was preparing its official response to the operational plan, which it had received on 27 September. In a note addressed to Prime Minister Urho Castrén on 30 September, the acting chairman, Lieutenant General Savonenkov, voiced his strong dissatisfaction with the situation and the operational plan. The high command of the Finnish army was trying to hold up the execution of the relevant clauses of the armistice agreement by whatever means possible. There was no sign of active military operations on any of the sectors of the front. Simply by following the retreating Germans, the Finnish military command was showing its lack of appetite for the terms laid down in the armistice. Savonenkov thereupon demanded a new plan for an offensive to be prepared for the Control Commission that very day and the commencement of active military operations in northern Finland by the following morning at the latest (0800 hours, 1 October 1944).[39]

A few hours later, the Control Commission was handed a single sheet of typed paper signed by Lieutenant General Airo. Entitled "Offensive operation for the internment of German troops," it listed the directions of advance and the forces mustered for these tasks.[40] From the Finnish point of view, the landings of Siilasvuo's troops at Tornio and the attack launched at the same time towards Kemi, a two-pronged operation that led to large-scale hostilities between Finnish and German troops, could not have come at a better time (the morning of 1 October). Rendulic's protests and appeals "to the common sense of the Finnish soldier" and to the agreements made were, in these circumstances, fruitless. With the expiry of its ultimatum on 2 October, the Mountain Army now regarded itself as at war with Finland. The Finns had not kept the promise that Haahti had made, evidently on his own authority, to inform the Germans beforehand if they intended to abandon the agreements. To hinder the advance of its new enemy and in revenge for the "betrayal" of the *Waffenbrüderschaft*, the Germans now began the systematic and extensive destruction of Lapland.[41]

To free their countrymen captured and interned in Tornio, the Mountain Army took hostages in northern Finland from among the Finns still remaining there, such as civil servants. Observing the instructions of GHQ, which were themselves based on positions adopted by the foreign ministry and the government's foreign affairs committee, Siilasvuo refused to enter into any negotiations over the agreements mentioned by the Germans because he did not recognize their validity. The government in Helsinki did not even know of their existence.[42] In addition to all this, the OKW bowed to pressure from the *Auswärtiges Amt*, fearful of a possible Swedish reaction, and ordered Rendulic to release the hostages immediately and unconditionally. This was done.[43] In a memorandum to Hitler on 5 October, Ribbentrop gave vent to his annoyance with Rendulic, who should have shown greater restraint and avoided trying to adapt the methods he had used in Croatia to Finland. Moreover, insults to the Finnish army would only make more difficult the efforts to organize a pro-German resistance movement in the country.[44]

The situation created by the events in Tornio aroused a good deal of anxiety in the OKW. Behind the operation was seen lurking once more "the hand of Moscow," stretching out towards Narvik. General von Buttlar of the OKW warned Rendulic and Hölter by telephone on 1 October about the bridges in Kemi and Tornio, which had at all costs to be destroyed. There must be no repeat of Arnhem, where the Allies had captured the bridges across the Rhine only to lose them again. Rendulic tried to calm down the führer's headquarters by assurances that the destruction of the bridges in the Oulu-Tornio region had been taken care of. It would take a long time to repair them. Moreover, Finnish and Swedish railways operated on different gauges, which would also slow things up.[45]

The OKW was also concerned about the overall strategic position of Finland and Scandinavia. With the loss of the French coastline, the importance of Norway as a base for German U-boats had greatly increased. The threat of active operations on the part of the Western powers had also fundamentally increased, in the opinion of the OKW, with the release of sea and air forces hitherto used by the British and Americans against bases in France. An invasion of Norway was therefore very much on the cards. The Western powers might try to cut off the vulnerable sea links of the 20th Mountain Army, especially as it had now lost the use of the ports of the Gulf of Bothnia. To shorten these supply lines and to avoid heavy losses, the Mountain Army was to withdraw to positions that were easy to defend on a narrow strip of land lying between the northern tip of Sweden and the Lyngen fjord before the expected Allied attack. By concentrating forces in this way, the Germans would have a better opportunity of repelling any possible Swedish attack on Norway. Northern Finland no longer was of much importance, especially as Reichsleiter Albert Speer had announced that German nickel reserves were sufficient. The withdrawal from Finland had of course to be coordinated with the movements of *XIX Geb. Korps*, which was retreating from the direction of Litsajoki and Petsamo. The population of northern Norway would be evacuated and (with suitable wasting tactics) the area could be made into a relatively effective no-man's-land, at least for the winter, between German and Russian troops. Hitler gave his final consent to this plan on 3 October 1944.[46]

On the same day, Rendulic was given advance notice of the decision by telephone from the OKW. Operation *Birke*, which had been intended to secure the line of Kaaresuvanto-Ivalo, was now replaced by Operation *Nordlicht*, a march directly to positions around the Lyngen fjord. The Mountain Army head-quarters confirmed at the same time that most of the German transports from the east and south had already passed through Rovaniemi on their way north. The town could therefore be abandoned in the near future without any serious consequences. Although fighting was still going on in Tornio, the situation had changed for the Germans. Rendulic's orders declared that it was no longer essential to hold the town of Tornio, which could be abandoned to the Finns. It was more important to keep open the road up the Tornio valley to Muonio for the troops retreating from the direction of Kemi. On 6 October, Rendulic broke off the assault on Tornio, and the withdrawal along the Rovaniemi and Muonio roads began the following day. Siilasvuo's troops sought to split up and destroy the retreating German units by flanking movements.[47]

For the Finns, the main objective of the Tornio and Kemi operations—the refutation of the Control Commission's accusation of collusion with the Ger-mans—had been achieved. Flanking movements on a large scale with the forces at the disposal of the Finnish army were in any event thought to be difficult because of the speedy retreat of the German units and the minelaying tactics and thorough destruction they employed. Nevertheless, the Finns had been able at least partially to tie down Rendulic's troops as Meretskov began his offensive on 7 October against Ferdinand Jodl's *XIX Geb. Korps* on the Litsajoki front. By the end of October, the Germans had suffered heavy losses and were pulling back westward through Petsamo and Kirkenes. On the face of things, the oppor-tunity for Soviet troops to attack southwards from Petsamo against Ivalo was now open.

As early as 5 October, the quartermaster-general, Lieutenant General Airo, had handed over a proposal to this effect from the Finnish GHQ to the Control Commission in the Hotel Torni in Helsinki. As they pulled out of Lapland, the Germans had to use two crossroads—Muonio and Ivalo. The capture of these two places would resolve the entire situation, for Rendulic's troops would then find themselves completely cut off and would be forced sooner or later to surren-der. The Finns would push ahead as fast as possible with their offensive from Tornio to Muonio to complete this stage of the operation. "As the seizure of Ivalo cannot be undertaken by the Finns, we suggest that the Soviet Union undertake to carry out this part of the operation, thereby giving Finland the assistance provided for in Article 2 of the armistice agreement." Two days later, the president and commander in chief drew attention to this issue in talks with the chairman of the Control Commission, General Zhdanov. With Meretskov advancing from Petsamo to Ivalo, the Germans retreating northwards from Rovaniemi would be surrounded.[48]

Stalin did not accept this proposal, however. The Finns received the official reply via the Control Commission a fortnight later, on 19 October. "Your proposal for assistance in the Ivalo area by Soviet forces is tardy and unrealistic.

The military leadership of the Soviet Union could not wait a month for the [Finnish?] military leadership to make a proposal about where Finland would need Soviet military assistance: the military leadership of the Soviet Union has therefore commenced those measures which it deems necessary.''[49] The precise motives for Stalin's attitude are unknown. It is natural to suppose that, even if he had succeeded in breaking through to Ivalo, Meretskov would have been throwing his troops into the breach against the Germans while the Finns tagged on behind at their own pace. In all probability, this line of reasoning may at least in part have persuaded Stalin to stay with the politically sensible line already established. It was up to the Finns themselves to free their own territory. The Kremlin's enthusiasm for joining in was hardly likely to be fueled by the fact that, because of the Finns' slow advance, Rendulic was able to transfer troops from the Finnish front to Petsamo.[50]

Matters would take on a different complexion, however, if the Western powers could be brought into a large-scale operation for the capture of Norwegian Lapland and the surrounding of the German forces in northern Finland. Stalin raised this with Churchill during the latter's visit to Moscow on 14 October. Churchill replied that the British could not spare the land forces for such an operation but that naval assistance could be provided. In addition, a "symbolic" Norwegian force of around 200 men could also be sent. Understandably, this was not good enough for Stalin, and the matter was dropped.[51]

Even before the arrival of Moscow's official answer, Zhdanov had warned Mannerheim in a note dated 16 October of the serious consequences of the "unsatisfactory" course of military operations in Lapland. The advance was slow and German losses were light. The favorable circumstances created by the seizure of Tornio and Kemi had been allowed to go to waste: protected by small rear detachments, the Germans' main force was continuing to withdraw in peace to the north. In particular, Zhdanov drew attention to the "ineffectual" activities of the Group Lagus, advancing along the Kemi River. The troop transfers to the north ordered by headquarters were still incomplete, and the handing over of German prisoners of war by the Finns to the Soviet Union had not even begun. The Finns had been unable to account for the dispositions of Rendulic's forces, even though "knowledge of the enemy and his intentions is a basic condition for the success of every operation." The Finnish military leadership now had to take energetic measures to repair this overall situation in the manner prescribed by the armistice agreement. "I have to inform you in advance, Mr. President and Commander-in-Chief, that unless this demand is fulfilled by the Finnish government and the high command, the Allied [Soviet] military command will be compelled to undertake those measures it deems essential."[52]

Mannerheim reacted swiftly. In a tightly worded telegram to Siilasvuo, dispatched that same day, he drew the general's attention to the gravity of the situation, in which the Germans were able time and again to break out of the positions to which the Finns' encircling movements had confined them. Sufficient forces were to be brought to bear in these operations.

I cannot understand why Major-General Lagus's forces appeared outside Rovaniemi and then did nothing but alert the enemy forces in the town, at a time when Major-General Pajari's operation against their rearguard communications had not yet had time to take effect. In these operations I see no sign of any purposeful efforts to surround and confine the enemy, which has been the main thrust of all my directive to you. The situation demands, urgently and without equivocation, a different kind of operational success rate than we have had up to now.[53]

In his detailed reply to Zhdanov, for which Mannerheim had been given two days' grace, the president stressed the great difficulties encountered by the Finns in the north. The conditions of the terrain (extensive bogland and few roads, which made bottling-up movements difficult), the miry state of the roads as a result of heavy autumn rain, the Germans' tough resistance and their thorough and effective mining and sabotaging tactics had regrettably slowed down the advance in certain areas. Nevertheless, "it is the unanimous opinion of the commanding officers taking part in military operations that the troops have, in these circumstances, acquitted themselves better than could reasonably have been expected."

The troop transfers ordered had been completed to the extent that men and equipment had been transported by train to the nearest railway terminals to the front. The transshipment of troops to Tornio and Kemi was dependent on tonnage that was not released until 17 October. General Zhdanov was right in saying that German prisoners of war had not yet been handed over to the Soviet Union. This matter had been left open because the Control Commission had not given any instructions as to how it should be done. For their part, the Finns were ready to hand over the Germans where and whenever the Commission chose.[54]

Mannerheim claimed that the Finns were sufficiently well informed as to the initial dispositions of Rendulic's army when the armistice had been signed. They had not been able to keep such a close watch over changes in the dispositions of the enemy thereafter, because the German prisoners generally did not reveal anything and only a few documents had been captured. Inquiries directed to the Soviet command about German troops and their movements in the direction of Petsamo and Kemijärvi had not met with any response. As regards intelligence supplied by agents, Mannerheim observed, this "had ceased completely when the Germans detained all Finns in their zones of operation. Agents were exposed with the aid of radio direction-finding equipment, and the placing of new agents in the wilderness is exceptionally difficult. The Russians, on the other hand, have their own excellent network of agents, established years ago." Air surveillance was also hindered at first by the ban on flying imposed on the Finnish Air

Force. After this ban had been lifted, reconnaissance flights had been carried out "to the extent that weather conditions and the exceptionally long flights for our limited resources have permitted."

Without wishing to deny that errors and failures had occurred in certain cases, the marshal gave assurances that the Finnish military command and troops would carry out their duties loyally and energetically in the exceptionally difficult circumstances. "I do not think I can conceal the fact that the carrying out of this campaign, in spite of all the good will and effort put into it, will probably take so much time that it may come into conflict with the deadline set down for demobilization in the armistice agreement."[55]

Zhdanov vehemently refused to discuss the time limits stipulated in the treaty for the demobilization of the Finnish army. In other respects, "I take note of your announcement that measures will be set afoot to speed up the disarming of the German troops in the north."[56] Zhdanov's attitude may have been influenced by news of the capture of Rovaniemi on the day when Mannerheim's letter was written. The advance now continued northwards, with Ivalo falling to the Finns on 4 November. The frontier was reached at Utsjoki on 20 November and in the direction of Karasjoki on the 21st.

In the "arm of Finland" sector, the Finns took Muonio after several days of fighting, the Germans having managed to evacuate the large ammunition dump located there. As Finland had been obliged to demobilize the wartime field army, in accordance with the armistice, the advance continued in difficult circumstances as a "children's crusade," with units composed of young conscripts pressing toward the northwest. Without taking advantage of their numerical and qualitative superiority, the experienced Alpine troops who comprised the *XVIII Geb. Korps* of General Hochbaum now retreated to the line of Kaaresuvanto and the positions prepared for Operation *Birke* in order to protect the right flank of the *XIX Geb. Korps*, which was marching westwards through Norwegian Lapland. When these troops had withdrawn far enough, the *XVIII Geb. Korps* detached themselves from their positions and moved behind the Lyngen line in January 1945. The extreme right wing of this position still reached into Finland in the direction of Kilpisjärvi. Rendulic had drawn Hitler's attention to this at the planning stage. Moving the position a little farther south from this spot would mean the cessation of hostilities with the Finnish troops, who were concerned only with pushing the Germans out of their territory, and would be to the advantage of the Mountain Army. Employing the arguments of a latter-day "Finlandizer," Hitler rejected Rendulic's proposal. The Finns would march wherever Stalin ordered them to. In planning the Lyngen line, there was no need to pay attention to anything but the suitability of the locality for fortification works.[57]

In actual fact, it was the expulsion of the Germans from Finland in accordance with the terms of the armistice that was at stake. The Soviet military command regarded the fighting in the arm as of secondary importance. Having inflicted a series of heavy losses on Jodl's *XIX Geb. Korps* in October, and having taken Kirkenes and Neiden, the Russians did not send their main forces in pursuit of the Germans as they withdrew westwards. Norwegian Lapland remained for the most part an empty no-man's-land throughout the winter. In his memoirs, Meretskov mentions the Finns' slow advance up the arm. "But it did not disturb us, because that distant sector had no essential significance."[58] This did not, however, prevent the Control Commission from sending a note about the slowness of the advance to the Finnish military leadership on 27 January 1945, to which the new commander of the defense forces, General Heinrichs, replied, pointing out the achievements of the Finnish troops in the face of difficulties.[59] The northwestern corner of the Kilpisjärvi area remained within the Germans' defensive zone, and the last soldier of Hitler's army did not leave Finnish territory until April 1945, a couple of weeks before the final collapse of the Third Reich.

PART II
The Allied Control Commission

4 The Early Days

After Prime Minister Hackzell suffered a stroke in Moscow on 14 September, it was obvious that a new government had to be formed. Protracted negotiations ensued, and the cabinet headed by the president of the Supreme Administrative Court, Urho Castrén, was able to take office on 21 September. The usual statement of aims was not issued by this government because it was taken for granted that its main task would be the carrying out of the armistice agreement, signed two days previously. The new government did not greatly differ in its composition from its predecessor. Carl Enckell continued as foreign minister, and he was to devote most of his time to looking after relations with the Control Commission. For this purpose, a special unit, the "B-section," was set up within the Foreign Ministry and headed personally by Enckell. Other affairs dealt with by the ministry were placed under the second foreign minister, Gen. A. E. Martola. Rudolf Walden continued as minister of defense. The act bringing the armistice into force, which authorized the government to determine by decree the exact details concerning the fulfillment and execution of the terms of the agreement, was approved by parliament of 20 September and confirmed by the president three days later.[1]

For the defense forces, contacts with the Control Commission were initially dealt with by Gen. Oscar Enckell. When the Commission expressed the view that the representative of the army headquarters should be a regular army officer, the president and commander in chief appointed Col. Ilmari Karhu as Enckell's assistant on 29 September. He was given the task of setting up the new headquarters liaison section; the name was changed on 4 December 1944 to the liaison section of the general staff of the defense forces. Colonel Karhu became the head of this section, responsible to the quartermaster-general and later directly to the chief of general staff. General Enckell was transferred to other duties soon after the founding stage of the section.[2]

On 5 October 1944, at 1:50 in the afternoon, a green Douglas aircraft piloted by Major Litvinov landed at Malmi airfield, and the chairman of the Allied Control Commission (ACC), Gen. Andrey Aleksandrovich Zhdanov, stepped out onto Finnish soil. Among the reception party were Prime Minister Urho Castrén, the members of the government's foreign affairs committee (Enckell, Walden, and the ministers Ellilä and Wuori), Minister of the Interior Hillilä, and senior members of the country's civil service and armed forces. The press paid particular attention to the fact that Zhdanov greeted Maj. Gen. Harry Alfthan's guard of honor in Finnish: *"Hyvää päivää pojat,"* to which they replied in due form: *"Hyvää päivää, herra kenraali."*[3] The top brass of the ACC was now in Helsinki, and work could begin in earnest.

According to the appendixes of the armistice agreement, the Control Commission was an instrument of the Allied (Soviet) military command whose main duty was to see that the Finnish government carried out the terms of the armistice to the letter and on time.[4] If it observed any breaches or shortcomings, the ACC was to make representations to Finnish officials for the relevant measures to be taken. The Commission, its members and authorized personnel, enjoyed diplomatic privileges and had unlimited access to all offices, institutions, and ports, and they had the absolute right to obtain all necessary information for the pursuance of their duties. The Commission, which had the authority to set up special subsections if necessary, was to be located in Helsinki.[5]

Special attention should be paid to the fact that the Control Commission functioned as an organization of Allied military command, and not (for example) as a kind of civil administrative supervisor for Finland. The word "Soviet" was always added in brackets after the term "Allied," as an indication that the Soviet Union was the real power in the ACC. Zhdanov's deputy and closest associate was Lt. Gen. Grigory Mikhailovich Savonenkov, who had worked with Zhdanov during the siege of Leningrad. Of the chairman's assistants, mention may be made of Maj. Gen. Sergey Fyodorovich Tokarev, who was in charge of general military and land force matters. The political section of the ACC was headed by the last Soviet minister to Finland before the Continuation War, Pavel Orlov, with Counsellor Y. Yeliseyev as his assistant. The liaison officer for the British members of the Control Commission was Colonel Vakhitov.[6]

After the signing of the armistice agreement in Moscow, steps were taken in London to organize the British representation on the Control Commission. The War Office showed little interest in the affair, seeing it as a job for political and economic experts in the first instance, and as having little direct military relevance. The Foreign Office, on the other hand, had to assume that Moscow would probably only allow the British members of the ACC to have access to Finnish officials via the leadership of the Commission. The moderate interest of the British government in Finland as a military concern is also reflected in the instructions given to the British members of the Commission. The British section, which comprised its leader, Commodore R. M. Howie of the Royal Navy, Lt. Colonel J. H. Magill of the army, and Group Capt. P. D. Kelly of the RAF, were to work in the closest collaboration with their Soviet colleagues. They were to remember that Finland lay within the Soviet Union's zone of operations as long as the war lasted, and for this reason Moscow had the right to make sure that the terms of the armistice were being enforced. Nevertheless, the British members of the Commission were to report immediately any signs of Soviet officials seeking to violate Finnish sovereignty without cause. On the other hand, cooperation with the Soviet Union was of great importance to the British government and this could greatly be affected by the relationships between Soviet and British personnel of the control commissions of different countries. Every opportunity should therefore be taken to forge open and cordial relations with Soviet colleagues. The British members of the Commission should not have direct or official contacts with the Finnish government. Even in unofficial contacts with Finnish officers and civilians, anything that might be seen in Soviet eyes as political plotting or military espionage was to be avoided. Finnish officials or private persons who tried to take advantage of the sympathies of the British members of the Commission were to be shunned in order not to arouse the suspicions of Soviet colleagues that the British were too friendly or too well disposed towards the Finns. The Finns were to be treated in an objective manner, within the terms of the armistice agreement.[7]

Because of the subordinate status of the British officers on the Control Commission, the government sent a special "political representative" to Finland as it had done in the case of Rumania, to maintain direct contact with the Finnish government; the restoration of diplomatic relations was not contemplated at this stage. Molotov gave his consent on 1 October 1944 to the British plan with regard both to Rumania and Finland, and with reference to the similar situation of the Soviet representative in Italy.[8] His Majesty's Government's political representative to Finland was to be Francis M. Shepherd, the British consul general at Leopoldville in the Belgian Congo, who arrived with the British members of the ACC in Helsinki on 18 October. The Allied Control Commission was now complete.

With the arrival of Commodore Howie's group, the head of the liaison section of GHQ, Colonel Karhu, ordered his assistant, Commander H. Gröndahl, to act as liaison officer to the British section of the Commission. When he presented himself to Howie on 21 October, Gröndahl mentioned that the liaison section was ready to give the British all the information they wished. Following his instructions, Howie observed that he was getting "at least for the time being" all the information he wanted from the Russians. Gröndahl's services were thus not needed, and the liaison section was forced to conclude that the British were content to play the role of mere observers.[9]

In a statement given to the newspaper *Uusi Suomi*, Shepherd also defined his task as "a watching mission."[10] Unlike the military members of the Commission, Shepherd did have authority to maintain direct contacts with Finnish officials. On the day after his arrival in Finland, he called on Foreign Minister Carl Enckell, who emphasized the determination of the Finnish government to carry out the conditions of the armistice. The Russians had behaved absolutely correctly in this respect, the foreign minister added. "He went on to say that the Russians themselves had, however, complained that Finland was not showing sufficient understanding of the Allied position and implied that they were using the word "Allied" to cover purely Russian cases." Shepherd avoided getting into a discussion of this subject, and the foreign minister assured him that a satisfactory solution would nonetheless be reached with the Russians. One of the practical problems in Finland was the lack of Russian speakers, which meant, for example, that he personally had to check and correct the correspondence in that language leaving his own ministry.[11]

After meeting the second foreign minister, General Martola, Shepherd thought it was too early to draw any conclusions from his discussions. The Finns were anxiously looking for signs that might indicate any possible excess of interest by the Russians in their country, and they hoped that the British in such instances would restrain Moscow. In general, however, it was acknowledged that the Russians had for the time being behaved extremely correctly. The Foreign Office viewed the contents of this report with satisfaction. The Finns seemed to be refraining from making complaints and were not trying to win British sympathy with tales of their troubles.[12]

Shepherd's account of his courtesy visit to the president at his residence at Tamminiemi did not have a favorable reception. "The Marshal was in uniform and his erect and commanding figure in the sunny and rather stagey setting of an old-rose carpeted salon looking out on the water and the autumnal birches gave the scene a strong flavour of royalty of the pre-Great War age: an impression which the Marshal's demeanour was not calculated to dispel." The president began the discussion, which lasted slightly less than an hour, by welcoming the representative of Great Britain to Finland, and he expressed his regrets that circumstances had conspired to place the two countries on opposing sides in the war. He stressed the difficulty of carrying out the military articles of the armistice agreement when the Control Commission was demanding the expulsion of the Germans and the demobilization of the Finnish army at the same time. The Soviet Union's negative attitude toward his proposal of an attack on Ivalo from Petsamo had also irritated the marshal.

Moving on to discuss general postwar political perspectives, Mannerheim gave vent to his suspicions of Russian attempts to ensure their security behind small buffer states. This could only mean a shifting of Soviet frontiers to those of the buffer states, after which new buffer states would be needed to protect these boundaries, and so on, in a never-ending chain reaction. "When I mentioned as an analogy our own reliance for our security on friendship and treaties with France and the small states across the Channel, he smiled sceptically and said he knew the Russians." The Porkkala base, in Shepherd's opinion, had strengthened Mannerheim's suspicions. "He thought that before this war there might have been some justification for such a demand, but now, with the south shore of the gulf in their possession and a powerful air force, nothing more was needed to protect Leningrad and to ensure free ingress and exit for the Russian Baltic Fleet."

In Shepherd's view:

> It was a little embarrassing for me to listen to these indirect aspersions on our Russian Allies, but in fact, apart from his insisting on always referring to them as the "Bolshies," Marshal Mannerheim, who speaks extremely careful and correct English, phrased his remarks so as to give no ground for demurring, though I was, of course, careful to take the opportunity to emphasise that our friendship and alliance with Soviet Russia was based on confidence in their integrity both as regards Finland and otherwise. The Marshal's distrust of Russian intentions is very widely shared by his countrymen.

Shepherd's report drew the following comments from the Northern Department of the Foreign Office: "Mannerheim has little faith in the future and clearly takes the lowest view of Soviet intentions. There was no 'New Deal' atmosphere about this meeting." Although the marshal's statements in themselves were only to be expected, Shepherd's conduct caused some disquiet in London. On the instructions of the under secretary of state, Orme Sargent, he was directed "to avoid listening to too much anti-Russian talk. Mannerheim obviously placed you in rather a delicate position; and you are no doubt taking care to make it clear to any Finns who take this line that they must not talk to you in this manner about our Soviet Allies."[13]

Although General Zhdanov received Shepherd on 22 October, the day after his visit to Tamminiemi, the conversation remained on a general level, with the ACC chairman not going into details about actual problems. The relations of the British political representative with the Control Commission continued to remain rather cool and distant. On 20 November, he had to report to London that Moscow still had not officially informed Zhdanov of the position of the British representative in Finland.[14] Even without having access to Soviet original material, it may be supposed that this was part of a general attempt to limit British involvement in Finnish affairs and the workings of the Control Commission as much as possible. This was emphasized by Moscow's very chilly reception of the idea of an American political representative coming to Finland, as we shall see later.

After he had been in the country a month, Shepherd made it clear to the Foreign Office that he had endeavored to steer clear of contacts with the Finns. He had done so in order not to depart from the Russians' own manner of conduct, and also to dispel the idea that the British political representative had arrived in Finland as some sort of softening influence upon the Russians. Nevertheless, it would in due course be useful to meet a few leading Finns, particularly from the commercial point of view. These people might then be able to form for themselves a picture of Britain's complete lack of interest in Finland. In a directive issued on 30 November, the Foreign Office noted that it could not see any obstacles to the forging of contacts with Finns. However, Shepherd had to avoid people like Ryti, Ramsay, and Tanner (three important wartime ministers), since meeting them might arouse Russian suspicions.[15]

Two days later, Orlov finally conveyed to the British the reassuring news that the Control Commission had now been told of Shepherd's official position by Moscow.[16] Even so, the British political representative was still complaining on 13 December to London that neither General Zhdanov nor Lieutenant General Savonenkov had turned up at the cocktail party he had organized to round off an evening of British films, in spite of his own diligent presence at every occasion organized by the Russians.[17] It seems as if Shepherd only met the chairman of the Control Commission once during 1944, with the exception of formal gatherings. Supervision of the execution of the terms of the armistice agreement in Finland remained firmly in the hands of the Russians.

During the first few weeks of its sojourn in Finland, the Control Commission concentrated on the expulsion of the Germans, as we have seen. Although this was without doubt the most important problem, it was by no means the only one. As soon as it had arrived in the country, the ACC had demanded an account of the withdrawal of Finnish troops to the 1940 frontier. The plans for withdrawal handed to the Commission on 28 September and 2 October prompted objections. The Finns were accused of acts deemed to be in contravention of the armistice agreement such as the removal or damaging of property. Mention was made of the machinery at the Enso, Harlu, and Värtsilä factories and the telephone exchange at Sortavala. In spite of the agreed timetable, there were still differences and misunderstandings—for example, when Soviet troops advanced in places too rapidly, in the Finns' opinion. The incidents that resulted were often difficult to untangle.[18]

Trying to arrive at common working procedures also took up time. When Enckell, Walden, and the commander of sea forces, Valve, arrived for the first meeting to discuss these matters, they were obliged to sit waiting in the lobby of the Hotel Torni for some considerable time before they were ushered into a room furnished with a large T-shaped table. The Finns were placed at a slightly lower, small table at the base of the T, a location that they interpreted as a sign of the subordinate position of the defeated.[19]

Article 3 of the armistice stipulated that Finland was obliged to hand over all of its south and southwest coastal airfields, with their installations, to the Soviet Union for use as bases for air operations against the German troops in Estonia and against Dönitz's sea forces operating in the northern Baltic. By October 1944, the Estonian mainland had already been taken, but German fleet movements were still a possibility. In addition to Malmi airport, which the ACC also needed for its own communications, the fields at Turku and Kymi, near Kotka, were handed over. The grass strip at Hanko, built by the Russians in 1940-41, was also on the list, but it turned out to be unfit for use. The fields at Turku and Kymi were not needed either, in the end, though their reservation remained in force. Only Malmi airport was used, and a closed military zone was placed around it. At the height of activity, Finnish estimates claimed, there were several squadrons based there. The ACC also inspected the other airfields in Finland and gathered information on the strength of the air force, its organization, weaponry, and so forth.[20]

The armistice agreement also obliged Finland immediately to set free those persons, irrespective of citizenship or nationality, who had been imprisoned for activities carried out on behalf of the United Nations or for showing sympathy for the cause of the United Nations, or because of their ethnic origins, and to rescind all discriminatory legislation and restrictions (Article 20). Article 21 obliged Finland to dissolve immediately all pro-Hitler political, military, and militaristic organizations operating on its soil, as well as other organizations conducting anti-United Nations and especially anti-Soviet propaganda, and in future not to permit the existence of such organizations. Only four days after the signing of the armistice, the Council of State (i.e., the Finnish government) issued a decree, emanating from the Ministry of Justice, on the release of political prisoners. This was swiftly put into operation by the ministry. On the same day, some four hundred associations were banned on the grounds that they came into the category of proscribed organizations according to Article 21. Most of these were local associations of the semi-fascist IKL (Patriotic People's Movement). The party's eight M.P.s were allowed to remain in parliament as "unattached": the parliamentary group thus had to give up its party identity. The IKL paper *Ajan Suunta* was banned on 4 October. Numerous tiny "national socialist" associations also disappeared from the scene, though most of these were merely names by the time of the armistice, the hobbyhorses of certain individual would-be politicians. This was not the case with the association for former members of the Finnish SS Battalion, nor the Academic Karelia Society (AKS), which had dominated student life before the war and whose membership at the time of its abolition was around three thousand.[21] After the Control Commission arrived in the country, the number of organizations forced to cease their activities increased still further.

In connection with the question of handing over prisoners of war, the ACC demanded separate explanations of any breaches of international regulations that had occurred in the prison camps, such as murders and acts of ill-treatment. On 19 October, General Zhdanov handed over to Prime Minister Castrén a list of 61 persons who were guilty of war crimes, largely involving prisoners of war, and demanded their arrest. "Further procedures against the listed war criminals after their arrest will be determined in due course by the ACC." Mistakes in the spelling of some of the names on the list made identification difficult and caused a number of mix-ups. Of this "list of 61," 39 persons were arrested in all, almost all of them having served in East Karelia during the war. The government feared that the Commission would take for granted the handing over of these men to the Soviet Union for judgment. It was also feared that there might be renewed demands of this kind in future. These forebodings were not realized, however. The list was to be the only one of its kind. Two of the men arrested, generals Aaro Pajari and Väinö Palojärvi, were released in December 1944 after the ACC confirmed that they had been imprisoned without cause; but the rest were kept in the prison at Riihimäki and an emergency jail in Miehikkälä, awaiting the further instructions of the Commission. They could not be dealt with because material for the prosecution could not be got out of the ACC before the signing of the Paris peace treaty. The matter was not finally cleared up until the autumn of 1947.[22]

While deprecating the treatment accorded to Soviet prisoners of war, the ACC also took the Finns severely to task for their too gentle handling of the German prisoners of war. Reference was made to quartering arrangements and to the flight to Sweden of a German medical corps in Tornio. Mannerheim sent Lt. Gen. Harald Öhquist to Tornio to investigate this particular incident. The civilian population moved to Finland from East Karelia and Ingria, and the so-called kith-and-kin battalions composed of Ingrian labor conscripts handed over by the Germans and prisoners of war of Finnic origin, created another problem. The Finns found themselves involved in protracted and complex correspondence with the ACC concerning the handing over of these people and the instances of escape that occurred.[23]

Of much greater significance for Finland's international position was the question of the demobilization of the army. Article 4 of the armistice obliged Finland to set its forces on a peacetime footing within two and a half months of the signing of the agreement—in other words, by the beginning of December. As the total strength of the defense forces in September 1944 was almost half a million men, demobilization would thus affect almost one in eight of the population of Finland. In addition, the war in Lapland had to be fought at the same time as demobilization was taking place, and the troops fighting there had also to be brought home within the general deadline.

To gain time and to relieve the prevalent labor shortage, GHQ issued an order on 25 September 1944 that all enlisted men, NCOs, and officers born in or before 1906 who had completed their period of military service were to be released by 5 October. (In the case of officers, due attention was to be paid to the prevailing needs of the military command.) The same held good for all born in 1926, irrespective of whether or not they had completed their military service.[24] Although the appendixes of the armistice clearly stipulated that the Finnish military command must reach agreement with the Soviet military command over the order in which the Finnish army was to be placed on a peacetime footing, this order was given and carried out without consulting the ACC. When the Control Commission got wind of it, however, lengthy and painful explanations were necessary.

The Control Commission got down in earnest to the question of demobilization on 12 October. It demanded to see a precise plan of demobilization by the 20th. The document handed over on the evening of 20 October by Lt. Gen. K. L. Oesch did not satisfy the representatives of the ACC, major generals Tokarev and Burmistrov, because there had been no time to translate into Russian the full text of the appendixes. The Finns were to hand over a complete version the following morning at 11 o'clock. Oesch's extensive reasoning in favor of a prolongation of the period of demobilization for the troops fighting in northern Finland did not give cause for further measures. In reply to the Finnish general's question about which task the Control Commission felt was the more important — the expulsion of the Germans from Finnish soil or demobilization — Tokarev replied that the armistice stipulated both tasks and that the Commission had no authority to change the deadlines or terms of the agreement. Its duty was simply to ensure they were carried out. The quicker operations in the north were brought to a conclusion, the more time there would be for demobilization. The two and a half months decreed by the agreement could be used as the Finnish military command wished. The main thing was that demobilization had to be completed by 5 December 1944.[25]

When Colonel Karhu arrived the following morning at the agreed time to hand over the complete translated text, Major General Burmistrov told him that he had relayed the main points of the previous evening's discussion to the chairman of the Control Commission. Lieutenant General Oesch had mentioned that the Finns considered a peacetime army, in the terms of the armistice, to mean a force similar to that which existed between the Winter War and the Continuation War. On the basis of two years' military service, this would mean a force of 63,820 men, with territorial functions continuing to remain in the hands of the Suojeluskunta, a paramilitary organization dating from the civil war of 1918. General Zhdanov declared that he could not accept this. The base month for the peacetime army was to be January 1939, not January 1941. No attention was paid to Karhu's counterarguments. Burmistrov also observed in passing that the ACC could see no obstacles to demobilization commencing straight away, but no exceptions to the deadline would be allowed. The Finns were obliged to add further details to the part of the plan dealing with the air and sea forces and the map appendixes, at Burmistrov's request, that evening and the following morning.[26]

Visiting the Hotel Torni for this purpose on 22 October, Karhu amplified his previous counterarguments, from which it could be inferred that GHQ took the same line. Did the Finns thus intend to ignore the warning that 1939 was to be taken as the model for a peacetime army? Would they continue to carry out demobilization in defiance of the armistice agreement's stipulation that this must be done in concert with the ACC? Lieutenant General Savonenkov now wrote on 24 October directly to Chief of General Staff Heinrichs, announcing in contradiction to the verbal statement of 21 October that only preparatory measures could be carried out in regard to the demobilization plan but that soldiers were not to be sent home from their units. The demobilization that had already taken place, of men of 38 or over and those born in 1926, was illegal.[27]

The Finns did not give way, however. In his reply of 25 October, Heinrichs observed that, because of the short period of time at their disposal, the army command had already issued the orders for the demobilization of the rest of the field army, and transports had been ordered as from the following day, 26 October; the ACC was thus requested to drop its ban on demobilization. However, the Commission stuck to its guns. On 28 October, it also demanded information for the following day concerning the strength of the Finnish army between 1937 and 1941. It was later revealed that the ACC needed such figures to help its deliberations as to the right size of a peacetime Finnish army.[28] As the situation became ever more complicated, the time for the Finns was beginning to run out. The men expecting to be sent home remained inactive in their units, not knowing the reason for the delay, a situation that might be expected to lead to difficulties in maintaining discipline. The most pessimistic rumormongers claimed that plans were afoot to use Finnish troops somewhere else in the European theater of war.[29]

On 30 October, Zhdanov gave Mannerheim his final reply to the Finns' demobilization plans. They were seen to be in contravention of the armistice agreement, as already explained. The basis for the peacetime army was to be that which obtained on 1 January 1939 and the total strength was to be 37,000 men, which would mean a reduction of the period of military service from two years to one.

The demobilization plan furthermore presupposes that the demobilized age classes will be placed at the disposal of the Suojeluskunta. The Suojeluskunta, as is well known, is a military organization with its own separate staffs, formations and numerous cadres. Moreover, the strength of the Suojeluskunta is nowhere specified, nor is it included in the strength of the army, although according to existing legislation the Suojeluskunta forms a part of the country's armed forces. This would permit any number of armed soldiers, over and above the age classes in the army, to remain in the Suojeluskunta.

From the documents presented, it is clear that only a part, and a small part at that, of the armed forces of Finland would consist of the age classes of the army. The greater part of its armed forces would be transferred in the process of demobilization from the army to the Suojeluskunta, where it would remain hidden in territorial formations of the Suojeluskunta, fully organized in the military sense, and ready at any moment to take up arms.

In the opinion of the Allied Control Commission, the preservation of an additional army in the guise of the Suojeluskunta would seem to be an attempt to avoid compliance with Article 4 of the armistice agreement and to preserve in one form or another a wartime army.

In addition to this, the Suojeluskunta, being a Hitlerite (fascist) type of military and political organisation, must be disbanded in accordance with Article 21 of the armistice agreement.

The Suojeluskunta organization was to be disbanded by 7 November 1944 and a new demobilization plan handed over to the Control Commission by 3 November at the latest.[30]

The question of the dissolution of the Suojeluskunta was not in itself a new problem. Shortly after his arrival in Finland, General Zhdanov had asked Prime Minister Castrén on 11 October whether the Suojeluskunta was not an organization to be disbanded. He mentioned the same thing to the Minister of Labor, Eero A. Wuori, on 13 October. The matter was also discussed publicly, for example, at a meeting of Swedish-speaking workers' associations four days later.[31]

Speaking to Shepherd on 19 October, Enckell emphasized the importance of the Suojeluskunta, now a fully integrated national organization (before the war, those of left-wing persuasion were not encouraged to join), for Finnish society. Its cultural and social activities, especially in the countryside, should not be belittled. The Russians had, however, discreetly pointed out that there was no reason to preserve an organization that was identified with the political antagonisms of the past.[32]

On a recommendation from President Mannerheim, the government's Foreign Affairs Committee decided on 29 October that it would be best to disband the Suojeluskunta organization before the Russians demanded this. That same day a bill was drawn up, with supporting statements, to be presented to Parliament. The government's official decision was held over for a couple of days at the marshal's request so that Lieutenant General Malmberg, the head of the Suojeluskunta, could come up with a request from the organization itself, which would propose its own dissolution. There was no time for this to be done, however. The feared demand was issued by the ACC the following day. The Finns had "missed the bus."[33]

After Zhdanov's note to Mannerheim of 30 October, things began to move rapidly. Thanks to preliminary preparations, the government was able to approve the bill to be presented to Parliament. At the same time, a meeting of the Suojeluskunta organization decided to abide loyally by this decision. In the afternoon of 31 October, the bill was laid before the house, where it passed through two readings that same day. The third and final reading, approving the bill, was on 3 November. The Women's Auxiliary Corps (Lotta Svärd) experienced the same fate two weeks later at the behest of the Commission.[34]

This eventual resolution of the issue came as a surprise to the British, in spite of everything. The British members of the Control Commission were only told of the letter sent to Mannerheim on 30 October the following morning. Bearing in mind his instructions from London, Commodore Howie did not raise any objections. When he met Savonenkov and Orlov that same evening (31 October), Shepherd expressed his doubts about the expediency of this measure, referring, as had Enckell, to the importance of the non-military aspect of the work of the Suojeluskunta in the countryside. Sticking to the position adumbrated by Zhdanov in his letter, the Russians refused to be budged. Shepherd now thought it best to retreat, though he did write a personal letter to Orlov in which he regretted that he and the British members of the Control Commission had been presented with a fait accompli. With an eye to the future, Shepherd suggested that open discussion should take place beforehand, and with plenty of time allowed to air matters, whenever political questions arose. This would also give him the opportunity, if needed, to consult London.[35]

The Northern Department thought Shepherd's letter unnecessary and, from the point of view of Anglo-Soviet relations, damaging. Moscow was fully justified in seeking the banning of the Suojeluskunta. "Neither we nor the Research Department have heard of this organization before, which suggests that it cannot be of such national importance to the Finns as Shepherd's report implies."[36]

In summing up the whole episode, Shepherd characterized the banning of the Suojeluskunta as a severe blow to the Finns, who would see this as an encroachment upon their independence, placing them even more at the mercy of the Russians. "They have however taken the blow sensibly and stolidly." Shepherd may have been aware of Foreign Office criticisms of his report, because he saw fit to defend his position yet again. The winding up of the Suojeluskunta might lead to the setting up of an underground organization, drawing its strength from a mood of misunderstood patriotism and powerful anti-Russian sentiment. The ending of the organization's social and other supportive activities in the countryside might lead to difficulties in these areas. Since the Suojeluskunta had opened its rank to social democrats, the government could have used the organization to advantage in building up friendly relations with the Soviet Union. The Russians, on the other hand, saw it simply as a fascist organization. The governmental crisis that was just then blowing up in Finland might in part be a result of the pessimism generated by the disbanding of the Suojeluskunta, the British political representative concluded.[37] But Shepherd's arguments were neither likely to affect the fate of the Suojeluskunta nor calculated to persuade His Majesty's Government to change its mind on the subject.

In accordance with General Zhdanov's deadline, the new demobilization plan, in which the demands of the ACC concerning the peacetime army had been obeyed, was handed over to the Commission on 3 November. The Commission gave a favorable response two days later, both to the proposed composition of the army and the demobilization plan, and the release of men from their units began. The Commission kept a very sharp eye on the progress of the release of troops and kept rigorously to the line it had adopted. In a number of separate instances, it was stressed verbally and in writing that the stipulated time limits must in no way be exceeded. During the demobilization stages, the ACC asked daily for detailed information about troops released. Every man had to be accounted for, and every weapon, vehicle, and horse put out of commission had to be detailed according to exact location. ACC observers diligently moved about the country seeing that agreements and directives were followed to the letter. The British officers also went along on these inspection trips once in a while. The ACC took a stiff line over faults that it came across, issuing reprimands and insisting that the chief of general staff take steps to punish those guilty of carelessness.[38]

The ACC approved the new plan for the release of troops on 5 November. There was thus exactly one month in which to carry out the plan. In view of the lack of transports, if for no other reason, the demobilization of the troops who had taken part in operations in northern Finland seemed very unlikely to succeed within the given time limits. Military personnel managed to cope with the task, however, and on 5 December 1944, the minister of defense, Lieutenant General Valve, could officially inform the ACC that the Finnish army had been demobilized in the manner stipulated by the armistice agreement. The Control Commission expressed its satisfaction with the achievement. The next day, Lieutenant General Savonenkov informed the British through Commodore Howie, whom he had invited to talks.[39]

In compliance with the articles of the armistice relating to economic matters, an agreement was concluded in December 1944 on the baselines for pricing arrangements for war reparations. This was a significant intermediary stage; indeed, as the year drew to an end, there was cause for satisfaction with the results already achieved. With the exception of the war guilt question, which was just beginning to raise its head, the execution of the terms of the armistice was proceeding more and more along established lines by the spring of 1945.

The work of the ACC took on a more routine appearance, and General Zhdanov, who was needed for important duties back home, was able ever more frequently (and for long periods of time) to leave the running of affairs in the hands of his deputy, Lieutenant General Savonenkov.

The easing of mutual suspicions, however, was a time-consuming task. There is an interesting eyewitness account of the initial situation and of the first impressions of the members of the Control Commission. John Scott, the ever-alert Stockholm correspondent for *Time* and *Life* magazines, who had visited Finland frequently and who had earlier spent several years in Moscow, rushed to Helsinki immediately after the conclusion of the armistice (20 September) and—with the exception of an occasional trip into the countryside—remained there until 13 October 1944. After he returned to Stockholm, Scott passed his extensive report to the American minister, Herschel Johnson, who sent it on to the State Department in Washington.[40]

In Finland Scott met, among others, the political adviser to the Control Commission, Pavel Orlov (whom he had known previously), and his assistant, Counsellor Y. Yeliseyev. Over lunch on 8 October, Yeliseyev was at pains to point out that the Soviet Union wanted nothing more from Finland than the unconditional fulfillment of the terms of the armistice, both in thought and deed. After that, "the Soviet generals walking around here now will go home, and we diplomats will become a regular Soviet legation." There was no question of Finland being "bolshevized." With the exception of military operations in Lapland and their slowness in rescinding discriminatory legislation (for example, with regard to political prisoners), the Finns had honestly sought to cooperate in carrying out the terms of the armistice. Yeliseyev made particular mention of the fact that most of them seemed psychologically to have buried their hatred and had decided to start promoting good relations with the Soviet Union. With regard to the Social Democratic Party, the problem was the dominant position of the "irreconcilable" Väinö Tanner, who was staking his hopes on a third world war. The overthrow of the Social Democratic Party leader was, however, a Finnish internal matter in which the Soviet Union could not interfere.

When Scott shifted the topic of conversation to the future leaders in government, Yeliseyev remarked that, in his view, Mauri Ryömä (a wartime dissident socialist and one of the founders of the Finnish People's Democratic Union) did not have the makings of a leader. Väinö Voionmaa (a cautious social democratic opponent of Tanner) was too old, Dr. Yrjö Ruutu (a rather belated convert to Marxism) was a good man, and Paasikivi of course was first class. When Scott asked how Yeliseyev would view the arrival of an American diplomatic representative in Helsinki, the Russian at first answered by saying he would think this perfectly natural. After a moment's reflection, however, he announced that he wished to withdraw his remark and to sound out Orlov on this matter.

Scott met Pavel Orlov two days later, on 10 October. In reply to the inquiry about the acceptability of an American political representative in Helsinki, Orlov said that he did not think this would be possible without prior discussion in Washington or Moscow, of which he would certainly have been informed. "Your question is therefore academic." Seen as a whole, the fulfillment of the terms of the armistice was proceeding in Orlov's view in a way that inspired hope for the future. Nevertheless, his list of comments was longer than Yeliseyev's. The Finns had broken the agreement by evacuating industrial equipment from the ceded territories, and they had been slow in releasing political prisoners. Russian prisoners of war had disappeared even after the armistice had come into force. Discriminatory legislation had not yet been rescinded, nor had the leaders of fascist organizations been put on trial. Many of Finland's wartime leaders were still occupying responsible positions and were exercising great authority. "Notwithstanding these facts, however," Orlov continued, "we look forward with confidence to the coming days and weeks because we believe that a foundation exists for the fulfillment of the armistice terms and for lasting peace and good relations between Finland and Russia."

Discussing with Orlov the arrangement of a press conference for Western journalists, Scott asked him to refrain from listing these complaints without presenting the other side of the picture, because otherwise the journalists and their readers could easily be given the impression that the Russians were simply drawing up a list of complaints as a springboard for renewed demands, as had happened in the case of Estonia in 1940. It would be unfortunate if such an impression were created. "Orlov laughed and said that of course there would be no question of an analogy with Estonia. 'We want an independent Finland, but a friendly Finland,' he said and added that the Soviet Union had learned much since 1940." Scott's impression was that the Russians were generally optimistic about the chances of forging good relations between Finland and the Soviet Union in the near future. They showed some skepticism and aversion toward the uncertain antics of the extreme left in Finnish politics, and they seemed to show a marked preference for a bourgeois democratic Finland.

Scott's overall impression was that the future prospects for an independent but at the same time pro-Russian Finland seemed at that moment to be "absolutely pretty good." The Finns were sincerely trying to meet their obligations towards Russia, and Scott believed that the Russians were seeking not only to tolerate but also to support an independent Finland. Both sides were beginning to see that they had been guilty of miscalculations: the Finns for thinking in the twenties and thirties that the state of weakness that followed the Russian Revolution would go on for ever, and the Russians for attacking Finland in 1939 for purely military reasons. It was not the concern of the United States to condemn the actions of the Soviet Union then, but there was no reason to shut one's eyes to the great suffering and sacrifices endured by the Finns in the fighting of recent months. This fight, in the last resort, was to free Finland from a situation that the events of 1939 had created.

In Scott's opinion, the Americans should view the new setup positively. For too long they had been inclined to reach highly polarized conclusions about Finland, seeing it on the one hand as a frontier post of Western culture against the Eastern barbarian, or on the other hand as a country that had fallen neck and crop into Russian hands. The United States now had to find a via media between these extremes. The Finnish people should be offered the moral support they deserved, but it should not look as if it were intended to "save the poor Finns from the Bolshevik bear." Even less should Moscow be left with the impression that the United States was trying to build in Finland "a base for the future against Russia." The United States ought to send to Helsinki as soon as possible a consul or a political and military representative, and should consider giving economic assistance after the restoration of diplomatic relations, in a manner that would not annoy the Russians nor arouse unnecessary illusions among the Finns. Both Soviet and Finnish officials deserved praise for the good state of affairs that was being created.

During the course of the autumn, however, the optimism of the Control Commission did at times slip. Orlov complained to Shepherd on 26 October of the Finns' slowness in carrying out the terms of the armistice.[41] Confidence in a future built upon a new foundation was by no means universal in the Castrén government. There were still suspicions that the Soviet Union, at least in the long term, was seeking to sovietize Finland. The old notions of relying on the help of the West still rose to the surface from time to time. At an evening sitting of the cabinet on 27 September, the second foreign minister, Martola, proposed that the Finnish minister in Stockholm be given the task of sounding out the chances of resuming relations once more with the United States. This idea fell through when others, including Minister for Social Affairs K. A. Fagerholm, took a negative view. Too much haste would only arouse suspicion because Washington would in any case sound out Moscow's opinion. Finland could not pin its hopes on the Western powers.[42]

A month later, the anxieties prevalent in government circles were not far from despair. The Swiss minister, Karl Egger, invited to talks with Martola on 25 October, was told that Finland was approaching the brink. Hopes of collaboration with the Soviet Union over the carrying out of the armistice agreement were fading alarmingly as the Control Commission continued to impose, in a threatening and arbitrary manner, new demands not in the agreement, which were quite simply beyond all reason. Counterarguments were not heeded, nor was any understanding shown of the Finns' goodwill or of the difficulties they faced. In particular, Martola was worried about the recent demand for the reparations payments to be fixed at 1938 price levels; by the "list of 61," because those mentioned therein would evidently find themselves outside the jurisdiction of the Finnish courts; and the simultaneity of the expulsion of the Germans and the demobilization. In addition to the indemnity, the interpretation of certain other articles of economic significance gave cause for concern. The intention of the Commission seemingly was to force the government into an impossible situation, which in a Finland that had lost faith and was divided could have catastrophic consequences. Martola wanted to make Switzerland (which was looking after American interests in Finland after the withdrawal of the U.S. diplomatic staff early in 1944), the other neutral countries, the western powers, and general world opinion aware of Finland's hopeless position so that they might influence Moscow to take a more placatory line. For this task of intercession, the foreign minister sought the assistance of the Swiss minister. Without revealing any sources, attempts had to be made to bring London and Washington together over the position of Finland. The foreign minister stressed the securing of American representation on the Control Commission. Links with the British section of the ACC were very weak, and there was no question of Shepherd acting as intermediary. After Martola had told him that a similar request for mediation would be presented to the Swedish minister to Helsinki, the Swiss minister deemed it wisest not to reject the proposal out of hand. He did, however, make quite clear the delicate nature of the proposal; it would involve neutral Switzerland in the affairs and relations of the Great Powers. He nevertheless promised to inform his government of the proposal. Because of the ban on coded messages, enforced since the signing of the armistice agreement, Minister Egger had to travel specially to Stockholm to relay Martola's request to Bern.[43]

The reply was predictable. Assuring the Finns of their heartfelt sympathy, the Politisches Departement — the Swiss foreign ministry — regretted that it could undertake no official action. At most, the attention of British and American representatives might be drawn, unofficially and in passing, to the matter in question; but there was no point in fostering false hopes as to the possible results of such a procedure.[44] Judging by the lack of positive activity, it would seem that Martola got the same sort of reply from Stockholm. Meeting Swedish Foreign Minister Günther on 26 October, Gripenberg hoped that he would have the opportunity in future to give an account of how things were going in Finland, "because nothing is so lamentable as being hung in silence." The foreign minister, who had listened sympathetically, burst out at this: "But we cannot do a thing for you."[45]

Shepherd and the British officers on the ACC took a different view. It was their overall impression that the Soviet representatives had shown an unexpected degree of reasonableness towards the Finns' inefficiency and equivocation. "I have not been able to establish any instance of the Russians having exceeded the Armistice terms."[46]

The same conclusion was reached by the British air attaché in Stockholm,

Wing Commander Fleet, when he visited Finland in November 1944. In his opinion, the Russian military authorities treated the Finns politely and correctly, but firmly. They hoped to gain plenty of experience in Finland that they could put to good use later in Germany. They affirmed that measures in Germany, which unlike Finland would be occupied, would nevertheless be completely different because they would not be restrained by the sympathy there was towards the Finns. The British officer reported that the Russians in a way held the Finns in high regard because of their *sisu*, or toughness and fighting spirit. They were also surprised at the relatively high standard of living in Helsinki. The Finns, however, were suspicious that the correctness of the ACC's attitude was only temporary. In Fleet's opinion, many officers who had been assigned to present certain points to the Control Commission "behaved like scared rabbits," but they could still arrange good dinners with plenty to drink.

The Finns' relations with the British, according to Fleet, were good. "The Finns are childlike in their attempts to show that they realize their mistakes and are grateful for any scrap of comfort, sympathy or understanding we show them. They are looking forward to the arrival of the Americans because anything that can be placed on the scales to counteract the power of the Russians is most welcome." At the same time, they seemed to overestimate the influence that Britain could wield, which might later give rise to reactions of disappointment.[47]

Shepherd believed that this last factor was not the main problem. The Finns were full of fear, scared out of their wits when they received the tightly worded notes of the ACC. This sort of attitude could easily lead to a lack of energy and self-confidence. Sometimes the government did not act because it did not know what it should do; it feared that, whatever course it chose, it would bring accusations upon its head from the Russians. This sort of mood could be explained to a large extent by the state of depression in which the country found itself, having lost the war and being faced with truly enormous difficulties. These included the surrender of Karelia and Porkkala, the resettlement of evacuees, the loss of merchant ships, the heavy burden of taxation, the lack of foodstuffs and fuel, the rising cost of living index, inflation, the reparations problem, and so on. Shepherd even added to his list the rains and darkness of autumn. "These are causes enough for depression, but not for hopelessness. I think the present pessimism is transient and will fade with time."[48]

Among the Finns themselves, doubts began to grow gradually about the ability of the Castrén government to carry out its tasks. In part, this had to do with the person of the prime minister himself. As early as 27 September 1944, the social democratic minister of social affairs, K. A. Fagerholm, noted in his diary: "It is a sad but undeniable fact that the Prime Minister will not be up to the job. He is out of his depth in the [political] world, and he seems not to have any policy of his own. He sees himself as a chairman — and even then, he's a bad one."[49] Gripenberg, visiting Helsinki, got the general impression of "all-around uncertainty. A guiding hand in foreign policy, especially in matters relating to Russia, is missing.''[50] Business kept on piling up, and the Control Commission became more and more impatient. Open and trust-enhancing cooperation was nowhere near getting off the ground. At the same time, the war-guilt question and the negotiations over reparations were getting bogged down. In Finnish political circles, it was also considered important that the government be reconstructed in order to broaden its base of support, especially in view of the rapid advances being made by the left at the expense of the strife-ridden Social Democratic Party. In the end, the Castrén government collapsed from within after the resignation of social democratic ministers Fagerholm and Wuori.

In the Paasikivi government, appointed in 17 November 1944, the posts of foreign, interior, and defense ministers remained in the same hands as before. General Martola was elevated to the rank of provincial governor and was replaced as second foreign minister by the social democrat, Reinhold Svento. After Rudolf Walden was stricken by serious illness on 27 November, he was replaced from 1 December by Lt. Gen. Väinö Valve. The Ministry of Justice, which was later to play a central role in the handling of the war guilt issue, was entrusted to Dr. Urho Kekkonen of the Agrarian Union. The communists were also represented in government in the form of Yrjö Leino, who took the post of second minister of social affairs. The recently founded left-wing party of the People's Democratic Union, in which the communists were to play a leading role, was also represented by Dr. Johan Helo, who had been imprisoned in 1941 for his opposition to Finland's participation in the war.[51]

The new cabinet immediately found itself having to grapple with a major diplomatic and military problem. When Col. Ilmari Karhu, the head of the liaison section of GHQ, had gone on 17 November to announce the current strength of the Finnish army (which had become almost a routine matter), he was greeted at the Hotel Torni by Major General Tokarev with a series of inquiries about the roads of northern Finland and the speed limits that their condition might impose for vehicles. In particular, Tokarev was interested in the routes between Rovaniemi and Ivalo and Rovaniemi-Kemijärvi-Salla. Finally, he came to the heart of the matter. "What would be the formal prerequisites for the transfer of Norwegian police units from Sweden via Ivalo or Salla to Soviet territory?" The formalities should be as simple as possible. If Sweden did not provide transport, one hundred lorries would be needed for the transfer operation.[52] Here it is relevant to note that the Finns had taken Ivalo on 4 November, so they had some idea of the damage caused and the state of the roads. Behind this proposal lay the desire of the Norwegians to transfer those refugees who had received training in Sweden to serve in their own country, in the areas of northern Norway liberated by the Russians.[53]

Tokarev's proposal did not come as a complete surprise to the Finns. On 6 November, Gripenberg had met the Norwegian foreign minister, Trygve Lie, en route for Moscow and had been given a preliminary account of the plan. On his return from the Soviet capital, Lie told Gripenberg that he had discussed the arrangement of transit with Dekanosov on the understanding that the Norwegian government would seek the necessary permission of the Finnish government. Dekanosov, however, took strong exception to this proposed method. All proposals on this matter had to come from the Allied Control Commission. Lie gave way to Dekanosov's demand, but he wanted to let the Finnish government know what was afoot via the Finnish minister in Stockholm. The Norwegian foreign minister also believed that it was vitally important to keep the matter hidden from the press.[54]

Tokarev's inquiries were, therefore, no longer unexpected in Helsinki. Having been in touch with the newly formed Paasikivi government that evening, Karhu was able to give the Control Commission a positive response in principle. The practical details would be dealt with by the ACC and Finnish GHQ for the route from Tornio through Rovaniemi to Ivalo. It was not thought feasible to provide Finnish vehicles for the operation.

The execution of the plan was held up, however, with the first Norwegian units not being ready for departure until January 1945. Their transfer by land to northern Norway at that stage posed something of a technical problem because of the length of the journey and partly because of uncleared roads. The same was true of the alternative route considered; up the arm of Finland to Kaaresuvanto and Kautokeino. The most practicable solution turned out to be the dispatch of the Norwegian troops (one battalion and a field hospital) by air, directly from Sweden to Kirkenes. This was carried out in January-February 1945 by an American transport squadron of ten DC-3 aircraft commanded by Col. Bernt Balchen, which had moved in to use the airfields of northern Sweden. At this time, it was mostly German planes that were the subject of shadowing operations in defense of Swedish neutrality.[55] When the Kautokeino road was opened in April 1945, two Norwegian companies used it to get to northern Norway. As a safety measure, talks between the Finns and the Russians on the use of the Rovaniemi route still continued. In April 1945, the Norwegians finally informed the Finnish government that, in view of technical difficulties, the transit by road of troops could not begin until June at the earliest.[56] As the German troops in Norway surrendered in May 1945, the last wartime transit plan to use Finnish roads was never put into operation.

Paasikivi's assumption of the post of prime minister in November 1944 brought to the forefront of Finnish government an experienced politician who, in the midst of difficulties, knew what he wanted. As Paasikivi took a firm grip of the reins, Mannerheim moved more and more into the background. Visiting the Stockholm legation of the United States at the beginning of December 1944 to sound out the possibilities of obtaining a loan to help meet reparations payments, Minister of Labor, Eero A. Wuori stressed the new government's firm position:

There is not the slightest evidence of Russian desire to gain control of the internal government of Finland, although those inclined to interpret all Russian actions at their worst can regard various measures as easing the way for future interference. Wuori does not take this pessimistic view but he does think Moscow will ruthlessly press all demands with the two-fold object of squeezing every possible material gain out of Finland and making sure that a "reliable" Finnish regime will arise and really hold power.

Moscow's numerous and categorical assurances that Finland's independence would be respected were, in Wuori's view, sincere; there were no dangers on that score, at least in the near future.

Cooperation within the government was proceeding successfully, Wuori believed. Paasikivi himself enjoyed the exercise of power and was in good health. He had shaken his head when he heard of the collapse of former government minister General Walden, and he had told Wuori that his own burden was also heavy. Nevertheless, when Wuori asked why he did not delegate some of his tasks to Deputy Prime Minister Mauno Pekkala, Paasikivi replied that everything that came up was so important that he did not wish to delegate anything.[57]

One week after the formation of the new government, the prime minister received the British political representative, Mr. Shepherd. Paasikivi took the opportunity to emphasize that his government's first objective was to carry out faithfully the terms stipulated in the armistice and to work in close liaison with the Control Commission.

M. Paasikivi looks all of his 75 years and although his mind is quite alert and his personality attractive, he stumbled a great deal in his speech. He spoke excellent French but my impression was that it was rather a strain for him to keep his mind on the business in hand and to express himself. He has, however, a strong personality and, in spite of his approaching senility, is very definitely no nonentity.[58]

5 The Question of American Representation in Finland

Ambassador Averell Harriman's reports from Moscow gave the State Department good cause to believe, by the autumn of 1944, that the Soviet Union was unlikely to welcome the arrival in Helsinki of political representatives of other U.N. countries, although the establishment of consulates might be permitted. In accordance with its general policy of regarding the preservation of good relations as paramount, Washington decided not to risk annoying the Soviet Union and dropped the question of representation for the time being.[1]

This policy soon began to encounter obstacles, mostly of a practical nature. The legation in Stockholm had difficulties in obtaining information from Helsinki and in looking after the interests of the United States and its citizens in Finland. Informing the State Department on 3 October of the dispatch of British representatives to Rumania, Bulgaria, and Finland, the Foreign Office asked the Americans to do the same as soon as possible in the case of Bucharest and Sofia. No mention was made of Helsinki for the time being. Compared to the Balkan countries, Finland, which had been spared military occupation, was of much less importance to Britain. On the other hand, many American-Finnish organizations and private individuals urged President Roosevelt and the State Department to restore official links with Finland. The U.S. legation in Stockholm, which had taken to heart the report presented by John Scott, took the same line. Minister Herschel Johnson thought it was strange that the United States should have kept up relations with the Finnish government when it was in the German camp, whereas now—when Finland was fighting against Germany and forging good relations with the Russians—Washington had not even sent a vice-consul to Helsinki. The Soviet Union, not to mention the Finns, might well take umbrage at this, seeing it as an indication that the United States no longer recognized Finland as an independent country.[2]

Encouraged by the Kremlin's consent to the sending of a British political representative to Rumania, Cordell Hull instructed Harriman on 12 October to find out how the Soviet Union would like American political representation in Bucharest to be arranged. In Harriman's opinion, the United States could not be satisfied with less than Britain: in other words, the United States should also have a political representative with direct access to Rumanian officials, in addition to the officers sitting on the Control Commission. After a wait of some two weeks, Harriman received a favorable reply from the Russians to this proposal.[3]

The United States had not been at war with Finland, and in this instance Cordell Hull adopted a more cautious line of approach. There could be no question of American participation on the Control Commission. Anything that hinted at the restoration of diplomatic relations had to be carefully avoided, and this included representation at a consular level. One possibility might be to send someone who could act as an intermediary between the American government and the Allied Control Commission and who would also look after the interests of the United States and its citizens in Finland. Harriman was now asked to say how he thought the Soviet government might react to such a proposal.[4] In his reply, the ambassador declared that he would like to know why the Soviet Union should not accept the dispatch of an American consul to Finland as a sensible solution. An intermediary between the U.S. government and the Control Commission was hardly likely to be able to work efficiently, since the person would clearly not have any access to Finnish officials.[5]

The American legation in Stockholm, asked by the State Department to comment on Harriman's suggestion, took a different line. Representation simply at consular level would place the United States in a subordinate position in comparison to the Soviet Union and Britain and would certainly cause the wrong conclusions to be drawn in Finland and elsewhere, including the Soviet Union. Washington should send to Helsinki a political representative enjoying the same status as the British counterpart, even though the representative would of course not be a member of the Control Commission.[6]

The State Department now looked into the possibility of sorting out this problem by continuing to place the supervision of American interests in Finland in the hands of the Swiss legation there. This would avoid stepping on the Russians' toes and, with an eye to American public opinion, the State Department's "responsibility" for what was happening in Finland would continue to remain minimal. The embassy in Moscow, however, doggedly pursued its earlier line. Harriman's deputy, George F. Kennan, reported having heard from the Commissariat for Foreign Affairs that the Finnish government, in accordance with the appendix to Article 5 of the armistice, had suspended all communications between the legations and consulates in Finland (including the Swiss legation) and abroad. There could be no question of countermanding or changing these orders as long as German troops remained on Finnish soil. It was Kennan's impression that Soviet officials were unlikely to understand why a third party should act as the guardian of American interests. It would be unclear to them why representatives of the United States were not able immediately to come and take care of American interests directly, in the same way as the British representatives had done. Moreover, the Soviet Union and Switzerland did not even have diplomatic relations with one another.[7]

Having learned that Moscow had agreed to the dispatch of an American political representative to Rumania, Washington was at last ready to take steps with regard to Bulgaria and Finland. In accordance with Roosevelt's decision of 11 November 1944, Harriman's former deputy in Moscow, Maxwell M. Hamilton, would be transferred to Helsinki "as the representative of the United States in Finland." He would look after his country's interests in the same way as the representatives sent to Rumania and Bulgaria. Although Hamilton held a personal title of minister, this was not intended as a restoration of diplomatic or consular relations, nor was it intended that he should take part in the workings of the ACC. The American representative and his staff were naturally to enjoy every possibility of maintaining links with the Finnish government and people and unlimited freedom of movement and communication, including the sending of coded messages. The second secretary of the legation in Stockholm, Randolph Higgs,[8] was to be sent without delay to Helsinki to prepare for Hamilton's arrival. Kennan was to inform the Soviet government of this decision without asking for its consent, seeking, however, to obtain verbal confirmation of the American supposition that there would be no objection to the American plan.[9]

Following his instructions, Kennan took up this matter with Deputy People's Commissar for Foreign Affairs Dekanosov on 17 November. Although unable to give a direct answer, Dekanosov stressed that the Finnish situation could not be seen as analogous to that of Rumania and Bulgaria. In Kennan's words:

> While the Soviet Government will no doubt proceed with characteristic circumspection to make sure that our step has no implications which could possibly be detrimental to Soviet interests or prestige, I believe that Dekanosov's reserve was due principally to the customary caution of Soviet officials in discussing matters on which they are not completely instructed.

It was difficult to see on what grounds the Soviet government could object to the arrival of an American representative in a capital where the legations of the neutral countries were still operating. However, it was within the bounds of possibility that Moscow would refrain from expressing a view, at least in the near future. In that event, the Americans could take silence to mean consent and could act as they then saw fit.[10]

But Washington preferred to err on the side of caution. In his instructions to Higgs on 5 December, Secretary of State Edward R. Stettinius made it clear that he was to stay in close contact with the Soviet minister in Stockholm, Mme.

Kollontay. He was only to go to Helsinki after confirmation that Soviet officials in Finland were aware of what was proposed and had begun to take the necessary steps to facilitate the journey of Higgs and his staff, such as arranging the usual diplomatic privileges. Higgs was not to get in touch with the Finnish legation in Stockholm, however, nor were the Finns to be asked to provide visas for Higgs and his staff. In Helsinki, Higgs was to take care of American political interests in Finland until Hamilton arrived and until normal diplomatic relations could be resumed.

> You will at all times bear in mind that although the United States and Finland have not been at war with one another, diplomatic relations between the two countries remain severed and Finland is still in a technical state of war with our Soviet and British allies. You will conduct yourself accordingly especially in your relations with Finnish officials.

All contacts with persons expelled from the United States were to be avoided.[11]

Three days later, Kennan outlined the instructions given to Higgs at a meeting with Dekanosov. The deputy foreign minister declared that his government had not yet come to a decision on the matter of American representation in Finland. General Zhdanov had been informed of the issue and had wanted to know the significance of the reference to American representatives in Rumania and Bulgaria. He had also raised doubts about the Americans' use of the term "mission." Placing Finland, with whom the United States had not been at war, in the same category as Rumania and Bulgaria was misleading. The word "mission" seemed to indicate the usual form of diplomatic representation.

Kennan argued that Finland could very well be taken as a special case. The term "mission" had been deliberately chosen to avoid giving the impression of a high-level diplomat being accredited to a particular government. Kennan hoped that these points would clear up any doubts Zhdanov had and would facilitate the prompt arrival of Higgs in Helsinki.[12] Kollontay nevertheless was obliged to inform Higgs on 14 December that permission to fly to Finland had not yet arrived from Moscow. She also avoided getting involved in a discussion about the purpose of Higg's journey. Clearly, the key to the problem was still in Moscow's hands.[13]

In his letter to Harriman sent on that same day, Dekanosov referred once more to the reservations Zhdanov had already expressed. The Soviet government would come to a decision only when it had heard Zhdanov's official view. In his reply, Harriman stated that he did not understand the reference to the lack of an analogy between the Rumanian and Bulgarian cases on the one hand and the case of Finland on the other. The Americans were not seeking to draw any parallel between Hamilton's functions and those of the American representatives on the Allied Control Commissions in Bulgaria and Rumania because the United States was not a party to the armistice agreement made with Finland. But this agreement made no mention of political representatives, and this was what was at issue. In Harriman's view, Kennan had drawn this parallel to help the Russians form a clearer picture of the position with regard to Hamilton. As this had not met with any success, Harriman suggested that the relevant passage of Kennan's dispatch be regarded as null and void.[14]

On 4 January 1945—evidently after sounding out the opinion of General Zhdanov one more time—the Kremlin was at last able to inform the Americans that it did not object to Hamilton's appointment as American representative to Helsinki. According to Dekanosov, his government had now concluded that the purpose of this move was not the restoration of normal diplomatic or consular relations.[15] Hamilton's road to Helsinki (in the first instance, that of Higgs) was now opened up in principle. As the Great Powers prepared for the summit conference planned for Yalta at the beginning of February 1945, the position of Finland was rapidly assuming a degree of stability.

PART III
The Ending of the War in Europe

6   From Yalta to Potsdam

At the Teheran conference in 1943, the question of the western borders of the Soviet Union was settled, in principle, in a manner acceptable to Stalin. The experiences of the world war had strengthened the unbending resolve of the Soviet leader to ensure that his country's security needs were met. The borders of 1941 were to be regarded as the basis for territorial settlements, and Stalin seems to have thought that there would be no question of a revival of the political, military, and economic *cordon sanitaire* around Russia that had prevailed throughout the interwar period. The Atlantic Charter, with its propagandistic phrases, was, by comparison, a secondary issue. Suspicion of the capitalist Great Powers and their leaders did not die away in Moscow, even at the height of the wartime alliance. These powers were still thought to be working for the ultimate destruction of the socialist Soviet Union. It was Stalin's belief that wars were inevitable as long as capitalism and its most extreme form, imperialism, existed. The Soviet Union could not therefore afford to rest on its laurels, even after victory in the war: it would have to remain alert and prepared to meet new ordeals.

After the Teheran conference, the fate of southeast Finland, the Baltic countries, and Bessarabia seemed to be settled. The real bone of contention between the Western powers and the Soviet Union was the Polish problem. These differences were not primarily caused by the eastern border issue, however, since the United States and Britain were prepared for political reasons to accept the Soviet demand for the Curzon Line (corresponding roughly to the present-day frontier), in spite of the opposition of the exiled Polish government in London. The Big Three had likewise envisaged an independent postwar Poland enjoying friendly relations with the Soviet Union. In the course of time, however, these vague phrases could no longer conceal the fact that they were interpreted in very different fashion in the East and in the West. The government in London, with

85

whom the Soviet Union had already broken off relations in the spring of 1943, was certainly not regarded as "friendly" by the men in the Kremlin. In his memoirs, the Polish ambassador to Washington, Jan Ciechanowski, even had Stalin complaining to representatives of the Western powers that he had been unable to find "a Polish Paasikivi."[1] The Mikołajczyk government, ignorant of the contents of the discussions in Teheran, remained firmly committed to the prewar frontiers of the Polish state and to a pro-Western foreign policy. The Kremlin believed that at Teheran the Soviet Union had been promised the Curzon Line and a friendly Polish government. The London Poles seemed disinclined to accept either proposition. The view of the Western powers was that no communist-led Polish government could be "independent" in the manner envisaged at Teheran and that this was more important than the frontier question. The situation became acute once more in 1944 as the Soviet troops advanced into Poland on the heels of the retreating Germans. A Polish "National Liberation Committee," in which the communists occupied a central position, was established behind the Soviet lines at Lublin; on the last day of 1944, the Kremlin officially recognized this committee as the legal government of Poland. A settling of accounts with the West over this issue could therefore no longer be avoided.

There were also problems in southeast Europe. In the autumn of 1944, the German grip on the Balkans finally loosened. Rumania and Bulgaria changed sides. In October 1944, Hitler's troops pulled out of Greece, while at the same time Tito's partisans were in control of a large part of Yugoslavia. These developments aroused mixed feelings in London. There was no longer any cause to doubt that Germany was sliding to defeat: a major bridgehead had also been established in western Europe, extending as far as Paris and Brussels. On the other hand, southeast Europe seemed to be sliding into Stalin's grasp at an alarming rate. In particular, the British were interested in the fate of Greece, which was vital for the control of the eastern Mediterranean. During the visit to Moscow by Churchill and Eden in October 1944, however, the two sides were able to reach agreement in secret discussions. Greece was assigned to the British sphere of interests, whereas the Soviet Union was to have the decisive voice in the affairs of Rumania, Hungary, and Bulgaria. Both sides were to have an equal interest in Yugoslavia. The agreement was limited to the Balkans, where Britain had clear interests; Finland was wholly omitted.[2]

President Roosevelt and Secretary of State Cordell Hull were not given full details of the Anglo-Soviet division of spheres of interest, though the Americans themselves refrained from taking any special notice of the agreement. The agreement did not formally involve them in the confused Balkan question. There was also good reason not to become mixed up in Eastern European affairs on the eve of the presidential elections, since this might have internal political repercussions. Furthermore, the "percentage agreement" was immediately put to test.

When the British troops sent to Greece crushed the communist uprising against the royalist government in Athens, Stalin did not interfere. When the Soviet-backed left wing, under communist leadership, overthrew the Radescu government in Rumania in February 1945 and forced King Michael to appoint a government under the leftist Petru Groza, Churchill in turn kept quiet. Dissatisfaction was shown, however, by the standard-bearers of the cause of democracy — the American government and press — in both instances. Although Washington did not for the present take further steps, these protests were a clear indication that the Americans were unlikely in the long run to concede the validity of the Churchill-Stalin agreement. The declining strength of Britain and the rise of America as a world power in the postwar years soon removed this agreement from any sort of position in which it might have influenced the course of events. Following its universalist principles, the United States was unwilling to limit in advance its freedom of action in any part of the world.

When the Big Three (after protracted preparations) assembled in Yalta at the beginning of February 1945, the collapse of the Third Reich was already in view. In these circumstances, discussion of purely military matters could be kept at a minimum. Nevertheless, the Western Powers attached some importance to Stalin's promise to enter into the war against Japan three months after the surrender of Germany. The main aim of the United States at Yalta was to ensure Soviet participation in a manner satisfactory to the Americans in the activities of the future world organization, the United Nations. The fate of mankind in the postwar years and the prevention of a new international catastrophe depended upon the continuation of cooperation between the West and the Soviet Union in the future. In this respect, Roosevelt could be well pleased with the compromise agreement reached over the right of veto of the permanent members of the Security Council. The problem of U.N. membership of the individual Soviet republics, which had dogged the allies since the Dumbarton Oaks conference in the autumn of 1944, was now resolved by limiting the right of representation to the Ukraine and Byelorussia.[3] It was decided to convene the founding conference of the United Nations in San Francisco in April 1945. Having won such important victories, Roosevelt now felt able to afford concessions.

There still remained the problematic Polish question, which took up more of the Big Three's time at Yalta than any other issue. In Western eyes, the Polish question had become a test case that would throw light on Stalin's broader ambitions. Moscow's security policy was all too easily interpreted in an ideological light. Appealing to the trust shown by American public opinion in the Atlantic Charter, and to the mood of the millions of Polish-born American voters, Roosevelt mounted an attempt to shift the town of Lwów and its immediate surrounding area back to Poland from behind the Curzon Line. Churchill for his part stressed the importance of Poland's "freedom and independence." This was a matter of honor for His Majesty's Government: Britain had, after all, gone to war to save Poland, and for this reason could not be indifferent to that country's fate.

In a pugnacious speech, Stalin bluntly outlined his position. For the Soviet Union, Poland was not merely a matter of honor but one of life and death. Poland formed a corridor along which attacks had been launched from the west against Russia time and again in the past. This route had now to be blocked once and for all. An anti-Soviet Poland could not, therefore, be permitted. Poland had to be strong so that it would be able in the future to resist attacks from the west. As for the eastern border of the Polish state, it had to be remembered that the Curzon Line had been drawn on the map at the Paris peace conference in 1919 at the instigation of *Western* politicians. Should he (Stalin) and Molotov thus return to Moscow with a poorer deal for the interests of the Soviet Union than Curzon or Clemenceau had offered? The discussion of the eastern border of Poland was concluded at this point. Warsaw would be given territorial compensation from Germany, though the size of this area was to remain undetermined for the time being.

Even more difficult was the question of who should govern in Warsaw: the exile government in London, regarded in the East as anti-Soviet; or the Lublin government, branded in the West as Stalin's puppet. The West now saw fit to try for a compromise by bringing the two competing groups together. After a lot of haggling, it was decided that the Lublin government would be reorganized on a broader democratic basis, with the inclusion of democratic leaders from Poland itself and from Poles abroad. This was to be arranged in further talks between Molotov and the British and American ambassadors in the Russian capital. Stalin promised that general elections would be held soon in Poland — perhaps within a month — and that a permanent government could then be formed on the basis of the election results. Roosevelt emphasized that the elections would have to be as clean and above suspicion as the morals of Caesar's wife, to which Stalin replied: "That is what they say about her, but in fact, that woman had her sins, too." In any event, the Great Powers had managed to avoid, for the time being, an open breach over the Polish question.

On Roosevelt's initiative, the Big Three also signed the so-called Declaration on Liberated Europe, according to which broad-based governments, representing all the democratic elements of the population, were to be established in Eastern Europe as well. Their duty was to organize free elections as soon as possible for the formation of governments representative of the will of the people. Against the advice of the State Department, Roosevelt refused to advocate any sort of follow-up mechanism. The declaration was important for him for specific internal political and cosmetic reasons. It was not wise to shake the faith of the electorate in the war propaganda phraseology of the Atlantic Charter as a basis for the future peace, because such a shock of disappointment could easily give rise to unfortunate consequences — as the fate of President Wilson in 1919-20 well illustrated. Were the United States to turn its back on the United Nations and return to isolationism, the mistakes of the era following World War I would be repeated. For this reason, great care and tact had to be used to bring the American public out of the dream world of wartime and into an appreciation of the realities of the situation. For the time being, the matter had to be postponed. A lot also depended on how far Stalin was prepared to work with Roosevelt in taking into account American public opinion. Perhaps the collapse of Germany would ease the situation by reducing the Soviet Union's acute need for security: in that event, the president believed, it might be possible to draw closer to a situation favorable to the Western-oriented phraseology of the Atlantic Charter.[4]

To all intents and purposes, Finland was ignored at Yalta. For the present, that country no longer occupied the attentions of the Great Powers. Parliamentary elections were due to be held there in the near future, and not one of the Great Powers at this stage believed that its interests demanded the raising of unresolved issues concerning Finland at the Yalta conference. In the opinion of the Big Three, there were far more important and pressing matters to be considered.[5]

Soon after the conclusion of the Yalta conference, it became clear that Stalin's willingness to make concessions did not stretch as far as Roosevelt, who was thinking of the reactions of the American public, had hoped. The formation of the Groza government in Rumania was seen in the United States as contrary to the principles of the Declaration on Liberated Europe. The discussions between Molotov, Harriman, and Clark Kerr, which had been agreed upon at Yalta, were bogged down from the start. Agreement could not even be reached on which Poles were to be invited to Moscow to work out the details of the new government. Molotov stuck rigidly to the letter of the Yalta agreement, maintaining that the Lublin government was to form the core of a new cabinet, with a few extra ministers to be added. The Polish government negotiators proposed by the West were only to be admitted to the discussions if they were acceptable to the Lublin government. The British and American view was that the Yalta agreement pre-scribed the setting up of a totally new government for Poland, which would include representatives of all political groups in the country. These differences proved irresoluble. Western feelings were not eased by the fact that several supporters of the exiled government in London were arrested and put on trial in Poland and were branded by Stalin as "saboteurs and diversionists."

As the war of words reached a peak, Moscow let it be known that Commissar for Foreign Affairs V. M. Molotov was otherwise engaged and would not have time to take part in the opening conference of the United Nations in San Francisco. To cap it all, Stalin saw fit to regard the American attempts to persuade the German troops in Italy to surrender in March-April 1945 as a plot concocted with Berlin, aimed at keeping Soviet troops out of Central Europe. "Frankly, I cannot avoid a feeling of bitter resentment toward your informers, whoever they are,'' Roosevelt cabled to Stalin, ''for such vile misrepresentations of my actions or those of my trusted subordinates.'' During the last weeks of his life, the president in private conversations accused Stalin of going back on the promises he had made at Yalta, thus causing the United States to rethink its policy towards the Soviet Union. ''We must not permit anybody to entertain a false impression that we are afraid. Our armies will in a very few days be in a position that will permit us to become 'tougher' than has heretofore appeared advantageous to the war effort,'' Roosevelt informed Churchill on 6 April 1945. The granting of loans for reconstruction could not be contemplated before Russia's intentions had become clearer, and the new weapon of destruction now being developed — the atom bomb — was to be kept a secret from the Russians for the time being.

This aggrieved reaction did not, however, lead to any fundamental revision of the policies of the United States. The fate of the postwar world depended upon the continuation of cooperation with the Russians. As late as the morning of 12 April 1945, Roosevelt sent a telegram to Churchill in which he expressed his belief that things would turn out for the best, in spite of everything. ''I would minimize the general Soviet problem as much as possible.'' In the afternoon, the president — after complaining of a severe headache — suddenly lost consciousness. A stroke ended Franklin D. Roosevelt's life a few hours later.

The new man at the White House, Harry S. Truman, knew very little of the worsening of American-Soviet relations because Roosevelt had almost completely excluded his vice-president from the management of foreign policy. The Missouri senator had earned his spurs in domestic politics. A typical Wilsonian traditionalist in his ideas, Truman was not at all familiar with the complexities of Roosevelt's two-tier diplomacy: ''realism'' in international relations and ''Wilsonian'' in regard to domestic opinion. Unsure of himself, but at the same time wanting to appear determined, Truman relied on the closest advisers of his predecessor as his mentors in foreign affairs — above all, Secretary of State Edward Stettinius, Ambassador Averell Harriman, and Admiral William Leahy. They all urged him to follow a tougher line with the Soviet Union. This advice accorded well with the personal disposition of the World War I captain of artillery. The new president told Harriman that he was not afraid of the Russians. In the end, ''the Soviet Union needs us more than we need them.'' The outlines of the future world would be created by joint effort at the San Francisco conference, and if the Russians did not want to be there ''they could go to hell.''

Abandoning his earlier decision, however, Stalin ''as a mark of respect to the memory of President Roosevelt'' ordered Molotov to lead the Soviet delegation in San Francisco. On his way to California, the people's commissar for foreign affairs was due to meet the new president in Washington. As might be expected, the meeting took place in less than favorable circumstances. Truman's state of mind was not improved by the news received on 21 April of the mutual assistance pact concluded between Moscow and the Lublin government. Molotov thus had to face some pretty tough talking at the meeting on 23 April. An agreement had been made at Yalta, the president thundered, and Stalin would have to stand by his word and abide by that agreement. When Molotov tried to explain that the Soviet Union was acting in a manner that it regarded as in accordance with the Yalta agreement, Truman cut him off in midsentence. The United States wanted cooperation with the Soviet Union, but the road to friendship was not a one-way street. According to those present at this meeting, the usually stony-faced Molotov displayed clear signs of discomfiture as the conversation proceeded. The people's commissar frankly admitted that "I have never been talked to like that in my life." "Carry out your agreements and you won't be," was the president's reply. Later, Truman boasted to Ambassador Joseph E. Davies that he had given "it to him straight 'one-two to the jaw.'" But the president's bravado ran out at this point; revealing his uncertainty, he asked: "Did I do right?"

This conversation between Truman and Molotov has sometimes been described as the opening shot in the Cold War, a sign of the new president's firm wish to change the American line of policy and to go for an open breach with Moscow. Certainly, Truman's rhetoric, especially when compared with the well-rounded diplomatic phrases of his predecessor, might have given that impression to the Soviet side. However, as John Lewis Gaddis points out, it was in the first instance little more than a question of rhetoric. Truman did not in principle wish to depart from the policy of his respected predecessor. In the last months of his life, Roosevelt, although not wishing to compromise the principle of cooperation, had begun to contemplate the adoption of a more "businesslike" approach to the Soviet Union. His closest political advisors were virtually unanimous in making the same point to Truman. Wishing to appear "firm" in the eyes of those around him, the new president, aware that he was a novice in the field of foreign affairs, aimed his sights too high, as he was himself later to admit.

Stalin for his part made his position on the Polish issue clear beyond a shadow of doubt in a letter to Churchill. In his view, the majority of the population supported the Lublin government. Furthermore, there was the question of security.

Poland has the same importance to the security of the Soviet Union as do Belgium and Greece for the security of Great Britain. . . . I do not know how truly representative is the government which has been formed in Greece, nor how truly democratic is the Belgian government. The opinion of the Soviet Union was not sought when these governments were being formed. The Soviet government does not wish to become involved in these matters, because it understands how important Belgium and Greece are for the security of Great Britain. It is incomprehensible why there is no corresponding wish to take into account the security interests of the Soviet Union in discussion of the Polish question.[6]

At the same time, Truman took steps to avoid clashing with the Soviet Union. In spite of his personal misgivings, he confirmed Roosevelt's promise of the three places to be given to the Soviet Union in the U.N. General Assembly, and he rejected Churchill's suggestion that the Anglo-American forces that had advanced east of the demarcation line in Germany remain there until Stalin showed a greater willingness to cooperate. Nevertheless, there were still plenty of differences of opinion. The Polish question remained an acute one, and the San Francisco conference seemed likely to turn into a public stage for these disagreements of the Great Powers rather than an occasion for constructive cooperation. After the Germans had finally surrendered on 7 May 1945, the Americans cut off deliveries under the lend-lease scheme to foreign countries, including the Soviet Union, with the exception of transports needed for the war against Japan. Although Truman later canceled this directive because of Moscow's forceful reaction, the incident did not improve relations between the two countries. The negative course that these relations were taking was beginning to cause alarm in Washington as well.

Wishing to do something to improve the situation, the political leadership of the United States decided in May 1945 to send Roosevelt's former confidant, Harry Hopkins, on a mission to Moscow, where he was held in respect. The circle was now about to close. In the summer of 1941, Hopkins had been Roosevelt's emissary to Moscow, where he had forged the basis for the Soviet-American wartime cooperation. He was now about to help bring to an end that period of history. In his instructions to Hopkins, Truman did not place any restrictions on the envoy's freedom of action. The "misunderstandings" that had arisen were to be corrected, and efforts were to be made to involve Stalin in cooperation, in which both parties would have to observe agreements made. "I told Harry he could use diplomatic language or he could use a baseball bat if he thought that this was the proper approach to Mr. Stalin." Hopkins' background would suggest that the latter alternative was unlikely to be resorted to.

Arriving in Moscow on 25 May, Hopkins entered into discussions with Stalin the following evening. He expressed his concern at the negative direction taken by American public opinion with regard to the Soviet Union over the past weeks. This phenomenon was dangerous in that it limited the freedom of action of President Truman, a man sincerely desirous of peace. The consequence might be the collapse of the global system of collaboration, which Roosevelt and Stalin had struggled so manfully to build up.

Stalin observed laconically that he for his part did not wish to hide behind Russian public opinion; rather, he wished to outline the unease felt by his government as a result of recent American actions. The attitude of the United States toward the Soviet Union had demonstrably cooled after it became obvious that Germany was beaten. It seemed as if the Americans were now saying that the Russians were no longer needed. Hinting at the Great Power status of his country, Stalin at one point in the discussions observed acidly that the Soviet Union was not any old Albania.

After Hopkins had raised the Polish question, Stalin began the discussion by confirming that the Soviet Union wanted a friendly Poland, whereas conservative circles in Britain were seeking to revive the old *cordon sanitaire*. Hopkins assured him that the United States would have nothing to do with such maneuvers, which Stalin had ascribed to the British. The Americans wanted a pro-Soviet Poland and *desired other states on the frontiers of the Soviet Union to adopt similar policies* (my emphasis). If this were so, Stalin said, it would be easy to reach agreement over Poland.

On other issues, Stalin was willing to show a spirit of compromise. On the matter of voting procedure in the United Nations, he rejected Molotov's arguments and came down on the American side. The marshal renewed his promise to enter the war against Japan and emphasized the importance of a powerful China, led by Chiang Kai-shek, for Asia. Hopkins was especially interested in Stalin's skeptical attitude towards the Chinese communists. The marshal also agreed to the joint Anglo-American proposal for a meeting of the Big Three in July 1945 at Potsdam, outside Berlin.

The major part of the talks between Hopkins and Stalin, which lasted almost two weeks, was devoted to the Polish question. Hopkins maintained that this had symbolic value for the American people and would show whether or not the United States and the Soviet Union were capable of cooperating together in peacetime. The United States itself had no direct interest in Poland. Stalin churned out in detail the historical and security reasons why a friendly Poland was vital for his country. The marshal did, however, repeat his consent to the Lublin government (now transferred to Warsaw) becoming the basis for a provisional government of Polish National Unity, which would hold office until general and free elections could be carried out. (The elections, which the Western powers did not acknowledge to be "free," were not held until 1947.) In the provisional government, those Polish groupings that were not among the original Lublin government supporters might be given five or six of the twenty or so ministerial posts. They would also have to be well disposed both to the Western powers and the Soviet Union. Agreement was also reached on the list of names of the Polish government negotiators.

Deadlock had now been broken. Recognizing their inability to do any more — for had the negotiations collapsed, the situation in Poland would have remained unchanged — Washington and London were at this stage ready to accept Stalin's offer. The dominant position of the Soviet Union in Poland would be preserved, but the West would at least have the opportunity to save face. The Polish provisional government formed at the beginning of July 1945 let it be known that it would follow the Yalta agreement in organizing free elections. The United States and Britain now recognized that government. Although the Polish problem was not finally resolved in the eyes of the Western powers, it could nevertheless be shifted to the bottom of the agenda and other pressing matters could be dealt with. Truman was thus compelled to learn the same lesson that Roosevelt had earlier. With the use of coercive methods ruled out, the most that could be hoped for in the case of Poland was that the pressure of Western public opinion might be able to bring about reasonably ''free'' parliamentary elections in that country.[7]

In the opening round of talks in Moscow on 26 May, Harry Hopkins had made it known that the United States hoped that all other countries bordering on the Soviet Union, in addition to Poland, would adopt friendly relations with the USSR. Stalin promptly took up this assurance to find out how much real substance it had. The following day, in identical letters to Churchill and Truman, Stalin proposed that the Allies restore diplomatic relations with Rumania and Bulgaria. More than eight months had elapsed since the signing of the armistice agreements, and these countries had shown their willingness to cooperate in practice by taking part in the war against Hitler's Germany on the side of the United Nations. ''At the same time the Soviet government considers it appropriate to resume diplomatic relations with Finland as well, since Finland is carrying out the terms of the armistice agreement and the principles of democracy are being consolidated in that country.'' A similar decision might also be made a little later in the case of Hungary.[8]

Ambassador Averell Harriman favored acceptance of Stalin's proposal. As Hopkins was still engaged in discussions in Moscow, Harriman's recommendation must be seen as representing his opinion too. The Russians were hardly likely to be disposed to allow the Western representatives any real influence now or in the future on the control commissions in the Balkan countries. ''We can therefore be no worse and possibly better off by handling as many questions as possible directly with the Governments concerned.''[9]

The Division of Eastern European Affairs of the State Department was of a different opinion. With the exception of Finland, the governments in question could not be regarded as democratic. The granting of recognition would thus create a false impression of the position of the United States. To succeed, Harriman's proposal would necessitate a freedom of action for these Balkan governments in their own countries. In the view of the division, these governments were little more than subdepartments of the Kremlin. Why then had not the Lublin government been accepted? By proposing recognition, the Soviet Union would be given — at least indirectly — a free hand to act in Eastern Europe as it chose, and the ''democratic elements'' in the three Balkan countries would also be deprived of their last hope of forging governments corresponding to the wishes of the majority. In a memorandum addressed to ''Doc'' Matthews, head of the Office of European Affairs of the State Department, Elbridge Durbrow, chief of the Eastern European Division, added: ''We have made too much of a fuss about getting a Democratic Government in Poland to through (sic) it all down the drain by this move." By recognizing the Balkan governments, the United States would be surrendering a useful means of exercising pressure and would be encouraging Stalin to try the same methods in other, more "Western" countries.[10] The State Department thus linked the Balkan problem to the precedent of Poland and to the supposed expansionist aims of the Kremlin.

President Truman acted in accordance with the recommendations of his State Department:

> I am . . . prepared to proceed at once with the exchange of diplomatic representatives with Finland, all the more readily of course, because that country has not been in a state of war with the United States, but also because through their elections and other political adjustments the Finnish people have demonstrated their genuine devotion to democratic principles and procedures.

Truman had not detected such encouraging signs in the cases of Rumania, Bulgaria, and Hungary. On the contrary, the governments of these countries were patently not expressions of the popular will of the inhabitants, and therefore recognition at the present time could not be entertained. However, as the normalization of relations was in itself a desirable objective, Truman proposed consultations between the Soviet Union, Britain, and the United States in the spirit of the Declaration on Liberated Europe in order to remove the obstacles to recognition.[11]

In Moscow, Hopkins and Harriman both felt that the President's letter might upset the talks still going on with the Soviet leadership. Dragging in the question of the former "satellite" countries might cause Stalin to link them with the Polish question and thus jeopardize the chances of reaching an acceptable agreement in the talks concerning Poland. Truman gave his permission to withhold the letter, which Harriman delivered to the Kremlin on 7 June, when Hopkins was already on his way home after the conclusion of discussions. The ambassador was not content simply to delay Truman's message, however:

> After full discussion with Hopkins and others here I took the liberty of eliminating the phrase referring to Finland not having been in a state of war with the United States as we felt strongly that this would cause a serious misunderstanding on the part of Stalin that we did not take sufficiently into account Finland's action with Germany against Russia.

Once more, the president gave way to his ambassador.[12]

But Stalin refused to make the recognition of Finland into a special case compared with the Balkan countries, as Truman desired. Conveniently forgetting the war in Lapland, the marshal observed that Finland, unlike Rumania and Bulgaria, had not participated in the armed struggle against Hitler's Germany. Public opinion in the Soviet Union would therefore be unlikely to understand why the Balkan countries were being discriminated against, in contrast to Finland. As regards the governance of Rumania and Bulgaria, Stalin felt that there were as good opportunities for democratic elements to play a part as there were, for example, in Italy, which had already been recognized by the United States and the Soviet Union. Therefore there was no reason to hold up the restoration of diplomatic relations with Rumania, Bulgaria, and Finland, and with Hungary a little later.[13] In his reply, Truman noted that the points of view of the United States and the Soviet Union differed, which was why this matter would have to be taken up at the Potsdam summit conference. Stalin agreed with this last point, but he still emphasized the need for speedy recognition of Rumania and Bulgaria.[14]

The Soviet leader had also informed the British on 27 May of his proposal concerning the Balkan countries and Finland. Supporting Washington's line, London had stressed the importance of the principles of the Declaration on Liberated Europe for Eastern Europe after the Yalta conference. Having lost hope of being able to exercise any influence on the affairs of Rumania, Bulgaria, and Hungary via the control commissions, the British arrived at an alternative that went even further than that adumbrated by Averell Harriman: the best thing would be to conclude final peace treaties with these countries and Finland as soon as possible. The situation would not get any worse. Mere restoration of diplomatic relations would be useless because it would not (for example) help rid the Balkans of Soviet troops. Churchill replied to Stalin on 10 June that his government intended in the near future to present the United States and the Soviet Union with "detailed proposals" concerning the Kremlin's initiative. With the Americans refusing to conclude peace treaties with governments not representing the will of the people, Churchill did not think it possible for Britain alone to push the matter any further. The question would thus remain open until the Big Three could deal with it at Potsdam.[15]

In April 1945, even before Hopkins was sent to Moscow, Truman had sought to strengthen his own position and had engineered a change in the leadership of the State Department. Edward R. Stettinius, regarded as Roosevelt's "hatchet man," who had only held office for a few months after the resignation of Cordell Hull in the late autumn of 1944, was replaced as secretary of state by James F. Byrnes. Unlike Stettinius, who had no party political affiliations, the South Carolina senator and wartime chief of operations designed to mobilize the American economy was firmly entrenched in political circles in Washington, where he was known as an energetic and skillful negotiator and as a tactician willing to compromise if necessary. Having fought Truman to the bitter end in 1944 for the Democratic Party nomination for the vice-presidency, Byrnes occasionally found it difficult to forget that with a little better luck he might have been the man in the White House instead of the Missourian, whom he held in scant regard. Truman preferred to seek conciliation with the disappointed but vigorous Southerner: Byrnes's presidential ambitions having come to nothing, he could at least console himself with the opportunity to be a peacemaker on the international stage. Although he had taken part in the Yalta conference as a member of Roosevelt's delegation, Byrnes had very little previous experience of foreign policy. As Stettinius was acting as host for the San Francisco conference, it was agreed that the formal change of appointments should take place after the meeting was brought to a close. This procedure was followed, and Byrnes took up his post on 3 July. Three days later, he set off from Washington with the president to what was to be the last round of meetings between the Big Three, at Potsdam.

Although fighting was still going on in the Far East, the settling of accounts for World War II was now at hand. At the opening session of the conference on 17 July, Truman took it upon himself to draw the attention of the participants to the mistakes that had been made at an earlier occasion:

> The experience at Versailles . . . does not encourage the belief that a full formal peace conference without preliminary preparations on the part of the leading powers is the best procedure. Such a conference without such preparation would be slow and unwieldy, its sessions would be conducted in a heated atmosphere of rival claims and counter claims and ratification of the resulting documents might long be delayed. I therefore propose as the best formula to meet the situation the establishment of a Council composed of the Foreign Ministers of Great Britain, the Union of Soviet Socialist Republics, China, France and the United States.

The first task of the Council of Foreign Ministers would be to draw up draft peace treaties for Italy, Rumania, and Bulgaria. Hungary and Finland were added to the American list at Potsdam. The preparation of a peace treaty with Germany, which was seen as a more difficult feat, would be left to a later stage on the agenda of the Council. Truman's initiative fitted neatly into the British plans. Stalin also accepted the plan in principle, but he raised the question of how far China could be expected to show interest and knowledge of problems concerning Europe. The Americans responded by pointing to the global nature of the war now ending and to China's position as a permanent member of the U.N. Security Council. After protracted wrangling, it was agreed that "for the discharge of each of these tasks the Council will be composed of the Members representing those States which were signatory to the terms of surrender imposed upon the enemy State concerned." It is worth noting that China was not a party to any of the "surrender agreements" made with European states. In the case of France, a specific exception was made to the general rule in that it was given the right to participate in the preparation of the peace treaty with Italy. In Stalin's opinion, however, France could have nothing to do with the agreements to be made with Finland and the Balkan countries. The Soviet leader, who naturally sought to limit the potential opposition round the negotiating table to as small a number as possible, held fast to this position. It was also agreed that the draft peace treaties prepared by the Council of Foreign Ministers should be submitted in due course for the approval of the United Nations. In what manner this approval was to be given remained for the time being an open question.

At the Potsdam conference, the Americans took a special interest in Italy. For influential Roman Catholic circles in the United States, Rome was still the spiritual and religious center of the world. Italian-born Americans and their pressure groups waged a constant propaganda campaign in favor of their former homeland, urging Washington to "pave the way for democracy" there. The restoration of stability and continuity in Italy was in the basic interests of the West, as the communist-fearing Churchill admitted, though he did not forget to mention Mussolini's "stab in the back" of Britain and France in the summer of 1940. After Italy had hastened to declare war on Japan, its former Axis partner, on 15 July – the eve of the Potsdam conference – President Truman was ready not only to ease the terms of the armistice, but also for a speedy peace with the Rome government; he was also prepared to assist Italy in becoming a member of the United Nations as soon as possible.

Stalin adopted the same position, in principle. In preparing the peace treaty, the foreign ministers could give the Italian question detailed treatment. In the same context, however, they ought also to study the corresponding problems of the other satellite countries – Rumania, Bulgaria, Hungary, and Finland. Stalin saw no reason to make a special case of Italy. To this, Truman had to agree. The mutual understanding broke down, however, when the Western powers explained that they would be prepared to renew diplomatic relations with the Balkan countries only when free elections had been held and the "undemocratic" governments reformed in accordance with the results. Stalin and Molotov for their part described the Italian and Greek governments as equally "undemocratic" because parliamentary elections had not been held in these countries either. Stalin's separate reference to the Greek civil war – compared with the "peaceful" situation prevailing in Rumania and Bulgaria – did not help Churchill to recall his own part in the October 1944 agreement on spheres of interest. The West's high-flown interpretations of the nature of free speech and unfettered opinion, in turn, left the Russians unmoved.

During this argument, Finland remained in the background, with both sides admitting that the parliamentary elections held there had been "free and democratic." In this respect, Stalin and Molotov were able at Potsdam to point to the northern republic as an instance of the "groundlessness" of Western suspicions. This cut no ice with Byrnes. "We would, frankly, always be suspicious of elections in countries where our representatives are not free to move about and where the press cannot report freely. Our representatives in every one of these countries had reported such conditions, but they had not done so in Finland." On the contrary, Byrnes said, the press had reported these elections freely, and the public was satisfied with the circumstances in which they had been held. Stalin then pointed out that, although Finland had not deployed such a large number of troops in defeating Germany as had Rumania and Bulgaria, it had nevertheless behaved well and deserved to have its situation eased and improved. The Western powers did not disagree with this. Although the question of recognizing Finland had in principle been settled before the Potsdam conference, the fact that it was being linked to the problematic issues of the Balkans and Italy seemed to be holding up any practical resolution of the matter. While Truman and Churchill objected to the "undemocratic" governments in the Balkans, Stalin persisted in refusing to make concessions to Italy unless the question of recognition of Germany's Eastern European satellites was resolved at the same time.

The conference also seemed to be heading for deadlock over the question of German reparations and Poland's western frontier. Remembering the experience of the 1920's, Washington and London believed that the $10 billion sum desired by Stalin would lead Germany into economic collapse. To prevent this, the Western powers would once more have to put their own resources at risk and in the last resort find themselves having to pay for war reparations. The Oder-Neisse line demanded by the Soviet Union and the Poles would also mean that millions of German refugees would be driven into the West's zones of occupation, increasing confusion and hardship there. It seemed as if agreement was as far off as ever, and the discussions at Potsdam threatened to be sucked into a whirlpool from which there was no way out. The news of the first successful test of the atom bomb, conveyed to Stalin by Truman, was not enough to persuade the Soviet leader to bow to the American demands.

With the British parliamentary elections of July 1945 returning a clear Labour majority, the government resigned immediately. In place of Winston Churchill, the new Prime Minister Clement Attlee arrived at Potsdam on 28 July; Anthony Eden's post was inherited by former Minister of Labour Ernest Bevin. Predictions of a change of political direction soon proved to be groundless. The Labour Party leaders could hardly be described as revolutionaries. In the view of French Foreign Minister Georges Bidault, "only the British with their splendid pragmatic tendencies could number men such as Attlee amongst the ranks of socialists." The new prime minister had from an early stage marked down the Russians as "ideological imperialists," and the former carter Ernie Bevin had a strong dislike of communists from his many years of struggle within the trade union movement. In the arena of foreign affairs, the change was largely confined to style, with the graceful phrases of the old Etonian Anthony Eden giving way to Bevin's blunt directness. Moreover, the British were well aware of the weakened reserves of strength in their country, of their dependence on the support of the United States, and of domestic opinion that was fed up with the war and "hard-line politics." In these circumstances, the newcomers to Potsdam thought it best to sail cautiously in the wake of the Americans.

With the talks in Potsdam seemingly stalled, the patience of the Truman delegation began gradually to crack. Instead of endless arguments, some decisions had to be reached. Many important matters were waiting to be settled back home, without mentioning the final settlement of the war in the Far East. On the other hand, the Americans did not wish to disturb Western public opinion by allowing the summit conference to break up in open conflict. The experienced politician Byrnes now offered the Russians a "package deal." In Germany, the victorious powers would each take reparations from their own zone; in addition, the Russians would be guaranteed certain additional deliveries from the Western zones, providing these were not vital to the German economy. In this event, the Americans would accept the handing over of the territories east of the Oder-Neisse line to Polish administration. The final destiny of these areas would be determined in the context of the peace treaty with Germany.

Byrnes' proposal concerning the German war reparations was a significant step towards the division of that country, since the erection of the planned central administration was now automatically delayed. Furthermore, if Moscow were to support the signing of a swift peace agreement with Italy and that country's admission to the United Nations, Byrnes announced that the United States would agree to the three governments examining "*each separately* in the near future, in the light of the conditions then prevailing, the establishment of diplomatic relations with Finland, Rumania, Bulgaria and Hungary to the extent possible prior to the conclusion of peace treaties with those countries" (my emphasis). Of "democratic governments" and the Declaration on Liberated Europe there was not a word. In principle, the Americans had not changed their views about the "democratic" nature of the Balkan governments, but Byrnes's formula did at least offer some hope that the negotiations would not break up in open quarreling. After a brief show of resistance, the British accepted the American position. Stalin was also prepared to accept, after a session of intense haggling, the basic contents of Byrnes's package. Stalin described Byrnes as "the most honest horse thief he had ever met": but the Potsdam conference was saved.

From the American point of view, Stalin's renewed promise to enter the war against Japan in the near future was a positive factor, even though this was less significant after the final successful testing of the atom bomb than it had been earlier. Japan's days were in any event numbered. On the other hand, the triumphant Stalin's interests now seemed to be extending even farther than the immediate security area of the Soviet Union's western borders. At Potsdam, he spoke among other things about the renewal of the Montreux agreement governing the control of the Dardanelles, the fate of France's Near Eastern mandates (Syria and Lebanon) and of Iran, of the division of the Italian colonies among the victorious powers as mandated territories, and of Soviet participation in the administration of the international territory of Tangier.

As a great power, the Soviet Union was naturally interested in how the bankrupt stock left by the world war would be divided up; but this interest was all too easily portrayed by the other side in gloomy colors. Moscow had now thrown off the mask and revealed "its real expansionist aims." Byrnes assumed that the Kremlin was seeking to use Libya as a base against the West and as a way into Africa toward the Belgian Congo, one of the world's most important sources of uranium. "Somebody had made an awful mistake," Byrnes complained to his aides at Potsdam, "in bringing about a situation where Russia was permitted to come out of a war with the power she will have. He said England should have never permitted Hitler to rise . . . that the German people under a democracy would have been a far superior ally than Russia. There is too much difference in the ideologies of the United States and Russia to work out a long-term program of cooperation."

In spite of these annoyed outbursts by the disappointed secretary of state, the public facade of cooperation was still kept up at Potsdam; in that sense, no "final" decisions were taken one way or the other. Byrnes himself maintained that the way was open for the discussions soon to begin in the Council of Foreign Ministers, and Truman assumed that some of Stalin's demands might be founded on bluff. On the other hand, as Daniel Yergin has pointed out, "the Great Powers had found that the best way to cooperate was to give each a free hand in its own sphere. Because they could not agree on how to govern Europe, they would begin to divide it." Looked at as a whole, this was indeed the most striking result of the Potsdam conference. The factor that had held the alliance together—the threat posed by Hitler's Germany—had vanished from the stage, and the way had opened up for the conflicts of interest between the Allies that had hitherto remained on the sidelines. "In whatever particular Hell he inhabited," John Gaddis remarks, "the Austrian corporal must have enjoyed a fleeting moment of consolation, for the coalition he had inadvertently forged had now, through the act of destroying him, begun to destroy itself."

Less than a week after the Big Three left Potsdam (the conference ended on 2 August), the Americans dropped the atom bomb on Hiroshima (6 August 1945). Two days later, the Soviet Union carried out its promise and declared war on Japan. The second atom bomb exploded over Nagasaki on 9 August, and on 14 August the Japanese government accepted the Allies' terms of surrender. World War II had ended.[16]

7 The Finnish Parliamentary Elections of 1945

Maxwell Hamilton had been appointed as United States political representative in Finland by President Roosevelt on 11 November 1944; he was preceded to Helsinki by Randolph Higgs from the American legation in Stockholm, who arrived on 16 January 1945 to organize the setting up of the mission.[1] At a meeting with Higgs on 25 January, Paasikivi, the Finnish prime minister, emphasized the importance of the war guilt question as Finland's major outstanding problem.[2] Pressure on the government on this issue had been steadily growing.

The question of the possible implications of Article 13 of the armistice agreement, concerning the punishment of war criminals, had occupied the minds of the Finnish delegation during their negotiations with the Russians in Moscow back in the autumn of 1944. The Finnish side had been unwilling at the time to explore all its possible ramifications for fear that any clarification of the way the article was to be interpreted would only make it less easy for the government to accept.[3] Fears on this point also seem to have been aroused in Stockholm. When Secretary-General Boheman of the Swedish Foreign Ministry, learned of the terms of the Finnish armistice, he made it clear to the American minister that—as far as granting rights of asylum to Finnish citizens was concerned—Sweden would not consider anyone a war criminal simply because the person was thought of as such by the Russians. As Johnson told Washington, "He [Boheman] said with considerable vehemence that it was not possible for any reasonable person to put Finland in the same class with Germany as far as war criminals are concerned."[4]

In discussions with Victor Mallet, the British minister in Stockholm, Boheman also made clear his concern about how the Control Commission would interpret Article 13. Was one to assume, Boheman asked, that it related to political decision makers as well as military ones? It would be impossible for the Swedish government to hand over to the Russians even "ordinary" war criminals arriving in Sweden, Boheman declared, unless they could be shown to be guilty of having committed wartime atrocities; even more, the Swedish government could not hand over past members of Finnish governments should they seek asylum in Sweden. The Foreign Office, while recognizing that the government did not consider any Finns as war criminals, was nevertheless convinced of the need to prevent Britain from becoming embroiled in any possible dispute that might blow up on this issue between the Soviet Union and Sweden.[5] When London learned of former Foreign Minister Rolf Wittings's arrival in Stockholm, the matter was simply described as "Sweden's headache, not ours." Although the Foreign Office thought Witting among those who had been especially responsible for Finland's fighting alongside Germany, it was felt that "he hardly deserves the death penalty usually handed down by the Russians to war criminals."[6] Because he died on 11 October 1944, however, Witting proved a short-term problem both for Britain and Sweden.

Following the delivery to the Helsinki government on 19 October of the Control Commission's list of 61 Finnish war criminals,[7] Shepherd, Britain's political representative in Helsinki, had cabled London at Prime Minister Urho Castrén's request for a definition of the term "war criminal." He was told by the Foreign Office that no generally accepted definition existed but that, in any case, no Finns were considered major war criminals. Shepherd was advised against taking too active a role on the issue, which was to be left to the Soviet Union to deal with.[8] The United States, which still lacked a representative in Helsinki in the autumn of 1944, remained noncommittal on the question, in line with its policy of nonintervention in Finnish affairs.

Following the tactics that had been adopted during the armistice negotiations with the Russians, the Finnish political leadership attempted to avoid doing anything untoward to arouse further Soviet interest on the matter. The war guilt issue had, however, been the subject of debate within the labor movement during the autumn of 1944. During the parliamentary debate of the government's review of events for 1943, Yrjö Räisänen, a member of a group of six Social Democratic antiwar dissenters, took up the question of what had led to the outbreak of war and demanded a full inquiry on the matter. Räisänen's demand was echoed in a communiqué issued after a meeting organized by the People's Democrats in Helsinki on 27 November. Although neither of these public statements actually made reference to Article 13 of the armistice agreement, "the fuse was already burning," in the words of Jukka Tarkka. The government, however, maintained its tactic of deliberately refraining from comment on the question, contending in private that Article 13 referred only to war criminals in a military sense and not to political figures.[9]

In discussions at the beginning of December 1944 at the American legation in Stockholm, Eero Wuori informed the Americans that the Soviet Union had yet to make any formal demands regarding the war guilt question. If this were to happen, he said, it would be difficult to know who would be required to stand trial. President Mannerheim had confided to Wuori that "what they really want to get at is me." Wuori, however, believed that the Soviet Union would, as likely as not, consider imprisonments and trials unnecessary if the Finnish authorities could ensure a complete purge of the political establishment and the removal of wartime policymakers from positions of authority. Wuori said that he had tried to persuade Ryti and Tanner to withdraw from public life, but so far without success. Internal political pressure from the Finnish left to arraign those held responsible for the war was growing with every day that passed, Wuori told the Americans.[10] Urho Kekkonen, the minister of justice, declared in a press statement in December 1944 that the nature of what constituted a war crime had remained largely undefined in Article 13; but he concluded that "we probably ought to bear in mind that international law generally defines actual war crimes as crimes committed by military personnel violating the generally agreed rules of war."[11]

By January 1945, the fuse appeared to have burned up. There was no longer any room for ambiguity in the Soviet Union's view that Finland was totally responsible for unconditionally complying with the terms of the armistice agreement and subject to the supervision of the Allied powers through the Control Commission; it was thus the Commission's duty to bring pressure on Finnish authorities when their policies failed to keep pace with the agreed terms. General Zhdanov had spoken to Wuori about the need to proscribe the Finnish Comrades-in-Arms (ex-servicemen's) Association immediately on his arrival in Helsinki in October 1944.[12] This, the country's largest popular organization, had more than 700 affiliated branches by the latter part of 1944 with a membership of about 240,000, drawn both from bourgeois circles and the labor movement, despite the suspicion that had existed between these two groups during the interwar years.[13] The association's activities had included acquiring about 4,500 farms for ex-servicemen, organizing between 25 and 30 million hours of voluntary cooperative work, and providing vocational education for some 2,000 war widows. Because any immediate end to the association's social activities would have made life even harder for many families that had suffered as a result of the war, the government had tried to keep the question of its dissolution quiet for as long as possible.[14] As Kyösti Skyttä has pointed out, however, both the People's Democrats and the Communists came to feel that the continuance of the association's activities would weaken support for the left in the coming parliamentary elections.[15] A meeting of delegates of the Finnish-Soviet Society in Helsinki on 14 January 1945 publicly demanded the banning of the Association, a political purge, and the handing-over of buildings previously owned by the

Suojeluskunta for use by the society. The same demands were presented directly to Paasikivi by a delegation from the society.[16]

Five days after this demand, *Tass* published a report reviewing Finland's progress towards full implementation of the armistice agreement. Though the report made a number of positive comments, it also saw legitimate cause for criticism.[17] The Finns, for instance, had been slow in expelling the German forces from Lapland and in releasing political detainees, the latter process only having begun to proceed smoothly after the appointment of Kekkonen as minister of justice. And "despite the demands of the Finnish people," the article went on, "the fascist Comrades-in-Arms Association has yet to be proscribed and remains active."

Speaking to a delegation of British and American journalists visiting Helsinki on 19 January, Orlov, the Control Commission's political adviser, declared that Article 21 of the armistice agreement also covered the Comrades-in-Arms Association. It would be unfortunate, Orlov said, if the association was not proscribed before the parliamentary elections to be held in March—especially in light of its potential, through its status as a mass organization, in influencing their outcome. It would clearly be the duty of the Control Commission to intervene in the matter if the Finnish authorities were not seen to be faithfully complying with the requirements of the article, Orlov concluded. This public clarification of the Commission's strong stand on the question was reinforced in a note handed to the Finnish government on 24 January. Paasikivi's cabinet was left with little room for maneuver and duly proscribed the association one day later. With an eye to securing his internal position from possible criticism, the prime minister requested that the minutes of the cabinet meeting should also include a reference to the note sent the previous day by the Commission.[18]

The British members of the Commission, together with Shepherd, Britain's political representative, accepted their ally's stand. The memory of the Finnish attempt in the autumn of 1944, against all but the strongest pressure from the Control Commission, to maintain an army almost twice the size of the country's normal peacetime one was still fresh in everyone's mind. The Russians, in particular, were suspicious that members of the proscribed Suojeluskunta had infiltrated other organizations, like the Comrades-in-Arms Association, and might be trying to continue their paramilitary activities outside the official army as the Germans had done after World War I. Shepherd was sympathetic in principle to what he saw as a legitimate Soviet security interest. Despite believing that the Russians were often given to exaggerated use of the term "fascist," there was no denying that organizations like the Comrades-in-Arms Association had shown clear anti-Russian and pro-German sentiments. On the other hand, proscription, in addition to putting a stop to the organization's positive social work, raised the possibility of pushing it and similar organizations underground and making their surveillance that much more difficult. Shepherd feared the proscription of the Comrades-in-Arms Association would in fact strengthen anti-Russian sentiment in Finland and slow down the country's positive development away from an anti-Soviet to a more pro-Soviet political outlook.

Shepherd also believed, by way of contrast, that the Finnish-Soviet Society had proved too left wing. Instead of advocating a policy of independent development for the two countries and mutual friendship based on their common interests, it seemed to be recommending that Finland should follow the Soviet example in terms of social and political issues, a view that Shepherd felt did not find favor with the mass of the population. Should the Control Commission demand the banning of other organizations, it was more than probable that relations between the Commission and the Finnish government would become increasingly difficult. Circumstances, in the shape of the recently concluded hostilities, effectively presented the Finns from making use of organizations like the Comrades-in-Arms Association to assist in reshaping the domestic political climate. As the Russians were unlikely to give much credence to Shepherd's cautious approach, however, the British delegation came to see the banning of the association as inevitable and concluded that little would be gained from pursuing the matter further.[19] The United States, not sitting on the Control Commission, took no part in the decision.

The *Tass* report published on 19 January also made some mention of Article 13 of the armistice agreement. Public opinion in Finland was described as demanding the beginning of proceedings to arrest known war criminals and bring them to trial.[20] In his statement to Western journalists on 19 January, Orlov carefully underlined the Soviet view that the country's approaching parliamentary elections would represent "the main test of Finnish good will." The Finns were faced with the dual task of dealing with their war criminals and those responsible for the war. What was to be done with the latter, whose names Orlov did not reveal, was up to the Finnish people to decide. "But the Soviet government," he went on, "must legitimately be suspicious of any Finnish government in which pro-German elements occupy positions of importance, or in which such elements are in a position to influence foreign policy." One can assume that these views were underscored in direct communications between the Control Commission and the Finnish government, although demands for the starting of actual indictments were apparently not made at this stage. The question of the possible existence of direct contacts between the Commission and the Finnish left must unfortunately be left unanswered because of the lack of documentary evidence. Addressing the same group of British and American journalists, Paasikivi emphasized that no government member or other official could be indicted under the Finnish judicial system for any actions or decisions they had taken that were in conformity with the country's constitution and legal code.[21]

In a subsequent conversation on 25 January with Randoph Higgs, the United States temporary representative, Paasikivi was at pains to stress the democratic nature of the Finnish political system. The forthcoming elections would offer all sections of society an equal opportunity to choose their respective representatives. The only democratic means of removing wartime leaders from the Finnish political arena was to give the people the chance of not reelecting them, Paasikivi explained. As the law did not allow for their summary indictment, no government could arraign them. The importance of this small group of individuals, numbering five or six, all of whom were now totally loyal to the country's new foreign policy, had in the prime minister's view in any case been significantly overestimated. The Control Commission had given the Finnish authorities to understand that it would try to avoid interference in the country's internal affairs, and this, according to Paasikivi, was just such an internal affair. Higgs described Paasikivi as saying that "agitation for prosecution of war culprits came from extreme left-wing Finnish politicians"; but "he evaded my question whether he thought they had had any outside inspiration." [22]

In the meantime, however, things had begun to snowball. The war guilt question had come before Parliament through a motion put forward by the Social Democratic "Group of Six" on 23 January. The six presented Paasikivi's government with a statement, which—in addition to underlining the "stubborn," "foolhardy," and "irresponsible" nature of the prewar government's policies and the "criminal machinations" of members of the wartime government—also requested information about the present government's intentions "to begin proceedings to clarify the possible responsibility of the President of the Republic in office in 1941, and of the members of the State Council, and if necessary of other persons holding high-ranking and responsible government office in 1939 and 1941, for the outbreaks of hostilities in those years, and to guarantee that those found guilty will be duly tried."

Paasikivi made his reply on 31 January in the presence of all the members of his government. He informed Parliament that the government had asked K. J. Ståhlberg, a previous president and leading expert on constitutional law, for clarification on the legal implications of the war guilt question. His opinion was that the commencement of hostilities, their continuation, their cessation, and the beginning of peace negotiations did not by themselves—under Finnish law—constitute actions implying war guilt because these actions were allowed for in the country's constitution. The president of the republic could only be held directly responsible for a war if his decisions as to whether the country was at war or peace constituted acts of high treason or treachery, whereas a member of the State Council could only be held similarly responsible if his actions while in office were linked with the beginning of hostilities through participation in obvious illegality or other acts contrary to the law. Acts that were politically or morally wrong, mistaken, or otherwise reprehensible did not by themselves constitute war guilt in any strictly legal sense. The constitution, moreover, did not allow for questions of war guilt to be dealt with in special courts. Nevertheless, Paasikivi told Parliament, the government believed that it would be best for those individuals who had occupied important political positions in recent years and had been most prominent in shaping Finland's policies during those years to withdraw from politics in order to aid the establishment of good relations between Finland and the Soviet Union and to dispel any doubts that might be entertained about Finland's present position. Parliament was also told that the government had decided to set up a committee to investigate Finnish foreign policy from 1938 onwards, particularly in relation to Finland's entry into the war. The committee, made up of Hj. Granfelt, K. R. Brotherus, Yrjö Ruutu, and Eino Pekkala, was to be chaired by Eirik Hornborg.[23]

Paasikivi's defensive tone taken toward Parliament was part of an attempt to win time. How far this tactic would work remained to be seen. The head of the Foreign Office's Northern Department in London, Christopher Warner, described the Finnish prime minister's response as "quite a skilful reply," but he added that he hoped "the exposé relating to the Winter War (1939-40) will not prove embarrassing to us."[24] But in a discussion of the situation on 10 February in Helsinki, Shepherd, despite Paasikivi's obvious anxiety, declared himself unable to provide any other advice beyond that of recommending following the course of action laid down by Finnish law. In line with Britain's policy of noninvolvement, the Foreign Office also warned Shepherd against giving Paasikivi any further direct advice. If Paasikivi should pursue the point, Shepherd was told to make it clear that the matter was completely in Finnish hands; but at the same time, he was not to give the impression that Finland need not do any more than it had already done.[25] In previous communications with London, Shepherd had made it clear that he believed the Russian position justified, in that the retention of leading wartime politicians in government office could only undermine the cause of developing good relations between Finland and the Soviet Union.[26]

Higgs, the American representative in Helsinki, was in contrast more ready to involve himself in the question. A conversation with Cay Sundström, a member of the Social Democratic Group of Six, failed to provide him with a straight answer as to whether those who had put the question in Parliament would be satisfied with the figures associated with responsibility for the war simply withdrawing from the political stage, or whether they would also demand legal action.[27] Johan Helo, the minister of finance, emphasized to Higgs shortly afterwards his belief that finding out whether any illegal agreements had been made with Germany was of central importance and that indictments would only need to be proceeded with if any were uncovered. Otherwise, an understanding that the wartime leaders would withdraw from public life would be sufficient. If that happened, Helo seemed confident that his group would take over control of the Social Democratic party, a point that Higgs thought particularly "interesting."[28]

During the course of his first meeting with Higgs on 25 January, Paasikivi had carefully avoided revealing to the Americans that he intended trying to persuade the country's leading wartime figures not to stand as candidates in the coming parliamentary elections. Higgs, however, had learned the same day from the Swedish minister in Helsinki, Beck-Friis, that Paasikivi was in fact well aware of the risks associated with an overly passive line on the part of the government and that moves were afoot, including possible use of the Swedish press,[29] to encourage the voluntary withdrawal of wartime politicians. The Swedish legation in Helsinki, convinced of the dangers Finland ran in letting all and sundry stand in the forthcoming elections, actively supported Paasikivi's efforts and indicated that it would willingly see the Americans join the campaign to persuade the wartime leaders to stand down.[30]

Some four days before his reply to the parliamentary question put by the Group of Six, Paasikivi had invited Eljas Erkko, whose paper *Helsingin Sanomat* had published an editorial the same day supporting the government and urging the wartime leaders to make a clean break with public office, to come and see him.[31] After questioning Erkko about his confidential contacts with the American mission, Paasikivi asked him to see if he could persuade the Americans to use their influence to prevent the wartime figures from standing as candidates. Their success in the elections, if they stood, Paasikivi feared, would be a foregone conclusion. The public at large was not in a position to appreciate the seriousness of the situation, according to Paasikivi, and even Mannerheim persisted in seeing the whole question in terms that were almost exclusively legalistic.[32]

Higgs's immediate reaction to the request passed on by Erkko was far from one of thinking that the Finnish politicians behind it were simply trying to embroil the United States in Finnish-Soviet relations, or that it was motivated by personal political ambition. On the contrary, he believed that it was in fact in America's interest to take a public stand against the election of specific wartime politicians to the Finnish Parliament. Such a stand would underline American solidarity with Moscow and at the same time help strengthen the basis for good relations between Finland and the Soviet Union.[33]

Randolph Higgs's view was supported by Averell Harriman, who saw such a move as likely to help improve U.S. relations with the Soviet government. "We are criticizing the Soviets for their activities in directions that we do not approve and it would seem appropriate for us to take a position publicly which would support them in this case where we think they are right," declared Harriman. By the time Harriman's telegram arrived in Washington, however, the State Department had already rejected Higgs's suggestion. The matter was not the concern of the United States, it was decided, but only of those countries that had signed the armistice agreement and that were represented on the Control Commission—in other words, the Soviet Union and Great Britain.[34] Although Washington approved in principle of the need for the wartime leaders to stand aside, its decision to avoid any public declaration on the subject was based on wider tactical considerations. Any statement on the issue, it was felt, was more than likely to give rise to a wave of accusations of American involvement in Finnish internal affairs, involvement that could also be construed as a direct infringement of Finland's democratic electoral freedom. As the United States did not have any direct interest at stake in the matter, it seemed to those in Washington more appropriate to remain on the sidelines.

Paasikivi was, in fact, not to need the additional support of the Americans. The Finnish government's overriding anxiety, as Jutila told Higgs at the end of January, lay in its uncertainty about how far the Control Commission intended to go with its demands in the future.[35] Despite their misgivings, however, the members of Paasikivi's cabinet decided to contact all the relevant parliamentary parties directly on the matter before the final day by which the lists of candidates for the elections had to be lodged with the central electoral committee. These discussions, in which the government mustered all its available authority, led to announcements by eleven Agrarian, Social Democratic, and National Coalition Party politicians that they were withdrawing their candidatures. No one from the People's Patriotic Movement (IKL) was allowed to stand.[36] Paasikivi's tone was decidedly determined in his comments to the Agrarian Party representatives he met: "The fact of the matter is that if my request is not complied with, the government will resign. We are already in deep water and cannot afford any more complications. I feel so tired and completely worn out that I cannot go on any more. The burden of work and all these sleepless nights are beginning to take their toll." The Agrarians, however, while expressing their appreciation of the responsibility shouldered by the prime minister, initially remained opposed to the government's request, emphasizing that "it was promised after all that there would be no intervention in our internal affairs. The constitution guarantees us electoral freedom." Paasikivi's response was sharp and to the point: "We are not independent. We are a defeated country and Zhdanov is now the one who makes the decisions. And after all neither Kalliokoski nor the others are indispensable in Parliament. There are always people available to replace them."[37] After some argument, the tired, 74-year-old statesman finally succeeded in getting them to agree.

In a radio speech two weeks before the elections, Minister of Labor Wuori described the Yalta agreement as implying that the Great Powers could "assist . . . previous Axis satellite states to reorganize their affairs on a democratic basis." He argued that it was therefore in Finland's own interest to ensure the elimination of what remained of national socialist tendencies and do all it could to ensure the democratization of the country, thereby making it unnecessary for the Allies to intervene. Far-reaching changes in the general state of things were thus unavoidable, Wuori emphasized, but neither the principle of private enterprise nor private land tenure, for instance (he went on), would need to be discarded overnight. If changes were not seen to be taking place soon, however, he concluded, "we will either find ourselves with a revolution, which will tear the country apart, or on a road where the traffic regulations are even less under our own control than the armistice agreement allows for."[38]

For foreign policy reasons, the internal political purge called for by Wuori was not publicly opposed; however, reaction to his speech was strong. Paasikivi himself attempted to quell public unease in a radio speech two days before the elections. It was not the government's aim, the prime minister said, to effect a radical upheaval in Finland's internal economic and social system. It was more a question of reducing the mistrust evident in the Soviet Union toward Finland and Finnish intentions. "If we simply say that those who up until only yesterday supported openly belligerent policies have now accepted a different approach, we are told: But that is pure political opportunism . . . we cannot trust such politicians. It may be unpleasant and difficult for us to hear this, but it is a fact which we cannot ignore. . . . People make policies. New policies, as history shows us, call for new people and new politicial leaders." Paasikivi concluded with a strong appeal for "new" faces in Parliament to replace those with "the burden of the past weighing heavy upon them," as he put it.[39] Paasikivi never subsequently disputed the exceptional and essentially antiparliamentary nature of this decision to address the nation so near to the elections. The government's main responsibility at the time, as he saw it, was to set forth its views as clearly as possible on questions that it saw as central to the country's future.

The early months of 1945 saw Britain continuing its adopted policy of noninvolvement with regard to Finland, a policy that—particularly as it affected the war guilt question—London did not fail to underline to Shepherd. The role of the British officers on the Control Commission also remained as subsidiary as before. Higgs got the impression that the Commission's Soviet members did not particularly respect their British colleagues, whom they tolerated largely to give meaning to the "Allied" nature of the organization.[40] The British, following the directives they had received in London in October 1944, had not attempted to play anything like a central role in the Commission's activities, and they seemed generally satisfied with the situation. The only real cause for complaint by Howie, Magill, and Kelly lay in the lack of information they received from the Commission's higher-ranking officials. The Soviet officers gave little away and were typically unwilling to volunteer anything to the British officers. The general state of Finnish affairs, however, had reached such a point that the Commission had little work left to do, with the majority of things running smoothly and more or less routinely. Now that the hectic days of the autumn of 1944 were a thing of the past, the focus of attention had largely shifted to technical issues; it seemed certain to some, like Shepherd, that the conclusion of the Commission's work was not far off.[41]

A meeting with General Zhdanov on 5 February offered Shepherd the opportunity for a wide-ranging discussion of the overall situation in Finland. On the question of Finnish compliance with the terms of the armistice agreement, Zhdanov believed that although Finland had adequately fulfilled many of the conditions, things were not completely perfect; the general picture was "speckled" rather than crystal clear. There had, for example, been shortfalls in the return of material belonging to the Soviet Union. Referring to the Finnish government's position on the war guilt question, Zhdanov said that "he was pleased with this as a first step, though he did not appear very enthusiastic and thought it should have been taken long before. The Finns were very slow to realise the situation but he understood that this was their nature." Zhdanov and Shepherd agreed on this point. On the question of Finnish public opinion, Shepherd told Zhdanov that he felt that the level of tension in the country had subsided significantly since the autumn, largely as a result of the proper and correct conduct of the Control Commission. In fact, the Finns seemed surprised by the Commission's behavior, and all the evidence pointed to the mass of the population genuinely wishing to maintain friendly relations with the Soviet Union. But the development of a feeling of trust to its full potential would take time, Shepherd believed. Zhdanov agreed, recalling that his first impression on arriving in Helsinki in October 1944 had been that the Finns had expected him to come with a tank regiment in one pocket and a squadron of fighter aircraft in the other.[42]

Suspicions, it was true, were not to be eliminated at the drop of a hat. Rumors circulating in Helsinki in February 1945 that the Swedes had begun to realize their assets in Finland led Colonel Magill, one of the British members of the Control Commission, to ask Randolph Higgs of the American mission whether he believed that the Soviet Union intended to occupy Finland in the near future. The same question had been put to the American diplomat a little while previously by Kaarlo Hillilä, the Finnish minister of the interior. Magill described the mood in the country as wary, with people constantly making comparisons between the present situation and what had happened in the Baltic countries in 1940. Higgs, however, reacted skeptically towards these speculations, particularly since Åke Gartz, the minister of trade, had recently told him of the success of the Finnish-Soviet trade negotiations held in Moscow.[43] An article by O. W. Kuusinen appearing under a pseudonym in the Moscow periodical *Voyna i rabochiy klass* at the beginning of March, which described President Mannerheim as being surrounded by a "fascist clique," also created a degree of unease in Helsinki. Answering subsequent American inquiries on the matter, Paasikivi declared that Mannerheim, together with 99 percent of the Finnish people, was convinced of the possibility of developing good relations with the country's eastern neighbor. Links with the Control Commission were described as "not bad," and relations with the Soviet Union in general were thought to be developing along the right lines, although the Finns felt that suspicions still existed on the Soviet side. Paasikivi said he was convinced, moreover, that Stalin had no wish to destroy

Finland and would allow the country to go on existing as an independent nation "in the way that small nations could have independence in the world today," as he put it.[44]

The American attitude to Finland in the first half of 1945 was characterized by a desire to avoid American involvement in Finnish affairs as much as possible, and not only on the question of the war guilt problem. The State Department's instructions to Maxwell Hamilton, issued on 30 January before his departure for Finland, typically emphasized the need for caution. "You should at all times bear in mind that, although the United States and Finland have not been at war with one another, diplomatic relations between the two countries remain severed and Finland is still in a technical state of war with our Soviet and British Allies."[45] A telling example of what that situation meant can be seen in the State Department's attitude to Hamilton's predecessor's request, made on 13 February before the former's arrival, for permission to talk on youth activities in the United States as a guest of the youth section of the Finnish-American Society. Washington refused permission because, as Higgs himself had said, "some members would like to use the society as an instrument to develop Finnish relations principally in the direction of the USA but also against the USSR." The State Department's decision was also probably influenced by Higgs's earlier comments on Soviet disquiet on the Control Commission at Shepherd's enthusiasm in developing the activities of the Finnish-British Society.[46]

The Americans also followed a cautious line on economic matters, and financial assistance for Finland in the form of loans was not seriously contemplated. Taking its cue from its experiences after World War I, the United States generally avoided funding the war reparations of other countries after World War II. In Finland's case, the uncertainty of the political situation also played a part. Randolph Higgs commented as early as November 1944 to the chairman of the British Trade Delegation, Daniel Caplan, there was no reason for the United States to put its money into what he described as the "Finnish mouse-trap." The process of restoring economic relations between Washington and Helsinki only began in earnest at the end of 1945, as a result of an upswing in American confidence in Finland's potential to come through its difficulties.[47]

Because of Zhdanov's temporary absence from Finland, Hamilton's first contact with the Control Commission after arriving in Helsinki was on 27 February when he met Pavel Orlov. Following the general tone of Zhdanov's earlier conversation with Shepherd, Orlov declared that although the Finns had somewhat inadequately fulfilled some of the terms of the armistice agreement, the situation on the whole was satisfactory and developments were proceeding in the right direction. Hamilton, in line with the instructions he had received in Washington, contented himself with expressing himself well pleased with the Commission's analysis; he refrained from putting forward any concrete initiatives of his own.[48]

Both Finnish foreign ministers, Enckell and Svento, communicated a similarly positive view of the situation to Hamilton. The Control Commission was fulfilling its responsibilities and the Finns had no cause for complaint, he was told. The worst of the difficulties associated with complying with the terms of the armistice agreement were also now past. Hamilton emphasized the strength and permanence of the cooperation existing between the United States, the Soviet Union, and Great Britain, both in the ongoing war and in the peace to come. "As a neighbor to the Soviet Union I thought it especially important that Finland develop good neighborly relations with the Soviet Union." The Finns agreed with this advice.[49]

When Hamilton finally met the chairman of the Control Commission on 13 March, Zhdanov reiterated the general view that the Commission's work had been much more difficult the previous October and November. Paasikivi's replacing Castrén had improved the level of cooperation between the Commission and the Finnish government, which the Soviet Union now thought generally good. The economic clauses of the armistice agreement, however, had in Zhdanov's view been complied with more willingly than the military and political ones. The disbandment of fascist organizations, in particular, had produced some difficulties. Although this process had now been formally completed, it was to be expected that some of the organizations might try to continue their activities underground. Zhdanov emphasized that he considered the parliamentary elections to be held in under a week's time to be a test of the resources of "reactionary and progressive" elements in Finnish society.[50]

Moscow's overall position toward Finland, although shaped to some extent by Finland's internal developments, was also colored by the Soviet Union's wartime experiences and its awareness of its international position. The fact that Finland had fought on the German side during the war was not to be easily forgotten, something that no doubt lay behind the repeated references in the Soviet press during the early spring to the significance of the Finnish elections as a touchstone of the country's new foreign policy.[51]

The Kremlin and the Control Commission also tried to influence opinion in Finland by more concrete means. The trade negotiations held in Moscow between the two countries were favorably concluded in good time before the elections. The securing of supplies of cereals and sugar was of particular importance to the Finnish negotiators.[52] It could also hardly have been mere coincidence that the Finnish public was allowed wide-ranging opportunities to learn more about life in their eastern neighbor through numerous visits by scientists, artists, and other prominent figures in the weeks immediately preceding the elections. The Red Army Choir, which gave a series of concerts all over Finland, enjoyed particular success. Cultural contacts and promotion of the Soviet image as a whole proved much less prominent later in the spring. Zhdanov and Orlov, it seems clear, saw the March elections as a kind of test of the efficacy and success of their policies.

8 The Problem of Military Cooperation

Finland's wartime army was demobilized, as set down under the terms of the armistice agreement, by 5 December 1944. The plan for the reduction of the navy, which was presented separately to the Control Commission on 4 November, envisaged a force comparable to that existing in 1939; a figure of 4,481 as the total strength of naval forces was accepted by the ACC on 26 November. The navy's internal organization, however, was subjected to significant modifications by the Commission: in particular, coastal defense forces were limited to a total strength of one artillery regiment and two separate coastal batteries — 1,616 men in all. This latter reduction was based on the shortening of Finland's coastline since 1939. General Zhdanov at the same time demanded that Finland should ensure that there would be a minimum of 200 vessels (1,986 men) engaged in minesweeping and clearance by 1 May at the latest. All material existing above and beyond that required by coastal defense and seaborne forces was, under the terms of the plan, to be removed and transferred to central storage depots.[1]

The head of the naval section of the Control Commission, Rear Adm. A. P. Aleksandrov, considered the last section of Zhdanov's requirement as implying that unmanned Finnish coastal defense positions should be dismantled and their equipment moved to storage depots on the mainland. The acting commander of Finnish naval forces, Rear Admiral Sundman, did not agree that this was a correct interpretation, as it would result in the weakening of coastal defenses to a level below that existing in 1939. With the situation deadlocked and the task of demobilizing the navy exceeding the deadline set by the armistice agreement, the president, in his personal capacity and as commander in chief, took charge of the Finnish side of the negotiations.

In a letter addressed to Zhdanov on 20 December 1944, Mannerheim observed that Finnish unmanned coastal defense positions formed an essential part of the country's pre-1939 defense system. They were a natural solution for a country like Finland, with insufficient numbers of personnel to operate all its defense positions in peacetime. And as the positions in question were located on islands and skerries off the coast, it would be impossible to transport and set up the heavy equipment they required after the commencement of an attack. The marshal mentioned, by way of example, that even without its breech mechanism the barrel of a 254-mm gun weighed 29 tons. The commission's demand for the dismantling of permanent armaments and their transfer to mainland depots would involve serious technical difficulties in winter conditions. The implications of military and political considerations both in the present and the immediate future also had a significant bearing on the matter. "As the war between the Great Powers has not yet finished and German naval forces are still operating in the northern parts of the Baltic, the preservation of the effectiveness of coastal defenses in the Gulf of Finland is a defense interest shared both by the Soviet Union and Finland." This was particularly important, in Mannerheim's view, in the case of the coastal zone west of Porkkala. "If those unmanned coastal positions west of Porkkala are demilitarized by moving their permanent armaments to distant central depots, we could well find ourselves in a situation in the future when both the Control Commission and the Finnish military leadership would have cause to regret this action."[2]

Zhdanov's answer took a couple of weeks to arrive. Mannerheim's request could not be agreed to. "The Control Commission considers it necessary to underline that the caliber of guns used in Finnish coastal defenses must not exceed 120 mm." The total number of guns was set at 140, of which 70 could be left not fully manned. The ACC agreed, however, because of the technical difficulties set out by the Finns, to extend the deadline for the removal of excess or over-caliber weapons to central depots on the mainland until 1 April. Zhdanov repeated his demand for 200 vessels to be ready by the summer for minesweeping operations. He also ordered the removal of propulsion engines and navigation and communication equipment, in addition to torpedoes and guns, from submarines belonging to the Finnish navy, a procedure justified because of "the superfluousness of submarines to direct coastal defenses."[3]

In his reply two days later, Mannerheim expressed his surprise that the question of the demobilization of the navy, which had already been agreed on, had been reopened on the submarine issue. While informing Zhdanov that he had given the necessary orders to comply with the measures demanded earlier, Mannerheim went on: "I consider it my duty, however, to bring to your notice, General, that some of the statements in your memorandum are not in my opinion based on the armistice agreement between Finland and the Soviet Union, but in fact imply partial disarmament. The placing of our coastal defenses on a peacetime footing cannot, as I understand it, mean that we lose weapons, the majority of which, such as large caliber coastal guns and submarines, we had for decades before the first year of conflict between our countries in 1939.'' Mannerheim saw the maintenance of a high level of coastal defense west of Porkkala as particularly important. ''The reduction of coastal artillery armament in this area so as to include weapons of a caliber of only 120 mm and less would be a particularly serious move.'' Artillery would naturally not be sited so that its effective range infringed the western border of the Porkkala area, unless the Soviet Union specifically wished for Finnish involvement, for example, in raising the overall effectiveness of coastal defenses.

On the submarine question, Mannerheim observed that the vessels under debate had been built years before the war. The placing of the armed forces on a peacetime footing as defined in the armistice agreement did not necessarily, in his view, presuppose their disarming. The general's demand would mean the total disabling of the submarines and the ending of training in underwater warfare in Finland.

> A speedy restoration of the submarine's military potential, if this should be called for by the Control Commission to serve our two countries' mutual purposes, cannot, under these circumstances, be guaranteed. I venture to hope that the General will discuss my suggestions at the Control Commission and that discussions will start from the basic premise that Finland and the Soviet Union have a common interest in respect of the defense of the northern Baltic and particularly the waters of the western Gulf of Finland, in which Finland wishes and is able, as an independent nation, sincerely and effectively to participate.[4]

These observations, although taking as their starting point the technical details of naval defense, embraced significantly wider issues. It was not merely a question of relative calibers and submarines, but more generally of the overall organization of relations between Finland and the Soviet Union. This clearly awoke Zhdanov's interest, and he visited Mannerheim personally on 18 and 22 January at the latter's official residence. The detailed content of their conversations remains unknown. Of interest, however, is a letter in Mannerheim's archives from Zhdanov, dated 19 January. Referring to their meeting the previous day, Zhdanov also attached copies of the treaties of cooperation that the Soviet Union had signed with France and Czechoslovakia.[5]

The same evening Mannerheim traveled on the night train to Mikkeli, the site of his wartime headquarters, to get the opinions of his close military advisers. In a handwritten memorandum to Mannerheim the next day, General Heinrichs declared himself in favor, in principle, of the idea of negotiating a treaty of military cooperation with the Soviet Union. Having thus recognized the security interests of Finland's eastern neighbor, it might then be possible, Heinrichs observed, to achieve some adjustments to those articles of the armistice agreement covering areas like Porkkala, the Saimaa canal, and Enso. Such adjustments would substantially aid the chances of the agreement being accepted in Finland. However, Heinrichs only thought it realistic to sign such a pact after the negotiation of a final peace treaty or simultaneously with such a treaty. Otherwise, the pact "would appear in the eyes of the majority of the population as only another step towards losing our national independence."[6]

On his return from Mikkeli and after a further discussion with Zhdanov at the presidential residence on 22 January, Mannerheim took up his pen and outlined in his clear, but by now slightly shaky handwriting, the first draft of a potential agreement between Finland and the Soviet Union. He wrote his outline, which ran to only three articles, in Russian, the result most likely of his being able to make direct use of the Czech and French agreements provided by Zhdanov. Mannerheim sketched the first article as follows: "Should an attack [*agressiya*] be directed against Finland, against the Soviet Union through Finland or against the two countries simultaneously, the High Contracting Parties bind themselves to give each other support and assistance in Finland, the northern part of the Baltic and in the Gulf of Finland, with all the forces at their disposal." In contrast to the agreements with France and Czechoslovakia, the embrace of this outline was clearly geographically restricted. An article specifying consultations between the two countries in the case of the threat of an attack was not included in this early draft.

The two remaining articles of Mannerheim's draft agreement covered the security interests of both parties, particularly the value of close and friendly cooperation after the restoration of peace; mutual respect of each other's independence and sovereignty; nonintervention in each other's internal affairs; postwar economic cooperation; and an undertaking "not to make any alliance or enter into any federative alliance directed against the other High Contracting Party." These last two articles follow almost word for word the text of the agreement signed between Czechoslovakia and the Soviet Union on 12 December 1943. Mannerheim sent his draft to Prime Minister Paasikivi the same day, 22 January 1945.[7]

Following their discussion in Mikkeli, Mannerheim requested General Heinrichs to continue work on outlining the general terms for a possible military cooperation agreement to be signed with the Soviet Union. Zhdanov's respect for Mannerheim was obvious to Shepherd, to whom Zhdanov described Mannerheim as "a remarkable man for his age."[8] But Zhdanov revealed nothing in this conversation with Shepherd about the topic or content of the discussions he had had with Mannerheim, and he probably had yet to receive the written outline prepared by the president. In fact, military and political realities were leading the Soviet and Finnish sides closer to each other; the road to mutual understanding was beginning to take shape. It was against this background that the troubled question of coastal defense was further discussed at the Control Commission. The matter's wider implications, however, required that it be referred back to

Moscow and Stalin for a decision, leaving the Finns with a lengthy wait for a definitive Soviet answer.

While underlining Finland's willingness to cooperate in the area of naval and coastal defense, Mannerheim was also keen to emphasize the limited and defensive nature of Finnish military interests. An opportunity to do this presented itself when the head of the naval section of the Control Commission, Rear Admiral Aleksandrov, suggested on 25 January that some small Finnish vessels might be used in the war against Germany outside Finnish waters, in addition to Finland's armistice agreement commitment to escort and other duties with Soviet vessels within Finnish territorial waters. The acting commander of Finnish naval forces, Rear Admiral Sundman, initially rejected the request, arguing that the navy was occupied with its minesweeping duties to such an extent that its participation in other operations was virtually impossible. At the back of Sundman's mind was the fear that acquiescence to the request would lead to the moving of the fleet far away from Finland's own shores. After outlining the Commission's demand to Parliament's foreign affairs committee, Sundman was also requested to report on the matter to Mannerheim. The president, after listening to Sundman's views, agreed and decided that the Russians would have to be told that the Finnish navy could not be used against German forces outside Finnish territorial waters. Enckell was entrusted with the task of communicating the decision to the Commission.[9]

By 2 March, the chairman of the Control Commission was at last ready to give what he described as his final reply on the naval defense problem, which had remained unresolved since January. Modifying his earlier position, Zhdanov declared that he accepted the proposal put forward by the Finnish military leadership of maintaining the present complement of coastal artillery (including large caliber guns) west of Porkkala, including that portion along the coast of the Gulf of Bothnia. After the demilitarization of positions on the Åland Islands, the number of coastal artillery pieces in the western zone, following the Finnish proposal, was to comprise 92 items.[10] As the total number of coastal guns was not allowed to exceed 140, the coast east of Porkkala, including the Helsinki area, was left with 38 guns of a maximum caliber of 120 mm. All other artillery, ammunition, and associated equipment above and beyond these restrictions were to be transported by 1 June 1945 to the two main storage depots of the Finnish navy. Demands for the stripping of Finnish submarines of their weapons were dropped; instead they were to be mothballed, by which the Commission made clear its opposition to their continued active use, preferring their preservation in a state of readiness in case of future need.[11]

Zhdanov's statement cleared the way, in Mannerheim's view, for progress toward mutually agreed policies combining the interests of both Finland and the Soviet Union. Three days later, Mannerheim informed Zhdanov that he had given the necessary orders and that the dismantling of coastal batteries west of

Porkkala had been halted. "The achievement of a final solution to this important question has in my view played a significant part in clarifying the situation in regard to the military and political position we have been in since last autumn and to which the Prime Minister referred in his recent statement recorded in the minutes of the State Council," he told Zhdanov.[12]

Mannerheim's latter point referred to Paasikivi's retrospective statement, given to Parliament at the beginning of March 1945, that a state of war had existed between Finland and Germany since 15 September 1944. This statement was largely the result of a memorandum prepared by the government's adviser on questions of international law, Erik Castrén. After demonstrating that such a declaration would largely be a formality, since the two former co-belligerents were effectively at war, Castrén had observed:

> The greatest benefit that Finland could derive in the future from a declaration of war might well be that, in any future peace negotiations with a defeated Germany, Finland might possibly be able to demand some kind of reparations for the destruction which has taken place in North Finland, together with other economic benefits. If Finland were able thereby to sit down at the same table at some future great peace conference alongside the "victors," her position would be much stronger than under the terms of a separate peace. . . . It is probable, however, that regardless of any declaration of war, Finland will be admitted in due course as a member of the new security organization to be founded at the conference to be held in San Francisco at the end of April, although she will not be allowed to participate in the planning of this organization. Certain long-standing neutral countries were only allowed admittance to this conference on condition that they had declared war on Germany before 1 March of this year, but this does not affect satellite states.

Although Castrén took the possibility of German countermeasures into account as a potentially negative aspect of the move, he felt that there was little cause for anxiety on this point, given the Germans' perilous military position.[13]

Castrén had concluded his memorandum with a recommendation that the prime minister present the statement in question to Parliament, which Paasikivi did two days later. As a precautionary measure, however, Paasikivi emphasized privately to Hamilton that the government hoped that Finland's action would not be interpreted as an attempt to gain admittance to the San Francisco conference, as it was realized that Finland would in any case be automatically excluded from those states invited.[14]

Zhdanov's and Mannerheim's discussions on the question of coastal defense had touched upon the problem of military cooperation between the Soviet Union and Finland in its wider context. The matter was further studied at Mannerheim's request during the spring of 1945 by the Finnish high command, as is clear from the detailed memorandums prepared by the commander of the defense forces, General Heinrichs.[15] These memorandums were also intended to serve as the groundwork for the deliberations of the committee set up to oversee the reorganization of the army and to produce a general review of defense forces. Heinrichs wrote:

> The bitter experiences of two wars oblige us to look for ways of finding our place in the world, which will not lead us into new conflicts with our strong eastern neighbor. We cannot shut our eyes to the fact that the Soviet Union's demands presented to us, in the form they appeared in the autumn of 1939, were clearly of a strategic nature. Without necessarily agreeing with their correctness, we can—and we must—see that behind those demands lay the Soviet Union's concern, as a Great Power, for its military security.

Heinrichs's overall conclusion was: "If the Soviet Union could be offered sufficient military guarantees that the Finnish area would form a trustworthy and sufficiently strong sector on the northern wing of a defense zone stretching across Europe and directed toward the West, there should not be any military reasons at least for further demands or a continued state of tension."

Satisfying the Soviet Union's security interests would, Heinrichs thought, also fundamentally strengthen Finland's political position in relation to the Soviet Union. Cooperation between the two countries would require a significant degree of trust by both parties as to the other's intentions. The Finnish army, as part of this, would have to remain an effective force to prevent Finland, as a small country, from being reduced to the status of a mere protectorate alongside her much larger partner. Military cooperation would, however, have to be strictly limited. "We cannot conceive," Heinrichs declared, "that Finnish forces—with the possible exception of our naval and air forces, and then only in a limited capacity—should be used in conflicts outside Finland's borders. . . . Within this geographically limited framework, Finland would use all the human and material resources at her disposal in the common cause." The question of possible Soviet assistance to Finland would have to be agreed upon separately. The Soviet Union's involvement in conflicts along other parts of its borders would not automatically involve Finland's participation, Heinrichs thought, and he advised that Finland should remain outside any such conflicts and maintain its neutrality.

Heinrich's outline agreement, which largely anticipated the Treaty of Friendship, Cooperation and Mutual Assistance that was finally signed between the two countries in 1948, nevertheless presupposed (as Heinrichs had made clear to Mannerheim back in January 1945) the prior existence of a peace treaty. The proposed agreement could be used, in Henrichs's view, not only as a bargaining counter to improve the possible terms of any peace treaty, but also as part of a concerted attempt "to hasten Finland's gaining a final peace before the negotiation of a wider-ranging European peace settlement." Obviously fearing that his views would shock those of more traditional schools of thought, Heinrichs concluded his final memorandum to the defense review committtee on 19 June with a direct appeal:

> Strange as this idea may seem to many in the context of Finland's history, it does perhaps offer one avenue for our political future, which will not inevitably lead to new military conflicts, at least not with our eastern neighbor. Marshal Mannerheim said in his last order of the day issued at the end of our heroic Winter War, that we had paid our debt to the West down to the past penny. I hope and believe that a courageous and unhappy period in our history has now come to an end, and I would be content if our defense forces could fulfil their duty in the future, as an instrument of the duly constituted leadership of our country, not only as in past years by shedding blood in what may have seemed hopeless situations, but by serving just as loyally and effectively in the shaping of a new type of foreign policy.[16]

Following the German surrender, Paasikivi suggested to General Zhdanov on 12 May the possibility of freeing Finland from certain restrictions imposed by the armistice agreement, a move allowed for under the agreement at the cessation of hostilities. Paasikivi specifically mentioned the return of certain airfields and allowing the use of codes in diplomatic communications by the legations of neutral countries in Helsinki. The chairman of the Control Commission, however, saw these as relatively minor problems alongside the major one of Finland's future relationship with the Soviet Union. Paasikivi stressed that his position on this was unambiguous, as he had tried to make clear in numerous speeches and public addresses—namely, that Finland could and would never again pursue policies directed against the Soviet Union. Referring to the agreements the Soviet Union had made with Czechoslovakia and France, Zhdanov asked whether Finland would be willing to consider a similar type of arrangement. Speaking personally, Paasikivi replied that negotiating an agreement similar to that signed between the Soviet Union and Czechoslovakia in 1943 was quite possible. Zhdanov felt able to conclude after this, as he told Paasikivi, that Finland and the Soviet Union had gone some considerable way toward developing good relations, and he promised to discuss the possibility of an agreement in Moscow. On his return to Helsinki, Zhdanov told Paasikivi on 26 May that the Soviet government would be sending the Finnish government an outline of a possible military agreement in the near future.[17]

In the meantime, Enckell set about preparing his own draft agreement for Paasikivi, in which he supplemented and amended the outline Mannerheim had produced in January. This new draft contained five articles in all. The additional articles provided by Enckell covered participation "in all international activities aimed at securing peace and security for all peoples" and in actions entered into in "a spirit of friendship and cooperation to develop and consolidate economic and cultural ties between both countries." While hoping to strengthen bilateral economic and cultural relations between the Soviet Union and Finland, Enckell also aimed at securing advance Soviet support for Finnish participation in the activities of the United Nations and its constituent organizations.[18]

In their various discussions in Helsinki with Gripenberg (the Finnish Minister in Stockholm), Mannerheim, Paasikivi, and Enckell all declared that they supported a possible pact so long as Finnish forces would only be called on to defend Finnish territory and would not be stationed outside the country's borders. They all agreed that such a pact would speed up the conclusion of a permanent peace and perhaps result in some reduction in the final amount of territory to be ceded to the Soviet Union; it would also mean the dissolution of the Control Commission. Paasikivi was particularly interested to know how Gripenberg thought Sweden would react to such an agreeement. Gripenberg supposed that Sweden would be sympathetic to the proposal. It would be absolutely necessary, however, to forewarn the Swedish government of any developments. Paasikivi agreed. Gripenberg repeated to all three men that he did not think that Finland would lose anything by signing such an agreement. In the event of a new war in Europe (which Gripenberg, it is true, did not think likely), Russia would occupy Finland in any case. "But we could perhaps avoid that calamity if in good time we declare ourselves ready to defend our own territory and by extension Russia as well."[19]

Following Paasikivi's instructions, Gripenberg, on his return to Stockholm, communicated in confidence the main points of the planned agreement to the Swedish government. Helsinki did not want to take any risks with Finland's most important trading partner. Hansson's cabinet, according to Günther, the foreign minister, refused to pass judgment on the proposed Soviet-Finnish military agreement, although as Günther later observed to Gripenberg, "not one voice in the cabinet was raised against the plan." Speaking personally, Günther went on to say that such an agreement could only be to Finland's advantage if through it Finland could achieve "a more secure position." It would mean, it was true, the dropping of all plans for a Nordic defense alliance; but Günther admitted that in any case he had not given the idea much chance. The cause of Scandinavian cooperation would certainly benefit from the defusing of the Finnish situation and the stabilization of the country's international position. Günther added that he was convinced that the Soviet Union did not intend to undermine Finland's independence.[20]

The outline text mentioned by Zhdanov, however, did not arrive from Moscow. After Hopkins's visit at the end of May 1945, Stalin began to prepare for the Potsdam conference, which was to deal with the question of the future of Germany's wartime satellites in its entirety. As a result, the Soviet Union refrained from negotiating cooperation agreements with Rumania, Hungary, and Bulgaria. The Great Powers only finally agreed on the principles to be followed in the preparation of the various peace treaties at Potsdam in July 1945, when a specially commissioned council made up of the foreign ministers of the Great Powers was entrusted with the matter. Although Finland's positive response, in principle, to a military cooperation agreement had been noted in Moscow, any implementation of such a pact would have to wait until after the negotiations on a peace agreement to be prepared jointly by the Great Powers. Paasikivi's cabinet saw no cause to press the matter of the pact in these circumstances; the issue, carefully kept under wraps, was allowed to rest.

Western diplomats stationed in Helsinki naturally tried as best they could to obtain any information about a possible Finnish-Soviet agreement. An editorial published on 5 May in *Vapaa Sana*, the main organ of the Finnish People's Democratic Union, describing the treaty recently signed between the Soviet Union and Yugoslavia as an appropriate model for future relations between Finland and her eastern neighbor, provided fuel for speculation. Hamilton's inquiries on the matter at the Finnish Foreign Ministry were met with a statement that there had been no discussions of that nature between the Finnish and Soviet governments, although the Ministry would have no a priori objections to the signing of such an agreement. Despite Hamilton's drawing an apparent blank, the State Department asked to be kept informed of the progress of negotiations as they transpired; however, Hamilton was instructed not to make any direct comments, either for or against such an agreement, to Finnish officials.[21] The American policy of noninvolvement was to be maintained.

The British for their part had not forgotten Stalin's statement made to Eden back in December 1941 of the Soviet Union's intention to demand military bases from Finland and to sign a Soviet-Finnish military treaty after the war. Shepherd reported in June 1945 that it was rumored in Helsinki that fortification work on the orders of the Soviet Union had begun on Finland's west coast and in the Åland Islands. Although Shepherd quoted Enckell as saying that ''a treaty of mutual assistance with Russia was not on the agenda,'' he nevertheless concluded on the basis of Enckell's choice of words that some form of agreement had been the subject of preliminary consideration, although it had as yet not been discussed in the government.[22]

In a memorandum prepared for the British delegation at the Potsdam conference, the Foreign Office declared that the guidelines of the future international organization then taking shape, the United Nations, specifically allowed for regional cooperation aimed at guaranteeing peace. The Kremlin no doubt would lay particular emphasis on this point. The memorandum continued:

It is for consideration whether we should attempt to dissuade the Soviet Government from concluding a treaty of alliance with Finland, since such a treaty would be likely to give them control of Finland's foreign and defence policies. It is clear that the Soviet Government will not again permit Finland to conduct an anti-Soviet foreign policy, with or without a treaty. It is equally clear that, in the event of trouble, neither we nor anyone else could prevent the Soviet Government from using any part of Finland as a military base. A Soviet-Finnish treaty of alliance would be unlikely to do more than confirm the actual state of affairs.

If Moscow was to sign such an agreement with Helsinki, it would be in Britain's interest, according to the Foreign Office, to propose Finland as a member of the United Nations as soon as possible after the conclusion of official peace negotiations, if only to reduce the level of Soviet influence in Finnish affairs marginally and to tie the country into a wider international context. Moscow would find it difficult immediately after having concluded an advantageous treaty to oppose a proposal of this sort.

The most disquieting aspect of the situation for the British was that the Kremlin's interest was hardly likely to be restricted to Finland: any treaty with Finland would be followed, and perhaps quickly, by similar treaties with Rumania, Hungary, and Bulgaria. With the Soviet Union's already close links with Poland, Czechoslovakia, and Yugoslavia in the forefront of their minds, the British saw Eastern Europe emerging as a powerful bloc that would be instrumental in accelerating the division of the whole of Europe into two separate camps. Fear of the Kremlin's intentions was growing in states in proximity to the Soviet Union, not least in Greece and Norway. If Stalin signed an agreement with Finland, Britain would probably have to act and sign a similar treaty with Norway. This would involve a number of problems, however, at a time when Britain did not even have formal ties of alliance with France. The British hoped that it would be possible to discuss the Finnish question at Potsdam with the Americans to find some means of pinning down the Soviet Union's intentions.[23]

Potsdam, however, gave the Big Three more than enough to think about without the Finnish problem. Moscow, contrary to the West's premonitions, made no attempt to promote the idea of a treaty with Finland, and the matter remained undiscussed. As a result, Bevin refrained from bringing up the question of a treaty during the visit of Norwegian Foreign Minister Trygve Lie to London in August 1945.[24] With the setting up of the special Allied Council of Foreign Ministers, the Foreign Office in any case considered any possible treaty between the Soviet Union and Finland unlikely until after the conclusion of official peace negotiations. There was thus no need for the time being to rush into negotiations with Norway, which London—with an eye to possible Soviet as well as American and French reaction—now thought would be premature.[25]

London maintained this line consistently in dealing with communications from the British members of the Control Commission in Helsinki during the autumn of 1945. In an extensive report filed on 30 October, Colonel Magill warned of the Soviet Union's "aggressive intentions" in the Scandinavian area. Britain, he said, needed to devise an integrated Scandinavian policy aimed at supporting the independence of these countries (Denmark, Norway, Sweden, and Finland) against the Soviet Union. Magill's idea met with a frosty reception at the Foreign Office, where it was thought that such a policy would only bring suspicion from the other Great Powers about Britain's intentions. More importantly, Magill also failed to provide any concrete evidence of what he described as Soviet expansionist policy toward Scandinavia. London thought Magill could more profitably use his time in acquiring such substantiating evidence. Obvious British activity along the lines suggested by Magill could, in the Foreign Office's opinion, only make Finland's position in relation to the Soviet Union more difficult.[26] Although no cause was yet seen for practical countermeasures, it is significant that rumors of a military agreement between the Soviet Union and Finland in the summer of 1945 clearly awakened in London the idea of Norway as a possible countering element in a future "Nordic Balance."

9 Toward Normality

The turnout at the polls in the parliamentary elections held on 17-18 March 1945 proved exceptionally high for the period (74.9 percent). The Finnish People's Democratic Union (SKDL), capturing 49 seats, emerged as a major new party; the Social Democrat's share of seats, previously 85, was reduced to 50, giving the nonsocialist parties a slender parliamentary majority with a total of 101 seats. There was a large number of first-time members, 92 in all, — the "new faces" Paasikivi had referred to in the days before the election — the majority naturally sitting for the People's Democrats. The other parties also had a larger than previous number of new members: half of the candidates elected for the National Coalition Party, nearly a third for the Agrarian Party, and a quarter for the Social Democrats were newcomers.

The change in the balance of power between the parties led to the forming of a political coalition by the three largest parliamentary parties at the beginning of the new parliamentary session on 6 April. A joint communiqué issued on 13 April by the parliamentary groups of the People's Democrats, the Social Democrats, and the Agrarian Party formally established the arrangement and outlined the coalition's future aims in the areas of foreign, internal, economic, and social policy. On the question of foreign policy, the communiqué stated that it was now necessary "resolutely to attempt to abandon once and for all the type of policies which have proved ruinous for the country and people, adopted by reactionary circles in Finland in recent years, if not thoughout the history of our independence." All three parties declared that they expected a speedy examination of all outstanding war-related problems and the implementation of the necessary actions to conclude them.

Paasikivi was entrusted with the task of forming the new government, his third, by President Mannerheim on 11 April. This government was duly sworn into office by the president shortly after on 17 April. The new government's policy program, which the Prime Minister presented to the State Council the following day, largely followed (albeit in more guarded language) the outline of the communiqué issued earlier by the three major parties. Foreign policy was to be managed "along the lines drawn up by the Allied powers and as allowed for under the terms of the Yalta conference." It was now time to draw the relevant conclusions from the facts as they had emerged regarding Finnish involvement in the war and, "acting in accordance with the present laws," to consider the appropriate courses of action. Each of the three parties received four ministerial portfolios. The People's Democrats were represented by Johan Helo, Yrjö Leino, Matti Janhunen, and Yrjö Murto; the Social Democrats by Onni Hiltunen, Eino Kilpi, Uuno Takki, and Eero A. Wuori; and the Agrarian Party by Kaarlo Hillilä, K. T. Jutila, Emil Luukka, and Urho Kekkonen. This apparent balance between the three was weighted, however, in favor of the People's Democrats because the government also included Reinhold Svento as the "prime minister's personal aide" and Mauno Pekkala as minister of defense; neither owed allegiance to the Social Democrats, and Pekkala in fact, officially belonged to the People's Democrats. From the foreign policy point of view, it was significant that both Enckell and Svento maintained a place in the new government; so did Urho Kekkonen, who, as minister of justice, was to play a central part in the handling of the war guilt problem. The government also included, as noncoalition members (in addition to Paasikivi and Enckell), Sakari Tuomioja of the Progressive Party as minister of finance and Åke Gartz, loosely connected with the Swedish People's Party, as minister of trade and industry.[1]

The Finnish elections received a favorable reception from the Allies. Hamilton, for the Americans, saw the election as clear evidence of a shift away from conservative groups and individuals friendly to Germany toward those favoring constructive and more positive relations with the Soviet Union. The elections themselves had, in his view, been peaceful and well ordered. Hamilton described Paasikivi's new government program as "a succinct and skilful statement, conducive to enlisting general support, of the principal problems confronting Finland."[2]

Shepherd, in conversation with Orlov (the Control Commission's political adviser), expressed his satisfaction that the elections had complied with the principles of the Declaration on Liberated Europe that had been agreed upon at Yalta. Orlov agreed with his British colleague. The elections had taken place "normally," and the result reflected in general terms the wishes of the Finnish people. All parts of the political spectrum appeared well disposed to developing friendly relations with the Soviet Union.[3] As the discussions at Potsdam later showed, this unanimously positive attitude toward the result of the Finnish elections was also shared by the leaderships of the three Great Powers.[4]

Moscow, however, took care not to give a public impression of the Soviet Union being unreservedly satisfied with events, if only to prevent the Finns from supposing that the work of building good relations was, as a result of the election, now largely over. The Soviet government paper *Izvestiya* emphasized on 22 March that, although the People's Democrats had indeed won 25 percent of the seats in Parliament, this did not in fact reflect the party's true standing in the country because of the disadvantageous position the party had been in during the election campaign in comparison with the other parties; for instance, it had lacked adequate meeting facilities. Reactionary groups were still strong in Finland, and much remained to be done in the Soviet view on such issues as the war guilt question.[5]

In a general survey of conditions in Finland sent to Washington on 23 May, Hamilton observed that, despite all the obstacles in its path, the Soviet Union's policy toward Finland had enjoyed some success since the autumn of 1944. Tanner's hold on the Social Democratic Party, together with that of other "conservatives," had been broken. Many politicians who had been associated with previous pro-German policies had not been reelected to Parliament. Parliament had got its "new faces." A more left-leaning government than that previously in office had been formed, and many of its key positions in terms of future social, economic, and political developments were held by people favorably disposed toward maintaining friendly relations with the Soviet Union, as was the three-party parliamentary coalition making up three-quarters of the members of Parliament. In fact, all the parties in Finland now supported cooperation with the Soviet Union. The government was actively working toward removing those associated with war guilt from governmental positions and directing its attention toward the purging of pro-German elements from the army, the police, schools and universities, and the state radio. The Finnish-Soviet Society had from modest beginnings become a politically important popular organization. Soviet economic interests were also being served by the Finnish government's strenuous efforts to fulfill the country's war reparations.

Although Soviet influence was clearly evident in Finland, conditions were altogether different, as Hamilton saw things, from those in Germany's other wartime satellite states. There were no Soviet occupation forces, and Western newspapers, magazines, and books were freely available. Civil administration, trade, postal and telegram services, and censorship remained completely in Finnish hands. The appointment of Zhdanov, who occupied an important position in the higher echelons of power in the Soviet Union, as chairman of the Control Commission reflected the particular significance given by Stalin to the Finnish question, which went beyond its obvious associations with the defense of Leningrad. Although Zhdanov and his Russian subordinates rarely departed from their strict interpretations of the clauses of the armistice agreement, they nevertheless seemed friendly toward the Finns. This favorable treatment accorded to the Finns was partly the result, in Hamilton's estimation, of the Russians' awareness of the Finns' longer experience in efficiently and effectively handling their internal affairs compared with the Balkan countries, and of Russia's respect for the Finns' capabilities as tough fighters, which had been demonstrated not least against the Soviet Union itself. Everything pointed to a greater degree of stability than might be expected from the other satellite countries. Hamilton also believed that Moscow was trying to use Finland as an example to demonstrate to the West that the Soviet Union was not in fact attempting to bolshevize those countries within its sphere of influence. Pointing to the freedom of the recent Finnish elections, Moscow could easily label Western attempts to supervise, for example, electoral freedom in the coming elections in the Balkan countries as unwarranted intervention in the internal affairs of those countries.[6]

On the question of the Soviet Union's possible long-term aims as regards Finland, Hamilton felt unable to offer any concrete predictions. Following the formation of Paasikivi's new government, the level of Soviet interest in the Finnish area appeared to have appreciably declined. The comments of the Moscow press on Finnish affairs were now fewer in number and had lost their earlier sharpness. This moderation of tone also extended to *Vapaa Sana*, the paper of the People's Democrats, which both the British and Americans saw as closely following and reflecting the opinions of the Control Commission. The "Finnish Freedom Radio" operating from the Soviet Union had also ceased its propaganda broadcasts. Taken as a whole, the Kremlin's policy toward Finland gave no cause for direct protest from the Western powers. That was not to say, however, that general basic questions—such as the meaning of the concept of democracy— were not still interpreted in sharply differing ways in the East and West.[7]

The British view of the situation followed that of the Americans. Moscow's "flexible" attitude toward Finland resulted, according to Sir Orme Sargent, the permanent under secretary of state at the Foreign Office, from the fact that the Finnish area was temporarily considered less important than the *cordon sanitaire* countries farther south.[8] The head of the British section of the Control Commission in Helsinki, Commodore Howie, saw the existence of the Soviet Union's "liberal" policy toward Finland as lending support to the view that Moscow was attempting to convert the Finnish establishment to a more favorable attitude toward the Soviet Union, rather than trying to liquidate it. Paasikivi's government's obvious cooperation with the Russians was, it had to be admitted, far from being simply submissive. But although a Soviet military occupation of Finland seemed improbable for the time being, Howie thought it certainly more than possible that the Russians might at some point in the future attempt forcibly to install a government ready to request the annexation of the country to the Soviet Union. A lot depended on the Finns' own determination to maintain their independence, a matter on which Howie himself felt far from certain.[9]

Howie drew attention yet again in his June report to London to the Commission's light workload. The British members had had practically nothing to do since March, he complained. The Commission had become little more than a "post office," as he put it, in Zhdanov's absence, with even the most minor questions having to be sent to Moscow for a decision. In any case, larger-scale problems of the type encountered during the previous autumn no longer existed, and routine took care of the rest. The Russians remained loath, as before, to keep their British colleagues informed, the latter typically finding themselves faced with faits accomplis. The general lack of work had led the British to begin reducing the number of personnel in the British section of the Commission from April 1945 onward. The Foreign Office, however, for reasons of international prestige, never envisaged Britain completely withdrawing her representation from the Commission.[10]

With the certainty of an imminent German collapse becoming ever clearer during April 1945, London began to direct its attention to the question of the future peace treaty to be signed with Finland. The Foreign Office initially thought it possible that a simple outline treaty could be signed even before a general peace settlement. This would be both economically and politically advantageous to Britain. Any treaty, however, would have to be signed by all those countries that had been at war with Finland.[11]

Shepherd, learning of these plans, which seemed to him to be in Britain's best interest, gave them his complete support. As long as the armistice agreement remained in force, the Finnish government and people would remain in a constant state of unease and fearful of Soviet intentions. This had been particularly apparent during the course of the Finnish-British trade negotiations held in Helsinki. A final peace treaty would undoubtedly free the Finns from a heavy burden of uncertainty about their future. It would also give new hope and strength to those Finnish figures who, while aware of the significance of friendly relations with the Soviet Union, were at the same time attempting to preserve as much of their country's independence of action as was practically possible. "These elements are at present suffering from very considerable depression, since they feel that Russian pressure is so imminently available in the form of the Control Commission that they are powerless to influence those elements in Finnish political life which are not only enthusiastically Russophil, but are even bent on a certain measure of slavish imitation of Soviet system."[12] Stalin's tying of the question of a Finnish peace on the eve of the Potsdam conference to the negotiation of agreements with Italy and the Balkan countries, however, saw the demise of British hopes for a separate solution to the Finnish problem. The plan discussed in the U.S. State Department in the spring of 1945, envisaging the setting up of a permanent Finnish legation in Washington without renewing official diplomatic relations also had to be shelved for the same reason. Hamilton's voice was nevertheless joined by that of George F. Kennan of the American embassy in Moscow in recommending that the State Department do all it could to strengthen Finnish self-confidence.[13]

The conflicts between the Western powers and the Soviet Union that emerged during the summer of 1945 also gradually began to make themselves felt in peripheral areas like Finland. Shepherd, for example, drew particular attention in one of his reports to the case of the People's Democrats' paper *Vapaa Sana* and to *Kontakt* and *Folktidningen*, which he described as mouthpieces of the Finnish-Soviet Society, and which had all accused Britain and the United States of pro-fascist tendencies and of fanning the flames of a third world war. Such articles could only be seen as directly inspired by Moscow, in Shepherd's opinion. The press attaché at the British legation had done everything he could to counter these "tendentious attacks," but it was unlikely that the left-wing press would publish any form of rebuttal. It was, Shepherd believed, a question of an organized campaign, and one to which attention should be drawn in the British press.[14]

The Foreign Office, however, disagreed. The matter was too insignificant to warrant beginning a war of words in the press, nor could an official protest be contemplated because the Finns would no doubt be tempted to point to the similar accusations that had appeared in the British left-wing press. Shepherd was, however, advised to let the Finnish government understand that such tendentious assertions, when they remained unchallenged, could do little to strengthen any general resolve for peace. It was hardly proper, moreover, for the press of a country that had fought on the side of the Nazis now to accuse the victors of the war against Germany of pro-fascist leanings.[15] Foreign Minister Svento agreed in his ensuing discussions with Shepherd on the subject that the prevention of such accusations in the press was desirable. The foreign minister added, however, to Shepherd's surprise, "that the journalists in question were not politicians." Despite this, Shepherd was able by the middle of July 1945 to report, with obvious satisfaction, that this type of press attack had completely ceased.[16]

The Control Commission also enjoyed a temporary new lease of activity. Speaking to Commodore Howie on 16 July, General Zhdanov made it clear that the end of the war against Germany would mean certain changes in the implementation of the armistice agreement. The airfields at Kotka and Turku would be returned to the Finns. The airfield at Malmi, however, would continue to be needed by the Control Commission to maintain its channels of communication. The restrictions on the movements of the Finnish navy and merchant fleet would also be removed, and Finnish military and civilian aircraft would be allowed to fly freely in Finnish airspace. Scheduled flights abroad would continue to remain forbidden, as neither Finland nor Sweden could be allowed to operate on routes that Britain and the Soviet Union did not operate themselves.[17] The danger of mines at sea would mean Soviet vessels continuing to use Finnish territorial waters, harbors, and port installations. The diplomatic community in Helsinki would be allowed to reopen postal, telegram, and telephone links abroad, but the ban on the sending of telegrams in code (with the exception of the American, British, and French legations) would continue in force. There was no cause yet,

Zhdanov argued, to allow neutral countries like Switzerland or Sweden full diplomatic rights in Finland, when the major Allied powers—including Great Britain—had yet to reestablish normal diplomatic relations.

Howie, however, felt himself duty-bound to observe that some of Zhdanov's suggestions conflicted with the terms of the armistice agreement. The use of airfields in south and southwest Finland by the Allies was restricted to wartime, as were the limitations on the movement of Finnish aircraft. Following the German surrender, there was no basis for even the partial maintenance of these restrictions, Howie suggested. The ban on the diplomatic use of code was also, according to the armistice agreement, supposed to apply only "until German forces have completely withdrawn from Finnish territory." Zhdanov refused to accept Howie's counterarguments, only repeating his suggestions and the reasoning behind them. Howie, satisfied that his opinion had for once been consulted before any final decision, was unwilling to damage his relations with the chairman of the ACC by pushing his opposition too far. In further discussions on 25 July, Howie restricted himself simply to demanding that the right of use of Finnish territorial waters and harbors should be extended to include ships of the other Allied powers, in addition to those of the Soviet Union. This was impossible, according to Zhdanov. The most that could be added to the terms would be a right of passage for British merchant vessels, but not for ships of the other Allies or for British naval vessels. Howie, however, could not agree to this.[18]

The chairman of the Commission ignored Howie's opposition and forwarded the adjustments to the armistice agreement that he had presented to Howie, together with the relaxation on the territorial waters question concerning British merchant ships, to Paasikivi the same day. Although Paasikivi had already drawn Zhdanov's attention to the effect that the ending of the war would have on the terms of the armistice agreement back on 12 May,[19] the Finns now found themselves in a difficult situation. Although the changes were clear relaxations of the earlier conditions, some of the restrictions initially limited to wartime now seemed destined to remain in force well into the future. Any changes in the terms of the armistice agreement, which had originally been accepted by Parliament, would logically also have to be put before Parliament for approval. Enckell emphasized to Shepherd that if this were not done they would be making the same mistake, at least in a technical sense, that Ryti had been guilty of in his agreement with Ribbentrop, and for which there were now demands that he be brought to book. Zhdanov, however, saw it as a question of "adjustments" to the agreement rather than large-scale changes, which did not require parliamentary approval. The matter could be dealt with by an exchange of correspondence between Zhdanov, as chairman of the ACC, and Paasikivi. The whole process would become unnecessarily complicated, according to Orlov in his discussions with Enckell, if every adjustment now and in the future had to be put separately before Parliament for approval. Enckell observed that a final peace treaty, negotiated as soon as possible, offered the best solution to the whole problem. Putting aside his legalistic anxieties, however, Paasikivi thought it expedient to accept Zhdanov's proposals, and he forwarded a reply to the chairman of the Commission on July 25, formally stating the Finnish government's acceptance of the proposed adjustments. Enckell added orally that in principle the matter required parliamentary approval.[20]

London was forced to respond. Howie's instructions, received from the Foreign Office on 29 July, made it clear that Zhdanov's position on the shipping question was not to be accepted. Matters of this type were to be decided collectively and not by the Soviet Union alone. Although hostilities against Germany had ceased, to all intents and purposes a formal state of war still existed. This being the case, the relevant clauses of the Finnish armistice agreement also remained in force, including those concerning Allied shipping as a whole. It had also to be remembered that Britain imported timber from Finland in ships of its allies (such as Norway) in addition to its own, and these had to have the right to move freely in Finnish territorial waters and harbors.[21] After duly listening to the Foreign Office position as communicated by Howie on 2 August, Savonenkov, Zhdanov's deputy, declared that the matter had already been agreed upon with the Finnish government and that, accordingly, the problem was now closed. Pressed by Howie, he said that Norwegian and Danish vessels employed on British business could be given the same rights as British merchant vessels. This had already happened in practice, as ships sailing under the two national flags in question had loaded timber from Finnish ports for shipment to Britain. Savonenkov argued, however, that although Norway and Denmark belonged to the United Nations, they did not constitute "allied states."[22]

London strongly resisted this latter interpretation. Howie was instructed to inform Savonenkov that Norway was both a member of the United Nations and an ally and that Britain similarly considered Denmark an ally.[23] The Foreign Office also considered it necessary to protest directly to Molotov over the schism that had developed within the Control Commission in Helsinki, drawing attention to both the shipping and code questions and to the fact that the recent modification of the terms on both went against the armistice agreement. "His Majesty's Government . . . must request that Colonel-General Zhdanov's communication, which is apparently based on a misapprehension of the position under the armistice terms of this matter, be withdrawn."[24]

But Moscow did not yield. In his reply sent on 2 September, Vyshinsky informed the British that demands for the right of use of Finnish harbors by Allied warships, other than those of the Soviet Union, were unjustified. The matter could not be postponed until the signing of a peace treaty with Germany. The appendix to Article 3 of the armistice agreement, allowing access for British and other Allied warships, was directed towards enabling them to take part in anti-German operations in the Baltic; but with hostilities now at an end, the

Royal Navy no longer had any need to make use of Finnish harbor facilities. The situation was somewhat different for the Soviet Union, as the Baltic formed part of its maritime frontier. On the question of access for merchant shipping, British protests were also unjustified in Soviet eyes because British ships already enjoyed complete freedom to use Finnish harbors, as did Norwegian and Danish vessels. Vyshinsky's reply made no mention of other allied states. Vyshinsky observed on the question of the right to encode diplomatic messages that Howie had not made any direct protest in his discussions with General Zhdanov on 25 July regarding the adjustments to the armistice terms to be presented to the Finns. The Soviet government did not as a result see any reason to alter any of the adjustments that had been made to the terms of the armistice agreement and that had been communicated to the Finnish government. [25]

By thus underlining its authority, Moscow had also strengthened Zhdanov's position. The British, however, could not resist the opportunity to press their point all the same. Howie seized the chance of a meeting with Zhdanov on 21 September to question him about the problem of Swedish vessels docking in Finnish harbors. Should the Control Commission, Howie asked, take steps to issue each vessel an official entry permit, thereby formally underwriting the existing state of affairs? Zhdanov (according to the account given by his British colleague), apparently showed clear signs of annoyance at the mere mention of Sweden. Any neutral state wishing to send vessels to Finland, Zhdanov declared, was responsible for requesting the necessary permission. As Swedish merchant ships nevertheless freely visited Finnish ports without any form of official permission, Howie concluded that there was little to be gained from pressing Zhdanov any further on the matter. [26]

The following day, however, Zhdanov suggested that Norwegian and Danish merchant vessels be issued official permits for docking in Finnish ports. Howie agreed to Zhdanov's proposal, while making it clear that the British government had not altered its earlier position on the issue. The Foreign Office found itself in what it described as an "absurd" position, both aware of the fact that Norwegian and Danish ships had been visiting Finnish ports for some time and yet unwilling to oppose the Soviet suggestion. Zhdanov expressed obvious satisfaction at the British government's positive response and promised to inform the Finns of the change. Both the Finns and Norwegians, however, not being party to the behind-the-scenes negotiations that had gone before, could make little sense of the practical significance of the new instructions. [27]

After the code question was decided in a manner satisfactory to the British, the only real bone of contention remaining was the right of use of Finnish harbors by the Royal Navy. The Admiralty in London saw little to be gained from opposing the Soviet position.

The Russians have, of course, a special interest in the defence of the Eastern Baltic, just as we consider we have a special interest in the defence of the Mediterranean and particularly the Eastern Mediterranean. The Chiefs of Staff have, as the Foreign Office will be aware, said that Finland is of no strategic importance to ourselves. We have indeed recognised the special Soviet interest in defence in Finland through our acquiescence in the cession of Porkkala Ud. Accordingly we should not wish to dispute any Russian claim to special defence responsibilities in the Eastern Baltic, provided that this claim did not extend to an exclusion of British warships from making normal courtesy visits. The Western Baltic is, of course, a very different matter, and we should certainly not agree that the Soviet Union has an exclusive special interest in the Western Baltic as a maritime frontier of the Soviet Union.[28]

This division remained. The days when, as the old Finnish song puts it, "Englishmen sailed off the coasts of Finland" were, except for normal courtesy visits, in the words of the Admiralty itself now part of history.

The Potsdam conference saw the Great Powers conclude that "all three governments [the United States, the Soviet Union, and Great Britain] agree individually to consider in the near future, in the light of prevailing circumstances, the establishment of diplomatic relations with Finland, Rumania, Bulgaria and Hungary, as far as it proves possible before the ratification of peace treaties negotiated with these countries." Moscow lost no time in acting. Within four days of the ending of the conference on 6 August, the Soviet government announced its decision to restore diplomatic relations with Rumania, Bulgaria, and Finland. The Kremlin, however, only informed Britain and the United States after the decision had been communicated to the countries concerned.[29]

London and Washington, which before Potsdam had treated Finland somewhat differently from the Balkan countries, now found themselves having to respond to the new situation created by Moscow's initiative. Britain, however, had previously made it clear to its allies that it would be unable for constitutional reasons to establish diplomatic relations with any country with which it was still technically at war. Conversely, there was no bar on "quasi-diplomatic relations," such as existed between the western Great Powers and Italy. Finland could send a representative to London who would be granted the personal title of minister. Shepherd's status in Helsinki would be similarly changed. Representatives of this sort would enjoy access to the governments of the countries in which they were posted, but they would not be diplomatically accredited. The Foreign Office communicated this possibility to the government in Helsinki on 18 August, carefully avoiding any reference to the term "quasi-diplomacy."[30]

Walsh, standing in for Shepherd, reported on 22 August that the Finnish government had received London's communications "with the greatest satisfaction." A representative would be appointed to London at the first opportunity.[31] Enckell's openly expressed admiration of Britain's respect for diplomatic convention and tradition surprised Walsh. "I had rather prepared myself to hear a mild complaint . . . in view of Russian readiness to appoint a . . . Minister immediately."[32]

With no state of war existing between the United States and Finland, the situation proved more straightforward for the Americans. In a memorandum to President Truman dated 17 August, Byrnes concluded that all the information he had received indicated that the parliamentary elections in March had been held completely in accord with the democratic wishes of the Finnish people and without foreign interference. Membership of the new government took account of the redistribution of power resulting from the election and represented a broad cross section of all the democratic elements of Finnish political life, all of which led Byrnes to recommend the reestablishment of diplomatic relations between the United States and Finland. Byrnes's particular emphasis on the democratic nature of the elections and the new government was clearly founded on a desire to underline the basis for treating Finland as a special case and as distinct from the Balkan countries, which remained diplomatically unrecognized. Obviously wishing to be seen to be acting in accordance with America's British ally, Byrnes cabled the decision to restore diplomatic relations to Helsinki the same day. President Truman's written confirmation came a day later on 18 August. As it is unlikely that Byrnes would have wished to present Truman with a fait accompli on such a delicate question, it seems plausible to assume that Truman gave his verbal agreement on 17 August at the latest.[33] The American decision was received in Helsinki with as much obvious appreciation as the British message had been received earlier, and the Finnish reply to both countries was almost identical. Speaking personally to Hamilton, Enckell added that he greatly appreciated the move, which he saw as indicative of American moral support for Finland.[34]

The appointment of diplomatic representatives to Finland by the Great Powers went ahead smoothly. Pavel Orlov, the Control Commission's political adviser, was named as the Soviet envoy. Francis Shepherd, now with the personal title of minister, continued as Britain's representative. Maxwell Hamilton's departure to the United States for a long visit on 22 August meant that Washington only asked for confirmation of his new status, which was duly forthcoming from the Finnish government on 19 September.[35] Benjamin Hulley served as chargé d'affaires during Hamilton's absence.

The appointment of Finland's representatives to the Great Power capitals took the form of a compromise agreed upon between the three major government parties. Cay Sundström of the People's Democrats was appointed to Moscow, Eero Wuori of the Social Democrats to London, and Kalle Jutila of the Agrarian Party to Washington. Wider discussion of the appointments in government circles only seems to have taken place in the case of the Washington posting, when G. A. Gripenberg, the Finnish minister in Stockholm, informed Enckell that he would like to be considered. Rejected as an "aristocrat" by the left, Gripenberg only gained the initial support of Enckell, Paasikivi, and Ralf Törngren, the new minister of finance. A later vote saw all three supporting Jutila's appointment in the cause of maintaining government unanimity. Under these circumstances, President Mannerheim—despite his personal views on the subject—did not believe himself able to support an alternative candidate.[36]

Benjamin Hulley, deputizing for Hamilton, thought the choice a good one and saw no reason to refuse Jutila's appointment. Jutila, who had previously been minister of agriculture, was friendly toward the United States and had visited the country many times; he spoke English "brokenly but fluently."[37] Caplan, who as leader of the British trade delegation that had visited Helsinki had come into a fair amount of contact with Jutila, was less enthusiastic. "Professor Jutila does not give one the impression of being a forceful personality capable of directing work on difficult problems." He was hardly likely to make a good impression in Washington, Caplan thought.[38]

The British looked on Eero Wuori, the Finnish appointee to London, more favorably. "Wuori is credited with a sound judgement and a good deal of shrewd common sense. He is quiet and a little reserved but friendly and likable and creates a good impression." Walsh considered Wuori's present position in the Finnish government as fraught with difficulties stemming from his simultaneously serving as chairman of the Finnish Trade Union Confederation (SAK). The unanimous opinion of the Foreign Office's Northern Department was that he would make "a good appointment."[39]

After the reestablishment of diplomatic relations between Finland and the Great Powers, there was no longer any reason to deny the right to use coded messages to the accredited representatives of other countries in Helsinki. General Zhdanov informed Commodore Howie on 4 September that he had received instructions from Moscow to allow the representatives of Norway, Denmark, and Brazil the immediate use of code and those of Sweden and Switzerland three or four days later. It was important to distinguish between those countries that had opposed Hitler and those that had not. As all the other foreign representatives accredited to Finland, with the exception of those of the four Great Powers already allowed the right to use code, resided in Stockholm, the question of granting them similar rights was not relevant. Howie naturally gave his approval to Zhdanov's proposal, which London—without distinguishing between two types of countries — had supported for some time.[40] The withdrawal of the restrictions on coded messages for Norwegian, Danish, and Brazilian diplomats was communicated to Enckell the same day; for those from Sweden and Switzerland, it was communicated five days later on 10 September.[41]

The Finnish government marked the surrender of Japan by sending telegrams of congratulation signed by Paasikivi to the victorious Great Powers. G. Warr, responsible for Finnish affairs in the Foreign Office in London, thought it "a little impertinent that a state, which is still technically an enemy should send this message." It would be best to ignore it, he recommended. Christopher Warner, the head of the Northern Department, disagreed. "The present Finnish Government's view is no doubt that Finland has been converted to the side of the Allies. I think this message is quite harmless." As a result, Walsh in Helsinki was instructed to convey His Majesty's Government's appreciation of the Finnish gesture.[42] With the exception of an official peace treaty, World War II was at an end for Finland.

PART IV
Political Deadlock

10   From Potsdam to Moscow

The Potsdam Conference held in the summer of 1945 had set up a negotiating body made up of the foreign ministers of the five Great Powers. This Council of Foreign Ministers was entrusted with drafting the peace treaties for Germany's European "satellites,"—Italy, Rumania, Bulgaria, Hungary, and Finland. The Council's first meeting was later fixed for 11 September at Lancaster House in London. The diplomatic rhetoric, which had been so much a part of the discussions at Potsdam, now had to be translated into workable political solutions.

The American delegation, which sailed to Europe on the *Queen Elizabeth*, was led by Secretary of State Byrnes. It knew in advance that the main differences of opinion between the five nations would focus upon the Balkan countries and the varying interpretations put on their electoral freedom and governmental democracy. Washington hoped that developments in Rumania, Bulgaria, and Hungary would follow the example of Finland. The State Department realized, however, that the United States had no real means of directly influencing what happened in southeast Europe because the area was under Soviet occupation. The Americans instead decided on a policy of pressuring all the relevant parties to accede to their interpretation of the Yalta agreement, following the tactics they had adopted at Potsdam. The United States, they declared, would not negotiate peace or reestablish diplomatic relations with Rumania, Bulgaria, or Hungary until the governments of these three countries had been replaced with ones duly elected by the majority of their populations and until Western journalists had been given the opportunity of unrestricted access and full reporting rights in the region to satisfy themselves of the rule of democracy.

Washington's initial negotiating position closely echoed the general tenor of American public opinion and the overall notions of "open-door" politics and the rhetoric of the Atlantic Charter. There was little public discussion, however, of the fact that unimpeded international trade was perhaps more than anything in the United States' own best interests, as an economic giant with an industrial infrastructure undamaged by the ravages of war. Balkan governments that had been freely elected, according to American criteria, could also legitimately be expected to respond more favorably politically to Washington than to Moscow.

Byrnes was optimistic about his chances of shaping what happened in London, and he believed that the foreign ministers would be able to conclude their work in a matter of a few weeks. After the outline of the treaty procedure had been agreed upon by the Council, the deputy foreign ministers (together with their respective delegations) would remain in London to take care of the finer details of the individual agreements. Byrnes's conviction was underpinned by his awareness of American economic might and the American atom bomb monopoly. Although he did not expect to have to resort to direct threats to use the atomic weapons, the secretary of state expected the facts of the situation by themselves to persuade the Soviet Union to take an accommodating line. The Americans were to be disappointed. Convinced that Western public opinion, at least for the time being, would not allow the use of the atom bomb against a wartime ally, the Kremlin refused to be intimidated. The Soviet delegation, led by Molotov, acted throughout as if the Western monopoly of the atom bomb was of no significance for the negotiations.

The Great Powers also found themselves faced with other complicated decisions in London, in addition to the problems surrounding the Balkans. Discussions on the Italian question got nowhere. A decision on the contested Italian-Yugoslav border and on the fate of Trieste had to be postponed for lack of adequate detailed information on contemporary ethnic and economic conditions in the area. Molotov suggested that Italy's colonies be divided among the victorious Great Powers as limited-term mandatory territories, and he expressed Soviet interest in acquiring Tripolitania. But the Western powers, assuming that Stalin was aiming for a military foothold in a strategically important area, refused to accept the Soviet argument that their merchant fleet needed base facilities in North Africa. Without access to Soviet documents, it is difficult to trace the reasons behind Moscow's demands as regards the Italian colonies. Stalin could well have been serious or he could have been aiming, in as tangible a way as possible, to prove to the Western powers the "unreasonableness" of their demands in the Soviet sphere of influence in the Balkans. Extreme initial proposals, in any case, allowed greater scope for subsequent compromises. The strong opposition of the Western powers meant that the Soviet proposals had no hope of being adopted at this stage. There was unanimity in principle, however, on the question of limiting the size of future Italian military forces, although the fixing of the restrictions was to require further discussion.

The problem of Italian war reparations saw Western and Eastern opinions in sharp disagreement. Soviet negotiators spoke of imposing reparation payments of $600 million, a proposal to which both Britain and the United States reacted skeptically. They believed that Italy would be unable to pay reparations of such magnitude; if forced to do so, Italy would only become a burden to the Great Powers. Molotov replied that if the United States and Britain were to forgo their shares of the reparations the total sum could be reduced to $300 million, to be divided between the Soviet Union, Yugoslavia, Greece, and Albania—with Moscow receiving $100 million. The damage caused by Italian forces on Soviet territory was such, Molotov argued, that the Soviet Union was unable to forgo its demand for reparations altogether.

Molotov seemed unwilling to understand the West's opposition. A number of small countries, such as Rumania and Finland, were already committed to reparations payments of $300 million. Was it not fair to demand a parallel sacrifice from a much larger country like Italy? Bevin retorted that Britain had only agreed to the inclusion of reparations clauses in the Rumanian and Finnish armistice agreements under protest and on the understanding that they would not be used as precedents. The Italian economy was on the brink of collapse, and a significant increase in the amount of Allied aid already being given would be required for the country to meet heavy reparations payments. "What would the British public say if [Bevin] agreed to fix a total of $300 million for reparations from Italy, and then had to admit that the British taxpayer was contributing towards payment of these reparations?" Bevin asked. The results of reparations arrangements following World War I had not been encouraging. The Americans, led by Byrnes, agreed.

Molotov saw nothing to be gained from comparing the present situation with the one after World War I. They should rather look to more recent experiences that had been much more positive. Finland, a country of four million inhabitants, on whom the greatest burden had been placed, was required to pay $300 million and yet was fulfilling its obligations and maintaining friendly relations with the Soviet Union. Molotov declared that he would not oppose any individual reparations demands Britain might make of Italy, but that if the Western powers as a whole were to demand reparations, the total sum would have to be $600 million. The question of Italian war reparations proved sufficiently intractable for further negotiations on the matter to be postponed to a later date.[1]

The Finnish problem came up in passing in London on the opening day of the conference of foreign ministers on 11 September in a discussion of the agenda. The conference's British hosts proposed that discussions on the Finnish treaty be treated separately from those for the Balkan countries. Molotov was unable to agree to this. Work on outlining the shape of the future treaties with Rumania, Bulgaria, Hungary, and Finland had been integrated at Potsdam and there was no good reason now to begin treating Finland—suspected in any case by the Soviet Union as being a favorite of the West—separately. The Western powers acceded and the agenda was changed in line with Molotov's argument.[2]

The following day, the Soviet foreign minister presented his colleagues with the Soviet Union's suggested guidelines for drawing up the peace treaties to be signed with the Balkan countries and Finland. The armistice terms then in force were described as offering a basic point of departure for all the countries concerned. In Finland's case, this would mean the retention of articles 6-14, 20, and 21, together with the appendixes of articles 7, 8 and 11 with appropriate modifications.[3] Article 16 of the armistice agreement would be replaced with an obligation on Finland, in line with the agreements made at Potsdam, to transfer all German assets on its territory to the Soviet Union. The Allies would assist Finland and the other satellite countries in becoming admitted to the United Nations, and these countries would be obliged to cooperate with the Allies in policies and actions promoted by them for the maintenance of world peace.[4]

The British delegation agreed that the peace treaties for Finland and the Balkan countries should be drawn up on the basis of their respective armistice agreements. The inclusion of an article banning fascist and anti-United Nations organizations and the propaganda of such organizations (Article 21 of the Finnish armistice agreement) was, however, unnecessary (in Britain's opinion) when all the governments concerned had shown themselves quite willing and able to act on this question. The British clearly wanted to prevent the Soviet Union and the Finnish and Balkan communist parties from using their own interpretation of the term "fascist" for "revolutionary" ends. Bevin's delegation went on to suggest that the peace treaties should define the type and strength of military forces allowed in the Balkan countries and Finland and should specifically limit their right to manufacture military equipment. Britain also suggested that military observers be jointly appointed by the Allies to oversee the implementation of the military articles of each peace treaty and that the respective control commissions be wound up after the treaties came into force. Allied (Soviet) forces could also then be withdrawn from the Balkans, and the Finnish government would be freed of the requirement to provide facilities of a military nature to the Soviet Union. Behind the British proposal lay the strong suspicion that the Soviet Union intended to negotiate military agreements with the countries in question. Thus it was only to be expected that everything would be done to hamper and weaken the emergence and content of such agreements in advance, as in the attempt to replace the control commissions (which had turned out to be poor channels of British influence) with Allied military observers.

The suspicion dominant among the members of the British delegation toward Soviet intentions was also reflected in the suggestion that, after the reestablishment of diplomatic and consular relations, each Allied power should be individually empowered to dictate the number of its consuls in the Balkans and Finland and their places of residence. To ensure the "democratic" nature of internal political developments in these countries, the Western powers also proposed that a separate

"Bill of Rights" modeled on the Italian example be appended to all the peace treaties, specifically guaranteeing the citizens of these countries the freedoms of speech, assembly, and religious and political opinion in accordance with the principles of the United Nations and affording adequate security and protection under the law to those supporting the cause of the United Nations and the various peace treaties. The satellite countries were also to be obliged to recognize the United Nations and its subsidiary organizations and its authority in replacing the League of Nations and the Permanent International Court of Justice. On the question of the maintenance, modification, or repeal of international agreements in force at the time of the signing of the treaties, each country would be required to follow Allied instructions.[5]

On the morning of 20 September, the foreign ministers moved on to a detailed discussion of the peace treaties to be agreed upon with the Balkan countries and Finland. The problem of the Finnish treaty, considered the most straightforward of the group, was dealt with first. Byrnes and Georges Bidault, his French colleague, restating the fact that neither of their countries was officially at war with Finland, made it clear that they would leave the bulk of the discussion to the Soviet Union and Great Britain as long as any decisions taken at the conference concerning Finland were not used as precedents in dealing with the other satellite countries. Events were to show that the insertion of this proviso by the Americans and French was well judged.

Molotov began the discussion on Finland by asking for Britain's reasons for wishing to limit Finland's peacetime military forces. Bevin replied that London thought it reasonable and right that the size of the military forces of *all* the satellite countries should be limited. The Council of Foreign Ministers had already agreed in principle to the matter in their discussions on Italy. Molotov did not accept this argument, explaining that in the Soviet view it was necessary to distinguish between the large Axis countries, like Germany and Italy, and the small countries, like Finland. It was impossible to imagine Finland ever being in a position to threaten peace in Europe. The Soviet Union, which was most likely to be affected in the case of any potential aggression, had not demanded restrictions on Finland's military capability in the peace treaty of 1940 and would not demand them now, Molotov declared. Finland could never begin a war of aggression without the assistance of a powerful ally like Germany; it would make more sense for the Allies, Molotov argued, to concentrate their efforts on preventing Germany from becoming capable of any further aggression than on presenting Finland unnecessary demands only likely to injure its national pride.

Bevin strongly disagreed. Simply to declare that a small country like Finland posed no threat to European peace was insufficient. The question of peace and security in Europe had to be seen in a larger perspective. Bevin remained adamant in his insistence on the necessity of including a clause restricting the size of military forces in the peace treaties to be signed with all the satellite states. The British delegation made Soviet acceptance of this point the condition for Britain's agreeing to the remainder of the contents of any final Finnish peace treaty.

Despite this unresolved disagreement, the preliminary discussion regarding Finland was allowed to continue. Molotov again inquired why the British proposed a clause allowing the Allies the right to determine the number and location of their consuls in Finland. No such demand had been made in the case of Italy! Bevin replied that the British intention was simply to ensure that no barriers were placed in the way of the appointment of consuls from the Allied countries to postings in Finland.

Molotov went on to say that Britain's proposal covering the United Nations and other international organizations effectively paralleled the Soviet Union's own suggestion for obliging Finland to cooperate with the Allies in actions initiated and approved by them that were aimed at maintaining world peace. The question of which of Finland's international agreements would remain in force and which would be nullified subsequent to the treaty, however, would require further deliberation—as would that of the freedom of Finnish citizens, although Molotov agreed in principle to the possibility of appending an article similar to the Italian one. Much work would be needed on the detailed drafting of these articles. Bevin and Molotov displayed a large measure of agreement on these points, in sharp contrast to their widely opposed positions on the military question.

Proceeding to the agenda of the conference, Molotov stated that the examination of the Finnish case had rested almost entirely with the British and Soviet delegations, with little participation from the others present. It would therefore be appropriate if a committee made up of British and Soviet delegates were empowered to draw up detailed provisions for consideration by the Council of Foreign Ministers, rather than having them discussed by the deputy foreign ministers. Bevin, realizing the potential of Molotov's proposal in setting a precedent for handling the peace treaties of the other satellite countries, refused to agree. He proposed instead that all preparatory work on the treaty, including reference to the British proviso on the restrictions of military forces, be given to the deputy foreign ministers. If Molotov agreed to this, Bevin said he would be willing to drop his earlier demand on the number and location of Allied consulates. Molotov, however, remained convinced of the practical value of the Soviet proposal. If it was unacceptable to the British, they would have to return to the matter later, he declared.

The British foreign secretary responded in like measure. The Soviet Union had proposed that the Allies support Finland's admittance to the United Nations, Bevin went on, but if this meant that the Allies had to agree to being bound in advance to support the Finns, Britain would have to dissent. Although he had "the highest regard for the Finnish people and his Government were determined to do all in their power to assist Finnish recovery," and he had no wish to oppose in principle the policy of supporting Finland's admittance to the United Nations, he and the British delegation nevertheless had to insist that they could not agree to any proposal that unconditionally bound the British government in advance. Molotov replied that the Soviet delegation would then have to resort to the same proviso with regard to the Italian problem.[6] The discussion, throughout which Finland's example had implicitly been treated as setting a precedent for consideration of both the Italian and Balkan questions, ground to a halt. The foreign ministers decided, this time unanimously, to break for lunch.

After the disagreements on the procedure for drawing up the Finnish peace treaty were again aired at the beginning of the afternoon session, discussion moved to the Rumanian and Bulgarian peace treaties. Hungary, where communist influence seemed slight for the moment, was treated separately. After the Budapest government had assured the Americans that they would hold free parliamentary elections in the near future, the United States announced on 22 September that it would be willing to restore diplomatic relations with Hungary. Behind this move lay, at least in part, Byrnes's desire—fearing the collapse of the London conference—to assure the Soviet Union of America's overall good intentions. No reason was seen, however, for concessions in the cases of Rumania and Bulgaria. The American delegation appended a statement to the outline treaty proposals it presented to the foreign ministers on 19 September:

> This suggested directive is submitted by the United States Delegation with the understanding that the United States will not negotiate a treaty of peace with Rumania (and Bulgaria) until there has been established a government broadly representative of all democratic elements in the population and pledged to the earliest possible establishment through free elections of a government responsive to the will of the people, which can be recognized by the United States.[7]

Molotov's reaction was unsurprising. Meeting Byrnes privately on 20 September (after lunch and the discussion on Finland), the Soviet foreign minister said that it seemed to be increasingly clear that the United States was using every means at its disposal to oppose the Soviet Union. The American delegation's statements concerning the Balkan countries could be considered little more than insults directed against the Soviet Union, to which he would be forced to respond. Why, Molotov wanted to know, had this been put on paper? Could Byrnes not withdraw the written proposals and satisfy himself with an oral statement that American participation in the drafting of the peace treaties was not to be interpreted as signaling American recognition of Rumania and Bulgaria? Byrnes, however, had gone too far to allow such a public retreat. Molotov was told that withdrawal of the American proposals was impossible. Then, Molotov replied, he would have to "reply to the attack on the Soviet Government." Byrnes, in keeping with his Southern temperament, retorted, "Of course you can answer it and when you do, I will answer you. Do you understand that?'' With that, the secretary of state snatched up his hat and walked out.[8]

Molotov now had no option but to go on the offensive the next day. The Soviet Union was ready to cooperate with the United States over the Italian peace treaty, he argued, but the United States seemed apparently unwilling to cooperate with the Soviet Union over the treaties for the Balkan countries and Finland. Security considerations made it impossible for the Soviet Union to accept hostile governments in the countries along its western border. Moscow was quite willing to allow the West complete freedom of action in Italy. But why, Molotov asked, did Washington, in its defense of democracy, refuse to recognize Bulgaria and Rumania and yet continue to maintain diplomatic relations with fascist dictatorships like Spain and Argentina? In fact, Molotov added, what did democracy have to do with the whole problem? How democratic was the Greek monarchist government, supported as it was by British bayonets? Byrnes answered Molotov's last charge by declaring that the American government had agreed to ensure that democratic elections would be held in Greece, to be followed by the setting up of a broadly based representative government. Foreign journalists were allowed to travel freely in Greece and report on conditions in the country, which was not the case, Byrnes observed, in Rumania (for example). Molotov suggested that one was forced to draw the conclusion that whereas the people were dissatisfied and the journalists happy in Greece, it was the journalists who were dissatisfied and the people content in Rumania. Which, he asked, was preferable?

Byrnes's response took the form of an extended account of American political ideals and democratic principles. If these were ignored in the drafting of the treaties, he concluded, the latter had little or no possibility of being approved by Congress in Washington. The discussion rapidly degenerated into a war of words, with accusations and counteraccusations filling the air. As a political realist, Molotov found it difficult to understand the Americans' persistent resort to abstract principles instead of practical national interests. The Russians were forced to wonder whether the American tactic was in fact serving to mask an as yet unrevealed political strategy. They remembered Roosevelt's constant references to American public opinion, but also his clear perception of Soviet security concerns in Eastern Europe. The motives behind the new administration's actions, however, must have seemed far from clear. Could the new American aim be to create an extensive anti-Soviet bloc to force the Soviet Union into making certain concessions? It must have been disconcerting for the Kremlin to witness the apparently unanimous behavior of the American, British, French, and Chinese representatives in London, behavior that had been conspicuously absent from the wartime conferences. It is another matter, however, as to why Moscow should have found it difficult to understand that the cause for this unanimity was largely suspicion of Soviet intentions. It would not seem too wide of the mark to assume that Molotov's delegation attached great importance to pinning down the Americans' "true" intentions. "I do not understand your Secretary of State," a member of the Soviet delegation was to say to Byrnes's assistant Charles Bohlen. "We have been told that he is a practical man, but he acts like a professor. When is he going to start trading?"

With the London conference stalled, or at best continuing as a display of shadow boxing, the Kremlin decided to tighten the screw. Molotov demanded on 22 September that an Allied control commission be set up in Japan to direct the actions of Gen. Douglas MacArthur and the American occupation forces. The Soviet Union, Great Britain, and China would be represented on such a commission, alongside the United States. Molotov also pointed out that there had been a procedural mistake in London because it had been agreed at Potsdam that France should only have the right to take part in the drafting of the Italian peace treaty and that China should be excluded altogether. The response of Bevin and Byrnes to the Soviet view was that it was "legally correct, but morally wrong." They believed that France and China should be allowed to take part in the discussions, but not to have the right to *vote* on any of the conference proposals. The public humiliation and exclusion of France and China (with the exception of French participation on the Italian question) would have meant, as everyone was keenly aware, a serious loss of authority and prestige for the Western powers. Tension in the conference room rose to a threatening pitch. Bevin's description of Molotov's position as the "nearest thing to the Hitler theory I have ever heard" provoked the Soviet foreign minister to rise and head decisively for the door; only Bevin's immediate public apology persuaded him to return.

The West was forced to take definite action. President Truman, at Byrnes's insistence, appealed directly to Stalin to act before the conference foundered. As the Soviet proposals in London must have been made with Stalin's knowledge and approval, his response was unsurprising. Stalin observed that Molotov's comments had been completely in accordance with the decisions taken at Potsdam and that this could not offend anyone. It should be remembered, however, that the question of French and Chinese participation was felt both in the East and the West to be only one sign of the deep disagreements existing between the Great Powers. Mutual suspicion of the other side's intentions, in fact, was growing apace.

In an attempt to defuse the situation, Byrnes suggested to Molotov the possibility of a four-power agreement guaranteeing the demilitarization of Germany for 25 years. Molotov thought the idea "interesting," but he did not return to it. The conference remained in the balance. This impasse was marked by the important role now assumed by Sen. John Foster Dulles, the Republican party's leading foreign policy specialist, whom Byrnes had personally invited to join the American delegation—partly as an attempt to secure advance support in

Congress for conference decisions. By 30 September, Byrnes was forced to concede in an internal discussion among the members of the American delegation that the war of words was becoming increasingly futile. They had to begin to look for a way to compromise. This clearly worried Dulles, who followed Byrnes up to his hotel room after the meeting to convince the secretary of state of the danger of any form of compromise. Mrs. Dulles was later to recall hearing her husband say that he had followed Byrnes as far as his bathroom. The secretary of state had to understand, Dulles argued, that a compromise at this stage would mean the first step on the dangerous road to appeasement. Had they not already had enough bitter experience of appeasing Hitler in the 1930s? Stalin had to be stopped in time. The need for the type of expedient compromises met with in the war years was rapidly receding. Peace was indivisible. ''Principle and morality must be reestablished in the world,'' Dulles declared. If Byrnes weakened in the face of the Russians he could be sure that he, Dulles, would organize an extensive campaign in Congress and the press against the secretary of state's appeasement policy. This bathroom discussion decided Byrnes: domestic consensus proved more important than consensus between the Great Powers. The London conference ended on 2 October with little achieved, not even a common final communiqué.[9]

All the Great Powers probably saw the conference's failure as something of a disappointment. The whole of Europe, every country that had suffered the ravages of the war, had expected and hoped for an outcome effectively underwriting the continent's future peace and security. The open conflict that was revealed between the Great Powers in London was a shock for the American public, which had trusted to the good faith of the anti-Hitler alliance and the hopeful words of the Atlantic Charter. Similar conferences and congresses in the past had ended in grand declarations of international accord and shared hopes for the future. The apparent total collapse of the London conference was especially difficult for the Truman administration, as the Americans had been instrumental in setting up the Council of Foreign Ministers at Potsdam. Similarly, the failure of Byrnes's publicly assumed role of peacemaker only weakened the secretary of state's position in the administration and the country. America's possession of the atom bomb had failed to have a significant effect on the Soviet position and had failed to help the West achieve the concessions it had hoped for in Eastern Europe.

The result was also unsatisfactory from the British point of view. The power of the Soviet Union seemed to be growing, and Molotov's interest in the Mediterranean area particularly worried the Foreign Office. Britain was also forced to admit, against its will, that British power in the postwar world was much reduced. Britain's ability to maintain its traditional presence around the world was declining rapidly. Alongside the emerging superpowers, Britain was increasingly assuming the status of a second-rank power. Even during the course of the London confer-

ence, the British delegation had been forced time after time to follow the exchanges between the United States and the Soviet Union from the sidelines, with
the Americans infrequently discussing common points of interest in advance.

The impression most likely gained by the Soviet Union during and after the
conference was one of increasing Soviet isolation. The West had managed to
present a surprisingly united front to the world in London. The obvious inconsis-
tencies in Western attitudes, however, must have aroused doubts and suspicion
on the Soviet side. What had happened to the agreement on spheres of influence
concluded in October 1944 between Churchill and Stalin, which the Soviet Union
had carefully observed in the case of Greece? President Truman promoted an
open-door policy on Rumania and Bulgaria, yet kept hold—following the tenets
of the Monroe doctrine—on the United States' own sphere of influence in the
Western hemisphere. Using the plea of national security, Washington demanded
certain islands in the Pacific and was doing everything in its power to keep the
other Allies out of the administration of the occupation of Japan. Against this
background, as Yergin has shown, Byrnes's and Bevin's strongly worded statements on Rumania and Bulgaria could hardly have been seen in Moscow as
anything but ominous attempts to rob the Soviet Union of its national security
and, by extension, of its status as a Great Power. What other options guaranteeing national security were open to the Soviet Union? The United Nations was
still in its early days and gave the appearance of being largely an American-
directed organization. The Kremlin's trust certainly did not stretch to relying on
the Americans for the security guarantees they needed. The Soviet solution was
to create an independent security policy based on a geographically dictated,
strategic protection zone. To American eyes, however, from the vantage point
of the Wilson inheritance, this policy appeared to indicate a dangerously expan-
sionist-minded state. Deadlock between the Great Powers seemed inevitable.[10]

How was the situation to be defused? Opinions in the United States were
divided. Many saw no possibility for an agreement between the United States
and the Soviet Union. Soviet policy seemed unrestrictedly expansionist, and
Western concessions were only likely to increase Stalin's appetite for more. The
United States and the Western European countries should instead, the argument
went, pool their military and economic resources in an attempt to maintain a
global balance of power to counter Soviet ambitions. Proponents of this argument
saw the "tough" line adopted by Byrnes in London as a step in the right direction.
But there was also belief in leading circles in Washington that the United States
and the Soviet Union shared a common interest in maintaining security across
the world and preventing the outbreak of future wars. Serious disagreements had
grown up between the two countries, it was true, but they could be overcome
if both sides showed themselves able and willing to negotiate and compromise.
Although not condoning Soviet actions in Eastern Europe, the proponents of this
argument questioned whether it was realistic to expect Stalin to loosen his control

there as long as the United States opposed Soviet participation in the occupation of Japan and the administration of Italy's ex-colonies. The wavering and uncertainty evident in American foreign policy during the autumn of 1945 was largely rooted in the unwillingness of Truman's administration to decide on the form of its long-term policy aims.

Byrnes, capitalizing on his public image as a peacemaker and with Truman's approval, decided to try to break the deadlock by sounding out the possibilities for a compromise. In a letter addressed to Stalin, delivered personally by Averell Harriman on 24 October, Byrnes emphasized the importance of continuing the discussions that had broken down in London. The United States was willing, according to Byrnes, to accede to ''limiting the drafting procedure of the peace treaties''; for its part, the Soviet Union would accede to the large-scale peace conference discussed at Potsdam, which would be charged with scrutinizing the draft treaties drawn up by the Council of Foreign Ministers. Stalin, after reading the letter, immediately observed to Harriman that no mention had been made of the Japanese occupation administration. Harriman replied that Washington was considering the possibility of setting up a mixed control commission in Tokyo, made up of military representatives from the United States, the Soviet Union, Britain, and China. In the case of procedural disagreements, however, the final decision in any such commission would lie with the American representative, General MacArthur. With the prospect of a compromise opening up on Japan, Stalin felt able to be more flexible on the problem of the peace treaties for Germany's European allies—particularly when Harriman confirmed that the preparatory discussions among the deputy foreign ministers in London would take place on a 4-3-2 basis. (In other words, the Soviet Union, United States, Britain, and France would prepare the Italian draft treaty; the United States, Soviet Union, and Britain those for the Balkan countries; and the Soviet Union and Britain that for Finland.) Stalin finally declared that the Soviet Union would be amenable to the American suggestion for a peace conference to be held under the aegis of the United Nations. It was now a question, in the Soviet view, of which countries should be invited to participate. What had Brazil, for example, to do with a Finnish peace treaty? What had Costa Rica to offer in drafting a treaty for Rumania? Harriman emphasized that European participation in the war should be seen as a whole. All the satellite countries had in some way assisted Hitler, and it was only right that all the Allied countries should have the right to be heard during the negotiations for a final peace. The Americans argued that all the European member states of the United Nations, together with those countries outside Europe that had taken a significant military part in the struggle against the Axis powers, should be invited to the conference, in addition to the five Great Power nations who were permanent members of the UN Security Council. The non-European countries would include Canada, Australia, South Africa, New Zealand, India, and Brazil — the last being the only Latin American country, which had sent two divisions to fight in the Italian campaign. Countries like Costa Rica, which had contented themselves with mere declarations of war, would not be invited.

Stalin could thus be certain that there would be no large contingent of Latin American countries at the conference attending in the train of the United States. He still saw no reason, however, for China's participation in the preparation of the European peace treaties, nor for that of small European countries like Holland and Norway, which had a legitimate interest in the form of the German peace treaty but none in the proposed Italian, Balkan, and Finnish treaties. Norway (as Molotov later pointed out to Byrnes) had never even declared war against Finland. Stalin also argued that India, lacking the status of a dominion, could not be counted as an independent state and should be treated as a British colony; Indian forces that had taken part in the struggle against Italy should properly be treated as British forces.

In his response, Harriman again pointed out the all-embracing nature of the war. It had been agreed at Potsdam that all peace treaties should be submitted for UN approval. Restricting the decision making solely to the Big Three would inevitably provoke dissatisfaction throughout the world; in any case, Harriman went on, the decisions and recommendations arrived at by a broadly based conference—in its role as a diplomatic ''safety valve''—did not necessarily have to tie the hands of the Big Three. Even though Holland and Norway had been occupied by German forces, their navies had fought on the Allied side and had taken part in action against Italy. Stalin refused to yield. If the Americans insisted on including these and similar countries in the discussions, Stalin argued, he would demand separate participation rights at the peace conference for the Soviet Union's sixteen republics, which had similarly fought and suffered. Stalin also rejected Harriman's argument about China's right to attend based on its status as a permanent member of the UN Security Council. The United Nations was a thing of the future but the peace treaties had to be drawn up now, Stalin declared. Harriman, seeing no point in continuing their wrangling, broke off the discussion.[11]

Back in Washington, Byrnes again tried to break the impasse by returning to the principle agreed upon between the Big Three at Yalta in February that their foreign ministers should meet at regular intervals to discuss issues of common interest. Byrnes instructed Harriman on 23 November to propose to Molotov that a meeting be held in Moscow some time in December.[12] By appealing to the Yalta decision, which was made *before* the setting up of the Council of Foreign Ministers, the Big Three could legitimately exclude France and China, whose participation had proved a stumbling block in the earlier discussions. Molotov thought Byrnes's idea a good one and gave it his full support. Following what was now becoming almost standard practice, the U.S. State Department did not inform its British colleagues until after the proposal had been put to

Moscow. Bevin, smarting from the Americans' "short-sightedness" and fearing concessions at Britain's expense, disliked the idea. There would not be enough time to prepare the necessary proposals, and French and Chinese suspicions would only be aggravated. Bevin's opposition, however, did not dissuade Byrnes. If the British preferred to stay away, Byrnes declared, he would have to go to Moscow without them. Angry but powerless, the British were forced to give way.

When Byrnes, Molotov, and Bevin finally met in Moscow on 16 December, their discussions at first got nowhere. Byrnes's two meetings on 19 and 23 December with Stalin on his return from the Black Sea coast were to prove decisive. Stalin, refreshed and relaxed, replied to Byrnes's polite inquiry about his holiday by saying that he had spent the time in Sochi reading Byrnes's speeches. The secretary of state's congratulations to the marshal on his good taste were met by the reply, "That was must reading for me." But Byrnes's attempt to pressure Stalin on the Balkan question failed. He began by saying that he had sent his good friend Mark Ethridge, a respected journalist known for his impartiality, to Rumania and Bulgaria to report on conditions in those countries. Ethridge's report, written on his return and made available to the Soviet government, made depressing reading on the questions of political democracy and freedom of opinion, Byrnes went on. Although he (Byrnes) did not doubt the truthfulness of Ethridge's information, he had decided against publishing the report for the time being for the cause of Allied unity. If the Moscow conference were to break up in failure, however, Byrnes threatened that publication would go ahead. Stalin replied that if that happened he would have to ask his friend, another journalist and one again known for his impartiality—Ilya Ehrenburg—to publish his views on the matter. Seeing that this would only lead to greater alienation between the United States and the Soviet Union, Byrnes withdrew his threat and did not return to Ethridge's report.

The American delegation confirmed what had been stated by Harriman earlier: they were ready to modify their previous position on Japan by allowing Soviet representatives to participate in the running of the control commission directed by General MacArthur. The final say on decisions, however, would remain America's prerogative, and there would be no question of dispatching Soviet forces to Japan. On the proposed peace conference, Byrnes emphasized that it was only envisaged as a forum to allow those member countries of the United Nations that had taken part in the war to voice their opinions on the draft treaties. The conference would not be empowered materially to influence the various proposed treaty conditions. Decision making would remain with the Great Powers, who would formulate the final versions of the treaties. Certain now of the harmlessness of the conference, Stalin yielded to the idea and accepted almost in its entirety the list of countries that the Western countries had drawn up. It was also agreed that the deputy foreign ministers would begin the preparation of draft treaties for Italy, Rumania, Bulgaria, Hungary, and Finland in London—

on the previously agreed 4-3-2 basis—without delay. This arrangement would include all the Great Powers that, with the exception of France, had originally signed the armistice agreements with those countries. After the draft treaties had been completed, the Council of Foreign Ministers would convene a peace conference by 1 May 1946 (at the latest) to be attended by the five Great Powers and all those member countries of the United Nations that had actively taken part in the campaign in Europe against the Axis states: the Soviet Union, Britain, the United States, China, France, Australia, Belgium, Brazil, Byelorussia, Canada, Czechoslovakia, Ethiopia, Greece, Holland, India, New Zealand, Norway, Poland, South Africa, the Ukraine, and Yugoslavia.

It was further agreed that, at the end of the peace conference, the Council of Foreign Ministers—following the division of responsibility previously agreed upon and after taking the conference's proposals into consideration — would prepare the final texts of the treaties. These treaties would be signed by the states that had attended the conference and been at war with the countries in question. Those other UN member countries that had declared war but had not actively participated in any campaigns (such as the smaller states of Central and South America) would be provided with the completed final treaty texts. The various treaties would come into force when ratified by the Great Powers (the signatory countries of the respective armistice agreements); the defeated countries in question would also have to ratify the treaties. The minor problem (from the Allied point of view) of perhaps allowing the former satellites the right to put their case at the conference was passed over. No available sources point to its even having been discussed in Moscow. The conflicting views among the Allies regarding the drafting of the treaties, which had caused the breakdown of the talks in London, had now been resolved to the satisfaction of all the Great Powers involved.

The foreign ministers also decided unanimously in Moscow to recommend the withdrawal of all foreign forces from Chinese territory, and they agreed that a single, independent, democratic state should be established in Korea that united the northern zone occupied by the Soviet Union and the southern zone occupied by the Americans. The question of withdrawing Allied forces from Iran was left open. In addition, an international atomic energy commission, to which the Soviet Union would also belong, was to be set up under the aegis of the United Nations to study the problems and potential of nuclear energy.

The question of the diplomatic recognition of Rumania and Bulgaria, one of the controversial issues that had surfaced in London, remained unresolved. Byrnes tackled Stalin on this question on 23 December. He suggested that Stalin formulate a plan for the participation of representatives from the leading political parties in Rumania and Bulgaria in the governments of those countries, which would in turn allow the United States to recognize them. Surely there were people in these parties who were well disposed to friendly relations with the Soviet Union.

While emphasizing that the Soviet Union presupposed that its neighbors would loyally respect its interests, Stalin admitted that there might be some noncommunists of the type described by Byrnes. Although he had been accused of interference in the internal affairs of other countries, Stalin went on sarcastically, "perhaps the Bulgarian parliament could be advised to include some members of the loyal opposition in the new Government." In the case of Rumania, he added, "it might be possible to make some changes in the Government there which would satisfy Mr. Byrnes and Mr. Bevin."—for example, to influence the Rumanians to introduce one representative from the peasant party and one liberal politician into the government, although the leaders of these parties (Juliu Maniu, Nicolae Lupu and Dinu Bratianu) would be unacceptable.[13]

Agreement was thus also reached on the Balkan question. Washington agreed to recognize the Bucharest and Sofia governments as and when the changes were implemented. Although the American negotiators had few illusions about the real import of what they had achieved, they had nevertheless found a way for the West, as in the Polish case, to save face. George F. Kennan, then attached to the American embassy in Moscow, described in his diary the agreements on the Balkan countries as "fig leaves of democratic procedure to hide the nakedness of Stalinist dictatorship." Byrnes's weakness (in Kennan's eyes) in his negotiations with the Russians was that he wanted "to achieve some sort of agreement, he doesn't much care what. The realities behind this agreement, since they concern only such peoples as Koreans, Rumanians and Iranians, about whom he knows nothing, do not concern him. He wants an agreement, for its political effect at home. The Russians know this. They will see that for this superficial success he pays a heavy price in the things that are real."

Kennan's sharp criticism came from someone who had been skeptical toward Roosevelt's policies and who was aware of the disappointment that would follow among those in the Balkan countries who had pinned their hopes on the West. However, as Yergin has pointed out, this criticism did not go to the heart of the matter. The Moscow conference had achieved its compromise conclusion, against all the odds, by confirming the fact of American dominance in Japan and Soviet dominance in the Balkans. Despite their apparent concessions, neither superpower had in fact reduced its dominant role either in Japan or the Balkans. Any change in this status quo would have required the use of military force, which neither side wanted. The drafting of the peace treaties for Italy, Rumania, Bulgaria, Hungary, and Finland could now be resumed. The virtue of compromise solutions in satisfying the national interests of the Great Powers, despite their increasingly cool relations, had been highlighted. Byrnes, careful of his adopted role as peacemaker, had acted throughout with a close eye to possible domestic reaction. The future was to show, however, that the decisions taken in Moscow were to become more of a liability than a benefit for him on the domestic political scene.[14]

11   A Delayed Peace

Throughout the world, the London conference of Allied foreign ministers in the autumn of 1945 aroused expectations of the rapid emergence of final peace treaties. The progress of the conference was, understandably, closely followed in Finland—both among the country's political leadership and throughout society as a whole. It was hoped that the government might be able to alleviate the severity of the armistice terms insofar as they would be incorporated into the final treaty. A delegation of Karelian members of parliament, led by Juho Niukkanen, called on Prime Minister Paasikivi as early as 30 August to underline the importance of bringing up with the Allies the question of the ceded territories. Paasikivi's reply was typically hardheaded:

> Finland's position may become worse. I don't have to remind you that back in the autumn of 1939 the Karelian cry was "Not an inch." "Harken to the sacred vow" was sung at the stations as I passed through on the way to the negotiations in Moscow. None of this helped. As I said, if there is the same sort of clamor again, Finland's position may be weakened. It is not the small nations which decide things now, but the large ones which draw the borders they want on the map; the victors decide." [1]

The Karelians, however, did not meekly accept Paasikivi's dressing down. Erkki Paavolainen, Wilhelm Wahlforss, Jussi Raatikainen, Väinö Huuhtanen, and Johannes Virolainen delivered a note on behalf of the Karelian evacuee population to Pavel Orlov on 21 September in which they requested the return to Finland of the territory ceded in Karelia. The note proposed granting the Soviet Union military bases in the areas in question complete with rights of transit if required. Finland would agree not to use any territory returned by the Soviet Union for military purposes and would station at most only the number of police necessary for the

159

maintenance of public order. A copy of the note was sent immediately after its delivery to Enckell at the Foreign Ministry.[2] Eero Wuori, who had been appointed as the Finnish representative in London after the resumption of diplomatic relations, was instructed by Helsinki the same day to establish "the procedure to be adopted over the Finnish peace treaty and related matters, such as where and when negotiations will take place."[3]

Paasikivi and Enckell took up the latter point for discussion with Zhdanov the day after the delivery of the Karelian note. Zhdanov claimed to know nothing more about the discussions in London than what had appeared in the official communiqués. Paasikivi then went on to outline the hopes of the Karelian community, and Enckell referred to the positive effect that the "return" of the province of Viipuri in 1811 had had in Finland at the time. Zhdanov commented that the Soviet Union would now be forced to conclude that the Karelian proposal was not solely a Karelian one, but was in fact supported by the government as a whole. There was no hope of its being acceded to, however, he explained, because changes in the territorial clauses of the armistice agreement were not envisaged. The Finns would have to blame their losses on their previous leaders and the policies they had followed. The position now apparently adopted by the Finnish government could have dangerous consequences. Paasikivi's cabinet, Zhdanov advised, should use its authority to convince the Karelians of the very real danger that pursuit of their demands held for Soviet-Finnish relations. Zhdanov described the affair as "disagreeable." Paasikivi replied that his government had little else but "disagreeable things" to deal with.

According to Enckell:

> JKP [Paasikivi] inquired as a result of Zhdanov's statement on the futility of any hopes for border changes, whether this was to be understood as the official Soviet view, to which Zhdanov replied (after what seemed a moment's hesitation) in the affirmative. I got the impression, both from my private conversation with him on 16 September and now, that Zhdanov did not have any knowledge of Moscow's plan for the peace and that he had instructions only to monitor fulfillment of the terms of the armistice agreement. As a result of his limited authority he found himself unable to say anything other than that border modifications ran counter to the agreement signed on 19 September 1944.[4]

Although Paasikivi's and Enckell's inquiries were rebuffed, Zhdanov nevertheless failed fully to convince the Finns of the futility of their hopes for border changes.

Enckell also tried to question Shepherd about the handling of the Finnish problem at the London conference. Shepherd, however, had little to say other than that the Soviet Union and Britain had both presented their views on the possible solutions. As soon as the general outline of the agreement had been agreed upon, its detailed drafting could begin, Shepherd explained. Only after the completion of the draft treaty could there be any question of discussions with Helsinki on its content. Shepherd got the impression, as he told London, that the Finns had concluded that their peace treaty would be agreed upon, if not ratified, at the London conference; consequently, they interpreted any delay as foreshadowing some unknown and ominous decision by the Allies.[5]

In addition to his discussions with representatives from the Finnish Foreign Ministry, Shepherd also attempted to dispel any widely held "illusions" on the matter by holding a press conference on 25 September. It was futile, he said, for the Finns to expect that he had returned from London with the complete peace treaty. The conference of foreign ministers was devoted to purely preparatory work. The world's press had exaggerated the level of disagreement among the Allies. "And finally in view of the tendency of the Finns to regard their own interests and necessities as paramount in Europe, it seemed to me advisable to attempt to induce some sort of proportion between the difficulties of Finland and those of other countries even more unfortunately situated."[6]

On his first visit to the Foreign Office on 25 September, Eero Wuori had the opportunity to discuss problems of interest to the Helsinki government with Christopher Warner, the head of the Northern Department. Wuori outlined the hopes of the Karelians from the ceded territories that border changes in Finland's favor would be included in the final peace. The Finnish government, Wuori went on, although uncertain of the possibility of such changes, would appreciate any indication of the likelihood of their being granted. Warner promised a reply if Wuori put his questions in writing. It would be futile, however, to hope for a positive response, Warner added, "unless Mr. Wuori was able to say that a similar approach had been made to the Soviet Government and had been sympathetically entertained. Mr. Wuori said that this was not the case." Warner commented that Finland would probably have to accept that the borders defined in the armistice agreement would remain unchanged.[7]

Warner was also less than forthcoming on providing details of the progress of the London conference. Discussions had been of a general nature and had not reached the stage of actually drafting the respective treaties. There was no reason, however, for the Helsinki government to expect any "surprises." The final drafting of the Finnish treaty could be delayed by the fact that there were many similar problems to be resolved in the case of all five ex-satellite countries. As to whether Helsinki would at some later date be officially consulted on the terms of the treaty, Warner replied that because such a possibility had not yet been discussed, it was impossible to offer Wuori any pointers as to what might happen.[8]

After the breakup of the conference in London, Soviet Ambassador Gusev told Wuori that Finland's future peace treaty—including the final border arrangements—would be based, in accordance with the Soviet proposal, on the terms of the armistice agreement. Gusev also mentioned Bevin's demand for the Allies to be able to appoint consuls independently of Helsinki, explaining that the Soviet Union had rejected this as unreasonable and unfair to Finland.[9]

Sundström in Moscow also tried to monitor progress on the peace treaty. In answer to his inquiry (on 15 September) about the likelihood of Finland's being invited to London, Vyshinsky, the Soviet deputy foreign minister, replied that it was a Soviet principle that treaty decisions should not be made without listening to the views of the country in question. Finland's position, he said, was comparable to that of Italy. Vyshinsky, however, said that he was unable to provide any final answers to Finnish questions while the discussions in London were still in progress. Dekanosov, the Soviet second deputy foreign minister, also informed Sundström that the Soviet Union had been ready to sign a final peace settlement at the time of the armistice negotiations in the autumn of 1944 but that the other Allies had resisted the move.[10]

On his return to Moscow from the London conference, Molotov told Sundström that the Finnish question had not been the cause of any significant disagreements between the Allies. "When pressed, he said there was no hope of any border adjustments. We discussed Finland's relations with Scandinavia. . . . Molotov said they had had unpleasant experiences of Scandinavian cooperation, did not approve of it and thought it unnecessary when Finland, sponsored by the Soviet Union, was to be accepted as a member of the UN." The Soviet Union's strongly negative attitude towards changes in the borders as defined under the armistice agreement was also made plain to Sakari Tuomioja, the director of the Bank of Finland, when he referred to the problems of Porkkala and the Saimaa canal during a visit to Moscow in October 1945.[11]

The picture that the government in Helsinki was able to construct of the London conference and what it had achieved remained necessarily superficial. It was possible to assume from Wuori's and Sundström's various communications[12] and from comments in the international press that disagreements over the procedural decisions taken at Potsdam had significantly held up the progress of the Council of Foreign Ministers. Detailed official information on these disagreements or on the precise content of the discussions that had taken place was unavailable. It seemed clear, however, that the Finnish question was a matter of interest primarily for the Soviet Union and Britain. The Foreign Ministry in Helsinki was nevertheless aware that decisions about Finland, a relatively small problem in itself, might be used later as precedents for those to be made about Italy and the Balkan countries. It was also unclear whether any of the countries in question would be allowed to present their own cases to the Allies. The possibility of a final peace within the foreseeable future seemed, to those in Helsinki, to be slipping away; but, as Eero Wuori emphasized in one of his reports, "Finland cannot gain anything by appearing impatient. . . . Seen from London it would seem best to concentrate on developing Finland's foreign relations in the hope that the Great Powers will come to an acceptable modus vivendi between themselves, which alone will open up the possibility of Finland being able effectively to pursue her affairs in the world."[13] In the circumstances, and after the Soviet Union had clearly expressed its opposition to any border adjustments, the Foreign Ministry in Helsinki decided to refrain from sending any list of possible border modifications, as suggested by Warner. Wuori was instead instructed to return to Helsinki to brief the ministry on the situation.[14]

Nevertheless, the eventual fate of the London conference was a disappointment to the Finns who had expected a rapid drafting of their treaty. President Mannerheim expressed his surprise in a discussion with Shepherd on 5 October that Britain was still, more than a year after the signing of the armistice agreement, unable to reestablish diplomatic relations. The placing of Italy before Finland in the order of countries most in need of a final peace treaty displeased the president. Shepherd commented later:

> I think that in the case of Marshal Mannerheim, this proceeds partly from amour propre, but I think also that he is most anxious to procure a peace treaty for his country as quickly as possible, as a successful culmination of his tenure as president during a very difficult period. The thought crossed my mind that the Marshal might only be waiting the signature of peace to retire from what must be in many ways a distasteful position. The state of his health has enabled him on two occasions to avoid performing official duties from which he was averse, but this is not a procedure that can be repeated too frequently.

Discussing the failure of the London conference, Mannerheim predicted that the Western powers would experience many more "surprises" from the Soviet Union—particularly in the Balkans—that would not, he said, be "pleasant." "I asked the Marshal whether, if he were, in fact, a Marshal of Russia, he would not desire to take such security measures as might ensure his country against such devastation as this war had caused, and he replied that he certainly would." Mannerheim, however, did not believe that Soviet policies were directed solely by security considerations.

> The Marshal is clearly just as mistrustful of the USSR as he was a year ago. He did not give any hint that he feared Russian action with regard to Finland but it was evident that he regards Russian designs in the Balkans as expansionist and perhaps ultimately imperialist. . . . The President looked a good deal thinner and older than when I saw him last year, but his mind, though evidently rather inelastic, is still clear and precise.[15]

Mannerheim's views, communicated by Shepherd to the Foreign Office in London, received as cool a reception as they had the previous autumn. "I don't think," commented G. Warr, "that we can regard Field Marshal Mannerheim as an impartial observer, and he is also now increasingly out of touch with affairs, even Finnish affairs. But I think that there is no doubt that the result of the Council of Foreign Ministers has increased Finnish nervousness of Russian intentions." [16]

Eero Wuori also exhibited a certain frustration with the situation in London in autumn 1945. Meeting Shepherd during his visit to Helsinki in October, he complained that he had not found enough to do in London.

> He did not seem greatly to enjoy his diplomatic functions and admitted that he would rather return to Finland and politics. Svento mentioned to me that he had told Vuori that he was an infant in diplomacy and that he would in due course find plenty to do, which suggests that the Government are not at present thinking of recalling him. I gathered that Vuori was a little hurt that he had not been received by the Secretary of State [Bevin], especially as the latter was a fellow Trade Unionist. [17]

Wuori's comments nearly twenty years later show that some members of Paasikivi's government had believed that Wuori would be able to make political use of his acquaintance with Bevin, which dated from the prewar years. [18]

The Finns achieved better results in Moscow. Although Molotov refused to countenance the possibility of any border adjustments, the Kremlin obviously thought it important, after the collapse of the London talks, to show an element of good will toward Finland. A cultural delegation led by Johan Helo, the Finnish minister of education, was allowed during a visit to Moscow on 8 October to have a wide-ranging discussion with Stalin and Molotov in the former's study. [19] Stalin opened the discussion, held at the Finns' request, by asking whether the visitors had any questions they wished to put to him. Despite this prompting, Helo launched into a long, prepared speech in which he described the recent war years when Finland had fought alongside Germany as a dark period in Finnish history. The Finnish nation was ready, however, to atone for its error and was sincere in its wish to earn a new place among the democratic nations of the world. Unfortunately, the war guilt question remained unresolved, despite the wishes of democratic circles in Finland. The eradication of fascism took time despite all their efforts. But changes had taken place—for example, in the management of the State Radio, which had been so much a source of fascist propaganda. Ironically, Hella Wuolijoki, the new chairman of the board of the State Radio and a member of the delegation, described Helo's speech to Shepherd on her return as "inept." The Foreign Office's opinion was similar. "Mr. Helo was outrageously sycophantic." [20]

Preferring to pass over the first part of Helo's speech, Stalin declared his agreement with Helo's conclusion that the Finnish and Soviet peoples had to live as friends from now on. "Nor do we wish anything else, and this is no empty phrase," the marshal added. Replying to Stalin's inquiry about the employment situation in Finland, Helo said that there was now little unemployment thanks to the war reparations industries. In a capitalist society, however, Helo continued, unemployment could appear at any time. This was not inevitable, according to Stalin. "If there are orders there is work. We shall trade with you and Soviet-Finnish trade may grow two or threefold. It is to the advantage of both peoples." Helo admitted Stalin's point and added that Finland could, if it wished, buy the majority of the products it needed to import from the Soviet Union, which had huge resources at its disposal. Stalin emphasized, however, that much still needed to be done to improve Soviet economy.

Helo replied to Stalin's question about the state of Finnish public opinion by declaring that long-standing traditions in education and the media meant that it might take decades to see a profound change of mind. Hella Wuolijoki, Eino Kalima, and Mauri Ryömä, however, disagreed, believing that developments could be more rapid. Stalin thought that anti-Russian sentiments were partly based on experiences from the czarist period that would disappear with time as the completely different policies followed by postrevolutionary Russia became better understood.

After listening to Helo's description of Finland's economic difficulties, Stalin asked whether an extension to the time-scale of reparations payments would be of any benefit. Hertta Kuusinen described what followed:

The delegation began rapidly to stir itself. We said that a concession of that sort would unquestionably be welcomed across the nation. Stalin and Molotov exchanged a few words and V. Molotov commented that Finland had conscientiously fulfilled her commitments up until now to the letter. The Soviet Union as a result agreed to extend the period of payment from six to eight years. When it became clear that the decision had really been made and that it was not to be kept secret and that the delegation could take the news back with them to Finland, it was obvious that something unexpected, with significant economic and diplomatic repercussions, had occurred, something which would be received back home with the greatest satisfaction.

Hertta Kuusinen went on to ask whether there was any truth in the notion that the Soviet Union and its leaders treated Finland more favorably that other countries. Stalin replied that Finland did not occupy any special position. The Soviet Union had helped its other neighboring countries, like Hungary, Rumania, and Bulgaria. "Revenge is no foundation for relations between peoples," Stalin added. This seemed particularly indicative in Helo's opinion of the Soviet Union's magnanimous intentions. Stalin's laconic comment was that it was not a question of good intentions alone, but of calculation. "We want good neighbors." The debts run up by the oppressive policies of the czarist regime had to be paid off to the Finns and other peoples, Stalin explained.

The visiting delegation, however, thrust on in typical Finnish fashion with its emotional line of argument. Helo suggested that the Russians felt a particular sympathy towards the Finns dating from the time of their shared struggle against czarism. "Stalin replied that it was true that individual friendships had sprung up. But we do not look positively on Finland because of individual personal relations, nor solely because the Finns are our neighbors. We like the Finnish people. They are a good people. Able and hardworking. God knows where you live. . . . You have built a country out of a marsh." Stalin's comparison of the Finns with the Belgians—to the effect that if the Finns had been in the Belgians' position they would never have surrendered to the fascists—particularly impressed itself on Lauri Viljanen's mind. A neighbor like that, the Finns were told, could be trusted.

The Finnish delegation declared in its turn that the Finns had received a good impression of the Russians. "Don't idealize the Russians," warned Stalin. "They have their faults like all individuals and peoples. But they are tough. They have had to endure a lot." Stalin, however, refused to accept the Finnish argument that the Russians alone had destroyed fascism. "We won the struggle in association with others. But there is no doubt that the Russian people can be justly proud of their fight." [21]

Stalin's comments to the Finns were noted with particular interest at the British legation in Helsinki, and the main points of Hertta Kuusinen's article on the visit in *Vapaa Sana* were sent on in translation to the Foreign Office in London. Shepherd emphasized Stalin's positive and apparently well-meaning stance toward the Finns and toward the future prospects of cooperation between Finland and the Soviet Union. Shepherd also drew London's attention to the Soviet leader's clearly expressed dislike of the signs of sycophancy shown by the Finnish delegation. [22]

Because of the lack of Soviet documentary material, the detailed thinking behind Stalin's position remains unclear. There seems no reason, however, to question the basic force of Stalin's statements. In international terms, it was probably important for Moscow to ensure that the Finnish reparations program should not be undermined through adherence to an overly strict timetable. Any extension could only help the image of the Soviet Union as a reasonable and flexible international partner. Relations between Moscow and Helsinki were characterized by a careful adherence to the terms of the armistice agreement in general and in the handling of the reparations commitments in particular. The War Reparations Committee (SOTEVA) had tried to maintain reparations payments as closely in accordance with the agreed timetable as possible, and any falling behind was generally ascribable to the insuperability of the task facing the Finns. The concessions granted by Stalin were, in his own words, by way of a sign of the Soviet Union's recognition of and trust in the Finnish nation. [23] They also boded well for the future. Stalin in fact, was to pay particular attention over the long term to developing a pattern of good relations based on an awareness of mutual interests between Finland and the Soviet Union after the war.

It was now decided in London that the time had come to improve relations with Helsinki, following the lead given by the Soviet Union. The War Office's instructions (drafted in cooperation with the Foreign Office) to the British section of the Control Commission on 22 October stated that Finland had completed with the majority of the terms of the armistice agreement, with the exception of outstanding long-term commitments like war reparations. Because diplomatic relations had been reinstated, to all intents and purposes, it was now thought appropriate to modify the strict procedural instructions that had been issued to the British officers on the Control Commission the previous October. They would now be allowed to establish closer (although it was not specified how close) contacts with Finns in the service of their work. Their major task, however, remained that of maintaining the closest possible cooperation with their Soviet colleagues; contacts with Finns known for their anti-Soviet or pro-German attitudes were to be avoided as before.[24]

But question of the future peace treaty remained a major worry for the Helsinki government. Wuori had to report from London as late as early December 1945 that little definite had been officially admitted about the fate of the agreement. The possible topics of discussion between Stalin, Byrnes, and Bevin in Moscow could only be speculated upon.[25] The situation was not significantly clarified when Wuori was finally able to meet Bevin on 11 December. Despite the apparent conviviality conveyed by the foreign secretary's usage — to the surprise of his Foreign Office officials — of the term ''brother'' in true trade-unionist manner to address the Finnish envoy, little of consequence was discussed. The international press had, Bevin explained, exaggerated the nature of the disagreements between the Great Powers. The discussions in Moscow would continue those that had taken place in London on the procedure to be adopted in the treaty negotiations. Bevin emphasized that there were no outstanding problems in British-Finnish relations, adding that if Wuori had any problems he could always come to him for assistance.[26]

The Finns similarly managed to find out little in Moscow. In a personal letter to Svento in Helsinki on 21 December, Sundström admitted that he knew nothing about the progress of the conference of foreign ministers then in session.[27] Sundström was later able to add that the ''obvious'' friendship displayed by the three leaders at a ballet performance organized at the Bolshoi on 23 December might point to some positive progress having been achieved. ''Molotov repeatedly complimented Byrnes and Bevin on their comments. During the interval it was said that the discussions were going well and that Soviet diplomacy had achieved a number of victories.''[28]

The Finns were able to conclude from the communiqué issued at the end of the Moscow conference that the drafting of peace treaties would continue under the aegis of the Allied deputy foreign ministers in London. The question of whether the ex-satellite countries would be given a chance to present their own views to the Allies remained unresolved. In response to Wuori's inquiry on the matter, the Foreign Office replied that no information was as yet available. After the British government had decided on its position on the question, any relevant material would be passed on to the Finns, the Foreign Office declared.[29] Helsinki deduced that, in the final analysis, it would be the Great Powers who would finally decide the content of the peace treaties and that the peace conference agreed upon in Moscow would only occupy a subsidiary role. Finland's own potential to influence the shaping of the treaty, which itself appeared to be slipping ever further into the future, seemed now to be minimal.[30]

12 Domestic Tensions

Until the summer of 1945, the Soviet Union seemed content to allow Finnish authorities sole responsibility for removing from public office those who had been prominent in the country's leadership during the war years and bringing them to trial. The Control Commission made no official comment on the parliamentary question put by the Social Democratic "Group of Six" on the issue and took no part in the debate that followed, preferring not to make use of the opportunity to assert its authority and wishes publicly. This attitude was typical of a general policy aimed at avoiding overcommitment of the Soviet Union throughout Europe until the Allies formally agreed on a policy for dealing with the leaders of the defeated countries.

The apparent restraint shown by the Commission, however, did not mean that the Finnish government could conclude that it had done all that was required of it. Speaking to Foreign Minister Enckell in January 1945, Zhdanov—while underlining that the war guilt problem was a domestic matter for the Finns themselves to solve—also emphasized the Soviet view that things would be much improved "if the Finnish government set about taking care of this matter to ensure justice is done"; he expressed his surprise that the government had not already moved to take the country's former leaders and present opposition figures into custody. Enckell's reply, that politicians of opposing views were able to coexist quite equally in Finland, only brought further expressions of surprise from Zhdanov.[1] Indirect pressure of this type was probably brought to bear by the Commission on other members of the Helsinki government. Despite the increasing insistence of the Finnish left that the government act on the war guilt question during the spring of 1945, however, Moscow avoided open involvement in the matter, except for occasional references in the Soviet press to the fact that the problem remained unresolved and to Finland's apparent delay in coming to terms with the issue.[2]

As the unresolved war guilt problem increasingly began to dominate political discussion in Helsinki, members of the Swedish People's Party and the Agrarian Party began to consider the possibility of putting a joint parliamentary question to the government on the issue. Both parties were convinced, in the words of the Swedish People's Party, that "the matter should not be dealt with out in the hubbub of the marketplace but in the country's appropriate representative bodies" and that the People's Democrats had to be prevented from "monopolizing" discussion on the issue. Urho Kekkonen of the Agrarian Party and John Österholm of the Swedish People's Party emerged as the main backers of the move. A question signed by fifty-five M.P.'s was finally put before Parliament on 29 June, asking whether the government was aware that the continuing unsettled situation surrounding affairs leading up to the start of hostilities and the continuing role played by individuals who had been in important positions during the war were undermining Finland's position both internally and externally, and further inquiring what the government—in the light of this—had done or intended to do.

In his reply on 4 August, Paasikivi pointed out that any assessment of the appropriateness or inappropriateness of wartime policies should not be confused with accountability before the law and liability for criminal punishment. The government, however, Paasikivi reiterated, was committed to effecting changes in personnel in government and other positions and hoped that those wartime politicians most under criticism would voluntarily withdraw from prominent public office. Paasikivi carefully directed the main burden of his reply to the latter half of the parliamentary question relating to the necessity for personnel changes in high-ranking positions. A long and occasionally sharply worded debate followed; but it ended with Parliament approving without a vote the government's reply, after which discussion moved, without any suggestion of a vote of no confidence, to the rest of the day's business. But Parliament's seal of approval for government policy could not disguise the fact that the very passion of the debate showed that a simple purge of leading political figures would not suffice as a definitive solution. Although Paasikivi stressed that any trial proceedings would have to take place within the contemporary legal framework, their possible form was left as open as before. The publication of the findings of the Hornborg Committee on 17 July did not materially affect the situation because the evidence collected by the committee proved inadequate, as far as the government was concerned, to serve as a basis for beginning proceedings.[3]

The Soviet Union, even at this stage, seemed reluctant to make its views known in the public debate. It is unlikely that the activities of the Finnish communists had any significant influence on the thinking of the Control Commission. As Kyösti Skyttä has suggested, the communists probably had some inside knowledge of Moscow's views and made use of this in their public statements. "But although the Soviet Union (and the Control Commission) scarcely allowed themselves to be influenced by the Finnish communists, they certainly had nothing against the latter pressuring the Finnish government."[4] By the beginning of August 1945, however, the "domestic" stage of the war guilt problem was drawing to a close.

On 8 August, before the setting up of the International Military Tribunal to oversee the war trials to be held in Nuremberg, the Allies reached agreement in London on what was to be understood by the terms "war crime" and "war criminal." The tribunal's charter distinguished between crimes against peace and war crimes in the more traditional sense. The former category of major war crimes embraced "(i) the planning, preparation, initiation and waging of a war of aggression, (ii) the planning, preparation, initiation and waging of a war disregarding international agreements and guarantees, and (iii) participation in a joint plan or secret alliance to carry out the crimes mentioned above." War crimes were defined as acts involving the breaking of the laws and conventions of war.[5]

Before the final outlining of the London agreement, the Soviet Union had begun to clarify its official position on Finland's progress towards compliance with Article 13 of the armistice agreement. After returning to Helsinki from Moscow, Zhdanov had discussions ranging over a number of topics on 19 July with Urho Kekkonen, the Finnish minister of justice and Johan Helo, the minister of education. At the end of the discussion, Zhdanov asked unofficially what further progress had been made toward settling the war guilt question. Kekkonen replied that he had been collecting material on the matter for the Commission and promised to discuss the details with Zhdanov at a later date. No direct sources relating to these later contacts between the Commission and the Finnish government at the end of July and the beginning of August appear to be extant; Tarkka, however, thinks it likely that the Commission was by this stage demanding the setting up of a special tribunal, whereas the Finns probably persisted with their legally based opposition to any such move.[6] Tarkka's speculations are given added credence by the entry for 8 August in Gripenberg's diary, in which he noted that during his visit to Helsinki, both Paasikivi and Enckell had said that the Russians had recently made *repeated* demands for action against those held responsible for the war. The Finnish side, including Paasikivi, had argued that war by itself, as understood in international law, did not constitute a crime. Crimes against the conventions of war were a separate matter. The Russians had refused to accept this argument, and both Zhdanov and Savonenkov had repeated their demands for proceedings to begin. "Savonenkov specifically said that 'war' is a 'crime.'"[7]

Nevertheless, the Kremlin decided to restore diplomatic relations with Finland at the beginning of August 1945, before having any guarantees that the war guilt question would be settled in a way acceptable to the Soviet Union. Because of the lack of Soviet documentary material, we cannot know the degree to which the achievement of an acceptable solution was considered a foregone conclusion by the Kremlin.

The war guilt problem was first debated by the government on 8 August, the day of the signing of the London agreement. Paasikivi briefed those who were present on his discussion a few hours earlier with General Savonenkov. Although expressing overall satisfaction with Finnish compliance with the armistice agreement, Savonenkov had directly referred to the delay in settling the war guilt affair. The Control Commission, it seemed, was becoming increasingly impatient over the Finns' lack of action, especially since the equivalent problem had already been dealt with in other countries that were in the same situation as Finland. The Commission, according to Paasikivi, hoped that Finland would be able to deal with the matter itself; but if no solution were forthcoming soon, things would have to be taken out of the hands of Finnish authorities. As Savonenkov had pointed out, this move would be likely to be disadvantageous to Finland.

Paasikivi had responded by maintaining that Article 13 of the armistice agreement, as interpreted in Finland, only referred to war criminals. Finnish law, in addition, made any trial of those allegedly responsible for the war difficult because retroactive legislation of the type required was not consistent with Finnish principles of justice. In reply, Savonenkov had stated categorically that a new law would have to be drafted, since the Control Commission could not allow what it saw as this failure to comply with the armistice agreement to continue.[8]

Zhdanov confirmed to Paasikivi on 22 August that Savonenkov had acted on his orders and that what he had said represented the Soviet Union's official position. Zhdanov also warned Paasikivi that the trial, as and when it took place, was under no circumstances to be allowed to degenerate into a comedy or farce. After much hesitation and after reflecting on the possibility of resignation, Paasikivi and his government decided that it would be in Finland's best interests to bow to Soviet pressure and draw up a bill to be put before Parliament enabling the setting up of a special tribunal to deal with the war guilt question. If the bill was not approved, the government decided that it would have no choice but to resign.[9]

The publication of the London agreement significantly reduced any room for Finnish maneuvers to ride out the problem without recourse to a full-scale trial. The actual role the Control Commission had in the drafting of the bill, by virtue of the pressure it was able to bring on the government, remains uncertain because of the lack of precise documentary evidence. Clearly, something took place behind the scenes to make Paasikivi accept a course of action that he had previously rejected, as Tarkka has observed. The very fact that this change of policy took place in secret marks the Finnish case off from those of the other defeated countries of Europe, where parallel events were relatively uncomplicated, speedy, and public. Paasikivi, although aware that he was acting in conflict with the constitution, believed that he had no other choice. It was the implications for Finnish foreign policy, above all, that determined his actions. Yrjö Leino's comment to Paasikivi at the time of the bill's presentation to Parliament to the effect that "If things were suddenly to change here, there wouldn't be any need for a special law to put you and me in prison" was met by Paasikivi's terse reply, "That's right." [10]

The proposed bill was first debated in Parliament on 23 August before being referred to the parliamentary constitutional committee. The committee in turn sought the opinion of the Supreme Court, which declared that Article 13 of the armistice agreement, which referred specifically to war crimes, did not impose an obligation to undertake the steps proposed by the government. Retroactive legislation was also not considered compatible with the constitution. Although this interpretation was accepted in principle by the constitutional committee, it found itself unable to oppose approval of the act because the government knew best those reasons that made this legislation necessary.

Despite these moves and the committee's recommendation, Paasikivi was subjected on 5 September to a sharp dressing down on the matter by Zhdanov. The chairman of the Control Commission emphasized that the Finnish Supreme Court was not in any position to pass binding judgment on an agreement made between the Allied Great Powers, and he expressed his surprise that he, as representative of the Allies in Finland, had not instead been asked for his views on the matter. If a retroactive component was not included in legislation of the type under discussion, Zhdanov argued, it would mean—for instance, in the German case—that neither Göring, Ribbentrop, or any of the other wartime leaders could be brought to trial. Zhdanov accused the Supreme Court of criticizing the principles of justice accepted by the Allies, of defending Ryti, and of endangering relations between Finland and the Soviet Union. "The Supreme Court's position, taken to its logical conclusion, will lead to a situation in which nothing less than a third war . . . is needed to finalize relations between Finland and the Soviet Union," Zhdanov concluded. [11] The Control Commission's view of the affair was thus communicated to the Finnish government in the strongest possible language. Without revealing its source of information and without undue recourse to scare tactics, Paasikivi's cabinet finally managed to instill an appreciation of the seriousness of the situation in Parliament. After the government had made it clear that it would regard rejection of the bill as equivalent to a vote of no confidence, it was passed on its second reading on 8 September.

Before the third and final reading, the Control Commission decided to make its views on the matter public to ensure that its previous communications with the Finnish government had in fact gone home—although it now adopted a somewhat more careful form of words than had been used with Paasikivi. In a communiqué appearing in the Helsinki papers on 11 September, the Commission formally stated that the parliamentary constitutional committee and the Supreme Court had willfully misinterpreted Article 13 of the armistice agreement, on which they were not, in any case, in a position to pass judgment. The thrust of the Commission's argument was that the requirements of the armistice agreement went above and beyond existing legislation and that if any conflict emerged between the two it was Finnish law, rather than the agreement, that required modification. The government's proposed bill was finally passed the same day by a special enabling act by a vote of 129 to 12.[12] The Finns' eventual willingness to accept the need for the move might also have been influenced by (in addition to the pressure from the Control Commission) the lingering hope of achieving a rapid peace treaty at the London conference of Allied foreign ministers.[13] The law was ratified by Paasikivi, standing in for Mannerheim who was on sick leave, on 13 September. The government was now faced with its practical implications.

Zhdanov had shown the text of the Commission's statement to Commodore Howie of the British section of the Commission before it was issued but after Moscow had approved it. Howie had unconditionally accepted it, but he later cabled London for further instructions. Christopher Warner's reply from the Foreign Office arrived in Helsinki some two weeks after the statement had been published. Warner argued that it was important to distinguish between ordinary and major war criminals; further,

As no atrocities or ordinary war crimes are known to have been committed by Finns against British subjects, His Majesty's Government have no interest in the former aspect of the question so far as it concerns Finland. As regards the second category of war criminals His Majesty's Government have not ever contemplated the Allied prosecution of members of the Governments of those Balkan countries which became German satellites and would not therefore wish to prosecute leading Finnish politicians responsible for launching an aggressive war.[14]

This can be taken as a clear instruction to the British representatives in Helsinki to avoid involvement in the whole war guilt affair. The United States, in line with its noninvolvement in the two Finnish wars and its nonmembership of the Control Commission, adopted a similar, if not more pronounced, low profile. Hamilton and Hulley contented themselves with simply keeping the government back in Washington informed of developments.[15]

After the necessary initial preparations,[16] the trial finally began at the House of Estates in Helsinki on 15 November. The accused included ex-President Risto Ryti; ex-prime ministers J. W. Rangell and Edwin Linkomies; ex-ministers Henrik Ramsay, Väinö Tanner, Antti Kukkonen and Tyko Reinikka; and former minister to Berlin, T. M. Kivimäki. The first part of the trial was given over to a general presentation of the prosecution's case by the acting prosecutor Attorney

General Toivo Tarjanne, and of various statements put before the court. Two days later, the tribunal decided to adjourn the hearing for three weeks to allow the defendants time to familiarize themselves with the prosecution's evidence. An interim judgment was also made on a vote allowing Tanner, Kivimäki, Kukkonen, and Reinikka to be released from detention but rejecting the other defendants' applications for release. The chairman of the tribunal, N. Hj. Neovius, the president of the Supreme Court, voted for the release of all the defendants.

The Control Commission reacted sharply to the tribunal's decision, which also came as a surprise to the Finnish authorities—especially in the light of Zhdanov's specific warning made to the government the previous day that none of the defendants was to be released before the conclusion of the trial.[17] Zhdanov told Paasikivi that he now regretted that he had allowed the Finns to handle the whole affair. Article 13 of the armistice agreement, Zhdanov argued, required cooperation between the Finnish government and the Commission on the handling of the trial; but Paasikivi's cabinet seemed to be hiding behind the tribunal's back and reneging on its obligations. Zhdanov described the overall atmosphere in the courtroom at the House of Estates as more like a club than a court of justice. The defendants were addressed by their former titles—Ryti, for instance, as Mr. President—and were even allowed to talk to members of the public as they entered and left the courtroom, Zhdanov complained. Unable to deny that this had indeed occurred, Paasikivi in reply tried to answer Zhdanov's criticisms by saying that he felt sure that "the majority" of the defendants would eventually be found guilty and sentenced. Zhdanov repeated his criticisms to five other members of the government who visited him on 27 November, and he argued that the Finnish right was using the trial as a vehicle for reactionary propaganda and was preparing the country for further armed conflict with the Soviet Union. The government had a duty, the ministers were told, to put a stop to this.

Zhdanov, however, did not content himself with merely dressing the government down. He also made the Commission's position clear to the wider body of Parliament in a meeting on 30 November with Juho Koivisto of the Agrarian Party, Onni Hiltunen of the Social Democrats, and Hertta Kuusinen and Yrjö Leino of the People's Democrats. Zhdanov traced the apparent difficulties that the Finns were experiencing in complying with Article 13 to their interpretation of war guilt in purely legalistic terms, whereas in fact the matter was largely political. Comparable proceedings elsewhere had all been based on the use of retroactive legislation. In Zhdanov's opinion, the Control Commission had shown a large degree of "leniency" toward Finland in the handling of the issue, by allowing the general public plenty of time to become acclimatized to the situation; by not protesting the fact that the necessary legislation had been unsatisfactorily drawn up, because it omitted reference to Finland's alliance with Germany; by not pressuring the government to increase the number of those to be tried; by giving complete jurisdiction in the matter to a Finnish court; and by not demanding the imprisonment of the accused before proceedings began. "The Finnish government, Parliament and Finnish democracy as a whole have been able to handle the matter in very easy circumstances, very easy indeed," declared Zhdanov.

Zhdanov went on to say that the preliminary stage of the proceedings had created a bad impression in the Soviet Union. Finland's handling of the affair had been decidedly slipshod and had "seriously undermined Finnish foreign relations. The freeing of four of the defendants . . . seems clearly deliberate, as if agreed beforehand." If the Soviet Union simply wanted revenge, Zhdanov said, the tribunal would be the least of Finland's worries. Nevertheless, Zhdanov declared, the Soviet Union could expect nothing less than that "the tribunal should act fairly and in such a way as not to endanger relations between our two peoples, that sentences should be discussed and that the proceedings should not be used for anti-Soviet or anti-United Nations propaganda." Zhdanov thus made it clear that the tribunal's role was simply one of adjudging the responsibility of those arraigned and not of specifying overall international responsibility in the war because the time was not yet ripe for dealing with this question without violating the prestige of the victorious Great Powers. "I have occasionally been asked," Zhdanov went on, "what will happen if the sentences are unsatisfactory. Will the matter then be taken out of Finnish hands? The defendants handed over to the United Nations or the Soviet Union? But this would be nothing compared with what would then lie ahead." Zhdanov concluded his sharply worded argument with an appeal to those present to remember the importance of maintaining good Finnish-Soviet relations.[18]

At the same time as Zhdanov was increasing his pressure on the government in Helsinki, Sundström in Moscow reported back to the Foreign Ministry that there was a distinct cooling in the previously friendly attitude towards Finland. The release of the four defendants had "caused surprise and ill feeling. The papers have begun . . . to print reports of protest meetings held to condemn the decision taken by the Finnish tribunal." The Moscow view seemed to be that the lenient treatment of the accused threatened to make a farce out of the whole trial. "The war guilt question is clearly seen as a test case for future relations between Finland and the Soviet Union and is being closely followed here," Sundström commented.[19] In contrast, interest in the affair in London and Washington was—according to Wuori's and Jutila's reports—slight. The tribunal's interim judgment had not caused any untoward reaction in either country.[20]

In Helsinki, Shepherd, in a discussion with Egger, the Swiss envoy, expressed sympathy with Zhdanov's obvious sense of disappointment and dissatisfaction with the Finns. The very appointment of a person of his rank to Helsinki underlined the significance that Stalin attached to developing good relations with Finland. "The progress of the trial up until now, however, has shown that both the tribunal and a large section of the population are clearly on the side of the defendants.'' The latter had been given free rein to voice anti-Soviet opinions during the trial. Shepherd thought that Zhdanov could well be tempted to interpret these statements, if not the whole course of the trial up until then, as directly undermining his authority and in some way indicating his failure as chairman of the Control Commission. These developments could have unpleasant consequences for his career, and ''nobody,'' thought Shepherd, ''knows the speed of the changes in the Kremlin's favour better than he does.'' Shepherd seemed sure that Moscow would not accept short sentences for the accused and thought it likely that if they were handed down, the Soviet Union would step in and take charge of the matter. ''This could undoubtedly lead to Paasikivi's resignation and have a whole series of internal repercussions which we can only guess at.'' [21]

Orlov also communicated his disappointment to Shepherd at the depth of anti-Soviet sentiment in Finland, insofar as it had emerged during the war guilt trial. ''Evidently, Orlov set his hopes too high on the effectiveness of his efforts to win friends in Finland, which from my observations have succeeded only in Left circles.'' [22]

The dissatisfaction felt by the Control Commission was matched by the Finnish government's own gloom at the way things seemed to be going. The government, however, was advised by Minister of Justice Urho Kekkonen to refuse General Savonenkov's demand that the released defendants be immediately redetained. The government had no option, in Kekkonen's opinion, but to wait for the tribunal to give a further interim judgment. Paasikivi, in a deeply pessimistic mood, agreed that the government was in no position summarily to detain the released defendants against the decision of the tribunal. The Commission's demand was thought totally ''unprecedented''; resignation seemed a very real possibility if the Commission maintained or increased its pressure on the issue. But Paasikivi was well aware that his cabinet had proved an effective coalition and that the government's resignation would be in no one's interest, least of all the Soviet Union's, ''as nobody knows what kind of government could follow.'' Despite his gloomy forebodings Paasikivi gave strict instructions to Kekkonen and Leino on 17 December, before their visit to the Commission, that they were ''not to give any indication that the government can or will influence the decisions of the tribunal.'' The government (the Commission was to be told) did not know of any intentions on the part of the released detainees to flee the country, a possibility to which Savonenkov had alluded. The Commission was also to be informed that the chairman of the tribunal had been made aware of its views and that the prosecution at the trial could be expected to demand redetainment for all the accused at the conclusion of the defense speeches. Savonenkov raised no objections to the government's explanations, saying that the Commission had always wanted the tribunal to redetain. The technical details were of secondary importance, as long as the final result was just. As Tarkka has pointed out, the government had won a tactical victory.[23] In a second vote on 21 December, the tribunal decided to redetain Tanner, Kivimäki, and Reinikka but to allow Kukkonen to remain free.

The government's other moves to eliminate those features of the trial proceedings that had attracted particular criticism from the Commission also no doubt contributed to the accord struck between the Finnish authorities and the Commission. N. Hj. Neovius, the chairman of the tribunal, was unhappy with his overall position and particularly with the position he found himself in after voting for the release of all the defendants; he tendered his resignation, which was accepted. Oskar Möller, an associate judge of the Supreme Court, was appointed to replace him. The public's contact with the defendants in the courtroom was restricted to prevent any recurrence of the alleged "club atmosphere." Censorship of the proceedings was also tightened in line with the Commission's wishes. When Ryti began his defense on 11 December, however, Zhdanov forbade its being published. Kekkonen, in discussion with Zhdanov, strongly disagreed with this; "denying the defendants the right of publication for their defense after the prosecutor has presented his case to the tribunal and it has appeared uncensored in the papers will have a far from positive effect on public opinion. People will easily believe that the defendant's evidence is too persuasive for us to dare to print it, because it would overturn the prosecution's case." All this could only serve radically to undermine popular trust in the justice of any sentences handed down, Kekkonen went on. Kekkonen also confirmed that the tribunal proceedings had been fully in accord with Finnish judicial practice and that neither the prosecution nor defense cases were allowed to be interrupted or contested before they had been concluded. Kekkonen's argument won through. After discussions at the Commission, Zhdanov informed the government that defense speeches could appear in the press as long as a check ensured that they did not give offense to the Soviet Union or go beyond assessing the specific charges faced by the defendants. The tribunal thus remained faced with ensuring a degree of censorship, a task made somewhat easier by the willingness of the defendants and their counsels to make use of an element of self-censorship.[24] The result was a tolerably effective compromise between a Western and a Stalinist style of proceedings at what was, as all were aware, a political trial.

The tribunal concluded its work on Saturday, 16 February 1946, deciding on sentences of eight years, imprisonment for Ryti, five years for Rangell, three years for Linkomies, two and one-half years for Ramsay, three and one-half years for Tanner, and two years for both Kukkonen and Reinikka; Kivimäki was found not guilty. The sentences, which were to be formally announced at the tribunal's final hearing two days later, proved harsher than the government had thought likely. Paasikivi was on record as saying to his government colleagues that the defendants had acquitted themselves well; he supposed that Ryti would most probably get six months and the others would be merely fined. Although the sentences were significantly more severe than this, they nevertheless failed to satisfy the Control Commission. (The following draws heavily on Tarkka's description of the events that ensued.)

General Savonenkov, the deputy chairman of the Control Commission, visited Paasikivi at home early on Sunday, 17 February. After explaining that he had heard about the sentences handed down the previous day, he again expressed his surprise that no effort had been made to contact the Commission before the decision, as had been discussed. The Commission, he went on, would not be satisfied with the sentences of less than five to ten years for Ryti, Tanner, Rangell, Linkomies, and Kivimäki; the three other defendants—Ramsay, Reinikka, and Kukkonen—should, in the Commission's opinion, be sentenced in line with what had transpired during the trial, but under no circumstances were they to be given nominal sentences. To allow these demands to be complied with, Savonenkov ordered that the sentences were not to be publicly announced on 18 February as agreed. The nature of Savonenkov's comments indicates that he must have been in prior communication with the highest echelons of the Allied leadership, probably Stalin, and that the demands were officially sanctioned. They also show that the Commission attached particular importance to sentencing Tanner and Kivimäki, as the sentences passed on Ryti and Rangell were within the limits presented to Paasikivi. The Commission's demand for stiffer sentences clearly reflected its view that Tanner and Kivimäki had been left off too lightly and that Linkomies, of the two former prime ministers in office during the course of the Continuation War, had been unnecessarily treated more favorably than Rangell.

After discussions with the chairman and various members of the tribunal, Paasikivi held an unofficial cabinet meeting to consider the matter. The atmosphere at this meeting verged on one of desperation. Paasikivi's opposition to acceding to Savonenkov's demands was apparent from the outset, with his declaration that the whole basis of the trial would be subverted if the length of the sentences were decided by anybody other than the tribunal. He forcibly expressed his belief that "Things will not be as easy as the Russians might think either, if they take the defendants to Petrozavodsk and execute them there." That would only make martyrs of them, he went on. The Soviet Union's giving Finland jurisdiction in the matter meant, in Paasikivi's view, that events were no longer open to direct Soviet influence or to Finnish government influence, for that matter, because the judiciary was independent of the government. "Möller has lost such a lot of weight brooding over the problem that it's pitiful to see him, and Castrén [president of the Supreme Administrative Court and a member of the tribunal] only groans. These men take their responsibilities seriously and they have the law on their side. . . . I can't be a party to this. I have principles too." Paasikivi's seeming intransigence was countered by the views of the others present that refusal to bow to the Commission's wishes would mean the loss of everything that had thus far been achieved; in any case, the Allies had the right under Article 13 of the armistice agreement to make known their opinion on the sentences handed down, and the government had a duty to inform the tribunal of the new situation. Kekkonen suggested that the tribunal be asked to postpone publication of the sentences and that its members be made aware of the Commission's interests in changing them. Kekkonen's suggestions were supported by the others present, and Paasikivi was forced to relent.[25]

The following day, in a public hearing lasting only two minutes, the tribunal decided to postpone announcement of the defendants' sentences to the following Thursday. The Finns had finally been forced to realize that Zhdanov had meant what he had said at the end of 1945—that the final sentences would have to be negotiated with the Commission. The Commission's lack of response, during the crisis that had blown up over the release of four of the defendants, to the government's solid defense of the tribunal's freedom of action under Finnish law had led the government (falsely, as it turned out) to assume that the Commission had accepted that the tribunal was not to be influenced. And although Paasikivi, subsequent to the trouble in December, might have expected that the Commission would wish to communicate its view of the sentences before their announcement, he had not felt it tactically wise to be seen to take the initiative by going to ask the Commission's opinion. If he had done so, his ability to pressure the tribunal over the sentences would have been much less than in the situation he now found himself, when it was he who was the object of outside pressure.[26]

Shepherd, despite Savonenkov's failure to inform the British section of the Commission before presenting his demands to Paasikivi, also felt it necessary to put his views of the situation to the Finnish authorities, convinced as he was that they should be prevented from acting against their own interests. Shepherd presented what he described as his "personal views" on the matter to Enckell on Monday, 18 February. He called the sentences of five to ten years demanded by the Soviet Union lenient and advised the Finns to accept their necessity. Enckell replied that the government thought the eight-year sentence passed on Ryti already harsh enough, and he believed that the Continuation War could not be treated separately from the Winter War. Shepherd repeated his advice that the Finns accept the changes sought by the Commission. In his report to London, Shepherd emphasized that the war guilt question was a matter of principle for Moscow and that the future of Finnish-Soviet relations depended on a solution satisfactory to the Soviet Union being found.[27]

Shepherd's advice to accept the Soviet demands was amplified by the Foreign Office's comments to Eero Wuori in London: the passing of overly lenient sentences could only harm Finland's position because of the "very unfavourable" impact they would have in the Soviet Union. Wuori was also told that Finland would be unwise to count on any disagreement emerging on the issue between London and Moscow.[28]

By the time Wuori's cable reached Helsinki, however, Paasikivi had already decided on his course of action. Since previous attempts to influence the decision of the tribunal had proved relatively ineffectual, he forced himself to put aside his personal qualms and sent a letter to the tribunal on Tuesday evening, 19 February, stating that the government thought it appropriate to inform the court that in passing sentence it should be aware of the need for an element of cooperation "on the basis proposed by the Allied Control Commission" and as referred to in Article 13 of the armistice agreement. Paasikivi signed the letter personally, "on behalf of the State Council." There was no countersignature. Paasikivi's position and personal role in taking responsibility for convincing the tribunal of the need for changes to the sentences was, as Tarkka has pointed out, probably decisive in convincing many members of the tribunal to reconsider their earlier judgment. The tribunal's final sentences were confirmed on 21 February. Ryti was given ten years of hard labor and Rangell, Linkomies, Ramsay, Tanner, Kukkonen, Reinikka, and Kivimäki were given six, five and one-half, two and one-half, five and one-half, two, two, and five years of imprisonment, respectively.[29] The Control Commission had achieved what it had demanded. London too was satisfied that the Finns had accepted the necessity of the situation. The British were aware that the Soviet Union could otherwise have made things very difficult for Finland, which in turn would have postponed the return of normal Anglo-Finnish relations.[30]

Taken as a whole, the sentences handed down by the Finnish tribunal were conspicuous in their lenience when compared with those passed on past political leaders in the other defeated countries of Europe. The different nature of the trials in these other countries was intimately linked with their significantly different political positions in comparison with Finland. The Finnish government, in particular, was able to keep charge of the trial proceedings and make the best use it could out of the limited room for maneuver allowed by the Soviet Union. In post-1944 Finland, the war guilt question was one of the first major issues that brought the public at large face to face with the conflict between the new style of foreign policy and the old, prewar political attitudes. Paasikivi and Kekkonen made no real attempt to adapt to public opinion but decided instead to lead it, "forcing" the country if necessary to understand where its best interests now lay. It proved impossible to handle the war guilt affair merely through recourse to legal principles and an appeal to moral justice. In the final analysis, securing the country's international position through a policy of practically minded political realism was considered more important. As Jukka Tarkka has pointed out, the solution of the war guilt dilemma was both a legal aberration and a political necessity.[31] Despite its drawbacks, however, the conclusion of the trial marked the ending of a long period of tension for the Finnish government. In a reception at the American legation on 22 February, Hulley was able to note that both Paasikivi and Enckell appeared much more relaxed and calm than they had of late. Enckell's observation that "though many troubles lie ahead it gives one a feeling of satisfaction to finish one great problem" seemed to sum up the Finnish view. The Soviet diplomats and members of the Control Commission present also expressed their satisfaction at the conclusion of the affair.[32]

It was thus Moscow's clearly voiced opinions that dictated the final form of the tribunal's judgment. Washington remained on the sidelines throughout, whereas London satisfied itself with advising Finland to accept the necessities of the situation to avoid the potentially more unpleasant consequences that could otherwise result. Why, then, was the issue so important to the Soviet Union? Faced with the inaccessibility of Soviet sources, any conclusions can only be provisional; but it seems clear that, in international terms at least, the problem for the Soviet Union was foremost one of prestige. Since the Allies had already agreed in principle that the political leaders of the defeated countries would be brought to trial, there was no reason to allow Finland to be an exception; only the actual handling of the problem turned out to differ from that used elsewhere. The Soviet Union also clearly had a wish to justify its wartime policies—policies that included Finland—in the international arena, and its allowing the trial to be abandoned or the tribunal to hand down minimal sentences would have raised the specter of a very visible loss of Soviet prestige.

Moscow's attitude toward the proceedings was also shaped by its assessment of the factors bearing on the development of future relations between Finland and the Soviet Union. Purging the Finnish political establishment of those figures identified with anti-Soviet sentiments was one of the Control Commission's long-term aims directed at easing Finland's shift to a new style of foreign policy commensurate with its changed position.[33] The creation of martyrs along the way, however, was far from being one of its intentions, as is indicated by the decision to allow the Finnish authorities to handle the trial proceedings. All the same, it is likely that Moscow, by failing to take sufficient notice of Finnish traditions, prejudices, and popular attitudes, overestimated the willingness of public opinion in Finland to come to terms with the country's past and in particular with a political trial—based on special retroactive legislation—of the country's past leaders. This interpretation would go some way toward explaining the obvious expressions of disappointment and frustration evinced by the Commission at the development of Finnish public opinion during the course of the trial. Aware of the problems that a trial would bring, Paasikivi had originally tried to oppose the whole notion of a tribunal. Once proceedings had begun, however, Paasikivi was well aware that they had to be brought to a satisfactory conclusion, if only to underwrite Soviet prestige. The experience showed that the work of building good relations between the two countries would demand significantly more time than perhaps had initially been expected and that the actual practical means of ensuring Finnish-Soviet cooperation would have to be fundamentally reassessed.

The end of 1945 had seen Finland faced with two major unresolved issues, as Paasikivi admitted at a press conference called on 13 December to state the government's case on the country's progress toward fulfillment of the terms of the armistice agreement. ''We have two difficult things still ahead of us. . . . One is the war guilt issue. The other problem is the arms dump affair.'' The so-called arms dump plan had its origins in discussions in autumn 1944 between Col. V. K. Nihtilä, head of the operations section at Finnish General Headquarters, and his assistant, Lt. Col. U. S. Haahti. The plan allowed for the setting up of secret arms dumps across the country to enable Finland to mount an effective resistance in the event of future conflict between the Western powers and the Soviet Union and Finland's being occupied contrary to the terms of the armistice agreement. Knowledge of the purpose and location of the dumps was restricted to a small number of army officers.

The state police uncovered the plan in the spring of 1945 through information it acquired in Oulu in North Finland; in May, the Control Commission sent Colonel Fedorov to Oulu to investigate the matter in detail. It did not take the Commission long to realize that, rather than a lone, underground ''fascist organization,'' they were dealing with one directed and controlled from Finnish military headquarters.[34] General Zhdanov was not, as has been widely suggested, satisfied with this conclusion. In a number of sharply worded letters sent to Paasikivi in June 1945, he demanded rapid and effective action to ascertain the full implications of what had been uncovered and to punish those involved. The Commission, he underlined, could not accept any delays.[35] The Soviet media also drew attention to the affair.[36]

A detailed understanding of the Soviet position on the problem would require access to the relevant original documents, but a number of general features stand out. The plan went against both the spirit and the letter of the armistice agreement, a fact that was heavily emphasized in the Finnish Communist Party's public statements on the matter. The Control Commission's demands, however, went much deeper than simply supporting the Finnish communists. When the Suojeluskunta had been banned, the Commission had paid particular attention to doing all it could to make any evasion of the rearmament restrictions in the armistice agreement—comparable to what had taken place in post-1918 Germany—impossible in Finland. The question of whether the plan constituted an ''underground Suojeluskunta movement,'' acting with the approval of Finland's highest leadership, must have been of central importance to Zhdanov and the Commission. Zhdanov waited to see how the Finnish government would react. Mannerheim's intervention and persuasion of Lt. Col. Haahti, one of the plan's central figures, to confess his involvement brought the details into the open.

Once the Commission saw that Finnish authorities seemed sincere in their desire to get to the bottom of the affair, it refrained from taking an active part in the investigations, although it naturally followed their progress closely. Pohlebkin considers the Finnish readiness to deal decisively with the affair as having contributed to the Control Commission's good opinion of the sincerity of their intentions. In turn, this readiness influenced the Commission's decision in the summer of 1945 to return full sovereignty over Finnish airspace to the Finnish authorities and to remove the wartime restrictions on maritime movements and general communications.[37]

Shepherd believed that the Russians "strongly" hoped that the Finns would be able to deal with the arms dump affair themselves.[38] In a parallel report to Washington, however, Maxwell Hamilton emphasized the difficulties that revelation of the plan had caused for Paasikivi's government, already embroiled in the problems of the war guilt issue.[39] The Western powers had no direct cause for involving themselves in the matter. On a visit to Stockholm in August 1945, Averell Harriman expressed his surprise to Östen Undén, the Swedish foreign minister, at the Soviet Union's apparently lenient treatment of Finland in comparison with its treatment of Germany's wartime satellites in Eastern Europe. If comparable arms dumps had been discovered in these other countries, Harriman seemed convinced that "a lot of blood would certainly have flowed."[40] Harriman, surprised at the apparent special relationship existing between Finland and the Soviet Union, could find no answer to this seeming conundrum. In the years to come, Harriman was not the only observer in the West to be brought up against the same problem of coming to terms with Finland's idiosyncratic relation with the Soviet Union. The arms dump case dragged for three more years, but the Control Commission showed no further interest in it.

After the appointment of Paasikivi's government in November 1944, President Mannerheim had played less of a part in the practical handling of the country's affairs. In fact, as an elder statesman belonging to what was now another era, Mannerheim became increasingly estranged from his presidential role as he gradually lost command of the various and ever-changing political and executive details that went with it. Enckell, for instance, complained to Gripenberg on one of his visits from Stockholm to Helsinki that Mannerheim "is beginning to get old and forget things." Gripenberg was struck by Mannerheim's "isolation," caused by the president's increasing reliance on a small circle of individuals — most of whom were old friends with little or no political significance.[41] Mannerheim's handling of foreign affairs was also colored by his isolationist stance. The president did not seem to have had any significant contact with the leadership of the Control Commission after his discussions during the winter of 1944-45 over coastal defense and military cooperation. Paasikivi was clearly in control. The new political realities of Finland's position told on Mannerheim's physical and psychological reserves, and he would occasionally sink into bouts of deep depression that did little to help his already heavily taxed prime minister. Paasikivi's outburst to Mannerheim (as recorded by Svento) has since become well known: "If what you predict is true, it would be better for both of us if we went out into the forest and put a bullet in our heads." Neither, however, was willing to follow Paasikivi's advice; but Paasikivi later recalled, with some satisfaction, that after this exchange Mannerheim exhibited less of his previous penchant for ominous warnings of the disasters ahead.[42]

Gripenberg's diary entries from the first half of 1945 onwards refer to a growing tension between Mannerheim and Paasikivi. Paasikivi, although aware of the decisive role that Mannerheim had played in leading the country out of the war, became convinced that as a president he was far from satisfactory. "If Mannerheim would give the government his full support we would be in so much of a better position, because he had the people's trust. But he has not done that."[43] Enckell later told Gripenberg that Paasikivi complained that Mannerheim "does not do anything," whereas Mannerheim thought Paasikivi "too submissive by far." "Unfortunately," added Enckell, "Mannerheim is losing more and more of his authority."[44] In discussions with Gripenberg, his relative and close friend, Mannerheim also repeatedly referred to his wish to resign, complaining that he was too old and did not have enough strength left. Time after time, however, appeals were made to him to remain in office.[45] Despite his increasing passivity and isolation, Mannerheim, as head of state, represented a father figure to a wide section of the population in the troubled times of 1945; his presence in the government was used by many to bolster their sense of national security and faith in the future. People simply did not want him replaced.

Despite his ebbing energies, the old soldier still had—as his discussions with Zhdanov during the winter of 1944-45 showed—a sharp eye for the political realities dictated by Finland's geopolitical position. What, then, prevented him from actively working to create an effective foreign policy based on these insights? The best answer is probably provided by some comments Mannerheim made to General Heinrichs, his long-standing and closest aide, in 1948. After listening to Heinrichs's positive remarks on Finland's new foreign policy and on the Treaty of Friendship, Cooperation and Mutual Assistance that had just been signed in Moscow (where Heinrichs had been acting as a military advisor), Mannerheim commented, "This might be alright in principle, but everything depends on who the other party to an agreement is. If Russia were still ruled by an autocracy or an ordinary government, it might perhaps be a clear-cut decision. But now . . . I'm too old to relearn things."[46] Little needs to be added to this. Weighed down with age and illness, this old czarist officer and aristocrat, for all his basically realistic outlook, was simply no longer able to see the logical necessities of his realism through into active policy.

Mannerheim's powers began visibly to weaken in the autumn of 1945. His physical illness—he was afflicted by a stomach ulcer—was complicated by the unpleasant experience of being forced, as part of the war guilt affair, to arraign his close wartime colleagues for decisions for which he himself had been, partly at least, morally responsible. His strong defense (in a discussion with Norwegian envoy Berg, to the latter's surprise) of the Ryti-Ribbentrop pact, which he described as "a bold act,"[47] and which he repeated to the Petäys commission before the setting up of the guilt tribunal, clearly indicated his attitude.

The increasingly public discussion (which was initially fired by the evidence put before the war guilt tribunal) as to how long Mannerheim would be able to remain as president was given further impetus by his departure, at his doctor's suggestion, to Portugal for health reasons at the beginning of November 1945. In a report filed to Washington on 27 October, Hulley, the American chargé d'affaires in Helsinki, suggested that it was unlikely that Mannerheim's term of office would last much longer. Mannerheim had been ill on 12 September when the war guilt legislation was ratified; after returning to office, he had again been taken ill in October, this time one day before the cabinet session that was due to name the defendants to stand trial before the war guilt tribunal. Mannerheim had also made diplomatic use of his ill health in March 1945 to avoid signing the government's proposal for compensatory payments to be paid out of state funds to communist underground opponents to the Continuation War who had been imprisoned during hostilities.[48] After Mannerheim had left for Portugal, however, and after discussions with Enckell and others, Hulley in his further reports emphasized that although Mannerheim's departure had been partly motivated by politics, his deteriorating health was becoming more and more of a factor. Gripenberg drew the same conclusion after meeting Mannerheim in Stockholm en route to Portugal. The war guilt issue might have been an added incentive for his departure, Gripenberg wrote in his diary, "but he is really ill."[49] Orlov, in discussions with his diplomatic colleagues in Helsinki, also referred to Mannerheim's deteriorating health, hoping that his stay in Portugal would improve things; but he refused to admit to believing that the war guilt case was in any way linked to the president's trip.[50]

Mannerheim's having to return to the hospital immediately on his return to Finland in January 1946 made it clear, however, that the trip had not had the desired effect. His personal doctor, Lauri Kalaja, in conversation with Speaker of Parliament K. A. Fagerholm, was forced to conclude that "the Marshal must leave his post as President. . . . he cannot manage his work. He is unable to make decisions and when something difficult comes up he falls ill again immediately." As time went on, Paasikivi increasingly complained of the heavy burden of looking after the tasks both of president and prime minister.[51] As a publicly declared presidential candidate, however, he was not in a position to be seen actively working for the departure of the incumbent. The opinion prevalent in government circles favoring a change in president had been communicated, through Fagerholm, to Mannerheim before his departure to Portugal.[52] The press also began increasingly to discuss the possibility of a change of leadership. Mannerheim, however, did not want to be seen as being forced to stand down from office, and he delayed a final decision. He was also influenced by a desire to wait until the war guilt trial had been concluded to avoid creating the impression of his resigning because of "a bad conscience" resulting from the evidence that had been put before the tribunal.[53] His resignation would appear more acceptable after the major hurdle of complying with the most important clauses of the armistice agreement (except for long-term commitments like the reparations payments, which would take years to complete) had been overcome.

The Western powers carefully avoided any direct or indirect involvement in the issue. Stalin respected the personal and other achievements of Finland's wartime commander in chief,[54] but as a realist he was aware that by 1946 the ailing marshal could no longer play an active and positive part in the work of developing Finnish-Soviet relations. His time was over, but the Soviet leadership felt unable to put it as bluntly as this to the Finns. Sundström in Moscow was aware of the general Soviet attitude, as is clear in a private letter he sent to Svento in which he commented that the general impression he had got from the Moscow press and from discussions with members of the local diplomatic community pointed to the Kremlin expecting a change in president in the near future.[55] Back in Helsinki, General Savonenkov visited Mannerheim on 27 January 1946 in the Red Cross Hospital to inform him, on Moscow's instructions, that the Soviet Union had no intentions of demanding action against him personally, despite the evidence that had emerged during the course of the war guilt trial.[56] Stalin had in fact made a similar promise to Boheman, the secretary-general of the Swedish Foreign Ministry, during the war.[57]

The war guilt trial having been concluded, Mannerheim tendered his resignation on 4 March. A period of Finnish history had come to an end.

PART V
From Moscow to Paris

13 Hardening Attitudes

On his return to Washington from the conference of foreign ministers held in the Soviet capital in December 1945, Byrnes found himself faced with a public increasingly ill-disposed toward the country's eastern ally. The view that Stalin was bent on a policy of unbridled Soviet expansion had gradually assumed greater currency in the United States throughout 1945, particularly in leading circles of the Republican party. Stalin, it was argued, could only be stopped by an American refusal to compromise and by recourse (if necessary) to the threat of force. For those who supported this line of argument, the American delegation led by Byrnes—referred to as "the eternal compromiser"—had made a series of "completely unnecessary" concessions in Moscow that would undoubtedly be interpreted by the Soviet Union as signs of weakness. Why, it was asked, did the United States, with its conventional strength already underwritten by its monopoly of atomic weapons, need continually to appease the Soviet Union?

The criticism directed at Byrnes was not restricted to Republican sources. Critical voices were also to be heard in the administration, and even in the State Department itself. Adm. William Leahy, personal chief of staff, for Truman and earlier for Roosevelt, was particularly vocal in his criticism of Byrnes when the secretary of state returned from Moscow. Leahy feared, as his diary makes clear, that the secretary had come under the influence of "communist elements" that had infiltrated the State Department. Leahy saw the actions of the State Department and the British Labour government in yielding to "Soviet pressure" in Moscow as little different from Chamberlain's behavior at Munich in 1938. The staff of the American legation in Bucharest, having similar views, had seriously considered resigning en masse after what emerged at the Moscow conference to protest what was described as the "sellout" of Rumania. Alexander Kirk, the American ambassador to Italy, afterwards described Byrnes's behavior in Moscow as "awful," resulting in the American delegation giving far too much away to the Russians."

More significantly for Byrnes personally, Truman himself began to show signs of inclining to the view that the Soviet Union's aims went beyond a simple desire to defend its security interests. Truman questioned the appropriateness of the flexible policy Byrnes had adopted in Moscow, a policy not helped in the president's eyes by what he saw as his secretary of state's somewhat arrogant manner of handling affairs without reference to his one-time political rival now occupying the Oval Office. Truman had received only one cable from Byrnes, and that couched in very general language, throughout the whole course of the Moscow conference. Byrnes's tone even in that one cable had been more like that of "one partner in business telling the other that his business trip was progressing well and not to worry," Truman was later to comment, than of a secretary of state reporting back to the president. The White House had also not been provided with a preview of the contents of the final conference communiqué before its issue.

Truman could keep his growing dissatisfaction silent no longer when he received his copy of the Ethridge report in January 1946, after it had been discussed in Moscow the previous December. Byrnes, summoned to see the president on 5 January, received a sharp rebuke from Truman, who made it clear that although members of the administration were given as much decision-making power as possible, there was no reason for them to suppose that the president had relinquished his role as the final decision-making authority. To maintain this role, the president had to be kept abreast of events, including the progress made at international conferences. The Ethridge report, Truman thought, showed that neither the Rumanian nor the Bulgarian government could be recognized until there had been radical changes in their composition. The Soviet Union, Truman went on, also showed no sign of withdrawing from those parts of Iran that it had occupied during the war, a fact that required a strong American protest. Truman also accused the Kremlin of aiming to move into Turkey to occupy the Bosporus area and the Dardanelles. The United States would have to stop "playing with compromises." If the Russians were not stopped now, a third world war was inevitable, Truman concluded. "They only understand one language: 'How many divisions have you?' . . . I'm tired of babying the Soviets."[1]

Truman's reaction was far from being merely the result of wounded pride. The latest opinion polls showed that the public's faith in the sincerity of Soviet intentions was steadily decreasing. Back in the autumn of 1945, at the time of the Japanese surrender, 54 percent of Americans had believed in the Soviet Union's desire for cooperation with the West in the reconstruction of the postwar world. Yet only two months later, after the failure of the London conference, the figure had dropped to 44 percent; by February 1946 it had dropped to 35 percent. Another poll conducted in March 1946 showed that 60 percent of those interviewed thought American policy toward the Soviet Union "too soft" and a mere 3 percent "too tough." Against this background of swelling discontent, Truman found it impossible merely to shrug his shoulders at the mounting criticism of Byrnes, coming not only from the country's politicians and the administration itself—embroiled as it was in reassessing the shape of future American foreign policy—but also from the public at large, which was full of the optimistic rhetoric of the Atlantic Charter and increasingly dissatisfied with the Soviet Union's current performance. Truman feared that this public dissatisfaction, if unchecked, could provide the Republicans with a dangerous weapon in the forthcoming congressional elections.

Despite Truman's tough stance, however, the question of the Kremlin's true motives remained the subject of controversy for some time to come, complicating the adoption of an integrated policy that could, if necessary, counter them. There were still those in the political establishment in Washington who considered the enmity between the Allied powers as being largely based on mutual misunderstanding, which could be eliminated by restraint on all sides and a sincere search for compromise solutions. Many remembered Truman's description of Stalin after the Potsdam conference as "a fine man, with the best intentions."

The spring of 1946, however, saw Washington finding the maintenance of a policy of cooperation increasingly difficult. Although it was found possible to recognize Rumania in February, after the governmental changes agreed upon at the Moscow conference had been made, continuing disagreements over the composition of the Bulgarian government meant that Washington finally reestablished diplomatic relations with Sofia as late as the autumn of 1947. The continuing presence of Soviet forces in Iran and Manchuria also raised the political temperature in the American capital. The Kremlin's obvious interest in the Mediterranean area and its demands for a share of the Italian colonies, border changes with Turkey, and the renewal of the Montreux Convention governing passage into the Black Sea only added to the sense of heightened tension. February also saw the Canadian government announce the arrest of several Soviet officials for "stealing" information on the development and manufacture of the atom bomb. A major speech by Stalin the same month reiterated the Soviet view that capitalism and communism represented inevitably opposing forces in the world. The Soviet Union, he warned, had to be constantly on its guard because future conflicts were merely a matter of time as long as capitalism and imperialism, its extreme form, continued to exist in the world.

Against this background, the State Department received the now-famous "long telegram" from George Kennan of the American embassy in Moscow, a statement of views that was fundamentally to shape the attitude of the government in Washington in its interpretation of the motives behind Soviet policies. Kennan believed that Russian hostility toward the West lay at the very base of Stalinism and that the Soviet dictatorship needed the image of a hostile world to justify its own autocratic form of government. Stalin was also ready to use any opportunity that presented itself to promote as large an expansion of the Soviet Union's sphere of influence as possible. Kennan's argument presupposed that no way of satisfying Stalin could or did exist. "Nothing short of complete disarmament, delivery of our air and naval forces to Russia and resigning the powers of the government to American Communists," he said, "would even dent this problem." "And even then," Kennan added in a later report, "Moscow would smell a trap and would continue to harbor the most baleful misgivings." His suggested solution to the problem involved increasing the West's strength to a level sufficient to provide effective immunity from the Soviet threat and then waiting for the Soviet system gradually to disintegrate. Kennan was not prepared to accept the possibility that the Soviet Union, weakened by its wartime struggle, was solely or even mainly concerned with ensuring its national security and, through compromise agreements, the stabilization of the international situation.

Kennan's views, despite their author's status as a junior diplomat, proved influential in Washington. Many of those in the administration believed that in them they had finally found an adequate and cogent explanation of Soviet policy and a basis on which to develop effective American countermeasures. A subsequent State Department memorandum concluded that it was up to the United States to demonstrate to the Kremlin "in the first instance by diplomatic means and in the last analysis by military force if necessary that the present course of its foreign policy can only lead to disaster for the Soviet Union." American policy toward its eastern ally had come to a decisive turning point. The uncertainty that had dogged the Americans through 1945—when the Truman administration had believed, despite its occasional public show of anger and irritation, in the possibility (at least in principle) of resolving disagreements with the Soviet Union through discussion and compromise—was gone. As John Gaddis has pointed out, the year 1946 saw American government policy, for both internal and external reasons, increasingly realigned to match the administration's uncompromising public rhetoric. From being an earlier (if increasingly distant) ally, the Soviet Union became a potential enemy whose interests could no longer be acceded to without undermining the United States position. It did not take Byrnes long, despite his earlier advocacy of compromise tactics, to realize that he too would be required to adapt himself to the general policy realignment. The concessions characteristic of his approach in Moscow in December 1945 were not to be repeated.

The hardening of American attitudes soon began to make itself felt in the international arena. Winston Churchill's "Iron Curtain" speech, for instance, delivered in March 1946 in Fulton, Missouri, before an audience including Truman, voiced strong criticism of the Soviet Union and appeared to meet with Truman's approval.[2] Aspects of the new policy were also evident in the American response to the Iranian crisis that developed after the Soviet Union tacitly refused to evacuate its troops by 2 March, contrary to the agreement that British and Soviet forces were to be withdrawn and despite the fact that the British had already left. No Soviet comment was forthcoming until the Americans put the matter before the UN Security Council. Tass officially announced on the day the issue was to be discussed that the Soviet forces still in Iran would be withdrawn in five to six weeks. Soviet suggestions that the matter required no further discussion were rejected by Byrnes, and the debate went ahead despite Moscow's protests; the Council approved a resolution based on the American case. Gaddis thinks it likely that this new determination by Byrnes was largely based on his reading of the changing attitudes in American domestic politics. Branded as an ''appeaser'' on a par with Chamberlain, Byrnes wanted to prove to his critics at home that he was able and willing to ''stand firm'' when the situation demanded.

The delivery of war reparations shipments from the Western zones in Germany to the East was halted in May 1946 and was followed three months later by a public announcement by Byrnes that the United States would assist the reconstruction of Germany with or without Soviet assistance. In July, President Truman agreed to the continued stationing of American troops in South Korea, an area that represented, in his words, ''an ideological battleground upon which our whole success in Asia may depend.'' The administration also decided to continue deployment of the US Navy in the eastern Mediterranean to counter what it saw as Soviet attempts to acquire bases in Turkey. An influential memorandum compiled by Clark Clifford, a White House aide, and by various foreign policy and military advisers recommended to the president that the ''government should be prepared . . . to resist vigorously and successfully any efforts of the USSR to expand into areas vital to American security.'' Despite the memorandum's restricted reference to areas of central importance to American interests, it was clear that the period of compromise politics was fast drawing to a close.

The conflicts between the Great Powers, which all parties had previously tried to keep hidden from public gaze, came increasingly into the open in 1946. The Western powers also embarked on a new policy of strengthening their armed forces to counter what they saw as the growing Soviet threat. The conflict between East and West, which had initially been restricted to Eastern Europe, seemed inexorably fated to make itself felt across the world. The wartime alliance had collapsed and the cold war had begun.[3]

14 The Deputy Foreign Ministers in London

The conference of foreign ministers, meeting in Moscow in December 1945, had decided to hold a peace conference in Paris to consider the Italian, Rumanian, Bulgarian, Hungarian, and Finnish draft peace treaties the following spring, by 1 May 1946 at the latest. The task of ensuring that the drafts were completed and ready by the time the conference met fell to the Council of Foreign Ministers.

The deputy foreign ministers of the four major powers met at Lancaster House in London on 18 January 1946 to begin work on the problem. James Dunn, Gladwyn Jebb, F. T. Gusev (standing in for Vyshinsky), and Maurice Couve de Murville represented the United States, Great Britain, the Soviet Union, and France, respectively. The Italian problem headed the agenda, but the disagreements that had emerged at the last London conference the previous autumn still remained on all the major questions. No agreement could be reached either on the size of Italian war reparations, the disposal of its colonies, or the redrawing of its borders. The ministers were able to decide to send a group of advisers to Trieste to study the area's geographical, ethnic, and economic situation.

While awaiting the adviser's findings on Trieste, the deputy foreign ministers (except for Couve de Murville, as had been agreed upon in Moscow) began discussions on 11 March on the draft treaties for the Balkan countries on the basis of outline agreements drawn up by the Soviet Union. As with the Italian question, however, progress was minimal and was confined to issues of secondary importance while the main problems remained unresolved. The ministers were able to agree, for instance, that the articles contained in the respective armistice agreements banning fascist organizations, preventing the dissemination of propaganda directed against the member states of the United Nations, authorizing the freeing of political prisoners, and repealing discriminatory legislation be included in the final peace treaties, together with an article guaranteeing human rights. No significant disagreements between the ministers emerged on these issues, although part of the drafting of various articles was postponed until later. These articles were mutatis mutandis to be identical in all five of the peace treaties.[1]

The Finnish question, generally considered the least important and least problematic of the group, first came up for discussion in its entirety in a joint meeting held on 5 April between the Soviet and British delegations. A Soviet draft dated 31 March 1946 and largely made up of the permanent clauses included in the armistice agreement was used as the basis for debate.[2] On the question of the strength of Finnish armed forces, an issue that had caused disagreement in London in 1945, Gusev, moving some way toward the earlier British position, proposed formally limiting Finnish ground, naval, and air forces to a size suitable solely for the maintenance of internal order, the local defense of the country's national borders, and any additional linked tasks given to them by the UN Security Council. Comparable articles, Gusev suggested, could be included in the other treaties. The British, however, were unwilling to accept Gusev's proposal as it stood, believing that more detailed restrictions were needed. The two sides decided to forward the matter for further consideration to the committttee of military advisers attached to the conference.

The proposed articles from the armistice agreement that were accepted in principle by Gladwyn Jebb included the reimplementation of the Moscow Peace of 1940, the surrender of Petsamo to the Soviet Union, the leasing of Porkkala, and the return of Hanko to Finland. He argued, however, that greater precision of expression would be needed in the final draft and that, in the case of the 1940 treaty, the exact articles to be superseded by the new agreement would have to be specified. Because the armistice agreement of 1944 would in effect be annulled by the signing of the final peace, Gladwyn Jebb also thought it preferable that instead of a mere reference to the armistice, the draft state that Finland and/or the Soviet Union *confirmed* the surrender of Petsamo, Porkkala, and Hanko, as laid down in the armistice agreement. The Soviet delegation agreed to consider the British suggestion.

The problem of the Åland Islands, however, saw the emergence of major disagreements between the two delegations. The Soviet draft article — stating that, ''in accordance with the armistice agreement, the effect of the agreement concerning the Åland Islands, concluded between the Soviet Union and Finland on 11 October, 1940, is completely restored''—proved unacceptable to Gladwyn Jebb. Not one but *two* international agreements defined the status of the Åland Islands, he argued, the convention of 1921 and the Finnish-Soviet agreement of 1940; the Soviet Union was not a party to the former and Great Britain was not a party to the latter. It would be impossible for the British government to commit itself to an agreement to which it was not a signatory unless the Soviet Union agreed to include a reference to the 1921 convention in the new treaty article. Gusev refused. Gladwyn Jebb concluded that they were left with two options: removing the Åland Islands article from the draft altogether or obliging Finland in advance, because of the lack of present agreement, to accept any later arrangement agreed upon between the Allies, until which time the islands would remain demilitarized. When agreement could not be reached on any of these proposals, it was decided to postpone further discussion of the whole Åland question.

Britain's evident aim in these talks was to maintain at least its nominal right to participate in any future decision on the demilitarization of the islands, thus preventing it from becoming a purely bilateral affair between Finland and the Soviet Union. Back in August 1945, the War Office had made clear its belief that fortification of the islands would improve the Soviet Union's potential for sealing off the Gulf of Bothnia and for attacking Sweden and possibly Norway as well.

> The Scandinavian countries represent an outer perimeter to the defences of this country. Indirectly, therefore, to permit the fortification of the Åland Islands is contrary to British interests. On the other hand . . . our interests are indirect only, and insofar as the Foreign Office state that our legal grounds for opposing the fortification of the Åland Islands are weak, it would appear profitless to press for a policy of demilitarisation once it has become plain that Russia, in whose sphere Finland lies, favours the reverse.[3]

Important as the question was to Britain, it was not central to its major interests.

Gladwyn Jebb also proposed some minor adjustments to the economic articles of the Soviet draft, although accepting without argument the Soviet demand for war reparations of $300 million. The Soviet proposal for a separate article covering Allied support for Finland's admittance to the United Nations, however, was thought unnecessary. Any such statement could be included in the preamble to the treaty, which in any case was to be identical for all five of the former German satellite countries.

In a second meeting between the Soviet and British delegations on 10 April, the latter took up the issue of the Soviet suggestion that Finland should be obliged to cooperate with the Allies in arresting and bringing to trial those individuals accused of war crimes. Had not Finland, the British wanted to know, already acted on this matter? Gusev replied that it was true that the Finns had sentenced some war criminals, but the proposed article aimed at underwriting their cooperation in acting against any war criminals who might request the right of asylum in Finland; as such, it warranted inclusion in the treaty. Although the British delegation did not have anything against this in principle, it nevertheless held out for the right to modify, if necessary, the article's actual form of words in line with similar articles to be included in the other treaties.

On the question of the strength of Finnish armed forces, Gusev stated that on the basis of further information he had received from the Control Commission in Helsinki, confirming that the Finnish army was in no position to threaten either the Soviet Union or any of the country's other neighbors, the Soviet Union still thought it unnecessary to include any additional restrictions, as proposed by Britain, to supplement the three principal restrictions laid down in the Soviet draft. Gladwyn Jebb's deputy, Lord Hood, strongly disagreed, maintaining that because the armistice agreement required the return of the Finnish army to its prewar strength, the peace treaty itself should also include restrictions—not only on manpower, but also on types of weaponry permitted, such as submarines. It was decided after additional discussion to pass the matter to the military advisers for consideration.

The same meeting on 10 April also covered the issues not included in the Soviet draft that had come up for discussion in London the previous autumn. Gusev's observation that there was no longer any need to require Finland to place military facilities at the Allies' disposal met with Lord Hood's agreement, since the leasing of Porkkala had already been separately arranged, and they agreed to omit any article on the matter from the final treaty. The two sides also agreed to omit any reference to the return of diplomatic and consular relations for similar reasons. The Soviet Union also did not oppose Britain's proposal to oblige Finland, in line with the other defeated countries, to accept the dissolution of the League of Nations and the Permanent International Court of Justice and subsequent Allied decisions to replace them. Finland was also to be pledged to recognize the peace treaties to be concluded with Italy, Rumania, Bulgaria, and Hungary and any later arrangements made between the Great Powers for dealing with Austria, Germany, and Japan. Comparable articles were to be included in all of the treaties under discussion. Further consideration, however, was thought necessary before a decision could be reached on the question of the effect of the peace treaty on Finland's other international agreements.[4]

In the three subsequent meetings between the two delegations on 16, 18, and 20 April, the Soviet representatives accepted Britain's proposed formal modifications to the treaty articles covering the Moscow Peace of 1940, Petsamo, Hanko, and Porkkala. The two sides were able to conclude that the majority of the political clauses of the draft treaty, both in terms of content and to a lesser degree form as well, required no further discussion. No agreement, however, was reached on the Åland Islands. Gusev continued to maintain that the Finnish-Soviet agreement of 1940, by virtue of its going beyond the convention of 1921 in requiring the islands' neutralization and demilitarization, remained the more important of the two agreements; he saw no reason to accept Gladwyn Jebb's suggestion that the 1921 convention be mentioned among the multilateral agreements still in force.[5]

With the exception of the Åland Islands, the restrictions to be applied to Finland's military capability, and the actual form of the preamble and the article covering war crimes, the deputy foreign ministers had reached almost complete agreement on the Finnish question. By the time the foreign ministers of the four major Allies met in Paris at the end of April, the majority of the work in drawing up the least contentious of the treaties had been completed.

15 The Foreign Ministers in Paris

With only a few days to go before the May 1 deadline agreed upon in Moscow was due to expire, the foreign ministers of the four major Allies met in Paris on 25 April to add their efforts to those of their deputies in completing the preparation of the five treaties. It was already clear, however, that any hopes of calling the planned peace conference by 1 May would have to be abandoned. The choice of Paris as the setting for the meeting was dictated by a general wish to allow France its turn to act as host country and by the Western powers' calculation that, in its desire not to undermine its popularity or standing with the French communists, the Soviet delegation would be unable to oppose French participation in discussion of all the draft treaties. The Soviet delegation, led by Molotov, possibly hoping for some support from France against the Americans and British, did not oppose the decision—a move that eliminated the possibility of the reemergence of the procedural disagreement that had marked the end of the London conference. None of the participating delegations, however, saw any profit in bringing up the question of China's possible participation in the talks.

The Americans went into the conference with a clear wish to prevent it from degenerating into a long round of unproductive negotiations. They hoped to complete final drafts as soon as possible to open up the way for the twenty-one nation peace conference they had proposed in Moscow, which offered the prospect of being the highpoint of Byrnes's international career. The solution of the Italian question was considered particularly important by the Truman administration because Italy was already receiving considerable American aid and assistance. From the outset, however, in line with their new "hardline" policy, the Americans were in no mood to make any significant concessions to the Soviet Union. Byrnes initially contented himself with a repeat proposal of the 25 year security agreement for Germany that he had suggested back in London and an additional proposal that the conference include discussion of the Austrian problem.

The Americans were well aware that the West would enjoy a considerable tactical advantage at the future peace conference, where the Soviet Union would find itself in a clear minority on the bulk of decisions. The speediest possible solution of the Austrian question would, the Americans hoped, most probably result not only in the withdrawal of the country's occupying forces but also the withdrawal from Hungary and Rumania of Soviet forces, which had been required up until then to maintain communications and logistics for the Soviet troops in Austria. Rapid and successful completion of the draft treaties would also strengthen the Democratic position in the congressional elections the same autumn, while at the same time removing many of the obstacles to a final resolution of the German question.

The American proposals, however, proved less than acceptable to the Soviet delegation. Molotov refused to countenance discussion of the Austrian question and was equally unwilling to enter into any talks on Germany at this stage. He reiterated that the present conference's main aim was to finalize the draft peace treaties for Italy, Rumania, Bulgaria, Hungary, and Finland.

Italy headed the agenda for discussion. The four delegates were able to agree that the promise of Allied support for Italian admission to the United Nations should be included in the treaty preamble and not in a separate article. This decision also meant the elimination of the question mark previously hanging over the inclusion of a similar promise in the parallel preambles of the other treaties. Agreement was also reached in principle on the limitations to be imposed on Italy's armed forces, which in turn cleared the way for dealing with the parallel clauses in the Balkan and Finnish treaties. Minor territorial adjustments to the Franco-Italian border in France's favor were also agreed upon, as was the rejection of Austrian territorial demands on the South Tirol.

Agreement between the ministers, however, did not go any further. On the major questions of Trieste, the Italian colonies, and the scale of Italian war reparations, the Soviet and Western positions remained as far apart as ever. Drawing on copious background material prepared by their respective advisers, Byrnes and Molotov quickly became embroiled in hours of historical arguments on the political history and ethnic composition of Trieste going back as far as the Middle Ages. The lack of simultaneous interpretation meant that these speeches had to be subsequently translated into the two other languages used by the delegations, a process that soon told on those present; some delegates, like Arthur Vandenberg and Tom Connally in the American delegation, found themselves occupying more and more of their time with elaborate doodling.

The presence of these two powerful senators in the American delegation was important to Byrnes as a way of protecting himself against possible domestic criticism of his handling of the negotiations. Their presence also strengthened the secretary of state's determination to continue pursuing the new, tough American line and to resist switching to a more concessionary approach toward the Soviet Union. The change in American tactics was also felt in the British delegation, led by Bevin, who now found himself largely playing second fiddle to Byrnes. As Bevin's personal secretary, Pierson Dixon, noted in a diary entry for 6 May: "The Americans were far tougher than at London or Moscow. . . . Byrnes is an admirable representative of the US, weak when the American public is weak, and tough when they are tough."[1] Byrnes also ensured, by keeping the American press and radio reporters in Paris closely informed of the conference's progress, that the American public at home remained fully aware of the tough line being taken in Paris.

The private feelers put out by Molotov in his search for possible compromises brought no response from the Americans. Sundström in Moscow learned privately from Aleksandra Kollontay, the former minister in Sweden, that the Soviet delegation was unhappy at the unwillingness of the American and British representatives to have any prior discussions on the issues put before the Paris conference and their obvious preference for presenting Molotov and his advisers, time and time again, with faits accomplis. Giving the details of unresolved questions to the sensation-hungry Western press to spread around the world similarly did little, in the Soviet view, to aid the progress of debate on the conference's more contentious issues or to develop effective international cooperation.[2]

On 8 May, the foreign ministers decided to end the fruitless public shadow boxing that had characterized debate of the Italian question and move on to discussion of the Balkan agreements. Although the Western countries by this stage no longer tried to influence the shape of the various border modifications, Byrnes, with British support, forcibly pressed the Western case for an open-door policy on Eastern Europe and, in particular, for free international traffic on the Danube—an idea that had been included in the American proposals made at Potsdam. Molotov's view that this was designed to return southeast Europe to "the enslavement of capitalism," however, meant that discussion on the topic got nowhere. There was similarly little movement in the debate on the war criminals clause, with the Western powers demanding a separate commission made up of Allied representatives to be set up in *all* the ex-satellite countries to oversee compliance with the clause, an idea found wholly unacceptable by the Soviet Union.[3] With the secondary problems already agreed upon by the foreign ministers' subordinates and the main problems seemingly insoluble, the conference's debate on the Balkan question had apparently come to an impasse similar to that reached over the Italian problem.

The Finnish question seemed to offer the only glimmer of hope. The deputy foreign ministers were able to conclude in a joint report to their superiors on 7 May that no unresolved details on the matter of the Finnish treaty requiring the foreign ministers' attention remained. Bevin concluded that the only significant point of disagreement that remained regarding Finland was whether reference to the 1921 convention should be made in the article on the Åland Islands. The finalization of the draft could nevertheless be left entirely to their deputies.[4] Molotov concurred, a decision that marked the end of ministerial debate of Finland in Paris.

By May 16, after three weeks of largely fruitless argument, the foreign ministers decided that they had had enough. The conference was adjourned at Byrnes's suggestion for a month, although it was agreed that the deputy foreign ministers should continue their work on the drafting of the treaties in the interim. No decision was taken on a date for the twenty-one-nation peace conference originally planned to begin on 1 May.[5]

After the foreign ministers had left the French capital, their deputies (together with their respective delegations and advisers) stayed on at the Palais du Luxembourg to iron out the details of the draft agreements. The intense negotiations that followed brought some progress. The British and Soviet delegates were finally able to agree on the form of words to be used in the article covering the Åland Islands. They decided as a compromise that, since Moscow was not a party to the 1921 convention and London not a party to the 1940 agreement, the text of the treaty should omit reference to both agreements and merely state that the Åland Islands were to remain demilitarized "in accordance with the present situation."

The foreign ministers' agreement in principle on limiting the size of Italy's armed forces opened the way for their deputies to negotiate the details of the military articles of the Balkan and Finnish treaties. It proved possible to draft the military articles of all the treaties virtually simultaneously because little variation between them was required, apart from the obvious linking of the upper limits put on the relative strengths of the different services in each country to that country's particular population and geographical position. But the discussions were not completely without disagreements. Although having withdrawn its overall opposition to specific restrictions of the armed forces of the Balkan countries and Finland, the Soviet Union still maintained that it would be sufficient merely to determine the maximum allowed figures for manpower strengths in the respective army, navy, and air forces. Relying on information from the Control Commission in Helsinki, the Soviet Union suggested figures for Finland of 34,400 men for the army (including antiaircraft and border units), 4,500 men for the navy, and 2,200 for the air force (later increased to 3,000 men).[6] Restrictions on weaponry for all the countries in question were considered unnecessary in the Soviet Union's opinion.

The British were unable to agree to this. They proposed instead that the treaties for the Balkan countries should include, in addition to manpower restrictions, specific armaments thresholds for such things as naval tonnages and numbers of air force aircraft. The British view was that "the smaller the forces of the Balkan satellites the better,''[7] a sentiment that the Soviet Union in all likelihood shared—not perhaps about the Balkan armed forces, but certainly about those of Italy. A figure of 10,000 tons was thought appropriate for the Finnish navy. In the case of the Finnish air force, in the light of its very restricted proposed manpower, the British saw no need in principle to specify a permitted upper limit for the number of aircraft. A maximum strength of 60 aircraft, however, was proposed to parallel the fixed restrictions for the Balkan countries.

This solution proved the basis for a practical compromise, although one that did not affect the other major controversies. Agreeing to the joint decision to limit the size of Italian forces, the Soviet Union accepted the West's proposals for restricting the manpower and armaments of the armed forces of the Balkan countries and Finland. A ban on the use by these countries of bombers, missiles, submarines, and some types of mines was also included. The acquisition and manufacture of military equipment beyond that required for defense needs was similarly banned. Any surplus equipment originating from the Allies or Germany would have to be surrendered to the Allies within a year after the signing of the treaties, whereas all other surplus military hardware would have to be destroyed by the same deadline. When the foreign ministers returned to Paris in the middle of June, the drafting of the military articles had, to all intents and purposes, been completed, a fact that marked a considerable step forward toward the final completion of the treaty drafts as a whole.[8]

The first week following the reconvening of the Council of Foreign Ministers on 15 June to continue talks on the draft treaties was dominated, as the first weeks of May had been, by lengthy and essentially fruitless ideological speech-making. The resulting stalemate was partially overcome after the beginning of informal discussions between the foreign ministers and their advisers, as proposed by Georges Bidault, on 20 June. A week later on 27 June, Molotov, to the surprise of the Western delegates, announced that the Soviet Union finally accepted the proposed changes to the Franco-Italian border and the transfer of the Dodecanese from Italy to Greece. Agreement was also quickly reached, in line with an American proposal, on the fate of the Italian colonies, a problem that had previously remained unresolved. It was decided to allow a period of one year for negotiating an acceptable solution, after which time—if the Allies were still unable to agree on the fate of the African colonies—the matter was to be handed over to the United Nations, as in fact finally happened.

After these Soviet concessions, Molotov thought it fair that the Americans make some of their own in return on the remaining major areas of disagreement concerning Trieste and the scale of Italian war reparations. Byrnes, supported by Vandenberg and Connally, refused to temper his earlier uncompromising attitude. Any significant concessions were out of the question, the Russians were told, and Trieste could under no circumstances be transferred to Yugoslav sovereignty. Molotov had previously refused to bow to American pressure and agree to the calling of the twenty-one-nation peace conference before the Council of Foreign Ministers agreed on the main content of the draft treaties under discussion. With this in mind, and aware of the need for a concession of some sort, Vandenberg and Connally advised Byrnes to propose that Trieste and its Italian-speaking hinterland be declared a free zone to be administered by the United Nations, while the border area with its Slav majority be transferred to Yugoslavia. Molotov took to the American idea and agreed to give it his approval, on condition that the Soviet Union be guaranteed Italian war reparations in kind to the value of $100 million. The Western powers accepted the Soviet proviso so long as the Soviet Union in turn agreed to supply Italian industry with the necessary raw materials to complete the deliveries and agreed to the calling of the peace conference (already months behind the previous timetable) for 29 July 1946, where the scale of reparations to be demanded from Italy for the other Allied powers would be decided. A solution acceptable to all sides, and covering all but the problem of free transit on the Danube, had finally been found. A clear breakthrough had been achieved with Allied agreement of the Italian treaty, generally considered the most obviously contentious of the five.

Breakthrough on the major problems also brought agreement on some of the secondary but still unresolved issues. It was decided in the case of the long-contested war crimes question that any disagreements on the application of the clause in the defeated countries should be put before the relevant local Allied diplomatic representatives who would be charged with settling the problem. For Finland, this would mean consulting the Soviet and British envoys in Helsinki.

When the foreign ministers outlined the agenda for the remainder of the conference on 26 June, they agreed that the Finnish draft treaty, the last to be discussed, was largely complete. Molotov proposed that the deputy foreign ministers be encouraged to complete any outstanding work on it as soon as possible. Byrnes agreed, adding that the foreign ministers themselves should continue to follow the order of precedence—beginning with Italy and running through Rumania, Bulgaria, and Hungary to Finland—that had been adopted at Potsdam, concluding that there was no reason to start at the end rather than at the beginning. Byrnes disliked the idea of postponing further debate on the Italian question in favor of the Finnish treaty, which had been drafted without American participation. For Bevin, as the British representative, the situation was somewhat different, and he invoked the Bible as justification for the last becoming the first. Molotov came to Byrnes's aid, saying that his proposal had only referred to speeding up the work of the deputy foreign ministers and not to changing the order of precedence established at Potsdam. In the words of one observer, "Mr. Molotov stated that he agreed that the Bible was a good thing, but in the present case the Conference could do without it." In conclusion, the ministers decided to continue discussion on the draft treaties in the agreed order, while at the same time encouraging their deputies to complete the remaining drafting of the Finnish agreement as soon as possible.[9]

The Finnish matter came up for discussion by the deputy foreign ministers the following day. The only still unresolved issue, it transpired, with the exception of a few economic articles shared with the Rumanian agreement, concerned the question of the treaty's interpretation. The foreign ministers had already agreed that the implementation of each treaty was to be monitored by the diplomatic representatives of the signatory Allied powers in each national capital for a period of a year after its signing. This monitoring would naturally involve a partial loss of national sovereignty for the countries in question, which was only thought appropriate for a limited period and would become redundant after the countries had been admitted to the United Nations.

Of course, it was possible that disagreements on the interpretation of the various treaty requirements might emerge at any time later than a year after their signature; to cover this eventuality, the Allies agreed to insert a separate clause in all five treaties. The Western countries proposed that any subsequent disagreements, insofar as they could not be resolved though diplomatic negotiations, should be put before the International Court of Justice. The Soviet Union thought such an arrangement impossible to agree to. A binding agreement to consult an international court, the Soviet Union argued, was unacceptable; all disagreements should be left in the hands of the relevant local Allied diplomats, who in the case of total disagreement should be empowered to call on a neutral arbitrator. The Soviet deputy foreign minister, Andrei Vyshinsky, emphasized that the Soviet proposal was better suited to the possible disputes over implementation of the economic articles of the various treaties and the delimitation of new boundaries likely to occur in connection with the Balkan countries and Finland; but at the same time he made it clear that, if the Western powers agreed to this, the Soviet Union would be willing to accept the possibility of appeal to the international court in the case of Italy.[10]

A compromise could not be struck. As no agreement on the content of the clause proved forthcoming, it was decided to append both the Western and Soviet versions to the draft treaties to be presented to the peace conference. This proved to be the only unresolved issue that remained in the Finnish draft treaty.[11]

The foreign ministers, however, found themselves faced with one last struggle in the shape of Molotov's refusal to agree to formal invitations being sent to the countries participating in the peace conference, scheduled for 29 July, until the agenda for the conference had been agreed. The matter was of especial importance to the Soviet negotiators because they were well aware that the Soviet Union, together with its supporters, would find itself in a minority at the conference. Although the main contents of the treaties had by now been jointly agreed, the Soviet Union still wanted to be in a position to prevent the West from being able completely to dictate the conference's decisions. It proposed an across-the-board principle of two-thirds majorities to be applied at both plenary session and commission levels. In the lengthy discussions that followed, in which Molotov refused to modify the Soviet position, Bevin's nerves soon began to get frayed. Returning one day from lunch to find that progress had still not been made, he got to his feet and, shaking his fist and addressing himself to Molotov, boomed in his broad West country accent: "I've had enough of this, I 'ave." As Charles E. Bohlen, one of Byrnes's aides, observed in his memoirs: "For one glorious moment it looked as if the Foreign Minister of Great Britain and the Foreign Minister of the Soviet Union were about to come to blows." [12] Molotov, however, was not to be intimidated and continued his speech unmoved. The exhaustion brought by a further week of continued fruitless discussion resulted in a final compromise being worked out in the shape of a "recommendation" from the foreign ministers for the conference to adopt the two-thirds majority principle, thus allowing for the participant countries to be formally invited. The foreign ministers decided to leave the formulation of the actual conference agenda to the conference itself.

Five more exhausting days of unproductive debate on the German and Austrian questions followed. By the end of the evening session on 12 July, Acting Chairman Ernest Bevin was finally able to say to his flagging colleagues, "Gentlemen, we shall meet at the peace conference." [13]

16   Finland Expectant

The communiqué issued at the conclusion of the conference of Allied foreign ministers in Moscow in December 1945,[1] confirming that the work of drafting the peace treaties for the defeated countries had recommenced in earnest, had brought some relief in Helsinki. The question of whether the Finnish authorities would be consulted as part of this process now became a major government concern. Wuori's initial inquiries on the matter in London immediately after the communiqué's publication yielded nothing definite and were met with a Foreign Office assertion that no decision on consultation had yet been taken.[2]

The exchange of notes that took place between the French government, as host to the peace conference, and those of the Big Three in January 1946 made it clear that the defeated countries were to be offered the opportunity of putting their views to the Allies.[3] French Ambassador Georges Bonnet in Washington, in a discussion with Jutila on 23 January, suggested that Finland would probably be able to put its case at some point to the Allied deputy foreign ministers then meeting in London. Jutila's attempts to get further confirmation of Allied intentions on the matter at a dinner organized the same evening by Hugh S. Cumming, the head of the Northern European Division of the State Department, were met by the latter's rebuttal of Bonnet's suggestion. The deputy foreign ministers, Cumming explained, were engaged on purely preparatory work for the Council of Foreign Ministers and were in no position to receive or act upon proposals from the defeated countries. Finland would instead be given the chance to make its views known at the twenty-one-nation peace conference scheduled to meet later in the spring.[4]

Wuori's efforts in London met with slightly better success than his colleague's across the Atlantic. On 17 January he was able after a discussion at the Foreign Office the previous day to confirm that Finland would indeed by given the

209

opportunity of presenting its opinions on the proposed peace terms to the Allies. "My question as to whether any possible discussion of the Finnish terms would take place in London received no firm answer. I suggest as a result, firstly, that inquiries should also be made in Helsinki as to where the eventual discussions will take place; secondly, that work on finalizing the details of our case should be completed; and, thirdly, that those whose task it will be to represent Finland should be prepared. . . ."[5] Wuori emphasized the same points to G. A. Gripenberg on 25 January when Gripenberg passed through London on his return from a holiday in the United States. Christopher Warner, the head of the Northern Department at the Foreign Office, told Gripenberg that Britain would willingly do what it could for Finland and assured him that "Finland will be able to express her views concerning the peace treaty to Britain and Russia," after which process the draft would then be put before the Paris peace conference for consideration.[6] Despite this assurance, however, Warner later told Wuori on 5 February that no decision had as yet been taken on the date for Finland to present its case, although he was able to say that the treaty would in large part be based on the armistice agreement then in force.[7]

The Finns also sought information on the matter from various Soviet officials. Deputy Foreign Minister Dekanosov confirmed to Sundström in January that Finland would in due course get the opportunity to put its views to the Allies, but he added: "Why are you asking this? Does the government intend presenting us with a counterproposal? Do you intend to demand Karelia back?" Sundström replied that there had been no ulterior motive behind his question.[8] Back in London, Gusev told Wuori on 4 February that the drafting of the Finnish treaty would probably be the last of the issues to be dealt with by the deputy foreign ministers. "Gusev asked whether Finland had any definite proposals. I replied that I, at least, had no knowledge of any. I referred to Finnish hopes for border changes, adding that we had not made any proposals to Britain."[9]

The government in Helsinki, in the meantime, followed Wuori's advice and began work on outlining the case to be put to the Allies on economic issues and the border question. Gen. Erik Heinrichs acted as the government's specialist adviser on the latter problem, and his memorandum dated 25 January had a major impact on subsequent government thinking. Heinrichs made clear his belief, one that he had emphasized to the defense review committee in 1945, that the border issue would only lose its critical military and political significance after the Soviet Union's security interests in the Leningrad region had been resolved through a defense pact with Finland (as the subsequent Treaty of Friendship, Cooperation and Mutual Assistance was then described).

Heinrichs was careful to stress his view that the government would be unwise to pursue major territorial changes, much less the reinstitution of the borders agreed upon under the Peace of Tartu in 1920.

Our previous border on the Karelian Isthmus was inappropriate for one between two sovereign states, being as it was only the border between the pre-1918 Grand Duchy of Finland and the main part of the Russian Empire. That that border (on the Isthmus) was ratified by the Tartu Peace Treaty as the border of the Republic of Finland with the Soviet Union can now be seen, against the background of the history of the two hundred years prior to Finnish independence and on the basis of our last two wars, as having been without doubt a fateful "achievement."

It should be accepted, Heinrichs continued, that "*the possibility of our being able to live in peace and as an independent state alongside our eastern neighbor diminishes the nearer our southeastern frontier is to Leningrad*" (Heinrichs's emphasis). Paasikivi used Heinrichs's argument, almost word for word, at a press conference he gave a couple of weeks later.[10]

Heinrichs thought it very unlikely that the Soviet Union would surrender its hold on east-west land communications to the north of Lake Ladoga.

If one were to try to sketch the possible adjustment of our border with Russia, taking into account the points already mentioned, one would be forced to conclude that *our southeastern border, in our own interests and irrespective of any possible changes in the international climate, must remain at a reasonable distance from the city of Leningard* [Heinrichs's emphasis]. In addition it is difficult, despite what we may hope, to envisage the border running close to the shores of Lake Ladoga, at least not before a sufficient psychological base had been created through conscious and time-consuming efforts for developing positive relations between the Soviet Union and Finland.

Heinrichs, however, did not think that the border agreed upon at the Peace of Moscow did much in itself to help the development of positive Soviet-Finnish relations. The loss of Viipuri had been a severe blow to Finland, whereas the advantage gained by the Soviet Union by possession of the northwest shore of the Bay of Viipuri as a military bridgehead was minimal. Similarly, the effective closure of the Saimaa canal weakened the Finnish economy while bringing no tangible benefit to the Soviet Union. If it were to prove possible, as part of the final peace settlement, partially to redraw the country's borders established under the Peace of Moscow, Heinrichs thought that Finland could, at most, realistically hope for the return of Viipuri and its environs. Nothing would be gained from pursuing the return of territory on the Karelian Isthmus; the Koivisto Islands south-southeast of Viipuri, in particular, would have to be considered as permanently ceded. Heinrichs suggested a border running from the southern end of Lake Immolanjärvi south-southwest to the River Vuoksi, skirting to the south of Viipuri, and ending up on the Bay of Viipuri—possibly at the mouth of the

River Rokkalanjoki. The tongue of land stretching north from the Koivisto mainland and cutting virtually all the way across the Bay of Viipuri would remain in Soviet hands to allow it to seal off the area in the event of a conflict. The northwestern shore of the bay would be returned to Finland.

"This or a similar border revision would create a completely new basis for the positive development of Finnish-Soviet relations and would offer the necessary psychological foundation to both sides for productive mutual cooperation," Heinrichs declared.

Soviet possession of Porkkala would become unnecessary if a military agreement proved forthcoming. Heinrichs was aware, nevertheless, that just as "mutual trust does not grow as quickly as grass on graves," Finland would have to do all it could to take Soviet views of the situation into account. It would probably be something of an achievement in itself, he was forced to conclude, if agreement could be reached on moving the northern border of the leased area far enough south to enable the reinstitution of a direct rail and road connection between Helsinki and Turku.[11]

Paasikivi invited Carl Enckell, Reinhold Svento, G. A. Gripenberg, and the experienced diplomats P. J. Hynninen and K. G. Idman to the State Council's formal conference and reception rooms on the evening of 19 February to debate the various issues relating to the eventual signing of the peace treaty. The result of this meeting was a unanimously approved proposal that a government delegation headed by Paasikivi be sent to Moscow in the hope of meeting Stalin to discuss possible changes to the armistice agreement. This decision to seek bilateral discussions at an early date was largely prompted by a general feeling that the Soviet Union was unlikely to want to make any concessions at the official peace conference; in any case, an overactive Finnish presence there might only serve to undermine Finland's relations with its eastern neighbor.

At the same time, the government was keen to avoid giving offense to the British by any such move. It was agreed that, after the Moscow trip had been finalized, London would be informed of the decision and of Finland's willingness to have separate bilateral discussions at a later date on those sections of the treaty concerning Britain. The Soviet Union was also to be informed of the intention to present Finland's wishes to the British. All those present at the meeting were clear that anything that might undermine Finnish relations with either Great Power was to be carefully avoided. The government saw it as good tactical sense, however, to refrain from inquiring in advance about which parts of the treaty had already been agreed upon between the Allies.

Although none of those present held out any great hopes of the Soviet Union agreeing to territorial changes, the meeting on 19 February nevertheless approved Heinrichs's border proposals both on Viipuri and Porkkala. Finland, it was thought, could offer the Soviet Union the Jäniskoski area in Lapland, which was important for the energy needs of Petsamo, as possible compensation. Svento disagreed, describing the proposals as serving no useful purpose and as being potentially harmful of Finnish interests. It was pointless, Svento argued, to propose any modifications to the territorial clauses of the armistice agreement. It also seemed far from likely that the Kremlin would agree to the proposal on the ceded territories that had been put to Orlov in the autumn of 1945 by a delegation representing the evacuated Karelian population. Although acknowledging that bringing up the matter in Moscow would probably be necessitated by the pressure of domestic opinion, the meeting postponed any final decision on including the issue in Finland's proposals. In the event of the Soviet side rejecting all territorial changes, the Russians were nevertheless to be requested to grant Finland the right to use the whole of the Saimaa canal and to allow transit traffic on the rail line between Helsinki and Karjaa running through the leased Porkkala area. Attempts were to be made to get some reduction in the total war reparations payment imposed on Finland. Paasikivi also emphasized that if the peace conference was, against all expectations, to present demands that conflicted with the maintenance of Finnish sovereignty, these were not to be acceded to.[12]

The same group, this time with Wuori replacing Gripenberg, was reconvened for further discussions on 1 March. Between the calling of the two meetings, Colonel Magill of the British section of the Control Commission had informed Enckell that the Allies planned reduction in the armed forces of all the defeated countries, and he had suggested that it might be appropriate for Finland to take some initiative in this area. The Finns, however, were opposed to such a move. Any external pressures were to be resisted. If demands for force reductions were to be made to all the countries that had fought on the German side, it was conceded that Finland would probably have little option but to agree. Any more general reduction of forces proposed under the umbrella of the United Nations would be a separate issue and would not need to be opposed. If restrictions affecting only some, rather than all, of the member states of the United Nations were made the basis for Finland's admission to membership, the government would be forced to reassess the ultimate value of joining the new organization. Membership, in the tense international situation, could cause Finland problems, in addition to any possible benefits it might confer.

The meeting was unanimous in regarding the Soviet Union as the major negotiating party in all matters relating to the peace treaty. Enckell made it clear to Wuori that discussions with Britain would take place only later and along lines laid down by the Foreign Ministry in Helsinki. There was also general agreement that the present state of domestic public opinion would force the delegation to initiate some discussion of the Karelian question in Moscow. Svento, now supported by Wuori, continued to oppose such a move. The delegation as a whole should avoid reference to the issue; any discussions, if they were thought necessary, should be restricted to direct talks between Paasikivi and Stalin.[13]

The resignation of President Mannerheim on 4 March and the change of government that followed delayed the outlining of the plans for the talks in Moscow. Mauno Pekkala was chosen to form the new government after Paasikivi became head of state; Carl Enckell and Reinhold Svento remained as joint foreign ministers. The overall handling of defense matters was divided between Pekkala and the Social Democrat Yrjö Kallinen. The new government included six People's Democrats, five Social Democrats, five Agrarian representatives, two members from outside the coalition, Enckell (belonging to no party), and Törngren from the Swedish People's Party. Kekkonen, Hillilä, and Gartz, the ministers of justice, supply, and trade and industry in the previous government, were omitted from the new cabinet; the move was considered at the time as signaling a strengthening of the left.[14] Paasikivi, however, warned Hamilton against overestimating leftist influence in the new government, emphasizing that on major issues he, as president of the republic, would remain in overall charge.[15]

The situation in Finland by the early spring of 1946, according to a report compiled by the American legation in Helsinki and sent to Washington on 12 March, was steadily stabilizing. The Soviet Union's main aim in the area seemed to be one of security, and events pointed to a sincere Soviet attempt to establish good neighborly relations rather than any desire to destroy Finland's independence. But the Russians were strict in requiring compliance to the letter with the terms of the armistice agreement, a fact that occasionally led to minor disagreements with the Finns over its interpretation. Hulley nevertheless underlined the fact that, although the Soviet Union was not bent on expansion along its northwestern frontier, Moscow kept a careful watch that Finland remained within its sphere of influence and showed obvious distrust of Helsinki's Scandinavian contacts. There was, however, no cause for open disagreement between the United States and the Soviet Union over Finland. At most it could be argued that reparations deliveries restricted and hampered the development of Finnish-American trade, but it had to be remembered that the final figure of $300 million had been decided upon with the full knowledge of the American government. As long as the peace treaty remained unsigned and the Control Commission remained in existence, both being circumstances that often prevented the government from making decisions on important questions, Hulley did not believe that the Finns could be masters of their own country.[16]

This latter point was mentioned by Carl Enckell in a meeting with Maxwell Hamilton on his return to Finland on 21 March. The signing of the treaty, Enckell emphasized, would have a great psychological effect on the whole country and would assure the people of the continuity of Finnish independence and national sovereignty, while at the same time bringing about the termination of the Control

Commission. Despite the disagreements that had erupted over the Commission's sphere of activity (and the foreign minister made no attempt to hide his criticism of that body), Enckell believed that in general the Commission had acted fairly and correctly. Enckell also emphasized the significance of good relations with the Soviet Union. Those handful of Finns who imagined that a clash between the Great Powers would bring any advantage to Finland were simply laughable, according to Enckell.[17]

Throughout the spring of 1946, the Finnish Foreign Ministry tried in vain— through its various representatives abroad—to learn what it could of the content of the peace treaty being drawn up by the Great Powers.[18] Wuori was able to report on 5 April that he had heard from Gusev that the latter had given the Soviet draft to the British and that discussions had begun; however, Wuori was told that the armistice terms covering the ceded territories and the size of Finland's war reparations would not be amended. Neither Gusev nor the British Foreign Office was willing to provide Wuori with a copy of the Soviet proposal. The discussions between the deputy foreign ministers on the draft were also declared secret.[19] The Finns now had little choice but to take some sort of initiative if they wanted to have any say in deciding their future.

A meeting of the government's foreign affairs committee on 9 April, chaired by President Paasikivi, was dominated by uncertainty as to whether the Soviet Union would look favorably upon separate bilateral discussions on the treaty with the Finnish authorities. It was finally and unanimously decided, providing a positive response was received from Orlov in Helsinki, to send a government delegation to Moscow, led by the prime minister, to put Finland's case. Paasikivi was particularly emphatic in his belief that no opportunity of advancing the Finnish cause should be left untried, "for the sake of our country and our future." Pekkala proposed that talks be prefaced with a survey of Finland's present problems, before any attempt was made to pass on to debate of the more long-term issues. Paasikivi reiterated his view that the territorial question should also be aired at some stage, despite the admittedly small chance of any Soviet concessions on the matter. "The issue has to be clarified one way or the other so that the government cannot be accused of having stood idly by," he declared. But the delegation would have to be particularly careful of its choice of words in any discussions and ready to adopt a flexible approach.[20]

Pekkala was able to tell the committee on 13 April that Orlov had confirmed that a Finnish delegation would be welcome to visit Moscow and would be received by Molotov and perhaps also by Stalin. Because Molotov would be taking part in the conference of Allied foreign ministers scheduled to begin in Paris on 25 April, it was suggested that the delegation leave as soon as possible. At Paasikivi's suggestion, Pekkala was joined on the delegation by Törngren, Leino, Svento, Takki, and Vesterinen, all government ministers. Pekkala proposed that the Finnish case to be put in the Soviet capital be drawn up on the basis of the discussions that had taken place in Helsinki during the spring, and in such a way as to allow the delegation a fair measure of room for tactical maneuvers. It might prove possible, Pekkala conceded, to bring up the views of the Karelian evacuees.

Paasikivi broadly agreed, while reiterating his conviction that the Saimaa canal, Viipuri, and Porkkala problems also warranted inclusion in the discussions. The Jäniskoski area in Lapland could be offered as compensation. The delegation was also instructed to lobby for the reduction of the war reparations payment to $200 million, in line with a proposal drawn up by Lauri Kivinen, the director of the War Reparations Commission. But the question of a defense pact with the Soviet Union was best left undiscussed, according to Paaskivi's instructions, until after the actual signing of the peace. "General Zhdanov referred to the matter last year in private conversations first with the then president and later with the prime minister, but little progress was made on the issue in Moscow, as we were later informed. There is no cause for us to refer to the issue at this stage, unless it is brought up by the Soviet side." [21]

Before the delegation's final departure for Moscow on 17 April, the government made an official announcement to the nation of its intentions and the prime minister gave a radio speech in which he warned against excessive optimism at what the delegation might be able to achieve. Referring to the possibility of the delegation's discussing the shape of the final peace treaty, Pekkala emphasized that as a defeated country Finland could do no more than present its wishes to the Allies. [22]

Although the Foreign Office had been warned by Wuori of the Finnish government's decision to send a delegation to Moscow, the news of its departure nevertheless quickly became the cause of intense speculation in London. The British initially seemed unwilling to believe that the initiative was Finland's, rather suspecting that it was part of a Soviet attempt to increase pressure on the Finnish government—possibly with the aim of forcing Finland to accede to a military treaty of some sort, or as a prelude to concluding a separate peace with Helsinki. Revealing its obvious unease at the development, the Foreign Office instructed Shepherd to make clear its view to the Finnish Foreign Ministry that nothing should be allowed to take place in Moscow that would adversely affect Finland's trading relations with the West. Enckell did what he could to allay these British fears. [23]

To avoid possible misunderstandings with the Americans on the matter, Enckell also decided to forewarn the United States of the delegation's departure. The visit, Enckell emphasized to Hamilton, was being undertaken on Finland's own initiative in an attempt to ascertain the nature of the eventual peace terms to be imposed on the country, to voice Finland's views on them before they were finally agreed upon, and to discuss possible Soviet grain shipments to Finland. The discussions were to take place in Moscow because the Soviet Union was the main Allied power affected by the Finnish treaty. General Zhdanov had made it clear to the Finnish authorities that his role in Helsinki was solely limited to monitoring compliance with the terms of the armistice agreement and that he was in no position to discuss their possible modification. The delegation specifically included members from all the government parties to allow them the opportunity, at the earliest possible stage, of building up a picture based on first-hand information of what Finland could realistically expect from the final treaty. Hamilton's question as to whether there was any intention of bringing up the matter of the defense pact broached the previous spring was met by a denial that such a move was contemplated. Any such pact was only possible after the peace treaty had been signed, Enckell declared. Hamilton's subsequent reports to Washington show, however, that he was not convinced that Enckell had (as he put it) told him "the whole truth." The Finns' "eagerness" to discuss the peace treaty could reduce the country's ultimate scope for maneuver with the Soviet Union. It seemed more than likely that the Kremlin would use the discussions to put new, probably economic, demands to the Finns. Helsinki would have done better, Hamilton concluded, to have let the treaty negotiations proceed at their own pace in Paris. Hamilton underlined his belief, however, that there was no reason for any American involvement in the new development.[24]

The events that followed soon proved the West's fears groundless. The Finnish delegation led by Prime Minister Mauno Pekkala arrived in Moscow on 17 April and received a warm welcome from Molotov and his deputy, Dekanosov. They met Stalin the following day.[25] Pekkala presented the Soviet Government with a comprehensive survey, based on the discussions that had taken place in Helsinki, of what the Finnish authorities hoped could be incorporated into the final treaty. Particular attention was drawn to the economic hardships that Finland was suffering as a result of the armistice agreement. Insofar as it was possible for Finland to have a say in the shape of the future treaty, the delegation made it clear that a reduction of $100 million in the size of the country's war reparations would be of major benefit and would assist Finland in complying with its other armistice obligations.

The closure of the Saimaa canal was also identified as the cause of significant damage to the Finnish economy while not being of any visible benefit to the Soviet Union. The delegation explained:

> If a way could be found to reopen the Saimaa canal to Finnish use, it would be logical to return, to Finnish administration, the Russian bridgehead on the northwestern shore of the Bay of Viipuri, which in any case probably has little military significance. The same would go for the town of Viipuri itself and its immediate environs. The present status of the Koivisto islands, on the other hand, would remain unchanged. The question of the harbor at Uuras at the mouth of the Bay of Viipuri and its future use is also naturally of great interest to the Finnish government.

Pekkala also expressed his government's hope that the northern part of the Porkkala area could be returned to improve Finland's internal communications, and he mentioned the possibility of ceding the Jäniskoski power station in Lapland, together with its immediate surroundings, to the Soviet Union as compensation.

Pekkala concluded his survey with a reference to the fact that the resettlement of the Karelian evacuee population was proving one of the country's most intractable problems. "There is still a strong hope among the Karelians that they may one day be able to return to their old homes, and they feel that some way may eventually be found to allow this to happen. The most optimistic of them think that a large part of Karelia and North Karelia, in particular, down to the River Vuoksi might be returned," Pekkala admitted.[26]

In his reply the next day, Stalin stressed the importance of the terms incorporated in the armistice agreement in forming the basis for the future peace treaty, especially on the question of the ceded territories. "Further inquiries as to whether any border modifications were in fact possible were met by a strong Soviet denial." Any reduction of Finland's reparations obligation would be difficult, but Stalin agreed nevertheless to consider the matter and return to it later. Stalin also invited his Finnish visitors to reflect on the fact that their country had not been occupied, something in itself of significant economic benefit. Svento described the Soviet leader as then going on to say, in something of a "dryly humorous vein," that he had heard that "being occupied is not in any case an especially pleasant affair." Stalin, however, agreed in principle to transit traffic on the Saimaa canal and on the Porkkala rail line, with the proviso that both matters would have to be separately agreed. The communiqué issued at the end of the talks only referred to the Soviet Union's positive attitude to "improving Finland's communications."

The major immediate economic benefit to result to Finland from the delegation's visit came in the form of the Finnish authorities being given permission to end the return of captured Soviet material as of 1 May. A $30 million trade exchange agreement was also signed on 30 April, giving Finland 100,000 tons of Soviet grain in return for supplying the Soviet Union with prefabricated wooden houses and temporary buildings, cellulose, and other goods. Finland also agreed in principle to grant the Soviet Union access to the Jäniskoski power station to guarantee the energy requirements of the Petsamo nickel mines.[27] While the Moscow talks thus clearly showed that the Kremlin wished to continue its policy of constructive cooperation with Helsinki, they nevertheless failed to provide any real sign of Soviet movement on the modifications to the armistice agreement terms to be incorporated into the final peace treaty that had been hoped for by the Finnish government.

The Foreign Office in London described the results of the Pekkala delegation's visit to Moscow as "interesting," primarily because there had apparently been no discussion of the signing of a joint Finnish-Soviet military agreement.[28] Shepherd reported from Helsinki that, despite the economic concessions that had been won, there was a general sense of disappointment in the country that no changes had been agreed upon concerning the territorial clauses of the armistice agreement, which seemed all the worse when there appeared to be even less hope of changes being achieved in Paris. The government view, as communicated by Enckell to Shepherd, seemed to be that the Allied foreign ministers, faced with having to resolve so many important and difficult problems, would as likely as not have little time to concern themselves with the details of a small country like Finland. It seemed that the Allies intended leaving Finland with no alternative beyond pleading its case at the twenty-one-nation peace conference, as and when it met—a course of action, Enckell complained, that did not readily recommend itself to the Finnish authorities. In fact, Enckell concluded, the Finnish government would perhaps be forced to decide that there would be little point in sending a delegation to Paris at all. Finland had lost two wars and would simply have to accept the terms dictated to it by the Allies.

Enckell emphasized the nature of the Continuation War as a Finnish-Soviet affair. Consequently, the peace settlement would largely be a matter between these two countries. Details of the treaty relevant to Britain could be discussed later. Finland's awareness of the Soviet Union's dominant interest in the treaty issue, Enckell explained, had decided the government to send a delegation to Moscow. There had, however, been high hopes of its achieving more than it did; despite the delegates' warm reception by the Soviet leadership, a general sense of pessimism together with a "feeling of helplessness" had subsequently begun to gain ground. The tense situation was further exacerbated by the events instigated by what Enckell described as "irresponsible elements" on the right and partly directed at the Control Commission which had taken place during the annual May Day celebrations, and various disturbances and demonstrations supported by the communists, in which it was feared the Soviet Union might be involved.

Enckell gave Shepherd the impression of being much more fearful of the Soviet Union's intentions than at any time since the autumn of 1944. Shepherd, however, warned the Foreign Office against reading too much into this apparent change of attitude, which could be purely temporary and likely to change as time went on. The fact of Mannerheim's recent resignation was also seen by Shepherd as a contributing factor in the increasing sense of gloom in the Finnish capital. Paasikivi, for all the respect he undoubtedly enjoyed, did not seem to be identified in the public mind as such an unbending defender of Finnish independence as his predecessor. The omission of Gartz, Kekkonen, and Hillilä from the new government did little to strengthen its hand, which Shepherd judged weaker than Paasikivi's previous administration. Although communist influence in the government appeared to be growing under the leadership of Yrjö Leino, the minister of the interior, Shepherd saw no reason for supposing that the Soviet Union was preparing to change its overall policy toward Finland, which up until then had been one of securing what had been achieved under the terms of the armistice agreement by purely legitimate means.[29]

There seems little reason to dispute the fact that the pessimism described by Shepherd did actually exist. Contemporary sources of the period abound with comparisons of the activities of the communists of the time with apparently parallel events in Estonia during the summer of 1940. It clearly served the purpose of the Finnish political leadership, however, to emphasize the difficulties facing the country to the British, thereby gaining some potentially useful sympathy from the latter, who had played no part in the negotiations that had taken place in Moscow. The Finns hoped that the Soviet Union's preeminent position as regards Finland, something that was particularly underlined to the British government, would also act as a form of preliminary justification for the low profile that would probably have to be adopted in any later discussions of the peace question.

Jutila informed the American government on 26 April of what had been achieved at the talks in Moscow. After listening to Jutila's account of the visit, drawn up in line with the instructions that had been circulated by the Foreign Ministry in Helsinki and carefully stressing its positive aspects, Hugh Cumming of the State Department seemed satisfied that Pekkala's delegation had scored a success.[30] Back in Helsinki, Hamilton was assured by Enckell that no decision on the signing of a military agreement had been taken in Moscow. The Finnish government, the latter explained, considered that issues of this type could only logically be discussed after the peace treaty itself had been signed. Enckell also used his discussion with Hamilton to reiterate the Finnish government's belief that only the speediest possible signing of the final peace treaty would allow the country to regain its equilibrium and independence and free itself of the presence of the Control Commission. Many of the details of the Control Commission's views on national issues would, if they were to become public knowledge, be instrumental in an upswing of anti-Soviet opinion, Enckell suggested. This had meant a heavy burden of responsibility both on the president and the government to resolve disagreements with the Commission with a minimum of fuss and publicity. The government was also obliged, Enckell argued, to do everything in its power to convince the Finnish people that unforced harmonious relations with the Soviet Union were in the country's best interests, a task that would be made much easier by the signing of the peace and all that it would bring in its wake. The Allies, however, had yet to inform Finland of the treaty's contents, the timetable of its drafting, or to what degree and when Finland's views would be heard as part of that process.[31]

Hamilton was well aware that the bilateral talks in Moscow would not by themselves automatically precipitate or require any change in America's established policy of noninvolvement in Finnish affairs. Enckell, in his various discussions with Hamilton, was careful not to give the impression that Finland was looking for overt American support, and he told Hamilton that the Kremlin would consider such an initiative on Helsinki's part as an unfriendly act toward the Soviet Union, thus worsening Finland's international position.[32]

Although agreeing with Enckell, Hamilton nevertheless feared that the situation facing the Finnish government might become more difficult after the signing of the peace agreement. Many Finns would then inevitably begin to question the value of continued close cooperation with the Soviet Union, after the policy had apparently served its main purpose of gaining Finland the best possible peace terms. It was important that American policy should do nothing to support any development of this kind of attitude because it would be both damaging to Finland's interests and, generally, "from the point of view of the kind of Finland we would like to see continue to exist." Future American policy toward Finland— after the signing of the peace treaty—although retaining its positive and friendly nature, should remain cautious. A reversal of this type of policy would probably not bring any large-scale conflict of interest between the United States and the Soviet Union, but it would probably cause an increase of Soviet pressure on Helsinki, which in the long run would be detrimental to America's presence and influence in the area. United States interests would best be served, Hamilton concluded, by a continuation of its previously adopted policy, with its strong emphasis on caution and overall restraint.[33] That *both* the superpowers continued to accept the status quo in Finland, considering it the best possible in their individual interests, only further underlined the country's unique position among the defeated countries of Europe on the eve of the Paris peace conference.

The spring and summer of 1946 saw the Finnish Foreign Ministry continue its persistent attempts to find out through its diplomats abroad what was happening in Paris; more precisely, they sought to discover when any information would be released on the contents of the treaty and where and how it could be commented on.[34] The results were modest. Johan Helo in Paris reported back to Helsinki in May that the Finnish question generally seemed to be considered relatively uncomplicated by the Allies; as a result, it had not generated much discussion. The apparent delay in progress on the treaty was largely caused by the other problems encountered by the Council of Foreign Ministers. "All are sympathetic toward Finland and hope the best for her, but feel that the solution to the problem lies with the Soviet Union and that Finland should avoid becoming overanxious and attempting to pursue the matter too intently."[35]

The Foreign Ministry in Helsinki wanted to know in particular whether Finland should take the initiative and send a delegation to Paris, as the Balkan countries had done, or whether it would be better to wait for an official invitation. Helo favored the latter option. The French disliked behind-the-scenes tactics, which would probably not do anything to advance the Finnish case, Helo suggested—a view supported by Soviet Deputy Foreign Minister Dekanosov.[36]

But the Helsinki government's anxiety continued to grow. Rumors reaching the Finnish capital described the British as having put forward proposals directly infringing Finnish sovereignty during the course of the talks in Paris, which the Soviet Union had opposed. Nobody seemed sure of what they might be, although Wuori speculated that they might have to do with the establishment of Allied consulates and restrictions on the army, which it was known the Soviet Union opposed.[37]

Wuori's further inquiries of Philip Noel-Baker at the Foreign Office, at the end of June, about information on progress in Paris and when the views of the defeated countries were to be heard met with little response. "Mr. Noel-Baker said that he thought it was very difficult to foresee the future, but that he would make enquiries from Paris and that if he had anything useful to say he would write to Mr. Wuori."[38] Noel-Baker kept his promise, writing to Wuori a month later; but by that time the Finnish authorities had managed to get the information they wanted directly from Paris. The French deputy foreign minister, Maurice Couve de Murville, told Helo on 8 July that the peace conference, rather than the Council of Foreign Ministers, would invite delegations from all the defeated countries to the French capital to put their views and that copies of the draft treaties would be included with the invitations. Delegations could arrive unofficially before receipt of an official invitation if they wished, Couve de Murville added.[39] Jutila in Washington, in contrast, was kept totally in the dark by the State Department on the whole question; he was told as late as 23 July that no information could be provided on issues in which the United States was not directly involved.[40]

Ironically, the Finnish authorities were nevertheless being criticized for their reticence in the recent handling of their affairs at about the same time by Hector McNeil, parliamentary under-secretary at the Foreign Office. Wuori's argument that Helsinki had considered the Soviet Union as Finland's main negotiating party failed to soften McNeil, who refused to be drawn out on the question of whether Finland could rely on Western support in the future talks. Wuori believed, as he told Helsinki, that McNeil's criticism was largely motivated by an attempt to place as much responsibility for the final treaty as possible on the shoulders of the Finnish government. If Helsinki failed to make any radical suggestions for changes in the draft treaty (which, despite all the government's requests, had yet to be seen), the West could always claim that Finland had not made use of the opportunities it had been offered. Wuori was forced to conclude in the circumstances that the task of any Finnish delegation in Paris would be far from easy.[41]

There was no doubt in Helsinki that it would be anything else but difficult.

Enckell, speaking at a meeting of the foreign affairs committee of the Finnish Parliament on 11 July, made every effort to counter the members' somewhat overly optimistic hopes. He underlined the fact that the Paris conference would be much less of a peace conference in the traditional sense of the term than perhaps they imagined; it would be much more of an intermediate stage (required for tactical reasons) in the treaty drafting process, preparatory to the treaties eventually being dictated to the defeated countries by the Allies. "This procedure is obviously intended to give to the peace treaties the character of agreements that have been generally approved and are to that extent just." The proposed invitation of the defeated countries to Paris to put their cases was part of the same arrangement; far from holding out the posssibility of real participation in the negotiations, it would as likely amount simply to providing any additional information as and when and if required by the Allies.[42]

The long-awaited treaty draft finally came into Finnish hands on July 23, in something of an unconventional and unexpected way. In the course of a routine call paid on Helo in Paris by a Chinese diplomatic colleague, who also happened to be one of his neighbors, Helo asked whether his colleague knew anything of the content of the Finnish draft treaty. The Chinese official replied

> that he certainly knew, because the whole proposal was at that moment in his briefcase. I was surprised at this openness, normally uncommon among diplomats. I was all the more surprised when the Chinese official took some papers from his case and showed them to me. I tried not to show my surprise and casually asked whether I might glance at them. Why not, was the reply. I looked at them and said that I would like to make some notes on various points. He nodded.
>
> I took the documents into the legation's office and marked those sections which I wanted copied quickly. I then returned to my office and did what I could to entertain my visitor. Every so often I went out to the office on some pretext to see how far the copying had got. By the time my visitor finally rose to leave the major part of his papers had been copied. I returned his proposal and thanked him, bowing as politely and as profusely as he did.[43]

It seems unlikely that the Chinese official's action in showing the draft to Helo formed part of any premeditated policy on China's part. Rather, it is more than probable that the Chinese diplomat merely wished to satisfy a simple request from a colleague and neighbor on a matter that held little or no significance for his country's interests. Helo received the official Russian- and English-language texts of the treaty a week after the unofficial version on 30 July, after the conference had already begun. A formal invitation for Finland to participate, however, was still not forthcoming.

PART VI
The Paris Peace Conference

17   Talks Get Under Way

The long-awaited twenty-one-nation peace conference was finally convened in Paris at the end of July 1946. Its task was to scrutinize the draft treaties drawn up for Italy, Rumania, Bulgaria, Hungary and Finland by the Allied Council of Foreign Ministers. Soldiers of the *Garde Républicaine,* resplendent in their red and white dress uniforms, lined the way when the fifteen hundred delegates (but not including those of the defeated countries) arrived at the official opening at the Palais du Luxembourg on 29 July. French Foreign Minister Georges Bidault formally welcomed everybody to the French capital "for the second time in less than thirty years to discuss the settlement of the postwar world." Bidault underlined his hope that, despite the difficulty of the task facing them, the assembled delegates would do everything in their power to come to "if not ideal, at least reasonable solutions."

Georges Bidault's anxiety soon proved justified. The first two weeks of the conference's plenary session meetings were taken up by a long series of largely rhetorical, mandatory opening speeches given by the delegates of each participant country. The conference's procedural committee, meeting simultaneously, initially proved the more important focus of serious discussion. Herbert Evatt, the Australian foreign minister, hoping to assert his leadership of the delegations from the smaller nations, proposed that all conference decisions be made "according to democratic principles" on a basis of simple majority decisions. Molotov, supported by the delegates from what was already a clearly defined "Eastern bloc" (made up of the Soviet Union, the Ukraine, Byelorussia, Poland, Czechoslovakia, and Yugoslavia), rejected Evatt's proposal, reiterating his advocacy of the Council of Foreign Ministers' recommendation of the adoption of a two-thirds majority principle—which Byrnes, on the other hand, emphasized had been nothing more than a recommendation. A compromise solution was suggested

227

by the British delegation, allowing the conference to present the Allied foreign ministers with resolutions approved both by simple majority and two-thirds majority decisions. After much argument, the conference's plenary session finally approved the British proposal on 9 August by fifteen votes to the six votes of the Eastern bloc. Byrnes considered the result a "moral victory" for the conference, entrusted as it was with the role of acting as the "world's conscience," and indicative of the freedom it gave small countries to voice their opinions. The Western Allies should take every opportunity, Byrnes thought, to underline the "undemocratic nature" of the Soviet Union and its policies. The very bitterness of the argument over the question of majority decisions showed that both sides held out little real hope of the conference being able to work on the basis of consensual decision making.

As part of his attempt to mobilize world opinion against the Soviet Union Byrnes demanded free access for journalists to all conference proceedings at both general assembly and commission levels to ensure what he described as public accountability. Nothing was to remain secret. The publicity surrounding Byrnes's proposal made it impossible for any of the other delegations openly to oppose its adoption: by acquiescing, however, they ruled out the possibility of any serious negotiations taking place during the course of the conference. Aware that what they said would be communicated to the world at large and not only to their fellow conference participants, delegates were forced to direct the main burden of their arguments to a notional international audience. After its resolution of the procedural disagreement over majority decisions on 9 August, the conference's general assembly decided to allow the representatives of the various defeated countries to put their views before discussion moved on to the detailed study of the treaty drafts by the conference's specialist commissions. The conference secretariat was rather slow in implementing this decision, however: Finland only received an official invitation to attend, through the legation in Paris, on 14 August.[1]

Before the final convocation of the conference, Britain's diplomatic representatives in the defeated countries of Europe had been asked by the Foreign Office for their opinions on the draft treaties proposed for their respective countries.[2] Shepherd considered the reference in the preamble of the Finnish treaty to Finland as an "ally" of Hitler's Germany inappropriate; he thought the term "associated state" more applicable. With regard to Article 7, covering the freeing of political prisoners and the repealing of discriminatory legislation, Shepherd thought that the Finnish authorities would probably like to have the section omitted in which they were to be obliged . . . "to complete these measures" because all the necessary action referred to in the clause had already been taken. Article 8, which covered the banning of fascist organizations and propaganda directed against the Soviet Union and other UN countries, was also thought unnecessary by Shepherd in the light of Moscow's possible aims, and more than a little dangerous because of its imprecise formulation. Shepherd's comments — that the British position adopted in the Anglo-Soviet argument over the interpretation and follow-up of the treaty had been better judged and more practical — are hardly surprising.[3]

Despite Shepherd's observations, the Foreign Office decided that the reference in the preamble to the alliance between Finland and Germany did not warrant modification; any changes could be left to the Finns if they wanted to contest the issue in Paris. There was no reason, furthermore, to oppose the Finns if (as Shepherd supposed) they wanted to shorten Article 7, providing they were able to show that they had already instituted action in all the areas required in the draft. Recommending the omission of Article 8, in contrast, did not appear possible; it had been jointly approved by the Council of Foreign Ministers, and the Russians would no doubt reply by demanding the omission of the comparable article from the Balkan agreements, "thereby depriving us of a lever, however weak it may be, against the creation of organizations which have as their aim a denial to the people of their democratic rights."[4]

The Foreign Office chose not to consult the British section of the Control Commission in Helsinki on the military articles of the draft treaty or the likely difficulties to be encountered in implementing and monitoring them, a fact that surprised and annoyed the British officers in Helsinki, frustrated as they were by lack of work. They nevertheless made their opinions known to London and in particular their uncertainty over what was meant by the phrase "local defense of frontiers," over who would be charged with deciding which particular fortifications were to be allowed, and over what was meant by the phrase "the situation as at present existing" with regard to the Åland Islands. They believed that, although the islands had already been demilitarized, it would be more precise to refer to their legal or "international status." The British officers also reminded London that any limitation of the strength of the Finnish navy had to take account of its present mine clearance duties, which were likely to extend some considerable time into the future.[5]

The Foreign Office in its reply to Helsinki and instructions to Paris accepted, in principle, the legitimacy of the Commission's comments on the Åland Islands and the fact that the proposed changes would clarify the article; nevertheless, it believed that it was probably too late to change the clause unless the Finns were to bring the matter up themselves in Paris. There was good reason, however, to include a separate clause in the draft treaty allowing for a temporarily larger Finnish navy to enable Finland to complete its task of mine clearance. The reference in the treaty to fortifications, the Foreign Office argued, was not of great significance in Finland's case and had been included mainly to cover the Balkan countries. If Finland at some time in the future was to initiate a conspicuously extensive fortification program, however, "the word [fortifications] would give us a handle by which we might investigate her motives." The term "local

defense of frontiers'' referred to a defense capability commensurate with countering aggression from small nations in the area, rather than one with a potential
to threaten neighboring countries.[6]

Shepherd described initial Finnish reaction to the peace terms as reserved;
there was some satisfaction that the Control Commission would finally disappear
and that Finland might be relieved of some of the economic burden imposed by
the armistice agreement. Although the Karelian evacuee population continued
to organize meetings across the country, drumming up support for proposals to
modify the 1944 borders, Shepherd nevertheless believed it unlikely that many
people still thought significant changes to the proposed terms likely, with the
exception of the war reparations clause.[7] The Finns' determined desire to try,
however, was to surprise Shepherd. Hamilton reported back to Washington that
Helsinki's main hopes were focused on the possibility of changes to the economic
clauses of the armistice, changes that Hamilton thought would be in American
interests to support.[8]

On one of Gripenberg's visits to Helsinki, Paasikivi had stressed his continued
belief in the necessity of making plain to the peace conference ''that we cannot
be satisfied with any arrangement which would irrevocably strip us of the province
of Viipuri. . . .'' Gripenberg agreed: ''Our delegates should ask—politely, but
firmly—whether we have the right to voice our opinions. If we are denied the
right to speak, we will have to remain silent, but if we are allowed to, we should
put our case.''[9]

The State Council met on 19 July at the prime minister's summer residence
at Kesäranta to select the delegation to go to the conference. In spring, Paasikivi
had proposed that Carl Enckell head the delegation. This was now countered by
a Communist proposal advocating the naming of Mauno Pekkala in Enckell's
stead, the inclusion of Yrjö Leino, minister of the interior, and the removal of
the foreign minister from the delegation altogether. Enckell, aware of the plan
to remove him beforehand, had offered his resignation to Paasikivi on 17 July,
but this had been refused.[10]

It was against this background that Paasikivi made his ''tactful'' comments
at the Kesäranta meeting when discussion moved to the roles to be assumed by
Leino and Pekkala. What had the ''minister of police'' to do in Paris, on what
was after all a matter of foreign policy? Paasikivi likewise expressed his opposition
to the idea of replacing Enckell with Pekkala as the head of the delegation.
''Mauno Pekkala is simply not suited to lead the delegation to the peace conference. . . . We have a foreign minister in any case, who can speak French and
is quite capable of representing his country.'' Leino relates how, at this point,
''Mauno rose sharply from the table and went out into a side room. A moment
or two later—he had probably gone to take some Dutch courage from the hip
flask he always carried—he came back and said: 'Well then, why didn't the
president choose Enckell as prime minister, if he is such a great man?' '' Heikkilä

describes Pekkala as walking down to a jetty on the seashore when he left the room. "He was beside himself. When he leaned over toward the water, one did not know whether he was judging the suitability of his reflected face for Paris, or whether he intended drowning himself in the momentary depression caused by the insult he felt he had suffered."[11]

The debate between the ministers went on for some time after Pekkala had returned and was only finally concluded by the latter's being chosen to lead the delegation, with Enckell as his deputy. There was also some argument over the proposed inclusion of Cay Sundström and Eero Wuori in the delegation, which was finally resolved by deciding to include them—together with Johan Helo—as "political advisers." Yrjö Leino from the Communists, Väinö Voionmaa from the Social Democrats, Lennart Heljas from the Agrarian Party, and John Österholm from the Swedish People's Party were chosen (in addition to Pekkala and Enckell) to make up the main body of the delegation. The delegation as a whole, including its specialist advisers, finally numbered about thirty. Tauno Suontausta was chosen to act as its main secretary.[12]

Enckell subsequently emphasized to Shepherd that the Finnish government's decision to wait for an official invitation to Paris before sending its delegation had not been the result of indifference on Helsinki's part, but rather a desire to avoid unnecessary political chicanery and to distance Finland from the actions of the Balkan countries with which Finland, with her strong democratic traditions, did not want to be too closely associated. Enckell complained that, despite this caution on Finland's part, the government had nevertheless been denied the opportunity of presenting its views to the Council of Foreign Ministers *before* the drafting of the treaty.[13]

The general instructions issued to the delegation going to Paris, signed by Paasikivi on 9 August, stated that it was to be remembered at all stages of the talks that "the achievement and maintenance of permanent and positive friendly relations with the Soviet Union lie at the very basis of Finnish foreign policy." The Finnish case was therefore to be put with the utmost care and caution. "The delegation should also avoid giving the Russians any impression that we are intriguing behind their backs against the Soviet Union," the instructions added. The delegation was further instructed to underline in any discussions on territorial matters the economic and historical significance that Karelia and Porkkala held for Finland. Their importance dictated that "the Finnish government, in its role as representative of the interests of the Finnish people, cannot avoid presenting Finland's views and hopes on the matter." Leino's doubts voiced during the preceding discussions as to the necessity of referring to the ceded areas had been countered by Paasikivi's reply that all that was envisaged was a simple statement of fact and by Pekkala's admission that, in the final analysis, the issue could not be ignored altogether.

On the question of Finland's economic situation and war reparations, the delegation was instructed to draw attention to the size of the burden imposed on the country in comparison with that of other reparations agreed upon after World War II and to do all it could to get the figure reduced. The instructions' declaration that "one of our most important aims in the talks is to ensure the maintenance of Finland's sovereign independence and her traditional Scandinavian democratic order" reflected Paasikivi's anxiety about Articles 6-9 and 33 of the draft treaty, which covered general civil rights and freedoms, discriminatory legislation, fascist organizations and propaganda, war criminals, and the subsequent monitoring of compliance with the treaty. The delegation was also given detailed instructions about specific articles of the treaty.[14] Paasikivi considered that many of the treaty's articles, as they stood, were imprecise and open to different interpretations—as his comment that "any Finnish law student who wrote such a text would be failed" makes clear.[15] An introductory speech to be given to the general assembly of the Paris conference, drawn up by Voionmaa, Enckell, and Suontausta, was approved at a meeting chaired by Paasikivi three days later on 12 August.[16]

The Helsinki government was aware from the outset that Finland would be unable to count on Western support for any of the changes it thought necessary to the treaty terms, terms that it was clear were largely of Moscow's making. Nonetheless, Paasikivi hoped to keep open the possibility of modifications to the terms at a later date in direct talks with Moscow; he underlined both to the government and the delegation the importance of Finland's being clearly seen in Paris as making some attempt to present its views and counterarguments to the Allies and not as simply accepting the terms dictated to it. The Kremlin, despite its uncompromising public stance, had expressed its surprise back in the spring of 1944 that the Finnish authorities had not made definite counterproposals to the terms then presented to Paasikivi and Enckell.[17]

The government was also aware that its public stance in Paris would, at least in part, have to reflect the feelings of the population at large. A large number of Finns—and not solely those from the ceded territories—conceived of the Paris peace conference as an international supreme court of sorts, called into existence to correct the injustices of the postwar world. This fact could not be brushed aside, despite all the demands that Finland's adoption of Realpolitik imposed, as Paasikivi admitted to a meeting of Parliament's foreign affairs committee. "When we are invited to Paris and asked to express our views, it will be difficult to go and simply say that we are satisfied with the treaty presented to us."[18]

The frequent references to the government's responsibilities to the people and to Finland's future, which were typical of Paasikivi's comments of the time, can also be linked to his early experiences as a peace negotiator. He had suffered sharp criticism for his part in the 1920 Tartu Peace Treaty between Finland and the Soviet Union, which had been widely attacked as a sellout by right-wing circles. Although the situation in 1946 was not directly comparable to the one

Paasikivi had experienced in 1920, he remained keenly and constantly aware of the government's need to be able to demonstrate to the public at large that it was doing all it could to lighten the burden that Finland had been made to bear as a result of its defeat. The government, Paasikivi was also aware, could not be indifferent to the sort of impression Finland's stance in Paris made on a world largely unfamiliar with Finnish affairs and politics and one from which Finland had been isolated by years of war. The government was faced, in broad terms, with two possible courses of action, as Max Jakobson has observed; "either that of taking the part of the criminal repenting his crime, who confessing to his guilt submits to his just punishment, or that of presenting Finland's case, without attempting to ask forgiveness for the past, in such a way as to highlight the country's new style of foreign policy, while at the same time bringing out the continuity of Finland's democratic traditions." [19] Paasikivi chose the latter option.

Helo's cable from Paris on 9 August indicating that Italy would be presenting its case to the general assembly of the conference the following day confirmed to Helsinki that Finland would not have long to wait for its turn. Although no official invitation had materialized by 13 August, the delegation finally decided to leave for Paris by air via Stockholm. A free morning in the Swedish capital provided most of the members of the delegation with a welcome opportunity to replenish their wardrobes (which had worn thin during the war years), while Pekkala and Enckell, accompanied by Gripenberg, paid a courtesy visit on Swedish Prime Minister Per Albin Hansson. The Finns, while carefully avoiding any discussion of the territorial issue, underlined their hopes to Hansson of negotiating a reduction in Finland's war reparations, which Stalin had earlier hinted might be possible. [20] Pekkala's delegation continued its journey to Paris by air later the same day.

18 The Finnish "Peace Crisis"

The second phase of the Paris peace conference began on 10 August 1946. One after another, the defeated countries presented their points of view to the assembled delegates. This done, the "ex-satellite" delegations were ushered out of the conference chamber. They were allowed no opportunity to listen to any discussion that their statements might spark off.

The first to speak was Alcide de Gasperi, the Italian foreign minister and prime minister. He pointedly referred to the harshness of the draft treaty for Italy and to its incompatibility with earlier Allied declarations of principle. De Gasperi was critical both of territorial readjustments and the claims for reparations, without presenting any concrete counterproposals. His speech was received in icy, hostile silence. But as de Gasperi left the rostrum and prepared to leave the chamber, Byrnes demonstratively rose from his seat and shook his hand. Justifying this action later, the American secretary of state claimed that de Gasperi had already suffered enough at the hands of Mussolini and the Nazis without the Allies adding to the burden of this old protagonist of democracy. As Byrnes openly admitted in his memoirs, however, he was seeking by this gesture "to win over the confidence and friendship of the new Italy" against the Soviet Union.

The foreign ministers of Rumania, Bulgaria, and Hungary, on the other hand, were eager to praise the generosity of the Kremlin toward them, as in the very reasonable demands for reparations. The demands for compensation by the Western powers and their nationals for property lost or destroyed were denounced as excessive. In addition, Bulgaria launched into an attack on Greek "imperialism" in justifying its own claim to Western Thrace, which it had occupied during the war with German assistance.

The statements of the defeated countries created a tense atmosphere in the chamber. Molotov maintained that de Gasperi's speech was in no way a disavowal of fascist imperialism; on the contrary, the new Italy seemed to be treading the same path as its predecessor. The Soviet Union supported Italy's economic revival, but the aims of the West seemed to be geared to bringing the country "under the control of trusts and cartels and certain foreign states." "Certain Great Powers" had taken advantage of World War II to ensure their own enrichment. In comparison with Italy, the situation was entirely different in the former enemy countries in the Balkans, which had resolutely set about realizing democracy in a manner that deserved full support. Molotov also announced that the Soviet Union viewed positively the territorial demands of Bulgaria in Western Thrace.

After Hungarian Foreign Minister Janos Gyöngyösi wound up his speech at the morning session of 15 August, Byrnes deemed the time ripe to launch a fierce counterattack. The object of his wrath was not Hungary, the country on the agenda, but the Soviet Union, "which has falsified our position and motives." The assertions that the Eastern European countries, tailoring their policies to suit Moscow, were more democratic than was Italy was sharply contested by Byrnes. In a strikingly emotional speech, the American secretary of state defended Greece and observed that Molotov, having spoken of "certain Great Powers enriching themselves," had not said anything about the $400 billion paid out by the United States during the war — a sizable chunk of which had gone to aid the Soviet Union in its hour of need.

Deputy Foreign Minister Vyshinsky retorted that it was pointless for the United States, striving for world dominance, to draw attention to the alms that it was distributing to further its own interests. Noticing that the neighboring Czechoslovak delegation was "enthusiastically" applauding Vyshinsky's accusations, Byrnes sent off a telegram during the luncheon interval to the State Department in Washington, directing that a loan to Czechoslovakia be immediately cut off.[1] When Georges Bidault, acting as chairman, opened the afternoon session by inviting in the last delegation to be heard—the Finns—the atmosphere in the conference chamber, especially between the superpowers, was anything but cordial.

The Finnish delegation had arrived in Paris on their own initiative on the evening of 13 August, almost at the last moment. When the long-awaited official invitation was received the following day, it was accompanied by an announcement that Finland would be afforded an opportunity on the 15th to present its views to the plenary session of the peace conference. In their first meeting at their hotel on 14 August, the delegates began to work out their tactics. The original plan was for Prime Minister Pekkala to address the plenary session in Finnish, with translations of his speech distributed to the participants. The "political advisers" on the delegation—Helo, Sundström, and Wuori—were doubtful, however, whether the draft speech approved in Helsinki would satisfy the Soviet Union. The parts dealing with the territorial question should be erased entirely, and the old policy condemned. Otherwise, Molotov might reply to Finland as he had to Italy. Sundström believed that they should follow the example of the Rumanians. Leino was of the same opinion: he suspected that Pekkala had compromised "under pressure" in agreeing to deliver the speech.[2]

At a meeting the following morning, Pekkala announced that he could no longer answer for the speech. Affairs had taken a new turn the previous evening, when the prime minister had visited Molotov in the company of Leino and Sundström. After Pekkala had outlined the details of the speech, the Soviet foreign minister had declared that Finland was now presenting quite new demands. Upon hearing of this visit the following morning—a visit that he regarded as an act of disloyalty by the communists—Foreign Minister Enckell believed that to make the speech now would be tantamount to a protest. The text had either to be changed or an adjournment had to be sought of the conference. After Österholm, Voionmaa, and Heljas had made known their dissatisfaction with the "premature" demarche by the prime minister, which had weakened their negotiating position, the delegation decided to choose the first alternative mentioned by Enckell. Although Leino still persisted in demanding the removal of all mention of territorial issues, he did not entirely get his own way. The text was indeed reworked and abbreviated. References to the Winter War and to Karelia having been, historically and ethnically, a part of Finland for centuries were left out. Instead, mention was made of the economic difficulties caused by the loss of territory—especially Viipuri—and the document stated: "It is understandable that the great significance of the territories to be surrendered has kept alive the hope that some alleviation of the territorial terms of the final peace treaty might be obtained."

It was also proposed that reparations might be reduced "for example, by $100 million," so that "Finland might more easily carry out her obligations." As a result of the events of the world war, "democratic Finland stands as a defeated former enemy before the victorious democratic countries." Reference was also made to Finland's "pioneering position as one of the first states to realize political democracy, which has been and is in stark contrast to Nazism." Having detected the maelstrom into which its war policy was leading the country, the Finnish people had made an end to it and were now "following a new line in order to participate in lasting cooperation with our great eastern neighbor to uphold the peace and good-neighborly relations in this part of Europe." According to a note in the minutes of the meeting of the delegation, the speech was to be made by Enckell, in place of Pekkala, who had disclaimed responsibility. As the final text was prepared only minutes before the delegation set off for the Palais du Luxembourg, it could only be transmitted to the Foreign Ministry in Helsinki after the event.[3]

Enckell read his speech in French to a half-empty chamber after the luncheon interval. After the Finnish delegation was ushered out, the general discussion continued. Theron for South Africa and Alexander for the United Kingdom hoped that the participants would strive to create a more harmonious atmosphere. The prevailing mistrust might seriously jeopardize the final outcome. Generosity should be shown toward the former enemies and especially toward Italy. Talk of the resurgence of fascism in that country was unjustified. Bidault professed his surprise at the great differences of opinion that had been revealed in the conference, not only with regard to the vanquished but also and above all in the relations of the victors. He appealed to all participants for objectivity and harmony. Following his French colleague, Molotov nevertheless regarded it as his duty to repeat the accusations leveled at the Western powers over the treatment of Italy and the Balkan countries. The draft treaties drawn up by the four-power Council of Foreign Ministers had to be adhered to. With regard to Finland, Molotov's speech showed that the last-minute amendments to the text of the speech compiled in Helsinki were not enough. "Forgetting" the Moscow negotiations, he now charged that Finland had made new proposals that had not been conveyed to the notice of the Council of Foreign Ministers. Molotov expected that the armistice terms, which had been signed by Britain and by Finland itself in addition to the Soviet Union, would form the basis of the peace treaty. Because of the security needs of Leningrad and Finland's earlier aggression, no territorial concessions in the direction of the city of the revolution could be agreed to. "I shall not dwell on other territorial questions."

On the question of the reparations obligation, which Finland was facing up to fairly and squarely, Molotov observed that the Soviet Union had already made significant concessions; furthermore, not having to pay the costs of occupation (the only one of the former enemy countries to avoid this burden) meant a considerable lightening of Finland's burden.

> The Soviet Union will pursue a good-neighbor policy toward Finland, provided that Finland also pursues a similar policy toward the Soviet Union, and does not again become yet again a weapon in the hands of other powers, directed against the Soviet Union. There may be those who would like to speculate on differences among the Great Powers. We would not advise our Finnish neighbors to associate themselves with such schemes, or to yield to pressure of this kind. The experiment, in which Finland was used as a tool of the Great Powers, proved to be very detrimental to her. This should not be forgotten.[4]

In an atmosphere heavy with the quarrels of the Great Powers, the Finns had been given a clearly worded warning. To drive home the message, Professor Hans Kruus, an Estonian member of the Soviet delegation, pointed out to his old acquaintance and colleague, the historian Väinö Voionmaa, that Enckell's speech had created a bad impression.[5] The Foreign Office in London also noted that Molotov's words had shut the door on any concessions as far as Finland was concerned.[6]

Molotov's warnings soon had the desired effect. In a telegram to Helsinki on 17 August, the Finnish delegation expressed the view that the territorial question had now clearly been decided once and for all. Paasikivi's idea—relayed to Paris by telephone via the Finnish Foreign Ministry—of some kind of public reaction to the part of Molotov's speech that claimed that Finland had only now expressed its wishes was seen by the delegation as serving no purpose.[7]

The position became clearer when Pekkala and Enckell met Vyshinsky on 19 August to discuss the easing of the terms of the armistice. Molotov's deputy openly expressed the dissatisfaction of the Soviet delegation with the Finns' attempt to procure "the support of fifteen nations against the Soviet Union." Helsinki seemed to be continuing its old policy. "Just try to get the frontier shifted closer to Leningrad with foreign aid, try to do the same with other requests, and you'll soon see where that will lead." The Finns' performance, said Vyshinsky, had put in jeopardy his government's intention of viewing favorably the request to make arrangements for traffic on the Saimaa canal. When Enckell observed that the Soviet Union was judging the Finns' action rather harshly, Vyshinsky replied: "I am not condemning, I'm only warning! . . . One cannot afford to be generous with one's own security." Enckell pointed out that Finland had consistently avoided and would in the future avoid seeking foreign aid, since the terms of the peace depended entirely upon the Soviet Union. Finland had not been offered at any time the chance to present its requests to the four-power Council of Foreign Ministers. Raising the territorial issue was a duty that Finland had to perform in view of the Karelians, living in difficult circumstances. The government, conscious of its responsibilities to the nation, had raised the issue in a modest way when the opportunity had eventually arisen. Finally, both Enckell and Leino acknowledged that the position of the Soviet delegation had now been stated, "and we will take note of it."[8]

With the relations of the Great Powers getting worse at the Paris conference, the Soviet Union did not wish the discussion concerning Finland to add more fuel to the flames. There had been enough displays of Western anti-Soviet feeling already. On the other hand, the Soviet Union was aware of the long-established sympathies for Finland in the West. This could be used by the West as propaganda, and a majority on the commissions might decide to back the amendments proposed by the Finns—which would not be in Soviet interests. This lay behind the warnings against intrigues; furthermore, such activity was no longer considered appropriate to the new framework of relations between Helsinki and Moscow. The Soviet Union had already clearly indicated its position on amendment proposals in April and had reiterated its views to Pekkala and Leino on the evening of 14 August. Had they not relayed the message to the other members of the delegation? Unwilling to accept that the Finns' actions might have an internal political dimension, Molotov saw them as evidence of collusion with the West. From the Kremlin's point of view, it was not possible in Paris to make concessions that had been rejected several months earlier in Moscow.

After the Finnish delegation had reported back to Helsinki on its visit to Vyshinsky, a meeting of the expanded foreign affairs committee was arranged in the capital on 20 August. President Paasikivi, who had returned from his summer residence, was also at the meeting. After a rather confused debate, it was decided to send a telegram to Paris. It said that Finland, having been invited to put its requests to the peace conference, could only put forward what it felt were the views of the people and Parliament. New instructions were not deemed necessary; instead, "the delegation, being on the spot and best able to assess the situation, shall have the necessary freedom of action." [9]

In Paris, the Finnish delegation had been very careful the whole time to avoid playing the "Western card." Contacts were restricted to formal visits according to protocol. The British were known to have left the Finnish peace treaty for the Soviet Union to work out. Enckell and Wuori chatted with Bevin for a quarter of an hour on 4 September, mostly about Finland's coal needs and the British problems of delivery. According to the report, Bevin finally smiled and said: "I'm aware of your difficulties and the fact that you can't talk about them." [10] The Finns were never in contact with the Americans, which could be explained on the formal grounds that the United States was not a party to the peace treaty with Finland. After the conference had ended, Assistant Secretary Dunn reported from Paris that the Finnish delegation had "avoided" the Americans. [11]

Enckell, in his account sent to Helsinki, noted that

the attitude of the Great Powers . . . is seen in the oft-quoted opinion of the Americans that Finland must make a deal with the Soviet Union without foreign assistance. If such a deal is not worked out, and Finland is unable to repel invasion and other measures linked to world events, then it will share the fate of the Baltic countries, which the United States does not seem able to prevent. [12]

Hopes could not therefore be pinned on the Western powers; on the other hand, Finland should in all modesty strive to maintain its dignity and, steering clear of deliberate provocation, should avoid giving the world an image of servility toward the Soviet Union.

Mistrust of Helsinki and its motives was so strong in Moscow that other means were sought to give it expression. The media in Finland had originally viewed Enckell's speech favorably, irrespective of party distinction. With Hertta Kuusinen and Ville Pessi in Moscow at that time, the Communist leadership back home allowed its newspapers to defend Enckell's speech—which, as Upton has written, doubtless reflected the virtually unanimous feelings of the Finnish people. According to the People's Democratic paper, *Vapaa Sana*, "the performance of the delegation was based on relevant issues, which are essential in dealing with the question of peace." [13] The Communist Party newspaper *Työkansan Sanomat* took the same line: "Our delegation has shown itself capable of thinking about the issues and the situation correctly, and has presented our country's point of view in a manner fully acceptable to the democratic section of our people." [14]

After the Soviet Union had voiced its displeasure and Hertta Kuusinen had returned from Moscow, the Finnish Communist Party had to make a sharp turn and condemn Enckell's speech as an attack inspired by reactionaries. The campaign set in motion by the Finnish Communist Party, which earned the epithet of the "peace crisis," with its press articles, workplace and street meetings and resolutions, culminated in the visit of a delegation demanding an explanation to President Paasikivi. The two-hour discussions proved fruitless. At a meeting of representatives of workplace gatherings next day, a resolution was approved stating that the president had not managed to persuade the delegation that the speech made on behalf of the peace delegation had not damaged Soviet-Finnish relations. The removal of articles 6 through 9 of the peace treaty, in the opinion of the meeting, would endanger the democratic rights won by the people. For members of the Communist Party, who still vividly remembered the "protection" afforded them in the thirties by the constitution, this last point was extremely important. Upton maintains that it was thanks to this that the Communist Party was able, in spite of its "slavish" attitude towards the Soviet Union, to turn the "peace crisis" to its advantage. The party had publicly identified itself as the watchdog for the maintenance of friendly relations with the Soviet Union and as the defender of workers' rights against reaction. As the future soon showed, it also seemed capable of forcing its opponents to give way. [15]

The signals sent out by the Soviet Union's delegation in Paris and via the Communist Party in Finland were not without effect. After the secretary-general of the peace conference asked the Finnish delegation to send its written submission regarding the draft peace treaty by 24 August, for the consideration of the commissions appointed by the conference, the delegation found itself having to work out what it should do. Following the Communist Party line, Prime Minister Pekkala, Minister of the Interior Yrjö Leino, and "political advisers" Helo, Sundström, and Wuori were at pains to point out that proposed amendments should be as few as possible. On the territorial issue, Enckell agreed with them. There was no point in imagining that the Soviet Union would change its mind during the deliberations of the commissions. The Finnish delegation had already fulfilled its duty to domestic public opinion with the speech made at the general session. Raising the territorial question once more would only be a demonstration that would weaken relations with the Soviet Union. "Britain and the United States will not put forward any concessions. If others do so, it will be in other than Finnish interests. Our main task here is to show that our international position is stable. We must not endanger our position by actions that could lead to occupation."

Voionmaa believed that Finland, having been invited to an international conference, had already stated its wishes publicly at the general session. It would therefore create a strange impression were the matter to be allowed to drop altogether. It was after all a question of wishes, not of voicing dissatisfaction with the decisions of the conference. Some reference at least might be made in the written submission to the territorial requests mentioned in Enckell's speech. Voionmaa, though supported by Heljas and Österholm, did not manage to win the debate. The bitterness in which it was conducted may be gauged from the fact that, as the accusations were flying about during the decisive meeting on the 22nd, the three ministers acting as political advisers walked out in protest in midsession. The territorial question, as far as the delegation was concerned, was now at an end. Nothing at all was said about it in the written submissions forwarded to the commissions for further consideration. After this decision had been made, Leino felt that he could agree to a request being made for the reduction of reparations by $100 million, which the delegation thereupon decided to do.[16]

It was also deemed wise to observe caution in dealing with the so-called political articles. Without making specific proposals for change, the delegation contented itself, with regard to articles 6 through 8, by pointing out that the rights therein mentioned were part of the Finnish legal code: all that was needed was a guarantee that they would be observed in the future. In this way, domestic public opinion could be shown that an attempt had at least been made to refer to Finnish laws. On Article 9, concerning the potentially explosive issue of war crimes, the delegation affirmed that Finland had already embarked upon "all possible measures to punish actual war criminals as well as the so-called war-guilty." Finland had scrupulously fulfilled the obligations laid down by the armistice agreement, and "the question of punishing the war-guilty has finally been resolved in a manner satisfactory to the Allied states by the medium of a special trial." The delegation also drew attention to the fact that Finnish citizens accused of crimes could not be condemned in foreign courts without a breach of the principle enunciated in the Finnish Constitution. "The delegation assumes therefore that this is a question of handing over the accused for conviction in Finnish courts." Fearful that the war-guilt question might once more be resurrected, the Finns were also thinking of the fate of the "prisoners of Miehikkälä," arrested in autumn 1944 on the basis of the so-called List of 61.

On the question of interpretation of Article 33 (Article 35 of the final peace treaty), which had so worried President Paasikivi, the delegation abided by the line it had taken in Helsinki—accepting neither the British nor the Soviet proposal. Differences of opinion were in the first instance to be settled as far as possible by diplomatic means. If this did not work, the issue was to be transferred, unless the sides could agree upon another procedure, to the Court of Appeal established by the 1907 Hague Convention.

On the military articles, the delegation suggested that the maximums specified for the navy and air force—10,000 tons and 60 aircraft—could be doubled. Surplus war matériel handed over to the Soviet Union might be regarded as part of the reparations payments, and that handed over to the British might correspondingly be set off against the Finnish war debt still to be amortized in Britain. Matériel scheduled for destruction might be suitable for civil uses, or an agreed upon portion could be handed over for general consumption. [17]

These written submissions having been prepared, and participation in the deliberations of the commissions having proved impossible, the sizable Finnish contingent in Paris found itself with time on its hands. The return home of what had proved to be an unnecessarily large number of experts was thus set in motion. As the "peace crisis" sparked off by the protests of the People's Democrats still seemed to be continuing, the delegation, at Pekkala's suggestion, was given permission to return home to give its account of the situation to the president, government, Parliament, and the parties. The delegation remained in Finland between 31 August and 20 September, leaving only Enckell, Österholm, and some of the advisers to hold the fort in Paris. Before returning home, the delegation, at Enckell's suggestion, unanimously agreed that although a large delegation had been sent to Paris,

> responsible circles in Finland have been aware from the start of the conference's significance, which is only relative, since the conference is only a kind of facade. In striving to fulfill our desires, we have to turn, not to the conference, but directly to the Soviet Union. . . . We cannot rely— that is now obvious—on the Western powers, but we must turn to the Soviet Union on our own initiative. As for the mood in Finland, it must be calmed; everything which has been written seems to stem from the fact that what the delegation has said has been wrongly understood. [18]

Receiving the delegation in the presidential palace on 1 September, Paasikivi voiced his approval of their decision not to raise the territorial question again. Molotov and Vyshinsky had made the Soviet position perfectly clear. The head of state also voiced his strong displeasure at the demonstrations organized at home by the communists. In future, he would no longer consent to receive their delegations. Turning to Leino, the irate president growled: "Your wife (Hertta Kuusinen] has organized these demonstrations." [19]

The Pekkala delegation followed the lines it had agreed upon in Paris when it presented its account. When addressing the parliamentary foreign affairs committee, the prime minister (who clearly found himself caught between two fires) blamed the difficulties that had arisen on the composition of the delegation.

Pekkala also—with some justification—claimed that when the situation was "critical" in Paris, the only instructions received from Helsinki were to act as they thought best. This is what they had done. In a later radio broadcast, Pekkala characterized the work of the delegation as "somewhat futile" because the Soviet Union and Britain would in any event dictate the contents of the treaty. The prime minister rejected the claim that the delegation had not broached the territorial question at all. Molotov had however, clearly announced that no changes in frontiers were to be expected.[20] As this central issue was about to be settled finally by the deliberations of the commissions in Paris, the "peace crisis" also faded from the political stage.

19 The Commissions and the Final Decision

With the general discussions concluded, the Paris peace conference split up into five political and territorial commissions (one for each of the defeated countries), a joint military and a joint juridical commission, and two economic commissions, one to deal with Italy and the other with the economic aspects of the draft treaties for the Balkan countries and Finland.

The political and territorial commission for Finland assembled for its first meeting on 16 August 1946. Its task was to go over the preamble, articles 1 through 12, and articles 32 through 34 of the draft peace treaty. Twelve countries were represented on the commission: Australia, Britain, Byelorussia, Canada, Czechoslovakia, France, India, New Zealand, South Africa, the Soviet Union, the Ukraine, and the United States. The Soviet delegation announced at the start that it was prepared to allow the United States and France, as nonsignatories of the armistice agreement, to participate in discussions but not to have the right of voting. The American delegation nevertheless believed it appropriate to avoid repercussions on the domestic front, to stay completely away from the workings of the commission. The Australian John Beasley was elected chairman, with the Czech Peregrin Fisa as his deputy and Lord Samuel Hood as the rapporteur.[1]

The commission continued to discuss the procedural problems at its second session on 19 August. The main issue at stake was how the Finnish representatives should be heard. At that moment, the Ukrainian representative noticed members of the Finnish delegation, including the prime minister, already sitting in the conference chamber in places reserved for the press. The chairman shared the Ukrainian's view that the presence of the Finns was undesirable at this stage of the proceedings; at the unanimous request of the commission, Pekkala and his aides were ushered out. The representatives of the press remained in the chamber. The proceedings were in principle public, however, and the Finns had simply used the tickets issued by the conference secretariat to get in. After this incident, the Finnish delegation did not again dare to try to listen to the discussion on the fate of their country. After their withdrawal, the Australian representative, Lieutenant Colonel Hodgson, announced that the conference secretariat was at that moment drawing up arrangements for the commissions to hear the views of the former enemy countries. It was thereupon decided to wait for these general guidelines to be completed before proceeding any further.[2]

When the commission met for the third time on 29 August, the conference secretariat proposed that any invitation to the former enemy countries to make an appearance and put their case should depend on the decision of the relevant commission. This recommendation was taken up with regard to Finland. When the political and territorial commission began to go over the details of the draft treaty, Beasley noted (in reply to his fellow countryman Hodgson) that the Finnish delegation in its written submission had said nothing at all about the territorial question (Article 1). Novikov for the Soviet Union confirmed this and maintained that it was no longer necessary to call the Finnish delegation before the commission. There was no vote on this: the commission unanimously approved Article 1 as it was. Similarly, articles 2 through 5 were approved without discussion. The frontier question, which had so exercised the Finns, was thus dealt with in a matter of minutes.

More time was taken up by the amendments and additions of a declaratory nature proposed by the Australian delegation. The commission unanimously decided to add to the fourth paragraph of the preamble the words: "conforming to the principles of justice." The text now read: "whereas the Allies and Associated Powers and Finland are respectively desirous of concluding a Treaty of Peace which, conforming to the principles of justice, will settle questions still outstanding as a result of the events hereinbefore recited and will form the basis of friendly relations between them. . . . " A corresponding addition was made to all five draft treaties.

An Australian proposal for a completely new article fared less well. This concerned the admission of Finland as a member of the United Nations Food and Agricultural Organization, the International Wheat Council, the World Health Organization, and other economic and social organizations functioning under United Nations auspices. In the opinion of the majority of the commission, this was not a pressing matter because Finland itself would have to decide in the future whether it wished to become a member of the United Nations and its subordinate organizations. The Australian proposal was rejected by a vote of nine to one, with New Zealand abstaining.

Article 6 of the draft treaty, on human rights, which the Australians also wished to amend, was postponed to the next session. Concerning articles 7 through 9, the chairman referred to the Finns' written submissions, but these interested no one. The articles were approved as they were without discussion, as were articles 10 though 12. At this stage, the chairman brought the session to an end. In less than three hours, of which the major part was taken up in dealing with the peripheral proposals of the Australians, the commission had settled the bulk of the important articles of the Finnish peace treaty.[3] Even so, according to the correspondent covering the session for the *New York Times*, the majority of the delegates were unable to conceal their boredom with problems that were to them both distant and of little concern. They whiled away the time reading newspapers and polishing their nails.[4]

Equally fruitless was Enckell's attempt to give a verbal account of the Finnish submission to the deputy chairman of the commission, Peregrin Fisa, who maintained that the articles were for the most part the same for all the former enemy countries.

> The relatively young Czech diplomat was charming, but there was a touch of arrogance in his voice. On this, as on many other occasions, the humiliating position in which the Finnish delegation to Paris found itself seemed a bitter one. The Finnish delegates do not dare to go to listen to the proceedings of the commission, which are public, for fear of being driven away—as has already happened; they are regularly not invited to the receptions organized [by Norway and France]. They have been invited to voice their opinions on the peace treaty proposals, but in fact they are only permitted to make explanations in accordance with the wishes of the victorious powers.[5]

The Australian delegation, fired by Wilsonian idealism and seeking to establish a leading position among the small nations, persisted nevertheless in pursuing its well-intentioned but disruptive role in the Finnish political and territorial commission, as well as in all the other commissions. The decrees concerning human rights (Article 6 of the Finnish treaty) were to be recognized in these countries as having the status of constitutional law. Furthermore, they were also to cover those people remaining behind in surrendered territories, which would mean that they would be binding upon the victorious powers as well. This proposal was unacceptable to Novikov, who maintained that the Finnish submission showed that the principles of Article 6 were already in force in Finland. Novikov also thought the Australian proposal an undemocratic deviation from the norms of international law. No country could have its constitution determined by external forces. There was a great difference between the International Court of Justice and the Australian proposal: the former was based on voluntary agreement, the latter was intended as a compulsory device. The other delegations took the same view, though they did not wish to deny the Australians' "noble intentions": but, as Lord Hood observed, they could not be attained "by such methods." The proposal was rejected by nine votes to two, with Australia getting the support of New Zealand. Article 6 thus remained in its original form.[6]

To the annoyance of their more pragmatic colleagues, however, the Australians did not give up. Oblivious to their defeat, they threw out the idea on 3 September of a totally new section to be added to the peace treaties with Finland and all the other enemy countries, which talked of the setting up of an international human rights tribunal. With the unity of the British Empire in mind, the British delegation tactfully proposed transferring the initiative to the juridical commission for further examination. Deputy Foreign Minister Vyshinsky, who happened to be present at the meeting of the Finnish commission, lost patience at this. The Australians' new proposal was simply a vague idea, and it was impossible to divine its concrete significance. How would the tribunal function? What principles would it follow in its deliberations, and what would be the limits of its powers vis-à-vis the sovereign states? The proposal was "irrelevant, useless and half-baked." On a vote, the British proposal to transfer the matter to the juridical commission won by six votes to five. Adopting his earlier tough line, Vyshinsky now objected to the right of France—which had tilted the vote in favor of the majority—to vote on the commission dealing with Finland.[7]

The controversy, which threatened to become serious, was taken up by the deputy foreign ministers of the Great Powers at their meeting on the following day. It was agreed unanimously that the Australian proposal could not be accepted. Assured that the Western powers had shifted the matter to the juridical commission for tactical reasons, Vyshinsky let it be known that he did not hold by his protest against France's voting rights in the Finnish political and territorial commission.[8]

The final articles, 32 through 34, still remained to be dealt with. When the Finnish commission resumed its deliberations on 5 September, Australia, true to form, proposed the setting up of an executive council to deal with the treaty, one for each of the former enemy countries. In addition to the United States, the Soviet Union, Britain, and France, three further members would be delegated by the Paris conference to deal with the execution of the treaty and with matters of interpretation. This proposal was rejected out of hand by nine votes to one, with New Zealand abstaining.

The Australians were likewise alone in their attempts to get a resolution accepted in which the commission was to determine the procedure to be followed in any future possible review of the peace treaties. For this, a separate article was to be drawn up. In the ensuing debate, Lord Hood for the British delegation strongly opposed the proposal. In his view, it was not a matter of the mechanism but of will. The machinery already existed in the shape of the United Nations, and there was no reason to start competing with the world organization. Once more, the commission voted nine to one, with one abstention, to reject the idea.[9]

In the draft peace treaty for Finland prepared by the Council of Foreign Ministers, the only issue still open concerned Article 33 (on the settlement of differences arising over execution and interpretation of the treaty), for which both Britain and the Soviet Union had made their own proposals. The British position won the day by a majority of seven to four on the Finnish commission. No one saw fit to pay any attention to the written submission of the Finnish delegation, which was not even mentioned in the minutes.[10] A similar division of votes occurred in the other commissions dealing with the former enemy countries. The meeting of the deputy foreign ministers of the Great Powers on 6 September was unable to break the deadlock and postponed settlement of this problem to a future date.[11]

The only other undecided business of the Finnish commission was that of the Australian proposal for a human rights tribunal. The juridical commission adopted the view—hardly surprising in light of the agreement reached by the deputy foreign ministers of the Great Powers—that the issue as such more properly belonged to the functions of the United Nations; for this reason, there was no point in pursuing the matter any further. After the majority of the Finnish commission adopted the same position at the last full working session on 12 September, the Australians, aware of the hopelessness of their case, withdrew their proposal.[12]

The Finnish political and territorial commission was the first to complete its task. Without the disruptive Australians, this task, seen as very straightforward from the start, would obviously have been over and done with in a much shorter time.

Of significance from the Finnish point of view were the military commission, which was to go through the military articles of the draft peace treaties, and the economic commission for the Balkan countries and Finland. On both these commissions, the articles concerning Finland were regarded as of secondary significance and relegated to the end of the list, which meant that they had not even been looked at as the middle of September approached.

The slowness of commission deliberations gradually began to worry the Great Powers. The General Assembly of the United Nations was scheduled to open in New York on 23 September, by which time the peace conference was supposed to be over. The matter was discussed at an unofficial meeting of the foreign ministers of the Big Four in Paris, and it was decided to suggest to Secretary-General Trygve Lie that the General Assembly be postponed for a month. The reply was favorable. The foreign ministers also agreed to speed up the work of the commissions by setting a deadline of 5 October. The conference as a whole would have to reach its conclusion by 15 October, a week before the opening of the UN General Assembly. The foreign ministers' proposal was approved at a general session of the peace conference on 27 September.[13]

The "peace crisis" at home having died down, most of the Finnish delegation left Helsinki on 21 September to return to Paris. It was known that the fundamental decisions had already been taken, but, to comply with formalities it was necessary to play the game to the end. There was no longer any hurry; at the wish of Prime Minister Pekkala, the delegates traveled first by ship to Stockholm and thence by train to the French capital. Heljas and Voionmaa, both teetotalers, deemed it wise to make their own way by air to Paris. After the jovial company of travelers had arrived in Stockholm, Gripenberg received a somewhat surprising request to obtain tickets for Pekkala and Leino for an evening performance at the circus. The Finnish prime minister and his companions were afforded the opportunity to admire a variety of tricks in the sawdust ring, including a fakir pushing a needle through his neck. After the prime minister and the minister of the interior had declined the honor of pulling out the needle, it was withdrawn by a Swedish policeman sitting beside them. And—wonder of wonders—not one drop of blood appeared on the fakir's neck! On the train journey through occupied Germany, the delegation was disturbed by the famished crowds of people begging for food at the stations. To top it all, the delegates had to make do with "a meager helping of fish" for dinner in the restaurant car, while a group of young officers of the occupying forces sitting at a nearby table enjoyed "the most delicious meat dishes." Remonstrations about the "important diplomatic mission" of the delegation proved futile. On their return to Finland, the delegates lodged a complaint at the British mission in Helsinki, and they were rewarded with an apology.[14]

Having reached Paris on 25 September (in spite of the lateness of the season, it was still hot), the delegation gathered once more to go through the same old daily routine—"to ponder upon the questions that may come up—if they will now come up."[15] Leino's reservation was indeed apposite, since the real problems had now narrowed down to one. According to a telegram received by the delegation in Paris, President Paasikivi had received Orlov's successor as minister to Helsinki, M. Abramov, on 24 September. From their discussions, it had emerged that no reduction in the amount of reparations was to be expected in the final peace treaty; but "the President of the Republic had formed the opinion that, in regard to the conditions for carrying out the treaty, the granting of easier terms . . . might be considered." Abramov thought it useful for the Soviet and Finnish delegations to keep in touch, a view shared by Paasikivi.[16]

When Pekkala and Enckell met Vyshinsky on 28 September, the deputy foreign minister inquired, after the Finns had spoken, what conditions for the execution of the treaty they meant. He was told that it was a question of the way in which reparations were to be paid, the payment of the German assets, and so forth. If the Finnish delegation were to return with their only tangible result being the knowledge that the terms of the armistice agreement were to remain as they were, this might arouse serious discontent back home. At the same time, the Finns stressed the desirability of a bilateral agreement with the Soviet Union.

Vyshinsky replied that the Soviet Union, in accordance with its principles, would pay heed to real difficulties. The good will of the Finns was not in doubt, but the Soviet delegation lacked the authority to enter into discussions of the details of reparations deliveries. This would be decided by Moscow, which Vyshinsky promised to inform in a manner sympathetic to the Finns.[17]

Paasikivi's last attempt to secure direct easing of the terms in Paris had failed. But the door to the future remained ajar, at the same time as the crisis of confidence between Finland and the Soviet Union was being settled. The Paris conference as a whole was following a relatively satisfactory course from the point of view of the Soviet Union—in its beleaguered minority position—and this was alleviating the tension of the strained Great Power relationships. Further surprises were hardly to be expected. With regard to the special problems of Finland, Moscow was convinced that the Finnish delegation had raised the question of easing terms independently, without seeking to conspire with the West against the Soviet Union. The atmosphere now changed entirely. Leino recounted a luncheon hosted by Molotov two days later:

> On a sunny September day, the Finnish delegation *in corpore* stepped into the elegant embassy building. We were received by Molotov and Vyshinsky, and from the start, the occasion was extremely friendly. Molotov seated Pekkala beside him, and spoke to him over lunch, as did Manuilsky and Vyshinsky with me, their neighbor at table. After lunch, we moved over to the coffee table, and the mood there was so cordial that—dare it be revealed—even the Rev. Heljas had a drink so as not to offend our hosts.[18]

The military commission, chaired by Polish Brig. Gen. Stefan Mossor, dealt with the Finnish question in two sessions on 30 September and 1 October. Following up a suggestion of the British section of the Helsinki Allied Control Commission, the British proposed a new article that would oblige Finland to take part in postwar mine-sweeping operations. For this purpose it would be possible to maintain extra tonnage and fifteen hundred officers and men in addition to the already stipulated strengths. After the Soviet member of the commission, Admiral Karpunin, had been assured by the Finns' military expert, Gen. Aarne Sihvo, that this was acceptable to the Finns, the initiative was unanimously approved by the commission. A similar article was also added to the Italian treaty.[19]

At the suggestion of Belgium, it was also unanimously decided to prohibit possession, preparation, and testing of atomic weapons by all the former enemy countries.[20] More difficult was the question of motor torpedo boats, which were not given separate mention in the draft articles approved by the Council of Foreign Ministers. The exception was the Italian draft treaty; France had insisted on a precise ban on motor torpedo boats and "specialized types of assault craft." As France was not involved in making the treaties with the Balkan countries and Finland, it was not interested in extending a similar prohibition to these countries. A detail of this nature easily escaped the notice of the Western powers at this stage. Greece drew attention to the issue when it began demanding a similar ban on motor torpedo boats for Bulgaria. The Western powers now became involved, proposing for the sake of conformity that the omission be rectified by adding a ban on motor torpedo boats to the peace treaties with all the former enemy countries. The Soviet Union was unable to agree to this, pointing out that there had never been any intention of prohibiting motor torpedo boats in the Balkan countries and Finland. This difference of views remained unresolved. In other respects, the work of the military commission did not encounter any insurmountable difficulties.[21]

The Finnish articles were dealt with quickly. Their contents had, in any event, become clear in the previously reviewed treaties for the other former enemy countries. Nevertheless, this was the only commission to allow the Finns to present their views, verbally. On the morning of 30 September, after the session had begun, General Sihvo was summoned by telephone; but he found himself having to hang about in the lobby with his aides while the commission approved the military articles of the treaty. Invited in at the end of the meeting, Sihvo simply expressed his thanks for the invitation and said that he had nothing more to add to the written submission made by the Finnish delegation. There were no questions. To the satisfaction of the commission, getting ready for lunch, the Finns' "guest appearance" was thus confined to a couple of minutes. The articles were formally confirmed by the commission without discussion the following day. At no stage had any attention been paid to the Finns' written submission.[22]

The economic commission dealing with the Balkan countries and Finland was in an even greater hurry. At the very last moment, the United States proposed, on 4 October, that the burden of Hungarian and Finnish reparations be eased by $100 million. After discussions with the secretary-general of the conference, the chairman of the commission declared that the proposals had been made too late to fit into the agenda agreed upon for the conference. He did not wish, however, to prevent discussion of them. The meeting of the commission on the evening of 4 October looked first at the Balkan questions. At seventeen minutes past midnight, with the Finnish business still to be discussed, the chairman declared a fifteen-minute break, which the weary delegates spent in the bar.

The session did not get under way again until almost one o'clock because the chairman, who had gone to the bar to drag the others back to the conference chamber, allowed himself to be tempted with a drink. When Reinstein of the United States delegation renewed the proposal to lower Finnish reparations, the Soviet delegate, Gerashchenko—already annoyed by the wrangling that a similar proposal for Hungary had provoked—announced that he would reply only in the presence of the secretary-general of the conference. Efforts were made to trace M. Duparc, but in vain. Instead, his assistant, M. Garnier, was dragged out of bed. When he arrived at the meeting, he contented himself with a reference to the agreed agenda. In other respects, it was the business of the chairman to run the meeting, he declared irritably, and went off to catch up on his sleep. At the same time, the Finnish delegates, aware of the agenda of the meeting, were waiting up at their hotel expecting a call that never came. After the commission had argued for another two hours or so, a vote was taken at 3:30 a.m.; the American proposal was defeated by nine votes to four. War reparations thus remained unchanged. The United States now announced that it would vote against the article in its entirety at the plenary session.[23] The other economic articles referring to Finland were dealt with by six in the morning, after which the commission turned to Bulgaria. Their work finally came to an end at 2:35 p.m., just within the agreed deadline.

Although the American delegation could base its case on the fact that the Finns had themselves sought a reduction in the reparations bill (this had not been the case with Hungary), the question of motives still arises. The delegation was aware that its proposal came too late in the day and was out of order according to the timetable and agenda. Gusev and Gerashchenko with good reason pointed out that the Americans had been offered the chance to voice their opinions on the terms for peace with Finland on numerous occasions during the past two years. Washington had, however, remained silent. Why did the Americans now choose to speak out? The answer is surely not to be found in the Finnish supposition that the Americans had felt their consciences pricked at the last minute. It would seem that Washington saw the main purpose of the Paris conference as being a useful propaganda forum for turning world public opinion against the Soviet Union. By appearing to be a defender of small nations such as Finland and Hungary against the "unreasonable demands" of the Soviet Union, at a conveniently late stage, the United States could avail itself of the opportunity to score a few welcome points. It should also be borne in mind that Sen. Arthur Vandenberg, who spoke for the United States at the general session of the conference, was deeply concerned about his own future in the forthcoming congressional elections in November: because of his lengthy stay abroad, the senator had been unable to campaign.[24] His biographer noted that Vandenberg had already become aware of the considerable numbers of Finnish-born electors in his home state of Michigan during the Winter War of 1939-40.[25] It is unlikely that Vandenberg, in his precarious position, would have ignored this fact.

On the other hand, the American delegation believed it inappropriate to present the world with an image of the United States as simply wishing to cause difficulties for the conference. For this reason, serious consideration was given to the possibility of economic assistance to Finland.[26] The uneasy atmosphere that had hitherto surrounded the Finns' requests for a loan now noticeably improved.

When the peace treaty with Finland came up for discussion at the general session of the conference on 14 October, there were no surprises. The nearest to anything untoward was the lengthy description by K. V. Kiselev of the Byelorussian delegation of the acts of destruction committed by Finnish troops, comprising several divisions, in Byelorussia during the war! Vandenberg's rhetorical speech supporting a reduction in reparations for Finland evoked a sharp response from Molotov, who claimed that the Western powers, by courting Finland, were trying to make it into the kind of anti-Soviet base it had been before. This attempt would not succeed, however.

When voting began on the political and territorial articles of the Finnish treaty, articles 1 through 12 and 32 through 34 were approved unanimously, with the exception of Article 33, which dealt with matters of interpretation. That was approved in the form proposed by the British by fifteen votes to six. In addition, Byrnes—still trying to score points—declared that the United States would refrain from voting on the first and second articles dealing with territorial questions. The military articles were approved unanimously with the exception of the clause referring to motor torpedo boats. On the vote, the British formula won the day over that of the Soviet Union by fifteen votes to six. The article on reparations remained as it was after a vote of eleven to five, with Britain, Byelorussia, China, Czechoslovakia, Ethiopia, France, India, Poland, the Soviet Union, the Ukraine, and Yugoslavia voting for the article to remain unchanged and with Canada, Holland, New Zealand, South Africa, and the United States voting against. Australia, Belgium, Brazil, Greece, and Norway abstained.[27]

When the Paris peace conference (a parody of Versailles in 1919, as Daniel Yergin has called it) concluded its labors on 15 October 1946, it had nevertheless approved fifty-three recommendations by a two-thirds majority and forty-one by simple majority. The Council of Foreign Ministers, meeting in New York on 4 November, was to scrutinize the recommendations in order to shape the final contours of the peace treaties. Although the quarrel over the powers of the governor of the international zone of Trieste had not been sorted out, there had been a noticeable rapprochement on the major issues. It had been decided that, in addition to a payment of $100 million to the Soviet Union, Italy should pay $100 million in reparations to Greece and the same amount to Yugoslavia. Ethiopia was to receive $25 million. Albania was to receive nothing at all. The contentious problem of freedom of navigation on the Danube was left unresolved, as the matter was postponed to a future special international conference.[28]

The Paris peace conference was first and foremost the result of the efforts of the Americans, particularly the secretary of state. The original idea of a "peace of peoples" was realized in a considerably more modest form at a conference attended by a mere twenty-one nations. Byrnes was, nevertheless, in his element: the conference forum was reminiscent of the Senate back home, where it was possible to juggle votes and play to the gallery. By making it clear that the Soviet Union was in a minority and by stressing the role of the small nations in peacemaking, Byrnes laid the foundations for his next appearance at the forthcoming meeting of the Council of Foreign Ministers. Ward, who has studied the subject in detail, commented:

Undoubtedly, he succeeded in marshalling public opinion against the Soviet Union, but without fully realising the cost involved. What the American Secretary of State saw as the conscience of the world speaking, Molotov saw as American-organised opposition to the USSR. At first, Molotov reminded Byrnes of the principle of unanimity within the Council of Foreign Ministers, but when that failed to influence American strategy, he resorted to using the press as Byrnes had. The result was the lowest point in American-Soviet negotiations to date. Inflamed rhetoric had proved itself to be a poor substitute for diplomacy.[29]

For the Finns, the Paris conference had produced no tangible results. By October, they were more or less in the same position they had occupied in August. Although the chances of amending the draft treaty had been small to begin with (Enckell admitted to Hamilton on his return home), Finland had faithfully taken up the invitation and the delegation had presented the Finnish case to the world in a careful and unassuming manner. At no stage had they resorted to asking other states for help. In Enckell's opinion, the later contacts between the Finnish and Soviet delegations showed that, in spite of initial mis-understandings, the relationship between the two countries was pretty firm. Now, it was important to reach a decision over the peace treaty as soon as possible.[30]

Pekkala was of the same opinion. The atmosphere in Paris at the end of the conference had noticeably improved, and Finland might be able later to obtain concessions in direct discussions. All in all, he was satisfied with the trip.[31] Although no tangible results had been obtained, the Finns could console themselves with the thought that the way still remained open for negotiations with the Great Powers. Moreover, Finland's separate status with regard to Italy and the Balkan countries had been outlined, principally in the opening speech. Had Finland stayed away altogether from the Paris conference, an unfavorable interpretation of its position might have been conveyed to the rest of the world.

PART VII
The Conclusion of
the Peace Treaty

20 Preparation and Signing

The recommendations of the Paris conference were to be taken up by the Council of Foreign Ministers, meeting in New York in November 1946. The Palais du Luxembourg, with its ceremonially dressed *Garde Républicaine*, was now to be replaced by a suite of rooms on the thirty-seventh floor of the Waldorf Astoria Hotel, with 150 ordinary military policemen to look after the safety of the participants.

Well aware of the time and trouble already spent on preparing the "satellite treaties," all the Great Powers were anxious to conclude their work: further interruption was commonly regarded as being in no one's interest. Nevertheless, finding a way to a compromise agreement, in the chilly atmosphere of the Cold War, was proving to be an ever more complicated business. It was not long before the task of going through the recommendations of the Paris conference turned into a futile wrangle, with the foreign ministers digging their heels in to their entrenched positions. To improve the atmosphere, Byrnes tried a new tactic by proposing a two-minute silence in memory of those who had fallen in the war, "which might help us achieve the common objectives for which our boys gave their lives." The meeting was silent for two minutes—and then the wrangling was resumed. This first session on the Paris recommendations was not entirely fruitless, however, with regard to secondary issues. Thus, on 11 November, Britain and the Soviet Union finally agreed upon the sum of $300 million of war reparations to be paid by Finland, with Byrnes recording in the minutes the dissenting view of the United States as a nonsignatory of the treaty.[1]

When the second round of discussions of the Paris recommendations began on 12 November, the most difficult problem was that of Trieste. In fact, as Ward has pointed out, the Council of Foreign Ministers transformed itself within a couple of weeks into a commission to determine the constitution of the free zone. For days on end, the discussion ebbed and flowed around the details of the frontiers of Trieste, the presence or evacuation of foreign troops, the powers of the governor, the organization of transport links, and so forth. The following exchange of words, recorded in the minutes and dealing with the details of rail links between Yugoslavia and the free zone, is typical:

Bevin: This seems like horse trading to me.

Molotov: I do not know how to horse-trade.

Byrnes: Find me a horse trader as hard as you are and I will give him a gold medal.

Molotov: I am learning.

Bevin: God help us when you have learned![2]

To break the deadlock, a further personal meeting between Byrnes and Molotov was necessary. The Soviet foreign minister stressed that something had to be offered to satisfy the Yugoslavs. Byrnes said that this could take the form of a gradual withdrawal of the troops of the Western powers, in agreement with the governor of Trieste. Molotov thought that this would be enough for the Yugoslavs, and the deadlock was broken. Bevin and Couve de Murville accepted this negotiated solution. The question of reparations was smoothed out by the proposal that Italy and Bulgaria would together pay $150 million to Yugoslavia and the same amount to Greece, with Italy separately paying $100 million to the Soviet Union and $5 million to Albania.

These major issues having been settled, the small problems solved themselves. Molotov expressed his amazement that such an insignificant issue as motor torpedo boats could provoke such lengthy wrangling. To push things forward, he suggested, this type of weapon should be prohibited for all the former satellite countries. The differences of opinion over the interpretation of the peace treaties, the Soviet foreign minister went on, could be resolved by making the secretary-general of the United Nations the final arbitrator, instead of appealing to the International Court of Justice. The Western powers raised no objection to this. The final open questions relating to the peace treaty with Finland were thus resolved.[3]

Having concluded their business, the Council of Foreign Ministers agreed upon a further meeting, to begin in Moscow on 10 March 1947, to prepare the peace treaties with Germany and Austria. It was also agreed that the final technical points of the peace treaties with Italy, Rumania, Bulgaria, Hungary, and Finland should be settled without delay and that the treaties would be signed in Paris on 10 February 1947. The foreign ministers of the Great Powers could ill afford the time to travel specially to the French capital; they therefore authorized their representatives to perform this task. The final session of the New York conference ended on 12 December 1946 with a brief vote of thanks by Molotov on behalf of the visiting representatives.[4] The end result was a compromise that merited no fanfare of trumpets from anyone but that all could nevertheless accept. Having brought the satellite peace treaties safely into harbor, James Byrnes, who had already lost the confidence of the president and who had considered resigning since the spring of 1946, asked to be relieved of his office.[5] Gen. George C. Marshall was named as his successor in January 1947.

The Finnish Foreign Ministry sought in vain to obtain detailed information about what had actually taken place during the foreign ministers' conference in New York.[6] On the eve of the final session, 11 December, the Finnish minister in Washington could report that he had heard from the State Department that no fundamental changes had been made to the terms of peace for Finland: more than this he hadn't been able to learn.[7]

As the thirty-seventh floor of the Waldorf Astoria Hotel returned to everyday use, the situation was, however, changing rapidly. Just two days after the Finnish minister's report was filed, the secretary-general of the foreign ministers' conference, Warren Kelchner, asked the Finnish legation in Washington for expert assistance in translating the text of the peace treaty into Finnish. The legation was asked to take on the complete task of translation, although to save time the work would have to be done in Washington rather than Helsinki, and the contents of the treaty were not to be revealed for the moment. Jutila gave his consent, and the English, French, and Russian copies of the peace treaty were delivered to the Finnish legation on New Year's Eve. Naturally, news of this also reached the Finnish Foreign Ministry.[8] Big surprises were thus no longer to be expected.

On 16 January 1947, Kelchner was at last able *officially* to deliver a copy of the peace treaty text to the Finnish legation; it was published in the newspapers the following day. It was to be signed at the Foreign Ministry in Paris at 6:30 p.m. on 10 February 1947, and the names of the plenipotentiaries were to be transmitted directly to the French government as soon as possible.[9]

President Paasikivi was particularly irritated by the phrase in the preamble to the treaty that spoke of a settlement in accordance with the principles of justice. Enckell confirmed that this had been added at the Paris conference at the suggestion of the Australians and that it appeared in the same wording in all five peace treaties. This explanation did not satisfy the president, however, who entrusted Enckell with the task of commenting on this matter when the bill concerning the acceptance of the peace treaty was put before the Parliament. After referring to the earlier submissions made by Finland for the peace terms to be modified, Enckell wrote: "As no such concessions have been made, the government does not see fit to comment upon how far the provisions of the treaty are in accordance with the principles of justice mentioned in the preamble." Nevertheless, the State Council decided in the end to leave this sentence out of the supporting statement for the bill.[10] Although he regarded the peace terms as severe enough in themselves and was angered by the moralizing of the Australians, Paasikivi was perfectly well aware of the positive significance of the final peace as a means of bolstering and establishing Finland's international position. In this respect, no room for doubt is left by the tone and contents of his subsequent utterances.[11] After the first flush of irritation had passed, the president was quite willing to accept the verdict of the State Council without demur.

The Pekkala government presented the text of the peace treaty for the approval of Parliament on 21 January 1947 "as a proposal for legislation to approve the peace treaty between Finland and the Union of Soviet Socialist Republics, the United Kingdom, Australia, the Union of South Africa, India, Canada, Czechoslovakia, the Soviet Socialist Republic of the Ukraine, New Zealand and the Soviet Socialist Republic of Byelorussia." After wrangling for some time in fine Finnish fashion over which party was to be held most or least responsible for the events of 1939-44, Parliament unanimously approved the bill at its final session on 27 January 1947.[12] After the usual internal political tussle, the members of the delegation to Paris were chosen. Enckell was to head the delegation, and its members were to be Johan Helo, already in Paris as Finland's minister; Vihtori Vesterinen, an Agrarian Party member of the government; and Social Democrat Väinö Voionmaa, the chairman of the foreign affairs committee of Parliament, Voionmaa was relieved of the task on grounds of ill health; because his place was not filled, the delegation ultimately consisted of three members.

Less than a week before the signing ceremony, the French Foreign Ministry announced that Finland's turn would be half an hour later than originally agreed, in the Salon d'Horloge at the Quai d'Orsay. The delegation led by Enckell was to appear at 7:00 p.m. Should the delegation wish to make a statement before the ceremony of signing the treaty, the text would have to be submitted to the secretary-general of the Paris conference at least one day earlier. After four days, however, the Quai d'Orsay canceled the last part of its announcement. No statements were to be allowed after all.[13]

The reason for this shift, which was never explained to the Finns, lay with the obduracy of the Italians. The government in Rome did not conceal from the victorious powers its opinion of the "unreasonable and unjust" nature of the peace terms, and it was seriously thinking of refusing to sign the treaty. Final ratification would, in any event, depend upon the approval of the National Constituent Assembly. Although the de Gasperi government finally agreed to sign the treaty "as a temporary solution," the Great Powers, at the suggestion of the Soviet Union, felt it would be wiser in the circumstances to prevent any declarations by the Italians or any of the other defeated nations at the signing ceremony in Paris. Written statements, which the secretary-general would file away in the archives, were not forbidden, however, an opportunity that was utilized by all the defeated nations with the exception of Finland.[14]

The ceremonies began on 10 February 1947, 11:00 a.m., at the Quai d'Orsay. The first treaty to be signed was that dealing with Italy; the signing was accomplished within half an hour, including the speech of welcome by Foreign

Minister Georges Bidault. The afternoon session got under way with the same formalities at three o'clock, when it was the turn of the Rumanians. The omission of declarations from the program meant that proceedings went ahead of the original schedule. The delegates thus had to spin out the extra time by chatting together in the corridors of the Quai d'Orsay.[15] As the Hungarian ceremony was nearing its end around five o'clock, boredom got the upper hand and Secretary-General Duparc telephoned the Finnish legation to ask Enckell and his delegation to arrive earlier than agreed upon so that the treaty could be signed at six o'clock. The delegation was gathered together in record time, and its members (with their aides) marched into the Salon d'Horloge through the guard of honor of the *Garde Républicaine* in good time before the third, and final, deadline.

In the Salon d'Horloge, the Finns were placed by the side of the delegations of the victorious powers, facing the chairman, the French foreign minister. After Bidault had fluently delivered himself for the fifth time of the same speech of welcome—mutatis mutandis—the matter in hand was approached. As Helo reported:

> When the speech had been translated into English and Russian, Bidault asked the representatives of the victorious powers to sign the treaty in the adjacent room. This room, like the former, was lit up for the purposes of filming the occasion. The representatives each signed in turn [at the desk of Louis XIV], the Soviet Union first, represented by Minister Bogomolov, and then the British representative, Duff Cooper, and so on . . . and finally, the representative of South Africa.

Obeying Bidault's instructions, the Finns then went into the room, appending their names to the document: Enckell first, then Vesterinen, and finally Helo. To cap it all, Helo's fountain pen gave out, and the final stroke of the pen that terminated the entire ceremonial proceedings had to be repeated with a borrowed writing instrument. "Having regained the Salon d'Horloge and seated ourselves, Bidault immediately declared the session over. . . . We all went out in a heap. . . . "[16] Cyrus Sulzberger of the *New York Times*, who was present at the occasion, was struck by "the lack of joy" in the Salon d'Horloge, and in Paris too, where the event was observed "with complete indifference."[17]

After traveling by car to Helo's residence, the Finns celebrated the signing of the peace treaty "with a simple champagne toast, with Minister Enckell proposing that we had to forget all the wounds caused by the war."

> The Soviet Union is an immense state, which has great influence upon our fate. The Karelian question must not become any sort of open sore. The population of Karelia has left its dwelling places, the province is now inhabited by Russians and will thus change its basic character, so that the situation is unlike that of, for example, Alsace-Lorraine, where the population during the German occupation remained.[18]

As prescribed in Article 36 of the peace treaty, the only copy of the signed document was handed over to the Soviet government, which was supposed to send verified copies to all the signatories for ratification. In accordance with this procedure, an official copy of the Finnish peace treaty was handed over to Minister Sundström at the Foreign Ministry in Moscow on 28 February for dispatch to Helsinki.[19]

21 Ratification

On 12 March 1947, President Truman addressed a joint session of Congress at which he proposed a grant of $300 million aid for Greece and $100 million for Turkey. In February, the British government, struggling with its own economic problems, had announced that it was abandoning economic and military assistance to the governments of these countries. Although the eastern Mediterranean had traditionally been regarded as within the British sphere of interest, the resources of the British Empire, weakened by war, were no longer sufficient to bear this burden alone. It was time for the Americans to step into the breach.

The prevailing view within the State Department was that "rejection" of Greece and Turkey would mean a communist takeover in these countries. The domino theory of the time saw the Near East and Africa as next in line, followed by Italy and France. Although Truman in his public utterances did not go so far, he painted a pretty gloomy picture of the situation to convince Congress, which held the purse strings. What was at stake was a global struggle between two ways of life. The "collapse" of Greece would lead to hitherto unsuspected consequences elsewhere. It must be American policy, Truman declared, to support free peoples who oppose attempts at subjugation by armed minorities or foreign pressure.

The president's statement, which was later to become famous as the Truman doctrine, did not in itself add anything of significance to the anticommunist consensus that had gradually established itself in leading American political circles since the war. What was new was the official proclamation of these thoughts in the form of a program of principles aimed at Congress and the great American public, an action that in its very generality was later to pose problems for the national leadership when it found itself having to sort out for itself and

263

for others the relationship between interests vital and marginal to the United States in different parts of the globe.[1]

In addition to Greece and Turkey, which had triggered off the Truman doctrine, much attention was still focused on Western Europe, suffering badly in the winter of 1946-47 from economic slump. Food shortages and a lack of raw materials were still pressing, exports were falling, unemployment was rising, and postwar reconstruction was being slowed down. In the Italian and French parliamentary elections, the communists greatly increased their support. Although the Soviet Union played no direct part in these developments, which were of an internal nature, the economic weakness of Western Europe was followed in Washington with deep concern. In the long term, the possibility of the inflamed situation giving rise to a communist victory either by a coup, or even through free elections, was not ruled out. Moscow would not let such an opportunity pass it by, it was thought, and thus the European balance would be seriously jeopardized.

The American response was contained in Marshall's speech at Harvard on 5 June 1947, which proposed an all-embracing plan to revive the European economy. If the resources of the European states were insufficient to meet this plan, the United States was prepared to give aid. For tactical reasons, the offer was directed to all the states of the Old World, including the Soviet Union. As the Americans had expected, Moscow turned down the offer, seeing the administration and control implicit in such economic aid as affording the Western powers an opportunity to interfere in the internal affairs of the Soviet Union in a manner that would jeopardize the future of the socialist system. From the American point of view, the Marshall Plan was not primarily intended to guard against a direct Soviet military offensive, which was regarded as relatively unlikely. What was more at issue was the prospect of economic debility sapping the self-confidence of America's Western European allies, which would lessen their chances of warding off the rise to power of native communists. The Marshall Plan was seen by the United States as a means of ensuring the political balance in Europe by utilizing what was traditionally a major source of strength—technology and economic might—instead of armed force. At the same time, Washington cut its aid to China and Korea. Alongside the general phraseology of the Truman doctrine, the Marshall Plan signified a far more clearly organized arrangement of political objectives, with Western Europe coming well to the fore in the campaign to hold back communism.[2]

During the famous "fifteen weeks" between the proclamation of the Truman doctrine and the Marshall Plan, the ratification of the peace treaties with the former "satellite" countries, already regarded as a side issue, was overshadowed by major events. The conference of foreign ministers from the Big Four in Moscow during March, which was intended to draft the peace treaties with Germany and Austria, also drew attention away from this matter. Because of sharp differences of opinion, the discussions were bogged down from the start.

As the quarrels of the Great Powers increased in intensity, the Soviet Union deemed it wise to await the actions of the other victorious powers in finally bringing into force the treaties with Italy, Rumania, Bulgaria, Hungary, and Finland.

In the peace treaties with the former satellites, it had been decreed that they were to be ratified by the relevant victorious powers. The defeated countries were to proceed in like manner. The coming into force of each treaty, however, demanded final confirmation only on the part of the Great Power signatories. Thereafter, the documents of ratification for Italy were to be deposited with the French government, those for the Balkan countries and Finland with the Soviet Union.

On 4 March 1947, Secretary of State George Marshall laid the Italian, Rumanian, Bulgarian, and Hungarian peace treaties before Congress for ratification. The chairman of the Senate Foreign Affairs Committee, Arthur Vandenberg, had great misgivings about the whole procedure. After ratification, Western troops were supposed to evacuate Italy, while the Soviet Union would be allowed to keep troops in Rumania and Hungary to maintain communications with the occupying forces in Austria. Delaying the ratification would thus strengthen the American bargaining position in the foreign ministers' conference just beginning in Moscow, which was to discuss the peace treaty with Austria.

The Truman administration did not think delay would serve any purpose. Leaving unratified treaties that had been negotiated after lengthy debate, even if the results were in part unsatisfactory, would mean a loss of face. Furthermore, relations with Italy would now be normalized on an acceptable basis. The occupation administration based on the armistice in Eastern Europe would come to an end, which would probably improve the economic position of these countries. Soviet troops would withdraw from Bulgaria. In a telegram to Marshall, who had traveled to Moscow, Assistant Secretary of State Dean Acheson emphasized the need to get the satellite treaties already agreed upon in Paris out of the way before dealing with the Austrian question. The policy advocated by Vandenberg would give the Soviet Union cause to level accusations of ill will, while bringing little or no benefit to the West. With the settlement of the German question in mind, there was also little reason to slam the door shut once and for all upon the Soviet Union. Marshall shared this view. Following Vandenberg's policy would mean that the Americans would find themselves saddled with the occupation of Trieste, since the British were pulling out militarily and economically, and it would also mean that the last remaining hope of doing anything about the placing of Soviet troops in the Balkans would be lost.[3]

Vandenberg did not give up, however, and there were frequent pleas from the government in Rome and visits of American-Italian pressure groups to the State Department (and to Vandenberg himself) to do something to alleviate the terms imposed on Italy as the ratification procedure slowly ground its way through the Senate Foreign Affairs Committee.[4] Vandenberg believed that the treaty in question was already out-of-date, since it had been drawn up at a time when the United States was still pursuing a policy of appeasement toward the Soviet Union. With the declaration of the Truman doctrine, the situation had totally changed. The fruitless talks in Moscow offered even less cause to speed up the ratification. By sticking to harsh terms, the United States could unwittingly steer Italy toward communism. At all events, Vandenberg believed that both Marshall and his predecessor Byrnes should appear in person on Capitol Hill to justify their position before the committee. Because the secretary of state was out of Washington at the Moscow conference until the end of April, the ratification procedure as far as the United States was concerned seemed to be stalled.[5]

The other Great Powers, who were following developments in the United States, were unwilling to rush ahead of events, though in the course of time the British could not conceal their anxiety. In an identical memorandum submitted to Moscow, Paris, and Washington on 11 April, London proposed the simultaneous deposition by the Great Powers of the ratification documents for the peace treaties of all five former satellite countries. This would avoid the possibility of tactical maneuvering that would be damaging to the relations of the four Great Powers. The first of May was a suitable date for such a procedure, in the view of the Foreign Office.

The Attlee government also drew attention to the fact that the former enemy countries seemed to be delaying ratification. The Italian government in particular seemed to think it was tactically more appropriate, in view of the prevailing unrest in the country, to wait until the Great Powers, and especially the United States, had irrevocably ratified the peace treaty before submitting it to the National Constituent Assembly. It was possible that other former enemy countries might be seized of the same idea in hopes of obtaining an easing of the terms at the last minute. The defeated countries might even fail to confirm the treaties. Although the ratification procedure by the vanquished was not a precondition for the final coming into force of the treaties, a favorable resolution was nevertheless of great importance. If the defeated countries could avoid ratification, they might later brand the peace treaties as externally imposed diktats, which the people had not approved and which there was thus no need to obey. To avoid such dangers, the Big Four would have to make clear to the vanquished that they expected the ratification of these treaties *before* they were finally brought into force by the simultaneous act of deposition of the Great Powers.[6]

But the Americans did not support the British view. Dean Acheson rejected out of hand the idea of setting a time limit, such as the first of May. Ratification had to be dealt with by the Senate, which would not tolerate any curbs on its powers by an external deadline. Even the mere suggestion of such an idea might decisively sour the mood on Capitol Hill. The decision already taken to wait for

Marshall's return from Moscow was naturally not mentioned by Acheson. He believed that the British would have to try to understand the position of the Italian government, which was holding back on the ratification of a treaty widely regarded as unfair in the country at large, while the U.S. Senate was still deliberating and the chance of some kind of easing of terms was still in principle possible. Once Washington had made its mind up and the possibility of amendment had finally been blocked, Rome was unlikely to cause trouble. In these circumstances, the United States could not agree either to the setting of a deadline or to the presentation of a demand to the vanquished nations that they ratify the treaties in advance.[7]

The British now had to give way. Not wishing to endanger relations with the transatlantic superpower, it was thought best to wait for the decision of the Senate. The Foreign Office believed that, if necessary, each former satellite could be dealt with separately. In other words, having reached agreement over the coming into force of any one peace treaty, the victorious Great Powers could settle the matter without resort to a simultaneous conclusion of the affairs of all five satellite countries. When the Senate had come to a favorable decision, it might be possible to issue a joint statement by the Big Four in which they would affirm that they regarded ratification by the defeated countries as an essential precondition for the coming into force of the peace treaties. Fearful of strengthening the Italian communists and sensitive to the reactions of American-Italian voters, Washington was unwilling to give its backing to this idea. No statement was necessary: instead, unofficial pressure could be brought to bear. In other respects, cooperation between the Great Powers was of course desirable, if need be in the form of enforcement of separate peace treaties.[8]

George Marshall returned from Moscow and duly appeared with his predecessor James Byrnes on Capitol Hill, where both spoke forcefully for ratification of the treaties. The Senate finally voted in favor on 5 June 1947 by a majority of 79 to 10, with 6 abstentions. President Truman confirmed the ratification of the treaties with Italy, Rumania, Bulgaria, and Hungary for the United States on 14 June.[9] France immediately followed the American example, Britain already having completed the process in May.

As well as letting its Great Power allies know that it favored ratification by the defeated powers as a precondition for the peace treaties coming into force, Britain also made these views known to the former satellites in April 1947. In Italy, which was still hoping for some sort of salvation from the U.S. Senate, this plea not unnaturally fell on deaf ears. The Balkan countries, with one eye on the Soviet Union, deemed it best to refrain from taking any steps for the time being. The exception was Finland.

The Finnish minister to Moscow, Cay Sundström, had already been instructed by Helsinki to ask Vyshinsky on 23 March what the position of the Soviet Union was with regard to ratification. Vyshinsky replied that this was not a pressing matter for his government, but Finland could of course proceed as it thought best.[10]

On 11 April, the British chargé d'affaires Ledward visited the foreign ministry to meet Head of Chancery Tapio Voionmaa. He informed Voionmaa that it was the wish of His Majesty's Government that Finland ratify the peace treaty before Britain, where it was expected that ratification would take place before the end of the month.[11] The same message was relayed to Helsinki via Eero Wuori. The British also let the Finns know that they were ready, provided the Soviet Union gave its consent, to bring the peace treaty with Finland into force irrespective of the other satellite states. No reply had yet been received from Moscow on this issue.[12]

For the Finns, desirous of a speedy peace and the return of normal conditions, the British initiative was a welcome one. Striving to do what he could to push matters forward and acting on the authority bestowed upon him by Parliament on 27 January 1947, President Paasikivi decided at a secret session of the State Council on 18 April to ratify the Finnish peace treaty. Finland was thus the first of the five former satellites to ratify a peace treaty. The document was dispatched without further delay to the Moscow legation for presentation to the Soviet Foreign Ministry. The deposition ceremony was postponed, however, after the Soviet Union announced (in accordance with its general policy) that it would return to the matter at a later stage.[13]

As the problem of ratification hung fire in the spring of 1947, internal political developments in Finland gave cause for anxiety among the three Great Powers. Ever since the parliamentary debate sparked off in the autumn of 1946 by an interpellation concerning the activities of the State Police, the Pekkala government had begun to show ever more unmistakable signs of disintegration as the Social Democrats and Agrarians sought to break free of their partner in government, the Finnish People's Democratic Union.[14] The problems of having to deal with wages and prices at a time of continual unrest on the labor market strained the relations of the government parties to the point where the 1945 agreement between the Big Three was virtually a dead letter. The situation was not improved by the low esteem in which Prime Minister Mauno Pekkala—"drinking excessively even by Finnish standards"—was held.[15]

The government had been held together so far by the uncertain state of Finland's international position. Western observers were conscious of the danger that, even though the peace treaty remained to be confirmed, the Finns might construe the signing ceremony in Paris as sufficient encouragement in itself to start squabbling among themselves. Unable to understand the "shortsightedness" of the ever-growing Finnish obsession with internal affairs and a change of government, American Minister Maxwell Hamilton felt it necessary as early as 3 February to deliver a warning through Foreign Minister Enckell. "I remarked that in the English language we had an expression of 'keeping the boat steady.' Finland still had to pay her reparations and 1947 was considered to be one of the specially hard years. Finland also wanted to become a member of the United Nations Organization. In all the circumstances it seemed to me that it was a good thing to keep the boat steady.''[16]

Some anxiety was also felt in the Soviet Union, where there were suspicions that the Finns were intending to readjust their new foreign policy. Taking advantage of the celebrations being held in Helsinki in honor of the signing of the peace treaty, General Zhdanov arrived in the Finnish capital in February 1947, the first time he had visited the city since December 1945. During his stay, the chairman of the Control Commission invited the chairmen of the parliamentary groups of the Finnish People's Democratic Union, the Social Democratic Party, the Agrarian Union, and the Swedish People's Party for talks. The meeting was a cordial one, and Zhdanov assured the Finns that the Soviet Union was not trying to interfere in their internal affairs or to change the system that the Finns thought best suited them. At the same time, however, Zhdanov made a point of saying that the Soviet Union and Marshal Stalin in particular believed the present composition of the government was a good one and saw no reason to change it.

The government question now ceased to be a matter of debate for the time being. In his reports to Washington, Hamilton believed that the chairman of the Control Commission had achieved his objective: "It is believed from the Soviet viewpoint that his mission was successful, assuring continuance of Finnish political orientation toward the Soviet Union upon arrival of actual peacetime conditions. No other motive or motives for his visit have been evident to date.''[17] Shepherd agreed with his American colleague.[18]

To this same period belongs the article published by Paasikivi in the Finnish-Soviet Union Society's journal on 12 February, in which the president made a point of stating that Finland would in the future fight side by side with the Soviet Union should attempts be made to attack the Soviet Union via Finnish territory. It was obviously intended to assure Finland's eastern neighbor that there would be no changes in Finnish foreign policy even after peace had finally been restored.

The calming influence of Zhdanov's visit did not last for long, however. Within a few weeks, the Finns were again at each other's throats. On 28 March, the People's Democrats presented demands for general wage increases, tight price controls, and transfer of powers of decision in wage questions from the government to the organizations in the labor market. Desirous of a cabinet more in line with the new balance of forces within its ranks, the Social Democrats responded by proposing the formation of a new cabinet to draw up a program for economic stabilization. Both parties — the People's Democrats, which were whipping up demands for wage increases, and the Social Democrats, with their campaign directed against "forced democracy"—had an eye on the approaching elections within the trade union movement. In the heat of the moment, the question of ratification of the peace treaty perforce had to take second place. On 10 April, exasperated beyond endurance by squabbles over prices policy, the Agrarian Union precipitated a crisis by withdrawing its members from the government. The Pekkala government remained in office, however, because Paasikivi refused to call elections before the parliamentary session had run its full course. Attempts to reconstruct the government finally ended in complete failure, and it was agreed that Pekkala would announce the withdrawal of his resignation on 20 May and that the old State council would be reappointed.[19]

The "primitive reactions" of the Finns were followed with baffled amazement by the Great Powers. In a telegram to Hamilton on 16 April, Assistant Secretary of State Acheson referred to Zhdanov's earlier recommendation and to the fact that the ratification process was still incomplete. What, then, had made the Finns choose this particular moment to provoke a government crisis—which by the very nature of things must mean a direct challenge to the Soviet Union?[20] In his reply, Hamilton dealt in detail with the internal background to the crisis, which had caused the pent-up desire for a change of government to "boil over." Had Zhdanov not visited Finland, the Pekkala government would clearly have collapsed much earlier. External considerations and the demands of national unity were beginning to take a back seat in Finnish thinking as the return to normality occurred and the memories of the armistice of 1944 gradually faded. It would have been wiser to let the government remain in office until the peace treaty was ratified or possibly until the parliamentary elections, due to take place in 1948.[21]

Hamilton told Enckell on 10 May that, in his personal opinion, it would be a very good thing if Finland kept quiet and got on with what needed doing. Changes and upsets in the economy which the Finns regarded as purely internal affairs, might in the prevailing confused global situation be seen by certain outside observers as having international ramifications. "I repeated that it seemed to me that this was a very good period for Finland to continue to have its own situation quiet and for Finland to saw wood." Enckell admitted that he was entirely of the same opinion.[22]

The Foreign Office also warned Helsinki against any change of government before the ratification of the peace treaty, in view of the close attention being paid by the Soviet media to the Finnish government crisis, which was portrayed as a "reactionary" attack on the "democratic" line and the new foreign policy. The foreign policy of the Pekkala government, in the British view, had been wise and successful. Extreme caution was therefore necessary.[23]

After the decision for the Pekkala cabinet to remain in office, however, the situation speedily returned to normal. As Ylitalo has rightly observed, those who sought to bring about a new government and who ignored Zhdanov's message had miscalculated the situation.[24] The armistice was still in force; the peace treaty had not been ratified. The People's Democrats, who never forgot Zhdanov's wishes for a moment, simply refused to back down and emerged from the crisis as victors, or at least not having lost ground.

There are no indications that the Soviet Union in the spring of 1947 had any objectives that went beyond the preservation of the prevailing status quo. This was the view of Paasikivi, who pointed out to Shepherd on 18 March the security policy aspect of Moscow's interest in Finland. The president was convinced that the Finnish people understood and approved of his policy of friendship towards the Soviet Union. The real problem was how to "manage" the extreme left, which comprised something like 25 percent of the members of Parliament. Paasikivi did not believe that the Soviet Union wished to force a communist administration upon Finland, since this would lead to chaos and compel Moscow to send in "thirty divisions" to maintain order. Finland was a country orientated toward the West, and toward Scandinavia in particular; Russia represented another world. "What the Russians required was security, and the conviction that Finland would not again be used as a jumping-off place for an attack on Soviet Russia, an attitude which he quite understood." [25] The head of the Northern Department at the Foreign Office, Christopher Warner, commented: "Mr. Paasikivi is a wise old man." [26]

After the trials and tribulations of the spring, the Finnish government adopted a cautious line on Marshall aid, the big question that loomed up in the summer of 1947. On 4 July, Bevin and Bidault issued an invitation to all European countries (with the exception of Franco's Spain and the Soviet Union, which had already adopted a negative attitude), to take part in a conference on European economic recovery to be held in Paris. One day later, the Soviet Union set out its objections to a number of the countries that had received invitations, including Finland, where the task was entrusted to Minister Abramov. Obedient to the Moscow line, the Eastern European countries turned down the invitations. In Finland, both the president and the government shared a strong desire to get hold of "free dollars." On 7 July, the deputy chairman of the Control Commission, Lieutenant General Savonenkov, made sure that Prime Minister Pekkala understood that the Soviet Union would oppose the participation of a Finnish delegation at the Paris conference. As Enckell later told Gripenberg, "that was that, as far as Finland is concerned." It is worth noting that the normal diplomatic channels—the Soviet legation in Helsinki—was not used to pass on this message; rather, the Control Commission did so, as if to emphasize the state of armistice.

On 10 July, Pekkala gave an account of Savonenkov's message to the foreign affairs committee of Parliament. In these circumstances, the government had decided to turn down the invitation, and this decision was not to be changed. Ignoring Pekkala's tough words, the committee nonetheless voted by ten to five to recommend acceptance of the invitation, the majority consisting of members of the Social Democratic, Agrarian, Conservative, and Liberal parties. After the prime minister's statement, no room for doubt was left as to the government's position. Because the majority was not prepared to press a vote of no confidence, however, its actions are difficult to separate from internal party and political calculations. The decision to turn down the "free dollars" was unpopular in the country, and it could now be conveniently shuffled off onto the shoulders of the president and the government.

The final decision to turn down the invitation was made a day later (the last day for replies) at a meeting chaired by the president at his summer residence. In its reply, the government stated: "As Finland's position as a state has not yet been established in the form of a permanent peace treaty, and since the Marshall Plan has developed into a matter of deep controversy between the Great Powers, Finland, wishing to stay out of global conflicts, regrettably does not regard it possible to take part in the said conference." The reply nevertheless went on to point out that Finland sincerely desired purely economic cooperation with other states and needed foreign aid in the work of reconstruction. For this reason, the government announced that it was willing to supply information on the Finnish economy.

Interest in economic cooperation was thus clearly underlined in the reply, even if the Finns were unable to participate in the Paris conference. Moreover, the Americans were left in no doubt that the Finns had not abandoned Marshall aid of their own volition, but because of Savonenkov's ban: Member of Parliament Onni Peltonen made sure, for example, that the minutes of the parliamentary foreign affairs committee were delivered to the American legation. The State Department was satisfied with the Finns' position. The Head of the Office of European Affairs, John Hickerson, assured Minister Jutila that the United States understood Helsinki's refusal and wished to keep Finland out of political complications.[27]

As the local government elections approached in the autumn of 1947, the political temperature in Finland once more began to rise in a manner that aroused anxiety among the Western powers. According to information received in London, the Social Democrats were planning to create a new government crisis. Without wishing to interfere officially, the Foreign Office asked the head of the Labor Party's International Department, Denis Healey, to make a confidential approach to his acquaintance Väinö Leskinen, the organizational secretary of the Social Democratic Party. Although it was not the task or the right of the British to hand out advice, Healey admitted:

I must tell you that we feel here it is of the greatest importance that the political situation should remain stable in Finland during the next few months. We have evidence to suggest that the Soviet Union is preparing to ratify all the "satellite" peace treaties in the immediate future. As soon as Finland is an independent sovereign state again the perspectives for your party will be completely altered. It is therefore essential that you should give the Russians no reason or excuse, either for delaying ratification of the Finnish treaty, or for pursuing direct action by force against Finnish democracy in anticipation of early ratification.[28]

It was not for nothing that Healey spoke about the approaching ratification. Britain, France, and the United States had all reached their decisions. Serious consideration was thus given in June 1947 to the idea that the new political representative about to travel to Helsinki to replace Shepherd, Oswald Scott, might formally be given the title of Special Envoy and Minister Plenipotentiary. In this event, it would also be possible to do away with the provisional nature of the Finnish mission in London. Careful to avoid making the already complicated problem of ratification even more difficult, however, the Foreign Office eventually decided to wait a while. Not wishing to offend the Finns by sending Scott to Helsinki as a "political representative," however, the government gave him leave to remain for the time being in London; the mission in Helsinki remained in the care of the temporary chargé d'affaires Ledward after Shepherd's departure on 8 July. At the farewell luncheon, Paasikivi felt obliged to say that for formal reasons he could not follow his usual custom and present the Order of the Finnish White Rose to the departing political representative, who had to be content with an autographed copy of a photograph of the president.[29]

Faithful to its adopted policy, the Soviet Union expected all the former satellite countries to complete ratification before it did. Once more, Italy proved to be a stumbling block. The reason for the delaying tactic this time was the thought that the Soviet Union would never complete ratification. To make matters worse, the prorogation of the Italian National Constituent Assembly for the holiday period in July-August threatened to prolong matters for several more weeks.

A way out of the seemingly deadlocked situation was found: under pressure from the Western powers, the Italian National Constituent Assembly agreed at the last moment, on 31 July, to ratify the peace treaty by 262 votes to 68 on condition that the Soviet Union did the same. Rumania, Bulgaria, and Hungary followed this example in August; finally, on 29 August, the Soviet Union decided to ratify the treaties. The Italian government ratified the peace treaty on 4 September.[30]

In accordance with the agreement reached by the Great Powers, the documents ratifying the Italian peace treaty were deposited at the Quai d'Orsay on 15 September and the corresponding Balkan and Finnish documents were left with the Soviet Foreign Ministry the same day. Finnish Minister Cay Sundström reported on the occasion:

> The days preceding it were difficult ones for the legations of the former satellite states, because when the ratification documents were checked, they were found to contain printing errors and other irregularities. Nevertheless, all managed to obtain new copies before the date for deposition except

Rumania, which had to leave a corrected copy, as there was no time to send a new one to Moscow.

The victorious powers deposited their treaties at 6 p.m., and the defeated countries two hours later, at the Foreign Ministry. . . . The protocol department of the Soviet Foreign Ministry had announced that the Russians would arrive in full-dress uniform, but that we would be free to choose our manner of dress. After conferring among ourselves, we decided to wear evening dress. Molotov received us cordially, and at 8 p.m., the deposition ceremony got under way. Rumania, which had an embassy, was first, followed by Bulgaria, Hungary, and Finland. When I handed the ratification document of the Finnish peace treaty to Molotov, he smiled and said: "It's very thin, but elegant." At six minutes past eight, Molotov and the undersigned signed the protocol, after which we shook hands, with Molotov expressing the desire for peace between Finland and the Soviet Union in the future. After this, we drank a toast to peace, and after familiarities were exchanged, the ceremony ended at 8:20 p.m.[31]

The peace treaty had finally come into force; the last remnants of the Control Commission, headed by Lieutenant-General Savonenkov, left Finland on 26 September 1947.

Conclusion

Conclusion
Finland and
the Great Powers,
1944-1947

On the international level, the year 1944 was something of a transitional period, in spite of the world war that was still raging. The fate of the Axis powers, politically and militarily on the verge of collapse, seemed to be sealed: it was now more a matter of how long they could last before they finally crumbled. The course of events on the battlefield, in fact, imposed an indelible mark upon the overall pattern of developments in 1944. The joint front of the Western Allies and the Soviet Union had been given firmer contours at the Teheran conference at the end of 1943, and this was to last until the end of the war. All efforts were to be bent toward defeating the common enemy. Neither side wished to risk provoking divisions by bringing latent differences out into the open. Although a start was made on the plans for the future world organization, the United Nations, at the Dumbarton Oaks Conference in autumn 1944, the details of the postwar world were for the most part postponed to a future date. This state of affairs did not change until the collapse of Germany and Japan in 1945, when a thorough sifting through of the debris left by the war could be postponed no longer.

For Finland, however, 1944 was a year of fundamental and far-reaching change; the country passed from alliance with Germany, concluded in the dying stages of the Continuation War, into an armistice agreement with the Soviet Union. The fulfillment of the terms of this agreement were to mark the beginning of a completely new phase of cooperation with the Soviet Union.

The overriding aim of the Third Reich in the first half of 1944 was to prevent Finland from concluding a separate peace. The methods and tactics employed were consistent to the end. It was not until Finland came under extreme pressure from the Red Army's massive offensive on the Karelian Isthmus in June 1944 that the circumstances were created for the Germans to tie the Finns more tightly

277

to their side. The end result was the agreement between President Ryti and Ribbentrop, which obliged Finland to abandon any idea of making a separate peace. Having succeeded in stemming the Russian assault, the Finns were able, with the aid of a change of president, to free themselves from the agreement Ryti had made in a personal capacity. The Germans no longer had the resources to keep Finland in the fold, nor were there quislings of any significance in the country on whom they could rely. The Germans therefore concluded that it would be best to leave the country, even though the evacuation of troops from Lapland turned out to be technically impossible to accomplish within the time limits laid down in the Soviet-Finnish armistice agreement. The Finns, weary of war and anxious to avoid further loss of life and property, strove as far as possible to smooth the way for a peaceful German withdrawal. The negotiations in Moscow during September 1944 convinced Mannerheim that the Soviet Union regarded active military operations in the north as essential for the fulfillment of the terms of the armistice. He had forced through the decision to commence an offensive against Finland's former comrades in arms in the teeth of opposition from GHQ in Mikkeli, which placed its hopes on the "autumn maneuvers" agreed upon between Finnish and German officers. By the end of 1944, Finnish territory, with the exception of the northwestern tip of Lapland, had been cleared of German forces. The last troops of the Third Reich left Finnish soil in April 1945.

The British had adopted a policy of noninterference towards Finland as early as the end of 1941. The settlement of the Finnish question, in which the British government had no vital interest, was seen as primarily a matter for the Soviet Union. The British were thus content to play second fiddle during the armistice negotiations in Moscow, with the exception of the issue of compensation for the Petsamo nickel mines, which was of direct interest to the British and Canadians. Nevertheless, the agreement made with Finland was kept under scrutiny as a possible precedent for future armistice and peace agreements that might be of more importance for Great Britain. The British were also quite happy to accept the very modest role, almost that of an onlooker, that was reserved for them by Zhdanov on the Allied Control Commission in Helsinki.

As the Continuation War unfolded, the United States had gradually drawn closer to the British policy of noninterference in the affairs of Finland. Washington too placed good relations with the Soviet Union at the head of its list of priorities, but the goodwill felt toward Finland had not completely disappeared. Wary of the reactions of an American electorate that took the phrases of the Atlantic Charter seriously, the Roosevelt administration emphasized the importance of Finland remaining independent, as Stalin had promised at Teheran. From Washington's point of view, the best solution would be for the Soviet Union and Finland to reach agreement without the American government having to play any part. Hence Washington refrained from comment on the terms offered to Finland by the Soviet Union in spring and autumn of 1944. The breach of diplomatic relations with Finland in June 1944 helped the Americans detach themselves from the final stage of the conflict, and the Ribbentrop agreement was sufficient to quiet American public opinion. This cautious line was observed after the armistice: 1944 was, after all, the year of the American presidential elections. It was vitally important for the Roosevelt administration not to shake the faith of the voters in the continuation of the close wartime bonds between the United States and the USSR, and the idealism that such bonds had generated.

Soviet policy toward Finland in the first half of 1944 followed much the same lines as it had done since 1941. Finland was to be forced out of the war on Moscow's terms, the main content of which had been accepted by the Western powers at Teheran. At stake was not simply the relationship between Finland and the Soviet Union; as Marshal Meretskov points out in his memoirs, the Soviet government had constantly to take account of its Western Allies, and also Scandinavia, in determing its policy toward Finland. "In practice, the Scandinavian countries' own appraisal of our foreign policy and their corresponding formulation of their own relations with the USSR were founded in the first instance on the way in which the relations of Finland and the USSR developed." [1]

The terms offered to Finland in spring 1944 were felt by the Finns to be excessively severe. In the prevailing atmosphere of distrust, they were seen as signifying merely the beginning of a road that would ultimately lead to the destruction of Finnish independence. Belief in a German victory, however, had long since vanished in responsible circles in Finland. In these circumstances, the Finns resorted to delaying tactics in the hope that the expected landing of the Western powers on the European mainland would act as a counterbalance to Soviet influence. It was even hoped that Finland might succeed in steering clear of the maelstrom by procrastinating until the eventual collapse of Germany and final settlement. Military events on the Finnish-Soviet front in the summer of 1944, however, knocked the bottom out of this policy of wait and see.

The sheer strength of the Red Army offensive in this northwestern sector of operations was a harsh reality that could not be ignored by the Finns. The kind of reference to an unbeaten army lying deep in enemy territory, made in the spring of 1944, was now no longer possible. In like manner, the theoretical possibility of a "stab-in-the-back" legend emerging some time in the future was laid low. On the other hand, the Finns, mustering all their resources, had at the last been able to halt the enemy advance, at least temporarily, and Moscow was not to repeat its demand for surrender made in June 1944. The psychological prerequisites for later coexistence, founded on mutual respect, were beginning to take shape.

The problem of provisions, which had earlier been held to be an unsuperable obstacle to the conclusion of peace, was solved in August 1944 when the Swedish government, having now abandoned its cautious passivity in the face of the German presence in Scandinavia, promised to send essential supplies in the

interim period following a ceasefire. The deep-seated fears and suspicions of the
Finns notwithstanding, the situation was thus prepared for the armistice agreement
of September 1944. It was to be the task of the Allied Control Commission,
dominated by the Russians, to make sure that the terms agreed upon in Moscow
were faithfully carried out in Finland.

How then did the Kremlin see Finland in 1944, especially after the conclusion
of the armistice agreement? It is essential to attempt some sort of analysis of
this central problem, even if original Soviet material is for the time being unavailable for research purposes. Was it intended, as many in Finland at the time
believed, to help the local communists to create the kind of conditions in which
they could be used as instruments for the bolshevization of the country? Several
political articles of the armistice agreement did give rise to this sort of interpretation at the time. The policy pursued by the ACC over the war guilt question
was even more alarming in this respect. It is clear that the ACC and the armistice
agreement, especially Article 13, offered in the short term an additional and
fundamental source of support for the radical left in Finland—in particular the
communists, whose whole ideological armory, political objectives, and earlier
experiences were geared to seeking revenge on those responsible for the previous
policies of the country. As Jukka Tarkka has shown, extreme leftists in Finland
strove to link their desire for revenge and their struggle for political power to
the question of responsibility for the war.[2]

The political left in Finland in the autumn of 1944 can in no way be described
as a united or monolithic grouping, and the full extent of its aims still awaits
detailed study. In the first number of the official Finnish Communist Party
periodical *Kommunisti*, Party Secretary Ville Pessi condemned those "extreme
left-wing elements" who in opposition to party policy expected the Soviet Union
to do their work for them. Pessi argued that they were incapable of grasping the
fact that "the Soviet Union will not interfere in our country's internal affairs.
. . . We have to look after our own affairs and we are able to do this, too."
Such people spoke of setting up a Soviet system in Finland, but (Pessi emphasized)
"our country is not ready to go over to such a system, however desirable it may
be. The overwhelming majority of the people of Finland are unwilling to go
over to the Soviet system."[3]

With or without good reason, Moscow obviously regarded the former leaders
of the country, who still enjoyed considerable support and prestige among the
Finnish public, as hindrances to the creation of a change of direction in Finnish
foreign policy. Seen in this light, the "branding" and removal from public life
of these figures proved to be a significant factor in the clearing of the way for
new, though not necessarily communist political leaders in Finland. It is quite
a different matter how far the popular mood was accurately gauged when those
accused of responsibility for the war were elevated to the status of martyrs and
expiators of the nation's guilt in the eyes of large numbers of Finns—something

that also made difficult the development of mutual trust in the relations between Finland and the Soviet Union.

In general, the claims that the ACC sought to bolshevize Finland must be seen as clearly inconsistent with the policy followed by Moscow toward Finland from the autumn of 1944. In spite of its stern exactions, the ACC cannot be said to have exceeded the bounds of the armistice agreement, even though opinions over the interpretation of certain details did widely differ. The possibility of an internal revolution (which, naturally, would not have been opposed by Moscow) seemed unlikely in the postwar social conditions in Finland, and relations between the two countries could not be based on such a vague hope. Stalin and Zhdanov were hardly likely to have forgotten the experience of the Terijoki government, set up at the outbreak of the Winter War and hastily abandoned after two months. It is my belief, which the original sources in due course may prove to be right or wrong, that the Control Commission, following the instructions of the Soviet leadership, *sought to smooth the way for the new Finnish foreign policy that was emerging* and that was later to be associated with the name of Paasikivi. In other words, a durable, long-term basis for mutual trust and cooperation had to be created.

*   *   *   *   *

The ending of the war involved more than just the collapse of German, Italian, and Japanese power. Of the victors, Britain had lost a great deal of its former might and, beset with internal political and economic problems and imperial worries, was fast sliding toward the status of a second-rate power. The same was true of France, now liberated from the occupation. The partial political vacuum thus created was filled by the two superpowers, the United States and the Soviet Union. Their comparative strength notwithstanding, neither superpower felt able to give way on what both regarded as vital security interests in the new "bipolar" international system that was emerging as a result of World War II. At first, attempts were made to keep differences over security policy, which were bolstered by economic and ideological quarrels, out of public view. As we have seen, the practice of putting off knotty problems to a future date and concealing differences of opinion in phrases of a sufficiently general nature had become the norm in wartime summit conferences, down to the meetings at Yalta and Potsdam. When the four-power (originally five-power) Council of Foreign Ministers began its deliberations in the autumn of 1945, however, and found itself having to deal with the concrete details of the postwar world, such problems could no longer be swept under the carpet.

The delegation headed by Secretary of State James F. Byrnes set off from Washington in September 1945 for the London conference, confident that the military and economic might of the United States, with its monopoly of the atom bomb, would be sufficient to persuade the Soviet Union to agree to the American line on the peace treaties, at least in general terms. American public opinion, nurtured on the ideals of the Atlantic Charter and the wartime alliance, expected swift decisions that would "bring the boys back home" and sort out the muddle left by the war in accordance with American ideals. At Lancaster House, however, Byrnes found that the Soviet Union expected guarantees for its own security and recognition of its Great Power position as revealed in the war. This involved, among other things, the question of the Balkans, reparations (seen as important for postwar reconstruction), and participation in the administration of the occupied Italian colonies and Japan. The Soviet demands ran contrary to the American interpretation of the principles of self-determination, free trade, and collective security; moreover, they were a challenge to the dominant position of the United States. These fundamental disagreements led to the collapse of the London conference. Byrnes, who had adopted the role of peacemaker, now sought to lay the blame for this unexpected failure upon the Soviet Union, which he accused in public of pursuing "expansionist aims."

American public opinion, weaned on the phraseology of the war years, had never been prepared for the problems of peacemaking by Roosevelt, whose policy operated in fact on two levels: "realism" in the international arena and "Wilsonian" ideals for domestic consumption. Hence, the frustrated reaction took the form of a growing anti-Soviet mood. As the 1946 congressional elections drew near, the shift in public opinion affected leading decision makers, including President Truman, and this in turn influenced American foreign policy. As Ward has shown, Byrnes also found himself having to operate a kind of two-tier diplomacy after his return from Moscow at the end of 1945 and in his efforts at the foreign ministers' meetings in Paris to secure the peace treaties. In public, the secretary of state adopted a tough line with the Soviet Union; but in private discussions, he displayed a degree of willingness to compromise in order to push things along.[4] In the open sessions of the Paris peace conference, the United States took an intransigent line, seeking to mobilize the "world conscience" against the Soviet Union, though with little success.

Although little progress was made on the German and Austrian questions, a compromise based on mutual concessions did appear to be within the bounds of possibility that autumn in New York. Months of tough and protracted bargaining had managed to overcome all difficulties and arrive at a positive outcome in that a decision was made to accept the peace treaties with the former "satellite" states. The final ratification process in the autumn of 1947 signified a degree of partial recognition by the Great Powers of the situation created in Europe by the war. In spite of dissatisfaction with many of the details, the final conclusion of these peace treaties was of major importance—among other things, in respect of the permanency of Finland's international position.

To bolster Britain's weakening Great Power status, the Foreign Office started planning, from the spring of 1944 onwards, a postwar Western European Union to which would belong (in addition to a dominant Great Britain) France, Belgium, Holland, Norway, Denmark, and Iceland and possibly Sweden, Spain, and Portugal. In this way, Britain's position would be strengthened politically, militarily, and economically in the face of the "young superpowers," the United States and the Soviet Union. These plans, supported by the British Chiefs of Staff, were to remain on paper only, both at the time and in the immediate postwar years. The risk of annoying both the Soviet Union and the United States was seen to be too great, which is why negotiations for a union with the Western European countries were not even started before 1947.[5]

From the start, Finland was omitted from even the theoretical plans for a Western European bloc. The position of the northern republic, which was seen as belonging to the Soviet sphere of interest, was clearly outlined by Anthony Eden in August 1944: "Although we shall no doubt hope that Finland will be left some real degree of at least cultural and commercial independence and a parliamentary regime, Russian influence will in any event be predominant in Finland and we shall not be able, nor would it serve any important British interests to contest that influence."[6]

The preservation of Finland's independence was indeed a positive option from the point of view of the interests of Great Britain—not least because of foreign trade considerations—but not to the extent of taking major risks on Finland's behalf. Much also depended on the Finns' capacity to hold out. In discussions held by foreign trade officials in London in August 1945, it was agreed that timber from Finland was important; but it did not justify supporting Helsinki by, for example, investing British capital on the politically unsound market of the northern republic. Shepherd, who was present at this meeting, voiced the opinion that the Soviet Union would in any event tighten its grip on the Finnish economy and that local politicians would gradually be pushed towards communism, although the entire process might well take time.[7]

On the other hand, the British did not conceal their belief that it was in the Finns' own interest to strive for good relations with the Soviet Union, while still maintaining their independence and Nordic social structure and system. The first condition would be an unswerving commitment to carry out the terms of the armistice. In accordance with their policy of noninterference, the British avoided involvement in the development of Soviet-Finnish relations, both in the ACC and elsewhere. Above all, there could be no question of supporting Helsinki against Moscow. Any noticeable activity by the British would arouse suspicion in the Soviet Union and would only serve to make the Russians take a tougher line, in the British view. His Majesty's Government noted with some satisfaction, in fact, that the Finns, after some initial hesitation, did not even attempt to seek British assistance.

At the Paris peace talks, Finland was of importance to Britain primarily as a test case and as a point of comparison with the former enemy countries of the

Balkans. The military leadership, including the Admiralty, had written off the northern republic even before talks got under way in Paris. Britain's military interests in the north embraced Norway, Denmark, and Sweden. With regard to Finland, the British contented themselves with seeking to preserve the Åland defortification clause. In this they succeeded, since the Soviet Union took the same view. In fact, the British were even prepared to give way on this issue if necessary. The British demands in regard to the limitations imposed upon the Finnish armed forces must be seen above all against the background of the Balkan problem. In general, the British accepted the Soviet position on the terms of the 1944 armistice as a basis for the final peace treaty with Finland.

In the course of time, British optimism about Finland's chances of survival was to grow. In a general survey drawn up in February 1947, after the signing of the Paris peace treaty, Shepherd underlined the favorable progress of Soviet-Finnish relations, which were based on common sense and moderation on both sides.[8] Shepherd wished to attribute a share of this successful outcome to the British, since they had consistently refused to encourage the Finns to seek support from the West. On the contrary, the Finns had been steered away from any "stubbornness" that might be detrimental to their own interests—for example, over the war guilt question. The British were later to recommend a similar policy of caution in spring and autumn 1947 in connection with the attempts to displace the Pekkala government. On the other hand, efforts were made to avoid any weakening of confidence and goodwill toward Britain. All in all, the British believed that they had done rather well in this balancing act. In spite of the increasing tension of the Cold War, Britain favored the development of good relations between Finland and the Soviet Union as the best solution from the point of view of its own interests.

The Finnish question did not rank very high on the American list of priorities in the aftermath of World War II. The goodwill of the American public had been eroded as a political factor during the years of the Continuation War, even if it had not entirely vanished. In refraining from declaring war on Finland, the United States was also able to remain outside the process of peacemaking—with the exception of a few short-term, tactical interventions—that was to be the concern of Britain and the Soviet Union. In comparison with the Balkan countries, political developments in Finland were seen in a positive light in Washington, as well as in London. After the 1945 parliamentary elections, recognized as being "free and democratic," the United States was ready to follow the Soviet Union in restoring diplomatic relations in the spring of 1945. Stalin had given assurances that he would respect Finland's independence—an issue of domestic importance in the United States—on numerous occasions; in other respects, Washington saw little reason to interfere actively in the Finnish situation.

Like the British, the Americans thought that the Finns themselves had to take responsibility and learn to get along with the Soviet Union without building on hopes of Western support. In a survey prepared for Secretary of State Byrnes in August 1946, the State Department noted that the United States was seeking to encourage the Finns to work sincerely for the promotion of harmonious and friendly relations with the Soviet Union, without at the same time compromising their independence. The future of an independent Finland might otherwise become problematic.[9] For the time being at least, Soviet policy toward Finland gave no grounds for serious misgivings in Washington or London.

The Americans frequently took the opportunity to let the Finns know their views, as did the British. It would be pointless to seek support from the West for anti-Soviet attitudes because the resurgence of such attitudes might provoke the Soviet Union to take countermeasures in a manner that would disturb the prevailing equilibrium and this could not be regarded as in the interests of the West. Although there was general acknowledgment of the Finns' toughness and ability to fight, the restrained and moderate line being followed by Moscow toward Finland was nevertheless noted in Washington and London with a mixture of suspicion and surprise: the Western powers evidently had difficulty in believing in the permanence of this line. Nevertheless, Charles E. Bohlen, one of the leading Soviet experts in the State Department, wrote as early as October 1945 that the Soviet-Finnish relationship in future would rest upon "a healthier foundation" from the point of view of the Soviet Union's own interests in comparison with many other states bordering on the USSR, which had not been shown the same degree of restraint.[10]

In accordance with their established policy of not financing the reparations payments of other countries, and wishing to keep an eye on the way things developed in Finland, the Americans were at first extremely cautious toward requests from Helsinki for economic aid. This situation changed by degrees from the beginning of 1946. As the Americans gradually became convinced of the Finns' ability to manage their relations with the Soviet Union and the West, they began to look more favorably upon such requests.

The policy of noninterference in Finnish affairs was consistently followed in its essentials down to the ratification of the Paris peace treaty. After Finland turned down Marshall aid in July 1947, the retiring head of the Office of European Affairs of the State Department, H. Freeman "Doc" Matthews, noted that the Soviet Union's policy toward Finland was now firmly established. Unless there was a panicky reaction to a possible general European crisis, changes in this policy were hardly to be expected, provided the Finns themselves did not give cause for such a change. In these circumstances, the United States had good reason to continue its former cautious policy. Economic aid for reconstruction could be granted, within suitable limits; but at the same time, the United States should avoid actions in Finland that the Soviet Union might reasonably interpret as a challenge to its own vital interests.[11]

In comparison with the other states that had fought on the German side during

World War II, only the Finnish "model" seemed to be acceptable to *all* the victorious Great Powers. From the Finnish point of view, however, the course adopted by the Soviet Union was decisive. The Western powers also kept a sharp eye on USSR policy before defining their own, though Moscow was constantly aware of the reactions of the Western powers and the Scandinavian countries when shaping its policy toward Finland. Seen over the perspective of four decades, however, Soviet policy has shown itself to be far too consistent to have been constructed simply as a consequence of these external influences. Although the lack of original sources means that any conclusions must for the time being remain hypothetical, the indicators seem to point strongly to a willingness on the part of the Soviet leadership—in spite of ideological differences—to trust in the durability of the new foreign policy being forged by Paasikivi and in the promising prospect of a satisfactory settlement of the interests of both sides that this offered. The knotty problems of 1945-47—the war guilt trials, the arms dump affair, and the "peace crisis" — were unable to break this basic equation. Gradually it could be seen that the Finns were working to secure this new policy, not simply because they were compelled to as a result of losing the war, but because the Paasikivi line offered a means in the long run of securing the country's own national interests. These conclusions were to be given a more permanent form in the 1948 Treaty of Friendship, Cooperation and Mutual Assistance after the legacy of World War II, in the matter of the relationship between Finland and the Soviet Union, had finally been settled by the Paris peace treaty in 1947.

Appendixes

Appendix 1
Armistice Agreement

Between the Union of Soviet Socialist Republics and the United Kingdom of Great Britain and Northern Ireland, on the one hand, and Finland on the other.

Whereas the Finnish Government has accepted the preliminary condition of the Soviet Government regarding a break with Germany and the removal of German troops from Finland, and whereas the conclusion of a future treaty of peace will be facilitated by the inclusion in an Armistice Agreement of certain conditions of this peace treaty, the Government of the Union of Soviet Socialist Republics and His Majesty's Government in the United Kingdom of Great Britain and Northern Ireland, acting on behalf of all the United Nations at war with Finland, on the one hand, and the Government of Finland, on the other hand, have decided to conclude the present agreement for an armistice, the execution of which will be controlled by the Soviet High Command similarly acting on behalf of the United Nations at war with Finland, hereinafter named the Allied (Soviet) High Command.

On the basis of the foregoing the representative of the Allied (Soviet) High Command, Colonel-General A. A. Zhdanov, and the representatives of the Government of Finland, Mr. Carl Enckell, Minister of Foreign Affairs, General Rudolf Walden, Minister of Defence, General Erik Heinrichs, Chief of General Staff, and Lieutenant-General Oscar Enckell, duly authorised thereto, have signed the following conditions:—

Article 1

In connexion with the cessation of military activities on the part of Finland on the 4th September, 1944, and on the part of the Soviet Union on the 5th September, 1944, Finland undertakes to withdraw her troops behind the line of the Soviet-Finnish frontier of 1940 in accordance with the procedure laid down in the Annex attached to the present Agreement. (See Annex to Article 1).

Article 2

Finland undertakes to disarm the German land, naval and air armed forces which have remained in Finland since the 15th September, 1944, and to hand over their personnel to the Allied (Soviet) High Command as prisoners of war, in which task the Soviet Government will assist the Finnish army.

The Finnish Government also accepts the obligation to intern German and Hungarian nationals in Finnish territory. (See Annex to Article 2).

Article 3

Finland undertakes to make available at the request of the Allied (Soviet) High Command the aerodromes on the southern and south-western coast of Finland with all equipment to serve as bases for Soviet aircraft during the period necessary for air operations against German forces in Estonia and against the German navy in the northern part of the Baltic Sea. (See Annex to Article 3).

Article 4

Finland undertakes to place her army on a peace footing within two and a half months from the day of signing of the present Agreement. (See Annex to Article 4).

Article 5

Finland, having broken off all relations with Germany, also undertakes to break off all relations with Germany's satellite States. (See Annex to Article 5).

Article 6

The effect of the Peace Treaty between the Soviet Union and Finland, concluded in Moscow on the 12th of March, 1940, is restored subject to the changes which follow from the present Agreement.

Article 7

Finland returns to the Soviet Union the oblast of Petsamo (Pechenga), voluntarily ceded to Finland by the Soviet State in accordance with the Peace Treaties of the 14th October, 1920, and the 12th March, 1940, within the boundary indicated in the Annex and on the map attached to the present Agreement. See Annex to Article 7 and map to scale 1: 500,000).

Article 8

The Soviet Union renounces its rights to the lease of the Peninsula of Hangö, accorded to it by the Soviet-Finnish Peace Treaty of 12th March, 1940, and Finland for her part undertakes to make available for the Soviet Union on lease territory and waters for the establishment of a Soviet naval base in the area of Porkkala-Udd.

The boundaries of the land and water area of the base at Porkkala-Udd are defined in the Annex to the present article and indicated on the map. (See Annex to Article 8 and map to scale 1: 100,000).

Article 9

The effect of the Agreement concerning the Aaland Islands, concluded between the Soviet Union and Finland on the 11th October, 1940, is completely restored.

Article 10

Finland undertakes immediately to transfer to the Allied (Soviet) High Command to be returned to their homeland all Soviet and Allied prisoners of war now in her power and also Soviet and Allied nationals who have been interned in or deported by force to Finland.

From the moment of the signing of the present Agreement and up to the time of repatriation Finland undertakes to provide at her cost for all Soviet and Allied prisoners of war and also nations who have been deported by force or interned adequate food, clothing and medical service in accordance with hygienic requirements, and also with means of transport for their return to their homeland.

At the same time Finnish prisoners of war and interned persons now located on the territory of Allied states will be transferred to Finland.

Article 11

Losses caused by Finland to the Soviet Union by military operations and the occupation of Soviet territory will be indemnified by Finland to the Soviet Union to the amount of three hundred million dollars payable over six years in commodities (timber products, paper, cellulose, seagoing and river craft, sundry machinery).

Provision will also be made for the indemnification in the future by Finland of the losses caused during the war to the property of the other Allied States and their nationals in Finland, the amount of the compensation to be fixed separately. (See Annex to Article 11).

Article 12

Finland undertakes to restore all legal rights and interests of the United Nations and their nationals located on Finnish territory as they existed before the war and to return their property in complete good order.

Article 13

Finland undertakes to collaborate with the Allied powers in the apprehension of persons accused of war crimes and in their trial.

Article 14

Finland undertakes within the periods fixed by the Allied (Soviet) High Command to return to the Soviet Union in complete good order all valuables and materials removed from Soviet territory to Finland during the war belonging to State, public and cooperative organisations, factories, institutions or individual citizens, such as: equipment for factories and works, locomotives, railway carriages, ships, tractors, motor vehicles, historical monuments, valuables from museums and all other property.

Article 15

Finland undertakes to transfer as booty to the disposition of the Allied (Soviet) High Command all war material of Germany and her satellites located on Finnish territory, including naval and other ships belonging to these countries in Finnish waters.

Article 16

Finland undertakes not to permit the export or expropriation of any form of property, (including valuables and currency) belonging to Germany or Hungary or to their nationals or to persons resident in their territories or in the territories occupied by them without the permission of the Allied (Soviet) High Command.

Article 17

Finnish merchant ships other than those already under Allied control shall be placed under the control of the Allied (Soviet) High Command for their use in the general interests of the Allies.

Article 18

Finland undertakes to transfer to the Allied (Soviet) High Command all ships in Finnish ports belonging to the United Nations, no matter at whose disposal these vessels may be, for the use of the Allied (Soviet) High Command for the duration of the war against Germany in the general interests of the Allies, these vessels subsequently to be returned to their owners.

Article 19

Finland will make available such materials and products as may be required by the United Nations for purposes connected with the war.

Article 20

Finland undertakes immediately to release all persons, irrespective of citizenship or nationality, held in prison on account of their activities in favour of the United Nations or because of their sympathies with the cause of the United Nations, or in view of their racial origin, and will also remove all discriminatory legislation and disabilities arising therefrom.

Article 21

Finland undertakes immediately to dissolve all pro-Hitler organisations (of a Fascist type) situated on Finnish territory, whether political, military or para-military, as well as other organisations conducting propaganda hostile to the United Nations, in particular to the Soviet Union, and will not in future permit the existence of organisations of that nature.

Article 22

An allied Control Commission will be established which until the conclusion of peace with Finland will undertake the regulation and control of the execution of the present Agreement under the general direction and instructions of the Allied (Soviet) High Command, acting on behalf of the Allied powers. (See Annex to Article 22).

Article 23

The present Agreement comes into force as from the moment of signature. Done in Moscow the nineteenth day of September, 1944, in one copy which will be entrusted to the safekeeping of the Government of the Union of Soviet Socialist Republics, in the Russian, English and Finnish languages, the Russian and English texts being authentic.

Certified copies of the present Agreement, with Annexes and maps, will be transmitted by the Government of the Union of Soviet Socialist Republics to each of the other Governments on whose behalf the present Agreement is signed.

For the Governments of the Union of Soviet Socialist Republics and the United Kingdom

> A. Zhdanov.
> M. P.

For the Government of Finland

> C. Enckell
> R. Walden
> E. Heinrichs
> O. Enckell
> l. p.

Annexes

To the armistice agreement between the Union of Soviet Socialist Republics and the United Kingdom of Great Britain and Northern Ireland on the one hand and Finland; on the other, signed in Moscow on the 19th September, 1944.

A. Annex to Article 1

The procedure for the withdrawal of Finnish troops behind the line of the State frontier between the U.S.S.R. and Finland laid down in the Peace Treaty of the 12th March, 1940, subject to the modifications arising from the Armistice Agreement signed on the 19th September, 1944, on all sectors occupied by Finnish troops, shall be as follows:—

1. In the course of the first day as from the moment of signing of the Armistice Agreement Finnish troops shall be withdrawn to such a distance that there shall be a gap of not less than one kilometre between the forward units of the Red Army and the Finnish troops.

2. Within forty-eight hours (two days), counted as from the same moment, the Finnish troops shall make passages through their mines, barbed wire, and other defences to a width of not less than thirty metres in order thereby to make possible the free movement of battalion columns with their transport, and shall also enclose the remaining mine fields within clearly visible marks.

The above-mentioned passages in the Defences and the enclosure of mine fields shall be made throughout the whole territory from which Finnish troops are withdrawn.

The clearance of passages by Finnish troops shall be made on all roads or paths which many serve for movement both in the neutral belt of one kilometre and also throughout the whole depth of the defences.

Towards the end of the second day the Command of the Finnish troops shall hand over to the appropriate Red Army Command exact plans of all types of defences with an indication on these plans of the passages made and to be made by the Finnish troops and also of the enclosures of all mine fields.

3. The Finnish Command shall hand over within a period of five days to the Command of the Red Army and Navy the charts, forms and descriptive maps at its disposal with legends for all mine fields and other defences on land, in rivers, and lakes and in the Baltic and Barents Seas together with data about the courses and channels to be recommended and the rules for navigation along them.

4. The complete removal of mines, barbed wire and other defences throughout the territory from the line occupied by the advanced Finnish units to the line of the state frontier, and also the sweeping and the removal of all defences from the channels on the approaches to Soviet territories, shall be made by the Finnish land and naval forces in the shortest possible time and in not more than forty days from the moment of the signing of the Armistice Agreement.

5. The withdrawal of Finnish troops behind the state frontier and the advance of the troops of the Red Army up to it shall begin as from 9.0 a.m. on the 21st September, 1944, simultaneously along the whole length of the front.

The withdrawal of Finnish troops shall be carried out in daily marches of not less than 15 kilometres a day and the advance of the troops of the Red Army shall take place in such a manner that there shall be a distance of 15 kilometres between the rear units of the Finnish troops and the advanced units of the Red Army.

6. In accordance with paragraph 5 the following limits are set for the withdrawal of Finnish troops on individual sectors behind the line of the state frontier:

On the sector Vuokinsalmi, Riihimäki the 1st October
On the sector Riihimäki, River Koitajoki, the 3rd October
On the sector River Koitajoki, Korpiselkä the 24th September
On the sector Korpiselka, Lake Pyhajärvi the 28th September
On the sector Pyhajärvi, Koitsanlahti the 26th September
On the sector Koitsanlahti, Station Enso the 28th September
On the sector Station Enso, Virolahti the 24th September.

The retreating Finnish troops shall take with them only such reserves of munitions, food, fodder and fuel and lubricants as they can carry and transport with them. All other stores shall be left on the spot and shall be handed over to the Command of the Red Army.

7. The Finnish Military Command shall hand over on the territories which are being returned or ceded to the Soviet Union in complete good order and repair all inhabited points, means of communication, defence and economic structures including: bridges, dams, aerodromes, barracks, warehouses, railway junctions, station buildings, industrial enterprises, hydrotechnical buildings, ports and wharves, telegraph offices, telephone exchanges, electric power stations, lines of communication and electric power lines.

The Finnish Military Command shall give instructions for the timely de-mining of all the installations enumerated above which are to be handed over.

8. When the Finnish troops are being withdrawn behind the line of the State frontier the Government of Finland shall guarantee the personal inviolability and the preservation of the dwelling places of the population of the territory to be abandoned by the Finnish troops together with the preservation of all the property belonging to this population and of the property of public, cooperative, cultural-social services and other organisations.

9. All questions which may arise in connexion with the transfer by the Finnish authorities of the installations enumerated in paragraph 7 of this Annex shall be settled on the spot by representatives of both sides, for which purpose special representatives for the period of the withdrawal of the troops shall be appointed by the Command to each basic route for the movements of the troops of both armies.

10. The advance of Soviet troops to the line of the State frontier on the sectors occupied by German troops shall be made in accordance with the instructions of the Command of the Soviet forces.

B. Annex to Article 2

1. The Finnish Military Command shall hand over to the Allied (Soviet) High Command within a period fixed by the latter all the information at its disposal regarding the German armed forces and the plans of the German military Command for the development of military operations against the Union of Soviet Socialist Republics and the other United Nations and also the charts and maps and all operational documents relating to the military operations of the German armed forces.

2. The Finnish Government shall instruct its appropriate authorities regularly to supply the Allied (Soviet) High Command with meteorological information.

C. Annex to Article 3

1. In accordance with Article 3 of the Agreement the Allied (Soviet) High Command will indicate to the Finnish Military Command which aerodromes must be placed at the disposal of the Allied (Soviet) High Command and what equipment must remain on the aerodromes and equally will lay down the manner in which these aerodromes are to be used.

The Finnish Government shall enable the Soviet Union to make use of the railways, waterways, roads and air routes necessary for the transport of personnel and freight despatched from the Soviet Union to the areas where the abovementioned aerodromes are situated.

2. Henceforth until the end of the war against Germany Allied naval vessels and merchant ships shall have the right to make use of the territorial waters, ports, wharves, and anchorages of Finland. The Finnish Government shall afford the necessary collaboration as regards material and technical services.

D. Annex to Article 4

1. In accordance with Article 4 of the Agreement the Finnish Military Command shall immediately make available to the Allied (Soviet) High Command full infor-

mation regarding the composition, armament and location of all the land, sea and air forces of Finland and shall come to an agreement with the Allied (Soviet) High Command regarding the manner of placing the Finnish army on a peace footing within the period fixed by the Agreement.

2. All Finnish naval vessels, merchant ships and aircraft for the period of the war against Germany must be returned to their bases, ports and aerodromes and must not leave them without obtaining the requisite permission to do so from the Allied (Soviet) High Command.

E. Annex to Article 5

1. By the rupture referred to in Article 5 of the Agreement by Finland of all relations with Germany and her satellites is meant the rupture of all diplomatic, consular and other relations and also of postal, telegraphic and telephone communications between Finland and Germany and Hungary.

2. The Finnish Government undertakes in future until such time as the withdrawal of German troops from Finland is completed to discontinue postal diplomatic communications and also any radiotelegraphic or telegraphic cypher correspondence and telephone communications with foreign countries by diplomatic missions and consulates located in Finland.

F. Annex to Article 7

The line of the state frontier between the Union of Soviet Socialist Republics and Finland, in connexion with the return by Finland to the Soviet Union of the oblast of Patsamo (Pechenga), shall proceed as follows:

From the boundary post No. 859/90 (Korvatunturi), near the Lake Jaurujärvi, the line of the State frontier shall be fixed in a North-westerly direction along the former Russian-Finnish boundary by boundary posts Nos. 91, 92 and 93 to the boundary post No. 94, where formerly the frontiers of Russia, Norway and Finland met.

Thence the line of the frontier shall run in a general North-easterly along the former Russian-Norwegian State frontier to Varanger-Fjord (see the attached Russian map, scale 1 : 500,000).

The line of the frontier, fixed from the boundary post No. 859/90 (Korvatunturi), to the boundary post No. 94, will be demarcated on the spot by a Soviet-Finnish Mixed Commission.

The Commission will establish boundary signs, will make a detailed description of this line and will enter it on a map of the scale of 1 : 25,000.

The Commission will be in its work on a date to be specified by the Soviet Military Command.

The description of the boundary line and the map of this line made by the abovementioned Commission shall be confirmed by both Governments.

G. Annex to Article 8

1. The boundary line of the area of Porkkala-Udd leased by the Union of Soviet Socialist Republics from Finland shall begin at a point of which the map references are: latitude 59° 50′ North; longitude 24° 07′ East. Thence the boundary line shall

proceed North along the meridian 24° 07′ to a point of which the map references are: latitude 60° 06′ 12″ North; longitude 24° 07′ East. Thence the boundary line shall proceed along the line indicated in the map in a Northerly direction to a point of which the map references are: latitude 60° 08′ 6″ North; longitude 24° 07′ 36″ East.

Thence the boundary line shall proceed along the line indicated on the map in a general North-Easterly by Easterly direction to a point of which the map references are: latitude 60° 10′ 24″ North; longitude 24° 34′ 6″ East. Thence along the line indicated on the map along the bay of Espon-Lahti, and further East of the islands of Småholmarna, Björkön, Medvastö, Högholm, and Stor-Hamnholm to a point of which the map references are: latitude 60° 02′ 54″ North; longitude 24° 37′ 42″ East, and thence the boundary line shall proceed South along the meridian 24° 37′ 42″ to the outer boundaries of Finnish territorial waters. (See the map, scale 1: 100,000 attached to the present Agreement).

The boundary line of the leased area of Porkkala-Udd will be demarcated on the spot by a Soviet-Finnish Mixed Commission. The Commission shall establish boundary marks and shall draw up a detailed description of this line and shall enter it upon a topographical map scale 1: 20,000 and a naval map scale 1: 50,000.

The Commission shall be in its work on a date to be specified by the Soviet Naval Command.

The description of the boundary line of the leased area and the map of that line prepared by the abovementioned Commission shall be confirmed by both Governments.

2. In accordance with Article 8 of the Agreement the territory and water in the area of Porkkala-Udd shall be transferred by Finland to the Soviet Union within ten days from the moment of signature of the Armistice Agreement for the organisation of a Soviet naval base on lease, to be used and controlled for a period of fifty years, the Soviet Union making an annual payment of five million Finnish marks.

3. The Finnish Government undertakes to enable the Soviet Union to make use of the railways, waterways, roads and air routes necessary for the transport of personnel and freight despatched from the Soviet Union to the naval base at Porkkala-Udd.

The Finnish Government shall grant to the Soviet Union the right of unimpeded use of all forms of communication between the U.S.S.R. and the territory leased in the area of Porkkala-Udd.

H. Annex to Article 11

1. The precise nomenclature and varieties of commodities to be delivered by Finland to the Soviet Union in accordance with Article 11 of the Agreement and also the more precise periods for making these deliveries each year shall be defined in a special agreement between the two Governments.

As the basis for accounts regarding the payment of the indemnity foreseen in Article 11 of the Agreement the American dollar is to be used at its gold parity on the day of signature of the Agreement, i. e. thirty-five dollars to one ounce of gold.

I. Annex to Article 22

1. The Allied Control Commission is an organ of the Allied (Soviet) High Command to which it is directly subordinated. The Control Commission will be the

liaison link between the Allied (Soviet) High Command and the Finnish Government, through which Government the Commission will carry on all its relations with the Finnish authorities.

2. The chief task of the Control Commission is to see to the punctual and accurate fulfilment by the Finnish Government of Articles 2, 3, 4, 10, 12, 13, 14, 15, 16, 17, 18, 20 and 21 of the Armistice Agreement.

3. The Control Commission shall have the right to receive from the Finnish authorities all the information which it requires for the fulfilment of the abovementioned task.

4. In the event of the discovery of any violation of the abovementioned Articles of the Armistice Agreement the Control Commission shall make appropriate representations to the Finnish authorities in order that proper steps may be taken.

5. The Control Commission may establish special organs or sections entrusting them respectively with the execution of various tasks.

Moreover the Control Commission may through its officers make the necessary investigations and the collection of the information which it requires.

6. The Control Commission shall be established in Helsingfors.

7. The members of the Control Commission and equally its officers shall have the right to visit without let or hindrance any institution, enterprise or port and to receive there all the information necessary for their functions.

8. The Control Commission shall enjoy all diplomatic privileges, including inviolability of person, property and archives, and it shall have the right of communication by means of cypher and diplomatic courier.

9. The Control Commission shall have at its disposal a number of aircraft for the use of which the Finnish authorities shall grant all the necessary facilities.

Appendix 2
The Paris Peace Treaty, 10 February 1947

The Union of Soviet Socialist Republics, the United Kingdom of Great Britain and Northern Ireland, Australia, the Byelorussian Soviet Socialist Republic, Canada, Czechoslovakia, India, New Zealand, the Ukrainian Soviet Socialist Republic, and the Union of South Africa, as the States which are at war with Finland and actively waged war against the European enemy states with substantial military forces, hereinafter referred to as "the Allied and Associated Powers," of the one part, and Finland, of the other part;

Whereas Finland, having become an ally of Hitlerite Germany and having participated on her side in the war against the Union of Soviet Socialist Republics, the United Kingdom and other United Nations, bears her share of responsibility for this war;

Whereas, however, Finland on September 4, 1944, entirely ceased military operations against the Union of Soviet Socialist Republics, withdrew from the war against the United Nations, broke off relations with Germany and her satellites, and, having concluded on September 19, 1944, an Armistice with the Governments of the Union of Soviet Socialist Republics and the United Kingdom, acting on behalf of the United Nations at war with Finland, loyally carried out the Armistice terms; and

Whereas the Allied and Associated Powers and Finland are desirous of concluding a treaty of peace which, conforming to the principles of justice, will settle questions still outstanding as a result of the events hereinbefore recited and will form the basis of friendly relations between them, thereby enabling the Allied and Associated Powers to support Finland's application to become a member of the United Nations and also to adhere to any Convention concluded under the auspices of the United Nations;

Have therefore agreed to declare the cessation of the state of war and for this purpose to conclude the present Treaty of Peace, and have accordingly appointed the undersigned Plenipotentiaries who, after presentation of their full powers, found in good and due form, have agreed on the following provisions:

Part 1. Territorial Clauses

Article 1

The frontiers of Finland, as shown on the map annexed to the present Treaty (Annex I), shall be those which existed on January 1, 1941, except as provided in the following Article.

Article 2

In accordance with the Armistice Agreement, the effect of the Peace Treaty confirms the return to the Soviet Union of the province of Petsamo (Pechenga) voluntarily ceded to Finland by the Soviet State under the Peace Treaties of October 14, 1920, and March 12, 1940. The frontiers of the province of Petsamo (Pechenga) are shown on the map annexed to the present Treaty (Annex I).

Part II. Political Clauses

Section I

Article 3

In accordance with the Armistice Agreement, the effect of the Peace Treaty between the Soviet Union and Finland concluded in Moscow on March 12, 1940, is restored, subject to the replacement of Articles 4, 5 and 6 of that Treaty by Articles 2 and 4 of the present Treaty.

Article 4

1. In accordance with the Armistice Agreement, the Soviet Union confirms the renunciation of its right to the lease of the Peninsula of Hangö, accorded to it by the Soviet-Finnish Peace Treaty of March 12, 1940, and Finland for her part confirms having granted to the Soviet Union on the basis of a fifty years lease at an annual rent payable by the Soviet Union of five million Finnish marks the use and administration of territory and waters for the establishment of a Soviet naval base in the area of Porkkala-Udd as shown on the map annexed to the present Treaty (Annex I).

2. Finland confirms having secured to the Soviet Union, in accordance with the Armistice Agreement, the use of the railways, waterways, roads and air routes necessary for the transport of personnel and freight dispatched from the Soviet Union to the naval base at Porkkala-Udd, and also confirms having granted to the Soviet Union the right of unimpeded use of all forms of communication between the Soviet Union and the territory leased in the area of Porkkala-Udd.

Article 5

The Aaland Islands shall remain demilitarised in accordance with the situation as at present existing.

Section II

Article 6

Finland shall take all measures necessary to secure to all persons under Finnish jurisdiction, without distinction as to race, sex, language or religion, the enjoyment of human rights and of the fundamental freedoms, including freedom of expression, of press and publication, of religious worship, of political opinion and of public meeting.

Article 7

Finland, which in accordance with the Armistice Agreement has taken measures to set free, irrespective of citizenship and nationality, all persons held in confinement on account of their activities in favour of, or because of their sympathies with, the United Nations or because of their racial origin, and to repeal discriminatory legislation and restrictions imposed thereunder, shall complete these measures and shall in future not take any measures or enact any laws which would be incompatible with the purposes set forth in this Article.

Article 8

Finland, which in accordance with the Armistice Agreement has taken measures for dissolving all organisations of a Fascist type on Finnish territory, whether political, military or para-military, as well as other organisations conducting propaganda hostile to the Soviet Union or to any of the other United Nations, shall not permit in future the existence and activities of organisations of that nature which have as their aim denial to the people of their democratic rights.

Article 9

1. Finland shall take all necessary steps to ensure the apprehension and surrender for trial of:

(a) Persons accused of having committed, ordered or abetted war crimes and crimes against peace or humanity;

(b) Nationals of any Allied or Associated power accused of having violated their national law by treason or collaboration with the enemy during the war.

2. At the request of the United Nations Government concerned, Finland shall likewise make available as witnesses persons within its jurisdiction, whose evidence is required for the trial of the persons referred to in paragraph 1 of this Article.

3. Any disagreement concerning the application of the provisions of paragraphs 1 and 2 of this Article shall be referred by any of the Governments concerned to the Heads of the Diplomatic Missions in Helsinki of the Soviet Union and the United Kingdom, who will reach agreement with regard to the difficulty.

Section III

Article 10

Finland undertakes to recognize the full force of the Treaties of Peace with Italy, Roumania, Bulgaria and Hungary and other agreements or arrangements which have been or will be reached by the Allied and Associated Powers in respect of Austria, Germany and Japan for the restoration of peace.

Article 11

Finland undertakes to accept any arrangements which have been or may be agreed for the liquidation of the League of Nations and the Permanent Court of International Justice.

Article 12

1. Each Allied or Associated Power will notify Finland, within a period of six months from the coming into force of the present Treaty, which of its pre-war bilateral treaties with Finland it desires to keep in force or revive. Any provisions not in conformity with the present Treaty shall, however, be deleted from the above-mentioned treaties.

2. All such treaties so notified shall be registered with the Secretariat of the United Nations in accordance with Article 102 of the Charter of the United Nations.

3. All such treaties not so notified shall be regarded as abrogated.

Part III. Military, Naval and Air Clauses

Article 13

The maintenance of land, sea and air armaments and fortifications shall be closely restricted to meeting tasks of an internal character and local defence of frontiers. In accordance with the foregoing, Finland is authorised to have armed forces consisting of not more than:

(a) A land army, including frontier troops and anti-aircraft artillery, with a total strength of 34,400 personnel;

(b) A navy with a personnel strength of 4,500 and a total tonnage of 10,000 tons;

(c) An air force, including any naval air arm, of 60 aircraft, including reserves, with a total personnel strength of 3,000. Finland shall not possess or acquire any aircraft designed primarily as bombers with internal bomb-carrying facilities.

These strengths shall in each case include combat, service and overhead personnel.

Article 14

The personnel of the Finnish Army, Navy and Air Force in excess of the respective strengths permitted under Article 13 shall be disbanded within six months from the coming into force of the present Treaty.

Article 15

Personnel not included in the Finnish Army, Navy or Air Force shall not receive any form of military training, naval training or military air training as defined in Annex II.

Article 16

1. As from the coming into force of the present Treaty, Finland will be invited to join the Barents, Baltic and Black Sea Zone Board of the International Organisation for Mine Clearance of European Waters and shall maintain at the disposal of the Central Mine Clearance Board all Finnish minesweeping forces until the end of the post-war mine clearance period, as determined by the Central Board.

2. During this post-war mine clearance period, Finland may retain additional naval units employed only for the specific purpose of minesweeping, over and above the tonnage permitted in Article 13.

Within two months of the end of the said period, such of these vessels as are on loan to the Finnish Navy from other Powers shall be returned to those Powers, and all other additional units shall be disarmed and converted to civilian use.

3. Finland is also authorised to employ 1,500 additional officers and men for minesweeping over and above the numbers permitted in Article 13. Two months after the completion of minesweeping by the Finnish Navy, the excess personnel shall be disbanded or absorbed within the numbers permitted in the said Article.

Article 17

Finland shall not possess, construct or experiment with any atomic weapon, any self-propelled or guided missiles or apparatus connected with their discharge (other than torpedoes and torpedo launching gear comprising the normal armament of naval vessels permitted by the present Treaty), sea mines or torpedoes of non-contact types actuated by influence mechanisms, torpedoes capable of being manned, submarines or other submersible craft, motor torpedo boats, or specialised types of assault craft.

Article 18

Finland shall not retain, produce or otherwise acquire, or maintain facilities for the manufacture of, war material in excess of that required for the maintenance of the armed forces permitted under Article 13 of the present Treaty.

Article 19

1. Excess war material of Allied origin shall be placed at the disposal of the Allied Power concerned according to the instructions given by that Power. Excess Finnish war material shall be placed at the disposal of the Governments of the Soviet Union and the United Kingdom. Finland shall renounce all rights to this material.

2. War material of German origin or design in excess of that required for the armed forces permitted under the present Treaty shall be placed at the disposal of the Two Governments. Finland shall not acquire or manufacture any war material of German origin or design, or employ or train any technicians, including military and civil aviation personnel, who are or have been nationals of Germany.

3. Excess war material mentioned in paragraphs 1 and 2 of this Article shall be handed over or destroyed within one year from the coming into force of the present Treaty.

4. A definition and list of war material for the purposes of the present Treaty are contained in Annex III.

Article 20

Finland shall co-operate fully with the Allied and Associated Powers with a view to ensuring that Germany may not be able to take steps outside German territory towards rearmament.

Article 21

Finland shall not acquire or manufacture civil aircraft which are of German or Japanese design or which embody major assemblies of German or Japanese manufacture or design.

Article 22

Each of the military, naval and air clauses of the present Treaty shall remain in force until modified in whole or in part by agreement between the Allied and

Associated Powers and Finland or, after Finland becomes a member of the United Nations, by agreement between the Security Council and Finland.

Part IV. Reparation and Restitution

Article 23

1. Losses caused to the Soviet Union by military operations and by the occupation by Finland of Soviet territory shall be made good by Finland to the Soviet Union, but, taking into consideration that Finland has not only withdrawn from the war against the United Nations, but has also declared war on Germany and assisted with her forces in driving German troops out of Finland, the Parties agree that compensation for the above losses will be made by Finland not in full, but only in part, namely in the amount of $300,000,000 payable over eight years from September 19, 1944, in commodities (timber products, paper, cellulose, sea-going and river craft, sundry machinery, and other commodities).

2. The basis of calculation for the settlement provided in this Article shall be the United States dollar at its gold parity on the day of the signing of the Armistice Agreement, i.e. $35 for one ounce of gold.

Article 24

Finland, in so far as she has not yet done so, undertakes within the time-limits indicated by the Government of the Soviet Union to return to the Soviet Union in complete good order all valuables and materials removed from its territory during the war, and belonging to State, public or co-operative organisations, enterprises or institutions or to individual citizens, such as: factory and works equipment, locomotives, rolling stock, tractors, motor vehicles, historic monuments, museum valuables and any other property.

Part V. Economic Clauses

Article 25

1. In so far as Finland has not already done so, Finland shall restore all legal rights and interests in Finland of the United Nations and their nationals as they existed on June 22, 1941, and shall return all property in Finland of the United Nations and their nationals as it now exists.

2. The Finnish Government undertakes that all property, rights and interests passing under this Article shall be restored free of all encumbrances and charges of any kind to which they may have become subject as a result of the war and without the imposition of any charges by the Finnish Government in connexion with their return. The Finnish Government shall nullify all measures, including seizures, sequestration or control, taken by it against United Nations property between June 22, 1941, and the coming into force of the present Treaty. In cases where the property has not been returned within six months from the coming into force of the present Treaty, application shall be made to the Finnish authorities not later than twelve months from the coming into force of the Treaty, except in cases in which the claimant is able to show that he could not file his application within this period.

3. The Finnish Government shall invalidate transfers involving property, rights

and interests of any description belonging to United Nations nationals, where such transfers resulted from force or duress exerted by Axis Governments or their agencies during the war.

4. (a) The Finnish government shall be responsible for the restoration to complete good order of the property returned to United Nations nationals under paragraph 1 of this Article. In cases where property cannot be returned or where, as a result of the war, a United Nations national has suffered a loss by reason of injury or damage to property in Finland, he shall receive from the Finnish Government compensation in Finnish marks to the extent of two-thirds of the sum necessary, at the date of payment, to purchase similar property or to make good the loss suffered. In no event shall United Nations nationals receive less favourable treatment with respect to compensation than that accorded to Finnish nationals.

(b) United Nations nationals who hold, directly or indirectly, ownership interests in corporations or associations which are not United Nations nationals within the meaning of paragraph 8 (a) of this Article, but which have suffered a loss by reason of injury or damage to property in Finland, shall receive compensation in accordance with sub-paragraph (a) above. This compensation shall be calculated on the basis of the total loss or damage suffered by the corporation or association and shall bear the same proportion to such loss or damage as the beneficial interests of such nationals in the corporation or association bear to the total capital thereof.

(c) Compensation shall be paid free of any levies, taxes or other charges. It shall be freely usable in Finland but shall be subject to the foreign exchange control regulations which may be in force in Finland from time to time.

(d) The Finnish Government shall accord to United Nations nationals the same treatment in the allocation of materials for the repair or rehabilitation of their property in Finland and in the allocation of foreign exchange for the importation of such materials as applies to Finnish nationals.

(e) The Finnish Government shall grant United Nations nationals an indemnity in Finnish marks at the same rate as provided in sub-paragraph (a) above to compensate them for the loss or damage due to special measures applied to their property during the war, and which were not applicable to Finnish property. This sub-paragraph does not apply to a loss of profit.

5. All reasonable expenses incurred in Finland in establishing claims, including the assessment of loss or damage, shall be borne by the Finnish Government.

6. United Nations nationals and their property shall be exempted from any exceptional taxes, levies or imposts imposed on their capital assets in Finland by the Finnish Government or any Finnish authority between the date of the Armistice and the coming into force of the present Treaty for the specific purpose of meeting charges arising out of the war or of meeting the costs of reparation payable to any of the United Nations. Any sums which have been so paid shall be refunded.

7. The owner of the property concerned and the Finnish Government may agree upon arrangements in lieu of the provisions of this Article.

8. As used in this Article:

(a) "United Nations nationals" means individuals who are nationals of any of the United Nations, or corporations or associations organized under the laws of any of the United Nations, at the coming into force of the present Treaty, provided that the said individuals, corporations or associations also had this status at the date of the Armistice with Finland.

The term "United Nations nationals" also includes all individuals, corporations or associations which, under the laws in force in Finland during the war, have been treated as enemy;

(b) "Owner" means the United Nations national, as defined in sub-paragraph (a) above, who is entitled to the property in question, and includes a successor of the owner, provided that the successor is also a United Nations national as defined in sub-paragraph (a). If the successor has purchased the property in its damaged state, the transferor shall retain his rights to compensation under this Article, without prejudice to obligations between the transferor and the purchaser under domestic law;

(c) "Property" means all movable or immovable property, whether tangible or intangible, including industrial, literary and artistic property, as well as all rights or interests of any kind in property.

Article 26

Finland recognizes that the Soviet Union is entitled to all German assets in Finland transferred to the Soviet Union by the Control Council for Germany and undertakes to take all necessary measures to facilitate such transfers.

Article 27

In so far as any such rights were restricted on account of Finland's participation in the war on Germany's side, the rights of the Finnish Government and of any Finnish nationals, including juridical persons, relating to Finnish property or other Finnish assets on the territories of the Allied and Associated Powers shall be restored after the coming into force of the present Treaty.

Article 28

1. From the coming into force of the present Treaty, property in Germany of Finland and of Finnish nationals shall no longer be treated as enemy property and all restrictions based on such treatment shall be removed.

2. Identifiable property of Finland and of Finnish nationals removed by force or duress from Finnish territory to Germany by German forces or authorities after September 19, 1944, shall be eligible for restitution.

3. The restoration and restitution of Finnish property in Germany shall be effected in accordance with measures which will be determined by the Powers in occupation in Germany.

Article 29

1. Finland waives all claims of any description against the Allied and Associated Powers on behalf of the Finnish Government of Finnish nationals arising directly out of the war or out of actions taken because of the existence of a state of war in Europe after September 1, 1939, whether or not the Allied or Associated Power was at war with Finland at the time, including the following:

(a) Claims for losses or damages sustained as a consequence of acts of forces or authorities of Allied or Associated Powers;

(b) Claims arising from the presence, operations or actions of forces or authorities of Allied or Associated Powers in Finnish territory;

(c) Claims with respect to the decrees or orders of Prize Courts of Allied or Associated Powers, Finland agreeing to accept as valid and binding all decrees and orders of such Prize Courts on or after September 1, 1939, concerning Finnish ships or Finnish goods or the payment of costs;

(d) Claims arising out of the exercise or purported exercise of belligerent rights.

2. The provisions of this Article shall bar, completely and finally, all claims of the nature referred to herein, which will be henceforward extinguished, whoever may be the parties in interest.

3. Finland likewise waives all claims of the nature covered by paragraph 1 of this Article on behalf of the Finnish Government or Finnish nationals against any of the United Nations whose diplomatic relations with Finland were broken off during the war and which took action in co-operation with the Allied and Associated Powers.

4. The waiver of claims by Finland under paragraph 1 of this Article includes any claims arising out of actions taken by any of the Allied and Associated Powers with respect to Finnish ships between September 1, 1939, and the coming into force of the present Treaty, as well as any claims and debts arising out of the Convention on prisoners of war now in force.

Article 30

1. Pending the conclusion of commercial treaties or agreements between individual United Nations and Finland, the Finnish Government shall, during a period of eighteen months from the coming into force of the present Treaty, grant the following treatment to each of the United Nations which, in fact, reciprocally grants similar treatment in like matters to Finland:

(a) In all that concerns duties and charges on importation or exportation, the internal taxation of imported goods and all regulations pertaining thereto, the United Nations shall be granted unconditional most-favoured-nation treatment;

(b) In all other respects, Finland shall make no arbitrary discrimination against goods originating in or destined for any territory of any of the United Nations as compared with like goods originating in or destined for territory of any other of the United Nations or of any other foreign country;

(c) United Nations nationals, including juridical persons, shall be granted national and most-favoured-nation treatment in all matters pertaining to commerce, industry, shipping and other forms of business activity within Finland. These provisions shall not apply to commercial aviation;

(d) Finland shall grant no exclusive or discriminatory right to any country with regard to the operation of commercial aircraft in international traffic, shall afford all the United Nations equality of opportunity in obtaining international commercial aviation rights in Finnish territory, including the right to land for refueling and repair, and, with regard to the operation of commercial aircraft in international traffic, shall grant on a reciprocal and non-discriminatory basis to all United Nations the right to fly over Finnish territory without landing. These provisions shall not affect the interests of the national defence of Finland.

2. The foregoing undertakings by Finland shall be understood to be subject to the exceptions customarily included in commercial treaties concluded by Finland

before the war; and the provisions with respect to reciprocity granted by each of the United Nations shall be understood to be subject to the exceptions customarily included in the commercial treaties concluded by that State.

Article 31

1. Any disputes which may arise in connexion with Articles 24 and 25 and Annexes IV, V and VI, part B, of the present Treaty shall be referred to a Conciliation Commission composed of an equal number of representatives of the United Nations Government concerned and of the Finnish Government. If agreement has not been reached within three months of the dispute having been referred to the Conciliation Commission, either Government may require the addition of a third member to the Commission, and, failing agreement between the two Governments on the selection of this member, the Secretary-General of the United Nations may be requested by either party to make the appointment.

2. The decision of the majority of the members of the Commission shall be the decision of the Commission and shall be accepted by the parties as definitive and binding.

Article 32

Articles 24, 25, 30 and Annex VI of the present Treaty shall apply to the Allied and Associated Powers and France and to those of the United Nations whose diplomatic relations with Finland have been broken off during the war.

Article 33

The provisions of Annexes IV, V and VI shall, as in the case of the other Annexes, have force and effect as integral parts of the present Treaty.

Part VI. Final Clauses

Article 34

1. For a period not to exceed eighteen months from the coming into force of the present Treaty, the Heads of the Diplomatic Missions in Helsinki of the Soviet Union and the United Kingdom, acting in concert, will represent the Allied and Associated Powers in dealing with the Finnish Government in all matters concerning the execution and interpretation of the present Treaty.

2. The Two Heads of Mission will give the Finnish Government such guidance, technical advice and clarification as may be necessary to ensure the rapid and efficient execution of the present Treaty both in letter and in spirit.

3. The Finnish Government shall afford the said Two Heads of Mission all necessary information and any assistance which they may require for the fulfilment of the tasks devolving on them under the present Treaty.

Article 35

1. Except where another procedure is specifically provided under any Article of the present Treaty, any dispute concerning the interpretation or execution of the Treaty, which is not settled by direct diplomatic negotiations, shall be referred to the Two Heads of Mission acting under Article 34, except that in this case the Heads of Mission will not be restricted by the time limit provided in that Article.

Any such dispute not resolved by them within a period of two months shall, unless the parties to the dispute mutually agree upon another means of settlement, be referred at the request of either party to the dispute to a Commission composed of one representative of each party and a third member selected by mutual agreement of the two parties from nationals of a third country. Should the two parties fail to agree within a period of one month upon the appointment of the third member, the Secretary-General of the United Nations may be requested by either party to make the appointment.

2. The decision of the majority of the members of the Commission shall be the decision of the Commission, and shall be accepted by the parties as definitive and binding.

Article 36

The present Treaty, of which the Russian and English texts are authentic, shall be ratified by the Allied and Associated Powers. It shall also be ratified by Finland. It shall come into force immediately upon the deposit of ratifications by the Union of Soviet Socialist Republics and the United Kingdom of Great Britain and Northern Ireland. The instruments of ratification shall, in the shortest time possible, be deposited with the Government of the Union of Soviet Socialist Republics.

With respect to each Allied or Associated Power whose instrument of ratification is thereafter deposited, the Treaty shall come into force upon the date of deposit. The present Treaty shall be deposited in the archives of the Government of the Union of Soviet Socialist Republics, which shall furnish certified copies to each of the signatory States.

Annexes*

I   Map of the Frontiers of Finland and the areas in Articles 2 and 4
II   Definition of Military, Military Air and Naval Training
III   Definition and List of War Material
IV   Special provisions relating to certain kinds of property
V   Contracts, Prescription and Negotiable Instruments
VI   Prize Courts and Judgments

*Not included here.

Notes

Notes

Chapter 1. Ceasefire (September 1944)

1. Cumming's memorandum to Cordell Hull, 6 May 1944; State Department 760d, 61/5-644. Cf. also Treatment of Finland, PWC-161, 10 May 1944. RG 59; PWC Committee Minutes, Meeting of 1 June 1944, pp. 4-5. Notter File, box 140, National Archives. Washington D.C. Ibid., Summary of Recommendations: Treatment of Finland, PWC-160a; Progress Report on Post-War Programs, book I, Finland 1, September 1944. Ibid., box 145. At the beginning of June 1944, the State Department published its "Black List" of Finnish firms trading with Germany. This was primarily a political action designed to mobilize Finnish business circles to urge their government to detach Finland from the war. It had little real effect, since relations were broken off at the end of June. Cf. FRUS II 1944, pp. 165-66, 169-71, 172-73.

2. Eden's memorandum, "Soviet Policy in Europe outside the Balkans," 9 August 1944; WP (44) 436, CAB 66/53. Cf. also Woodward (1972-74), vol. III, pp. 123-31 and Nevakivi (1976), p. 191.

3. Harriman from Moscow, 26 August 1944; FRUS IV 1944, pp. 196-97.

4. The main details of the terms of the armistice had already been sent to the Antonescu government in the spring of 1944, but they had been rejected. On the Rumanian armistice, see FRUS II 1944, pp. 133-232; Woodward (1972-74), vol. III, pp. 136-38; Lundestad (1978), pp. 225-29; Novikov (1976), pp. 217-34. The terms of the armistice with Bulgaria— which were drawn up in autumn 1944, after Finland had already left the war—followed for the most part the pattern established in the Rumanian case. Hungary did not detach itself from the alliance with Germany until the winter of 1944-45.

5. Gripenberg's diary entries for 14-16 and 22-25 August 1944; G. A. Gripenberg Papers, VA. Gripenberg (1961), pp. 264-68. Tanner (1952), pp. 357-66. Cf. Johnson from Stockholm, 14 August 1944, FRUS III 1944, pp. 609-11.

6. Gripenberg (1961), pp. 269-76. The telegram is reprinted in extenso in Tanner (1952), p. 268. The meetings between Gripenberg and Kollontay on 25 and 29 August took place at Counsellor V. Semyonov's flat in Lidingö because (as Mme. Kollontay put it) "there were rather too many Germans" at the hotel in Saltsjöbaden, where she lived. The preservation of secrecy was important for the success of the discussions.

7. Harriman from Moscow, 26 August and 4 September 1944; FRUS III 1944, pp. 611-12, 615.

8. On this meeting, see Tanner (1952), pp. 368-71, and Linkomies (1970), pp. 397-98.

9. Gripenberg from Stockholm, 31 August 1944; UM 110 B 3. Cf. Gripenberg's diary, 31 August 1944.

10. Cf. the telegram from the Finnish Foreign Ministry to Kivimäki, 1 September 1944 (UM).

11. Gripenberg from Stockholm, 2 September 1944 (UM).

12. It seems that Moscow also learned a lesson from the failure to take Finland out of the war in the spring. Similarly, the Russians were contemplating a time limit for the evacuation of German troops from Rumania in August 1944. This idea fell through when Hitler abruptly mounted military countermeasures.

13. Mannerheim's telegram to Stalin, 1 September 1944; UM 110 3 B and FRUS III 1944, pp. 615-16. Gripenberg handed it to Semyonov in Stockholm on the following day. For details of this and General Enckell's journey, see Gripenberg's diary for 31 August-2 September 1944 and Gripenberg (1961), pp. 278-81. Boheman thought Mannerheim's proposals were "reasonable," and Semyonov had received them sympathetically; Johnson from Stockholm, 2 September 1944, State Department 740.00119 European War 1939/9-244.

14. Gripenberg from Stockholm, 2 and 4 September 1944; UM 110 B 3. See also the memorandum "Samtal Boheman-Semjonov 4 September 1944" (UM). FRUS III 1944, p. 616.

15. Heinrichs (1959) pp. 401-2.

16. *Eduskunnan pöytäkirjat* III (1944), p. 58ff. Soikkanen (1980), p. 214.

17. Linkomies (1970), p. 399.

18. Gripenberg (1961), pp. 282-83. Palm (1971), p. 60. Puntila (1972), p. 220. Mannerheim's reserves of strength were also beginning to give out in the autumn of 1944. Cf. Heinrichs (1959), pp. 397-98. For the German minister's version of his meeting with Enckell, see Blücher (1951), pp. 437-38.

19. Gripenberg's diary, 3 September 1944.

20. Boheman (1964), p. 261. Gripenberg (1961), pp. 283-84.

21. Gripenberg, ibid. Cf. UM 110 B 3 (Pamyatnaya zapiska) and FRUS III 1944, pp. 616-17.

22. Gripenberg's diary, 3-4 September 1944. Gripenberg (1961), pp. 282-84. Meretskov (1968), p. 389.

23. Gripenberg from Stockholm, 2 September 1944; UM 110 B 3. Heinrichs (1954). Paasikivi, regarded as too "soft," was deliberately passed over. On the setting up of the delegation, see Soikkanen (1980), p. 214; Linkomies (1970), pp. 399-401; Tanner (1952), pp. 379-83; and Nykopp (1975), pp. 141-43.

Chapter 2. The Moscow Negotiations

1. Clark Kerr from Moscow, 5 September 1944; FO 371/43164 N5379/30/56. The Foreign Office's earlier requests for information about the armistice terms for Finland had met with no response from Moscow; cf. FO 371/43160 N2441/30/56 and FO 371/43161 N3128/30/56. Equally fruitless was the American-backed British initiative designed to raise the Finnish question in the European Advisory Commission, which was set up at the Foreign Ministers' Conference in Moscow in 1943. The Finnish question never featured on the agenda of the commission; FRUS III 1944, pp. 608-9.

2. Clark Kerr from Moscow, 6 September 1944; FO 371/43164 N5604/30/56. Harriman from Moscow, 6 September 1944; FRUS III 1944, pp. 617-18.

3. The Western ambassadors were not informed of Zhdanov's membership of the delegation until 14 September. Harriman surmised that this was not an unexpected decision, since Zhdanov was the secretary of the Leningrad Committee of the Communist Party and had been closely involved in the Soviet Union's Finnish policy. Rear Adm. A. P. Aleksandrov later took Tributs' place in discussions with the Finns.

4. This was dealt with in the following manner: Clark Kerr gave the Finnish delegation in Moscow a note to be sent to Helsinki, the contents of which the Finns obeyed by breaking off

relations with Japan on 22 September. Clark Kerr had followed the same procedure in the case of Rumania.

5. For the briefing session of 6 September, attended by the British and American ambassadors, see Clark Kerr from Moscow, 7 and 8 September 1944; FO 371/43164 N5605/30/56 and N5469/30/56. Harriman from Moscow, 6 September 1944; FRUS III 1944, pp. 618-19. The Soviet draft is to be found in the archives of the British Embassy to Moscow; cf. FO 181/987.

6. Cordell Hull to Harriman, 7 September 1944, State Department 740.00119, European War 1939/9-644.

7. Harriman from Moscow, 7 September 1944; FRUS III 1944, pp. 619-20.

8. Polvinen (1978), pp. 406-8.

9. Warner's memorandum, 8 September 1944; FO 371/43164 N5604/30/56.

10. Ibid., and FO to Clark Kerr, 8 September 1944; FO 371/43164 N5604/30/56.

11. Clark Kerr from Moscow, 9 September 1944; FO 371/43164 N5476/30/56.

12. The rest of the Foreign Office comments relate to the details of the economic stipulations of the draft treaty. Cf. FO to Clark Kerr, 10 September 1944, FO 371/43164 N5476/30/56, and 12 September 1944, FO 371/43165 N5688/30/56. See also Winant from London, 14 and 15 September 1944; State Department 740.00119, European War 1939/9-1444 and FRUS III 1944, pp. 621-22.

13. Clark Kerr from Moscow, 9 September 1944; FO 371/43165 N5477/30/56.

14. FO 371/43165 N5477/30/56 and N5509/30/56.

15. FO to Clark Kerr, 13 September 1944; FO 371/43165 N5553/30/56. Clark Kerr from Moscow, 14 September 1944; FO 371/43165 N5588/30/56. The FO also informed the State Department of this arrangement. Cf. Winant from London, 14 and 15 September 1944; State Department 740.00119, European War 1939/9-1444. FRUS III 1944, pp. 621-22. The Anglo-Russian protocol was finally signed in Moscow on 8 October. The Soviet Union agreed to pay the Canadian government $20 million within six years. The Canadians, who had originally demanded $50 million and payment within three years, were forced to back down. Cf. FO 371/43169 N6242/30/56, FO 371/43166 N5716/30/56.

16. Clark Kerr from Moscow, 14 September 1944; FO 371/43165 N5586/30/56.

17. FO 371/43166 N5643/30/56.

18. Cf. Clark Kerr's telegram of 14 September 1944 and Harriman from Moscow, 15 September 1944; FRUS III 1944, pp. 621-22. On the Dumbarton Oaks Conference, Russell and Muther (1958), pp. 421-77, and *Sovyetskiy Soyuz na mezhdunarodnykh konferentsiyakh . . .* III, passim. FRUS III 1944, pp. 713-959. Berezhkov (1972), pp. 225-364. Woodward (1972-74), vol. V, pp. 135-180. *The Diaries of Sir Alexander Cadogan* (1971), pp. 653-669.

19. Cf. Boheman's information to the American Minister in Stockholm: Johnson from Stockholm, 16 September 1944; State Department 740.00119, European War 1939/9-1644.

20. Hackzell from Moscow, 9 September 1944; UM Incoming telegrams, 1944, Stockholm (Moscow). Gripenberg's diary, 11 September 1944.

21. The decision to evacuate northern Finland was taken on 7 September; Tuompo (1968), p. 296. Söderblom for his part kept Harriman well informed of the contents of his discussions with Hackzell; Harriman from Moscow, 10 September 1944, State Department 740.00119, European War 1939/9-1044.

22. On the mood of the Finnish delegation, and Hackzell's illness, see Heinrichs (1959), pp. 407-9, and Nykopp (1975), pp. 144-45.

23. Molotov had raised the same issue with Hackzell on the 8th. See Hackzell's telegram of 9 September 1944.

24. Palm (1972), p. 57. Clark Kerr from Moscow, 15 September 1944; FO 371/43165 N5588/30/56. Harriman from Moscow, 15 September 1944; State Department 740.00119, European War 1939/9-1544.

25. The Finnish protocol of the first day's negotiations in extenso in Palm (1971), pp. 97-103.

26. Palm (1971), pp. 104-14, 117-19, 137-38, 146-47. Clark Kerr's reports from Moscow, 18,

18, and 20 September 1944; FO 371/43166 N5661/30/56, N5686/30/56 and FO 371/43167 N5753/30/56.

27. Heinrichs (1959), p. 413.

28. Protocol in extenso in Palm (1971), pp. 97-152. The corresponding English minutes, which do not differ significantly from the Finnish are in FO 371/43170 N8137/30/56. Cf. Shtemenko (1973), pp. 397-400.

29. Cf. Foreign Ministry to Finnish delegation in Moscow, 17 September 1944; UM Outgoing telegrams, 1944, Stockholm (Moscow). Carlgren (1973), pp. 522-26. Rystad (1968), pp. 1-23.

30. Palm (1971), pp. 127-29, 145-46. Cf. also Palm (1972), p. 110.

31. Enckell from Moscow, 18 September 1944; UM Incoming telegrams, 1944, Stockholm (Moscow). Palm (1972), p. 62. Heinrichs (1959), pp. 407-9. According to Nykopp, Enckell was "very depressed" after his visit to Molotov; Nykopp (1975), p. 149.

32. Palm (1971), pp. 150-52.

33. Linkomies (1970), pp. 404-5. Tanner (1952), pp. 300-301. Tuompo (1968), pp. 298-300. Käkönen (1970), p. 143.

34. Carlgren (1973), p. 522.

35. Gripenberg's diary, 18-19 September 1944.

36. Johnson from Stockholm, 19 September 1944, State Department 740.00119, European War 1939/9-1944. Mallet from Stockholm, 18 September 1944; FO 371/43166 N692/30/56. Jägerskiöld (1981), p. 53.

37. Eden's memorandum to the War Cabinet, 24 September 1944; FO 371/43168 N5896/30/56.

Chapter 3. The War in Lapland

1. Rendulic (1952), p. 239. Rendulic, who had begun his career in the Austrian army, had previously commanded the Second Panzer Army, fighting against Tito's partisans in Yugoslavia.

2. Polvinen (1979), p. 248.

3. Ziemke (1960), pp. 277-78 and sources cited therein. See also Vuolento (1973), pp. 12-15.

4. Ibid.

5. Rendulic (1952). pp. 283-85. Mannerheim (1952), pp. 413-14. Erfurth's diary entry, 2 September 1944; Kriegstagebuch 1941-44, VA. See also Menger (1979), p. 301 and sources.

6. Erfurth's diary, 2 September 1944.

7. Ziemke (1960). pp. 292-93. Erfurth (1950), pp. 287-88. Salewski (1975), pp. 466-67.

8. Erfurth's diary, 8-9 September 1944. On the plans to recruit volunteers, see KTB OKW IV/1 1944, pp. 897-88, and Ziemke (1960), p. 290.

9. Exchange of telegrams between Ribbentrop and Blücher, 5-7 September 1944; AA, Botschafter Ritter, Finnland 1469/367684 and 387688. On the intelligence service and the Germans' attempts to set up some sort of resistance movement in Finland in 1944-45, see Alava (1974), passim.

10. Erfurth's diary, 4-5 September 1944.

11. Ibid., 6-13 September 1944. Blücher (1951), pp. 405-9.

12. Vuolento (1973), p. 34 and 61 and sources. On the destruction of the airfield at Pori, see also (Geb) AOK 20, Ia, KTB 6 September 1944; AOK 20 65635/2; MF. With the departure of the last German ship from Kemi harbor on 21 September, some 7,000 soldiers, almost half of them wounded, had been shipped out of Lapland, together with some 300 evacuees and 700 vehicles. Of the total volume of around 180,000 tons of matériel belonging to the Mountain Army, 47,000 tons was taken off by sea, 17,700 tons by land. Some 30,000 tons was later transported overland, some was sold to Finland (including 20,000 tons of coal), and the rest either destroyed or left behind in the withdrawal.

13. Ziemke (1960), p. 293.

14. Erfurth's diary, 9-11 September 1944.

15. Haahti's notes, and those of his assistant, Capt. Eino E. Suolahti, of their discussions with the Germans in Rovaniemi, and other documents, are in the files of the Chief of General Staff, Ye pääll/PM T21622/22-23, SA. Vuolento (1973), pp. 24-26. Haahti (1979), pp. 698-700.

16. Haahti (1979), pp. 698-700.

17. Vuolento (1973), pp.27-28 and sources. Haahti (1979), p. 700.

18. Vuolento (1973), pp. 29-31 and sources. Haahti (1979), p. 700.

19. Ziemke (1960), pp. 296-97. Mannerheim (1952) pp.418-19. See also Meister (1958), pp. 96-99, and Käkönen (1970), pp. 135-36.

20. Vuolento (1973), p. 40. Haahti (1979), p. 701.

21. Vuolento (1973), pp. 40-43 and sources. Haahti (1979), pp. 701-4.

22. Tuompo (1968), pp. 298-99.

23. Cf. Enckell's coded telegram from Moscow, 17 September 1944, UM 110 B 3 and Haahti's undated notes, PM T21622/22, SA. Cf. also Kuosa (1979), pp. 252-53.

24. Ziemke (1960), p. 297 and sources. After his talks with Haahti on 18 September, Rendulic finally acknowledged that there was no point in the Germans hoping for a breakdown in the talks in Moscow, with the Finns returning to the joint front, as had occurred in the spring. Cf. (Geb) AOK 20, Ia, KTB 18 September 1944; AOK 20 65635/2, MF.

25. It was not possible to save all the movable goods in Lapland. Puroma and Sonck (1958), p. 391. Boheman (1964), pp. 263-65. Gripenberg (1961), pp. 286-88.

26. (Geb) AOK 20, Ia, KTB 21 September 1944; AOK 20 65635/2, MF.

27. Ibid., KTB 26-27 September 1944, MF.

28. Ibid., KTB Anlagenband 16-31 September 1944; AOK 20 65635/6, MF.

29. Vuolento (1973), p. 53.

30. Cf. *Pravda*, 20 September 1944.

31. Ziemke (1960), p. 297 and sources. Haahti (1979), p. 705.

32. Shtemenko (1973), pp. 394-97. Meretskov (1968), pp. 392-95.

33. Shtemenko (1973), pp. 400-41. The crossing of the frontier at Suomussalmi and Kuusamo, mentioned earlier, was something of an exception that was clearly carried out for political purposes. Soviet troops withdrew from these areas in November 1944. On operations along the shores of the Arctic Ocean, see *Istoriya vtoroy mirovoy voyny 1939-1945*, vol. 9, pp. 148-53, and sources.

34. Käkönen (1970), pp. 147-48. Seppälä (1974), p. 287.

35. The plan is dated 27 September 1944; Op 1/PM T 15706/11, SA. Cf. Vuolento (1973), pp. 13-16. On the setting up of Siilasvuo's corps, see Seppälä (1974), p. 270.

36. Rendulic to Willamo, 30 September 1944; Op 1/PM T 21622/22, SA. On the incidents, see Ursin (1980), pp. 21-22.

37. III Army Corps (Siilasvuo): order of the day, 30 September 1944; Op 1/PM T 19498/8a, SA. On the government's attitude, Fagerholm (1977), pp. 179-80.

38. Fagerholm (1977), pp. 179-80. See also Lieutenant General Siilasvuo's telegraphed message to GHQ, 30 September 1944; Op 1/PM T 15706/11, SA. Seppälä (1974), pp. 270-71.

39. Allied Control Commission note and telephoned message from the Foreign Ministry, 30 September 1944; Op 1/PM T 15706/5, SA. See also Martola (1973), p. 240.

40. Offensive operation for the interment of German troops; Op 1/PM T 15706/11, SA.

41. Ziemke (1960), pp. 299-300 and sources. Colonel Willamo and his staff left Rovaniemi on 6 October 1944. See *Yhteysesikunta Roin historiikki 1942-1944*, pp. 253-55, Col. O. J. Willamo papers, file 1241, SA.

42. Foreign Minister Martola's telephoned message to GHQ, 2 October 1944. "As there are references in Rendulic's telegram to agreements between Finns and Germans, the government's foreign affairs committee feels obliged to ask for information if such agreements have been made, and if so, when." Gustaf Mannerheim Papers, VA, file 622.

43. On the question of hostages, see Ziemke (1960), pp. 299-300. A detailed Finnish account

of the landing at Tornio is provided by Halsti (1972), pp. 10-198, esp. 70-73. The German fleet high command (OKM) warned Hitler and the OKW in October of the fateful consequences of Sweden joining the war; Salewski (1975), p. 450.

44. Ribbentrop to Hitler, 5 October 1944; AA, Botschafter Ritter, Finnland 1469/367671-74.

45. (Geb) AOK 20, Ia, KTB 1 October 1944; AOK 20 65635/2, MF.

46. KTB OKW IV 1 1944, pp. 903-4, MF. Ziemke (1960), pp. 300-32.

47. Ziemke (1960), pp. 300-302. MF.

48. Lieutenant General Airo signed the ''Further operational plan for the disarming and internment of German forces in northern Finland'' on 4 October 1944; Op 1/PM T 15706/11, SA. See also U. S. Haahti's memorandum of 27 April 1945 in the Erik Heinrichs Papers, file 45, SA.

49. Gustaf Mannerheim Papers, VA, file 615. Molotov had already adopted a negative attitude during the Moscow talks to Heinrichs's idea of joint operations around Petsamo. Cf. Palm (1972). pp. 124-25.

50. Ziemke (1960), pp. 304-8.

51. FRUS: ''The Conferences at Malta and Yalta, 1945,'' pp. 364-65, 368. Riste (1979), II, pp. 190-91, 195-97, and sources.

52. Zhdanov to Mannerheim, 16 October 1944; archives of the liaison section of GHQ, T 19498/8a, SA. The original copy of the letter is in the Gustaf Mannerheim Papers, VA, file 615.

53. Mannerheim to Siilasvuo, 16 October 1944; archives of the liaison section of GHQ, T 1949/8a, SA.

54. In practice, most of the German prisoners (around 2,500 men) were not handed over until a year later, autumn 1945. See the summary of the work of the liaison section, p. 40, T 20362/1, SA.

55. Mannerheim to Zhdanov, 17 October 1944; archives of the liaison section of GHQ, T 19498/8a, SA.

56. Zhdanov to Mannerheim, 22 October 1944, ibid. MF.

57. KTB OKW IV/1 1944, p. 905.

58. Meretskov (1968), pp. 394-95, 407-9. Ziemke (1960), pp. 292-310. Puroma and Sonck (1958), pp. 389-556. For a good summary of military operations in northern Finland, based on German and Finnish material, see Ahto (1980), passim.

59. Summary of the work of the liaison section, p. 13; T 20362/1, SA.

Chapter 4. The Early Days

1. On the formation and composition of the Castrén government, see Hyvämäki (1977), pp. 243-44.

2. Résumé of the activities of the liaison section; T 20362/1, SA. See also Blinnikka (1969), pp. 14-15. The attitude of the Control Commission toward the former czarist officer, General Enckell, may have been influenced by his participation in counterrevolutionary activities during the Russian civil war.

3. Blinnikka (1969), p. 9.

4. See specifically articles 2-4, 10, 12-18, 20, and 21.

5. See the appendix to article 22.

6. A detailed (though incomplete) list of the members of the Commission can be found in the archives of the liaison section; T 20362/1, SA. Regional subcommittees were also set up —for instance, in Kotka, Kokkola, and Rauma.

7. FO 371/43167 N5780/30/56. FO 371/43196 N5957/5799/56, N6108/5799/56, N6463/5799/ 56, and N6746/5799/56.

8. Harriman from Moscow, 1 October 1944; FRUS IV 1944, p. 244.

9. Karhu to Airo, 24 October 1944, and the appended memorandum by Gröndahl; archives of the liaison section, T 19498/8a, SA. According to Eero Wuori, ''the British had no real authority

on the Control Commission, they just happened to be members''; interview on 25 February 1963, Eero Wuori Papers, VA, file 10.

10. *Uusi Suomi*, 21 October 1944.

11. Shepherd from Helsinki, 19 October 1944; FO 371/43203 N6823/6290/56.

12. Ibid., and Foreign Office comments.

13. Shepherd from Helsinki, 21 October 1944, and appended documents; FO 371/43203 N6825/6290/56.

14. FO 371/43196 N6826/5799/56.

15. Shepherd's report, 20 November 1944; FO 371/43203 N7290/6290/56 and Foreign Office directive, 30 November 1944; ibid., N7418/6290/56.

16. Shepherd from Helsinki, 3 December 1944; FO 371/43203 N7589/6290/56. See also Winant from London, 5 December 1944; State Department 740.00119 Control (Finland) 12-544. According to Warner, the British Embassy had taken up the matter three times in Moscow.

17. Shepherd from Helsinki, 13 December 1944; FO 371/43203 N8142/6290/56.

18. See Blinnikka (1969), pp. 17-18.

19. Ibid.

20. Ibid., pp. 19-20, 39-40.

21. Hyvämäki (1954), pp. 19-21. Fagerholm (1977), pp. 179-80. Problems of interpretation occurred in connection with the release of political prisoners when the charges had been related to criminal activities, desertion, etc.

22. The release of Pajari and Palojärvi might have had something to do with the successful conclusion of the reparations negotiations in December 1944. President Mannerheim reacted forcefully to the arrest of his generals; he told Gripenberg, for example, that he would rather put a bullet through his head than surrender Palojärvi and Pajari to the Soviet Union. When the order for release came through, Mannerheim went personally to announce it to the generals in custody. Gripenberg, diary entry, 3 November 1944, 6 January 1945.

23. On the prisoners of war, see Blinnikka (1969), pp. 26-37. Halsti (1972), pp. 80-81. Tarkka (1977), pp. 67-72.

24. Sarva (1952), pp. 17-18, 49.

25. Col. Ilmari Karhu's memorandum on Lieutenant General Oesch's visit to Hotel Torni, October 20 1944; archives of the liaison section of GHQ, T 1949/8a, SA.

26. Colonel Karhu's memorandum on his visit to Hotel Torni, 21-22 October 1944, ibid.

27. Karhu's memorandum on his visit to Hotel Torni, 25 October 1944, Ibid.

28. Ibid. and Blinnikka (1969), pp. 42-43.

29. Blinnikka (1969), pp. 43-44.

30. Zhdanov to Mannerheim, 30 October 1944; Erik Heinrichs Papers, file 1172/46, SA.

31. Fagerholm (1977), pp. 190-91. Martola (1973), p. 240.

32. Shepherd from Helsinki, 19 October 1944; FO 371/43203 N6823/6290/56.

33. Martola (1973), pp. 248-51.

34. Ibid., p. 251. Raikkala (1966), pp. 433-36.

35. Shepherd from Helsinki, 31 October 1944; FO 371/43169 N6668/30/56.

36. Ibid. See also N6944/30/56.

37. Shepherd from Helsinki, 8 November 1944; FO371/43170 N8137/30/56.

38. Blinnikka (1969), pp. 44-45. See also Shepherd from Helsinki, 24 November 1944; FO 371/43169 N7359/30/56.

39. Howie from Helsinki, 6 December 1944; FO 371/43170 N7729/30/56. On the release of troops, see Sarva (1952), passim. Blinnikka (1969), pp. 1-104.

40. Johnson from Stockholm, 9 November 1944; State Department 740.00119 EW/11-944.

41. Shepherd from Helsinki, 26 October 1944, FO 371/43169 N6668/30/56.

42. Fagerholm (1977), p. 184.

43. Egger from Stockholm, 28 October 1944; Politisches Departement, E 2300, Helsinki 5, Bundesarchiv Bern. Martola makes no mention of this episode in his memoirs. The Swedish Foreign Ministry also conveyed to the Americans the information that the Soviet grip on Finland was tightening. No concrete proposals for measures to be taken were made. Johnson from Stockholm, 4 November 1944; State Department 740.00119 Control (Finland) 11-444.

44. Politisches Departement to Egger via the military attaché, Major Luthy, 1 November 1944; Politisches Departement. E 2300, Helsinki 5, Bundesarchiv Bern.

45. Gripenberg's diary entries, 26 October and 4 November 1944.

46. Shepherd from Helsinki, 14 November 1944, FO 371/43202 N7190/6093/56 and 24 November 1944, FO 371/43169 N7359/30/56. See also Magill from Helsinki, 29 November 1944, FO 371/43196 N7988/5799/56.

47. Fleet's extensive report of his impressions of Finland are in FO 371/43170 N7909/30/56.

48. Shepherd from Helsinki, 24 November 1944; FO 371/43169 N7359/30/56.

49. Fagerholm (1977), p. 185. Linkomies, a wartime prime minister, held much the same view (Linkomies [1970], pp. 408-9), as did Eero Wuori (interview of 25 February 1963), Eero Wuori Papers, VA, file 10.

50. Gripenberg, diary entry, 4 November 1944. For a negative Soviet view of the Castrén government, see Ingulskaya, (1972), pp. 96-98, and Pohlebkin (1980), p. 108.

51. On the collapse of the Castrén government and the formation of the Paasikivi cabinet, Hyvämäki (1977), pp. 248-51; Fagerholm (1977), pp. 184-205; Voionmaa (1971), pp. 388-99; and Linkomies (1970), pp. 408-9. At a meeting held at Tamminiemi on 3 November, Väinö Tanner in particular recommended Paasikivi to head the new government. Mannerheim was still reluctant to take this step, however, because Paasikivi had refused to join the Castrén government. Furthermore, according to the president, Paasikivi was "impossible, talking endlessly but achieving nothing." Gripenberg, diary entry, 3 November 1944.

52. Blinnikka (1969), pp. 57-58.

53. On the activities of the Norwegian refugees in Sweden, see Grimnes (1969), pp. 278-81. The Swedish government gave its consent in principle to the transfer of the Norwegian troops to Finnmark on 30 October 1944.

54. Gripenberg, diary entries, 6 and 16 November 1944. On Lie's trip to Moscow and its background, see Lie (1958), pp. 126-29, 147-61; and see Riste (1979), pp. 172-204, 208-10. Moscow strongly opposed Lie's alternative plan for the transfer of the Norwegian units to Finnish Lapland to fight against the Germans. The Finns themselves were to disarm the Germans, as they had promised. Riste (1979), p. 191.

55. The report of Air Attaché Maj. Birger Ek, 8 February 1945, in the papers of the Stockholm military attachés; UM. Grimnes (1969), pp. 279-80. Riste (1979), pp. 212-14.

56. UM 110 F 4 (transport of the Norwegian police units via northern Finland).

57. Johnson from Stockholm, 8 December 1944; State Department 760d. 61/12-844.

58. Shepherd from Helsinki, 25 November 1944; FO 371/43170 N8137/30/56.

Chapter 5. The Question of American Representation in Finland

1. See chapter 2.

2. Winant from London, 3 October 1944; State Department 740.00119 Control (Finland) 10-344. For expressions of American-Finnish opinion, see ibid. 711.60d/12-1144 and those following. Johnson from Stockholm, 3 November 1944, Ibid., 711.60d/11-344. See also Official File 434 A Finland, Franklin D. Roosevelt Library.

3. FRUS IV 1944, pp. 249-52. Lundestad (1978), pp. 227-28.

4. Hull to Harriman, 13 October 1944. FRUS III 1944, pp. 624-25.

5. Harriman from Moscow, 16 October 1944; Ibid., p. 625.

6. Johnson from Stockholm, 25 October 1944; State Department 124.60d/10-2544.
7. Kennan from Moscow, 1 November 1944; FRUS III 1944, pp. 625-26.
8. Higgs had served in this post since the beginning of April 1944.
9. Stettinius to Kennan, 14 November 1944; FRUS III 1944, pp. 626-27.
10. Kennan from Moscow, 17 November 1944; FRUS III 1944, pp. 627-28.
11. Stettinius's directives to Higgs, 5 December 1944; FRUS III 1944, pp. 628-30.
12. Harriman from Moscow, 8 December 1944; FRUS III 1944, pp. 630-31.
13. Johnson from Stockholm, 14 December 1944; FRUS III 1944, pp. 631-32.
14. Harriman from Moscow, 17 December 1944; FRUS III 1944, pp. 632-33.
15. Harriman from Moscow, 5 January 1945; FRUS III 1944, p. 633.

Chapter 6. From Yalta to Potsdam

1. Ciechanowksi (1948), p. 248.
2. After tough bargaining between Eden and Molotov, the following percentage figures, regarded as indicators for the future, were arrived at: Rumania—90 percent (to the Soviet Union): 10 percent (to Britain); Bulgaria—80 percent: 20 percent; Hungary—80 percent: 20 percent; Greece—10 percent: 90 percent; Yugoslavia—50 percent: 50 percent. For more details, based on British sources, see Resis (1978), pp. 368-87, and sources. Soviet historiography has challenged the existence of this agreement on spheres of interest, as it has challenged the existence of the additional secret protocol to the Hitler-Stalin pact of 1939.
3. On the quarrel over the United Nations, see Russell and Muther (1958), pp. 411-514, and sources.
4. On the Yalta conference, see FRUS, "The Conferences at Malta and Yalta, 1945," passim.; *Sovetskiy Soyuz na mezhdunarodnykh konferentsiyakh perioda Velikoy Otechestvennoy Voyny 1941-1945 gg*, vol. IV. (*Yalta*), passim; Woodward (1972-74), vol. V, pp. 261-319; Yergin (1978), pp. 61-67; Gaddis, (1972), pp. 160-171; Davis (1974), pp. 172-201; Wheeler-Bennett and Nicholls (1972), pp. 206-50; Israelyan (1964), pp. 473-512; *Istoriya vneshney politiki SSSR*, vol. I, 1917-1945, pp. 466-79.
5. In the 283-page "Briefing Book" prepared for Roosevelt's use at Yalta, the State Department devoted about three sheets to the Finnish question; it was content merely to describe the events of 1944 in that country and refrained from making proposals for actions to be taken. See State Department, "Briefing Book for Yalta Conference - 1945"; Rg 43, Records of International Conferences, box 3. For the origins of the Briefing Book see Walker (1965), pp. 36-37.
6. Stalin to Churchill, 24 April 1945. *Perepiska Predsedatelya Soveta Ministrov SSSR*, I, p. 335.
7. On the development of relations between the Western powers and the Soviet Union in the spring of 1945, see FRUS, "The Conference of Berlin (Potsdam)," I, pp. 3-81; Woodward (1972-74), vol. III, pp. 490-595, and vol. V, pp. 320-655. See also Feis (1960), p. 3-151; Wheeler-Bennett and Nicholls (1972), pp. 251-321; Davis (1974), pp. 202-81; Israelyan (1964), pp. 513-81; and Raysky (1979), pp. 22-36.
8. Stalin to Truman and Churchill, 27 May 1945. *Perepiska*, II, p. 236.
9. Harriman from Moscow, 30 May 1945; FRUS V (1945), p. 548.
10. FRUS (Potsdam), I, pp. 359-60. Davis (1974), pp. 282-84.
11. Truman to Stalin, 2 June (7 June) 1945; FRUS V (1945), pp. 550-51. *Perepiska*, II, pp. 238-39. Davis (1974), p. 284. The letter had been drafted in the State Department and Truman had approved it without amendment. The president also sent a copy of his message to Churchill.
12. Hopkins, Harriman, and Truman: exchange of telegrams, 3-7 June 1945; FRUS V (1945), pp. 551-52.
13. Stalin to Truman, 9 June 1945. *Perepiska*, II, pp. 240-41. FRUS V (1945), pp. 554-55.
14. Truman and Stalin: exchange of telegrams, 19-23 June 1945. *Perepiska*, II, pp. 245-47. FRUS V (1945), pp. 558-59, 560.

15. Churchill to Stalin, 10 June 1945. *Perepiska*, I, p. 369. Woodward (1972-74), vol. III, pp. 585-94. Davis (1974), pp. 284-87. Rumors of the Soviet Union's intentions of restoring diplomatic relations also reached Finland via the Swedish legation in Moscow. Carl Enckell's memorandum, 6 June 1945; Carl Enckell Papers, VA, file 84.

16. On the Potsdam conference, see FRUS (Potsdam) I-II, pp. 169, 230-31, 370-72, 589-90, 736-37 and passim; *Sovetskiy Soyuz*, vol. VI, passim; Woodward (1972-74), vol. V, pp. 401-99; Yergin (1978), pp. 109-22; Gaddis (1978), pp. 171-74; Feis (1960), passim; Wheeler-Bennett and Nicholls (1972), pp. 321-43; Davis (1974), pp. 288-313; Curry (1965), pp. 105-28; Israelyan (1964), pp. 581-606; *Istoriya vneshney politiki SSSR*, vol. I, pp. 481-86; Beletsky (1980), pp. 98-179. On Stalin's comment about Byrnes, Blum (1975), p. 475.

Chapter 7. The Finnish Parliamentary Elections of 1945

1. See chapter 5 above and FRUS IV 1945, pp. 598, 624-25. Zhdanov met Higgs on 20 January 1945. Their conversation, which emphasized the willingness of both sides to cooperate, did not reveal anything new. Cf. Higgs from Helsinki, 20 January 1945; FRUS IV 1945, pp. 625-26.

2. Higgs from Helsinki, 25 January 1945; FRUS IV 1945, pp. 598-60.

3. Tarkka (1977), pp. 51-54 and sources.

4. Johnson from Stockholm 19 September 1944; State Department 740.00119 European War 1939/9-1944.

5. Mallet from Stockholm, 29 September 1944; FO 371/43168 N5982/30/56 and the attached FO comments.

6. Ibid., N5994/30/56.

7. See chapter 4.

8. FO 371/43205 N6692/6692/56. Giving a clerical error as an excuse, the Soviet side of the ACC sent the list to the British about a month after it had been presented to the Finns. Cf. FO 371/43205 N7335/6692/56.

9. Tarkka (1977), pp. 71-75 and sources.

10. Johnson from Stockholm, 8 December 1944; State Department 760. 61/12-844. In an interview given to the Swedish newspaper *Aftonbladet* at the end of November, Deputy Prime Minister Mauno Pekkala had publicly supported the removal of wartime policymakers from positions of authority. Cf. T. Heikkilä (1965), pp. 22-23.

11. Skyttä (1969), p. 250.

12. Fagerholm (1977), p. 190.

13. Hyvämäki (1954), pp. 42-43. For the activities of the Comrades-in-Arms Association generally, see Kulha (1980), passim.

14. On the internal political difficulties of the government in making a decision about the proscription of the Comrades-in-Arms Association, see the statement made by Minister K. T. Jutila to Higgs on 27 January 1945; State Department 860d. 00/1-2845.

15. Skyttä (1969), pp. 246-47.

16. Hyvämäki (1954), p. 43. The Comrades-in-Arms Association thereupon issued a statement to the press denying any charges of "fascism" and clarifying the nature of its activities.

17. See, for instance, *Helsingin Sanomat*, 19 January 1945.

18. Hyvämäki (1977), p. 253 and sources. For Orlov's statements, see *Helsingin Sanomat*, 25 January 1945; Shepherd from Helsinki, 26 and 29 January 1945, FO 371/47369 N860/33/56 and N1042/33/56. The memorandum of the British section of the ACC, WO 32/14556. For the proscription of the Comrades-in-Arms Association, see Kulha (1980), pp. 236-43.

19. Shepherd from Helsinki, 30 January 1945; FO 371/47369 N1495/33/56. Howie from Helsinki, 18 March 1945; FO 371/47400 N3005/979/56. For the opinions prevailing among the members of the Finnish government, see Skyttä (1969), pp. 246-47.

20. See, for example, *Helsingin Sanomat*, 19 January 1945.

21. *Helsingin Sanomat*, 25 January 1945. Cf. also Higgs from Helsinki, 22 January 1945; State Department 740.00119 Control (Finland) 1-2245. Shepherd from Helsinki, 26 January and 6 February 1945; FO 371/47369 N860/33/56 and 371/47400 N979/979/56. Tarkka (1975), p. 75. Skyttä (1969), p. 248 and sources.

22. Higgs from Helsinki, 25 January 1945; FRUS IV 1945, pp. 598-99.

23. Hyvämäki (1977), pp. 258-60. See Soikkanen (1980), pp. 122-25.

24. Warner's comment, FO 371/47403 N1043/1043/56. After the completion of the committee's report the following summer, the Foreign Office did not, however, consider it expedient to demand that the parts concerning Britain's role in the Winter War be kept secret. The government subsequently gave way to the demand of the People's Democrat ministers and decided to keep the whole report secret.

25. Shepherd from Helsinki, 14 February 1945; FO 371/47403 N1824/1043/56.

26. Shepherd from Helsinki, 6 February 1945, FO 371/47400 N979/56.

27. Higgs from Helsinki, 29 January 1945; State Department 860d. 00/1-2945.

28. Higgs from Helsinki, 1 February 1945; State Department 860d. 00/2-145. The war guilt question became, at least outwardly, a fundamental cause of disagreement in the internal wrangles of the left during the winter of 1944-45. On 13 January 1945, the Social Democrats were offered an electoral alliance by the People's Democrats on condition that such "war culprits" as Tanner, Hakkila, Salovaara, and Aaltonen not be nominated as parliamentary candidates. The leadership of the Social Democratic Party considered the conditions humiliating; at its meeting on 21 January 1945, the party committee rejected the People's Democrats' alliance offer by a majority of one. The way to cooperation with the communists was now blocked and for example, Mauno Pekkala stood as a parliamentary candidate of the People's Democrats. In February, the Social Democratic party council took the view that Pekkala and J. W. Keto had resigned from the party.

29. Cf., for example, *Svenska Dagbladet*, 20 January 1945. It seems that Paasikivi was behind this article, which aroused a great deal of attention. Higgs from Helsinki, 26 January 1945, State Department 860d. 00/1-2645; Higgs from Helsinki, 25 January 1945; FRUS IV 1945, p. 599. Hyvämäki (1954), p. 46.

30. Higgs from Helsinki, 29 January 1945; State Department 860d. 00/1-2945.

31. *Helsingin Sanomat*, 27 January 1945.

32. Higg's account of his conversation with Erkko on 28 January 1945; FRUS IV 1945, pp. 600-601. On Mannerheim's "legalism," see the comment to Higgs made by Wuori, the minister of transport. Wuori likewise referred to the importance of American help in making the Finnish people appreciate the international repercussions of their attitudes toward their wartime leaders. Higgs from Helsinki, 28 January 1945; State Department 740.00119/9 Control (Finland) 1-2845.

33. Higgs from Helsinki, 30 January 1945; FRUS IV 1945, pp. 601-2.

34. Harriman from Moscow, 1 March 1945, and Under Secretary of State Grew to Higgs, 3 February 1945; FRUS IV 1945, pp. 602-5.

35. Higgs from Helsinki, 28 January 1945; State Department 860d. 00/1-2845.

36. The candidates concerned were Kalliokoski, Kukkonen, Tarkkanen, and Reinikka (Agrarians); Tanner, Salovaara, Hakkila, and Aaltonen (Social Democrats); and Linkomies, Horelli, and Lehtonen (National Coalition). On 6 February 1945, Tanner resigned his seat. This purge was also extended to some leading members of the administration and the business world. Thus Ryti and Rangell left the Bank of Finland, Tanner the Cooperative Association Elanto, J. V. Vakio the Finnish Radio, L. Arvi P. Poijärvi the Schools' Administration., Rolf Nevanlinna the University of Helsinki, and so on. Cf. Tarkka (1977), pp. 78-79.

37. Skyttä (1969), p. 249 and sources. See also Sorvali (1975), pp. 184-97.

38. *Helsingin Sanomat*, 3 March 1945.

39. *Helsingin Sanomat*, 16 March 1945. Tarkka (1977), pp. 81-82. Paasikivi's comment was based on remarks made by Zhdanov on 8 March 1945. Enckell's *Anteckningar*, 8 March 1945; Carl

Enckell Papers, VA, file 79. On the 1945 elections as a test case, see Bartenyev and Komissarov (1977), pp. 60-61.

40. Higgs from Helsinki, 19 January 1945; State Department 740.00119 Control (Finland) /1-1945.

41. Shepherd from Helsinki, 6 February 1945; FO 371/47400 N979/56. Cf. the memorandum of the ACC's British section, WO 32/14556, and Magill (1981), pp. 109-10, 113-14, 122-24.

42. Shepherd from Helsinki, 6 February 1945; FO 371/47369 N1600/33/56. On the Finnish fears, see also interview statements made by Orlov and Savonenkov to Pohlebkin; Pohlebkin (1980), pp. 106-8.

43. Higgs from Helsinki, 10 February 1945; State Department 760d.61/2-1045. On the trade negotiations in Moscow, see Blinnikka (1969), pp. 78-80.

44. Hamilton from Helsinki, 9 March 1945; State Department 860d.00/3-945. Cf. Baltiyskiy (1945).

45. Directives from the State Department to Hamilton on 30 January 1945; FRUS IV 1945, pp. 627-28.

46. Higgs from Helsinki, 13 February 1945, State Department 711.60d/2-1345, and State Department to Higgs, 17 February 1945, ibid, 711.60d/2-1745. For the note from the ACC, see Higgs from Helsinki, 19 January 1945; State Department 740.00119 Control (Finland) 1-1945.

47. On the economic repercussions of the Western powers' policy toward Finland cf. H. Heikkilä (1983), pp. 154-81 and passim. Washington's noncommittal line was a disappointment to the British, who, to secure the vital supply of Finnish timber, had hoped for some American measures to alleviate the difficult economic situation in the northern republic. Great Britain itself, being sustained by American credits, was not able to give any support to the Finns.

48. Hamilton from Helsinki, 27 February 1945; State Department 740.00119 Control (Finland) 2-2745.

49. Hamilton from Helsinki, 3 and 5 March 1945; FRUS IV 1945, pp. 605-6. In his conversations with Svento and Commodore Howie, the head of the British section of the ACC, Hamilton expressed his surprise at the small number of Soviet troops in Finland. Thereupon he was enlightened by both men that there were, indeed, none except in the zone northeast of Iñari where the Petsamo border issue had not yet been settled, the Porkkala zone, and (of course) the staff of the ACC in Helsinki.

50. Hamilton from Helsinki, 15 March 1945; FRUS IV, pp. 607-8.

51. Krosby (1978), pp. 56-57 and sources.

52. On the trade negotiations see H. Heikkilä (1983), pp. 96-101.

Chapter 8. The Problem of Military Cooperation

1. Zhdanov to Mannerheim, 26 November 1944: Archives of the liaison section of GHQ, T20362/1, SA. Cf. Blinnikka, (1969), p. 45 and sources.

2. Mannerheim to Zhdanov, 20 December 1944; liaison section of GHQ, ibid.

3. Zhdanov to Mannerheim, 6 January 1945; liaison section of GHQ, ibid. On the minesweeping preparations and their practical accomplishment in the years immediately after the war, see Mattila (1968), passim.

4. Mannerheim to Zhdanov, 8 January 1945, liaison section of GHQ, ibid.

5. Zhdanov to Mannerheim, 19 January 1945; Gustaf Mannerheim Papers, VA, file 615. Cf. Gripenberg's diary entry for 28 May 1945.

6. Heinrichs's memorandum, 20 January 1945; Gustaf Mannerheim Papers VA, file 614. Heinrichs had drafted his memorandum either in a hurry or for security reasons in only one handwritten copy.

7. Mannerheim's outline with its first draft; Gustaf Mannerheim Papers, VA, file 614. In the same file are copies in Russian of the Soviet treaties with Czechoslovakia and France. The relevant sections of the Czech treaty have been published in Finnish as an appendix to Söderhjelm's memoirs;

Söderhjelm (1970), pp. 217-18. The treaty between the Soviet Union and France in extenso in *Sovyetsko-frantsuskiye otnosheniya vo vremya Velikoy Otechestvennoy Voyny 1941-1945. Dokumenty i materialy*, (1959) pp. 383-85. The copy of Mannerheim's draft in Paasikivi's own handwriting is in the Carl Enckell Papers, VA, file 84. Leino later claimed in his memoirs that Paasikivi had been present at the discussions between Zhdanov and Mannerheim, but this may be a slip of memory; cf. Y. Leino (1958), pp. 226-27. It is evident from the first draft in Mannerheim's archives that the marshal also knew of the treaty concluded in December 1939 between the so-called Kuusinen Government and the Soviet Union, the third article of which stated that "the Soviet Union and the Finnish People's Republic bind themselves to give each other all manner of assistance, also including military assistance in the case of an attack or a threat of an attack by any European state against the Soviet Union via Finnish territory." Gustaf Mannerheim Papers, VA, file 614. The treaty with the Terijoki Government in extenso cf. *Suomen historian dokumentteja* (1970), vol. 2, pp. 406-7.

8. Shepherd from Helsinki, 6 February 1945; FO 317/47369 N1600/33/56. Shepherd himself went considerably further in describing Mannerheim to Zhdanov as "an impressive figure" and "a strong personality who commands respect."

9. Mattila (1968), p. 252. Blinnikka (1959), pp. 49-50.

10. On 23 November 1945, Lieutenant General Airo had delivered to the ACC a detailed account of the discussion of the Finnish desiderata between Zhdanov and Mannerheim concerning the dismantling of coastal artillery. UM 110 E 11 ("The demobilization of the Sea Forces").

11. Zhdanov to Mannerheim, 2 March 1945; liaison section of GHQ, T20362/1, SA.

12. Mannerheim to Zhdanov, 5 March 1945; liaison section of GHQ, ibid. In the opinion of legal expert Erik Castrén, submitted to the president on 3 March, the matter only necessitated a decision by the president and commander in chief; the consent of Parliament was not necessary. Castrén's statement, 3 March 1945, ibid. At the beginning of June, Mannerheim informed Zhdanov that the arrangements agreed upon had been completed according to schedule. Mannerheim to Zhdanov, 1 June 1945, ibid.

13. UM 110 F 4 (Erik Castrén's memorandum, 1 March 1945).

14. Hamilton from Helsinki, 9 March 1945; State Department 860.00/3-945.

15. Heinrich's memoranda, 27 March, 15 May, and 19 June 1945; chief of general staff, secret correspondence 1940-46, T20117/40, SA. UM 110 A 3c. Gustaf Mannerheim Papers, VA, file 614.

16. Heinrichs's memoranda mentioned earlier. In a meeting on 27 June 1945, where these ideas had a mixed reception, the defense review committee decided to postpone the matter because the views of the Finnish government and the Soviet Union were not yet known. The minutes of the defense review committee, 27 June 1945, T19572/376, SA.

17. Gripenberg's diary entry for 24-28 May 1945.

18. When preparing his draft, Enckell took into consideration the treaties concluded by the Soviet Union with Poland and Yugoslavia in the spring of 1945. Enckell's draft was written in Russian and was sent to Paasikivi after it had been translated into Finnish by Departmental Secretary Jorma Vanamo on 23 May 1945. In the archives of the Finnish Foreign Ministry there are no copies of the texts. Even Enckell himself did not have a copy of the Russian version, and on 16 November 1947 (when the whole question cropped up again with the visit of the Pekkala delegation to Moscow) he personally transcribed it from Paasikivi's original. Cf. Carl Enckell Papers, VA, file 84. There is a copy of Vanamo's Finnish text in the Carl Enckell Papers, file 116. Cf. also K. G. Idman's memorandum with Enckell's comments in the margin, 12 June 1945, UM 110 A 3c; Tauno Suontausta's memorandum, 18 May 1945, "On the Soviet cooperation and alliance treaties," Tauno Suontausta Papers, VA, file 3.

19. Gripenberg's diary entry for 24-28 May 1945.

20. Gripenberg's diary entry for 9 June 1945. Former Swedish Minister to Moscow Assarsson went even further when he said to Gripenberg that a military agreement between Finland and Soviet Union would be "an excellent development" if it were to reduce significantly the pressure upon

Finland. Gripenberg's diary entry for 5 June 1945. Cf. Carl Enckell's *Anteckningar*, 10 June 1945; Carl Enckell Papers, Va, file 84.

21. Hamilton from Helsinki, 12 May 1945, and Under Secretary of State Grew's answer; State Department 760d. 61/5-1245.

22. Shepherd from Helsinki, 26 June 1945; FO 371/47408 N4243/1131/G56. Cf. Shepherd's telegram of 8 June 1945 for his conversation with second Foreign Minister Svento. FO 371/47408 N6630/1131/G56.

23. FO memorandum, 24 July 1945, and attached documents; FO 371/47408 N8592: 1131/G56.

24. Bevin's memorandum of his discussion with Lie, 29 August 1945; FO 371/47528 N11314/716/30.

25. FO 371/47408 N8584/1131/G56. Cf. Roberts from Moscow, 5 October 1945; N13744/1131/56.

26. Magill's report, 30 October 1945, and attached FO comments; FO 371/47450 N15473/10928/G63 and N17623/10928/G63.

Chapter 9. Toward Normality

1. For the parliamentary elections, the "Big Three" communiqué, and the formation of Paasikivi's government see Hyvämäki (1954), pp. 53-60; ibid. (1977), pp. 260-63: Tarkka (1977), pp. 82-83. Cf. Sorvali (1975), pp. 206-23.

2. Hamilton from Helsinki, 23 March and 25 April 1945; FRUS IV 1945, pp. 611-13.

3. Hamilton from Helsinki, 23 March 1945; FRUS IV 1945, pp. 609-11.

4. Cf. above, pp. 31-32.

5. *Izvestiya*, 22 March 1945.

6. This weapon was, indeed, used by Moscow, Cf. Molotov's comment to Harriman on 11 April 1945 on the Bulgarian elections. Harriman from Moscow, 15 April 1945; FRUS IV 1945, p. 186.

7. Hamilton from Helsinki, 23 May 1945; State Department 740.00119 Control (Finland) 5-2345. Cf. ibid., 28 April 1945; FRUS IV 1945, pp. 613-15.

8. Winant from London, 22 March 1945; State Department 740.00119 Control (Finland) 3-2245.

9. Howie from Helsinki, 18 March 1945; FO 371/47400 N3005/979/56. Cf. Howie from Helsinki, 6 June 1945; WO 32/14558. In the latter report, the commodore expressed the view that Finnish "apathy" had increased to a worrying extent.

10. FO 371/47400 N4579/979/56. FO 371/47370 N5610/33/56. FO 371/47408 N6372/1131/56. Cf. Hamilton from Helsinki, 28 June 1945; State Department 740.00119 Control (Finland) 6-2845.

11. FO 371/47370 N5034/33/56. FO 371/47370 N5610/33/56.

12. Shepherd from Helsinki, 30 May 1945; FO 371/47370 N6459/33/56. Magill (1981), pp. 120-21.

13. In the spring of 1945, Paasikivi's government made several attempts to obtain permission for the Finnish representatives to travel to Washington for the negotiations regarded as vital for the supply of raw materials for industry. FRUS IV 1945, pp. 640-41, 646-48, 649-50. Cf. Rautkallio (1979), pp. 32-34. The United States raised the possibility of setting up a permanent legation in Hungary but not in Rumania and Bulgaria. Cf. Lundestad (1978), p. 122.

14. Shepherd from Helsinki, 12 June 1945; FO 371/47399 N7238/550/56. Cf. Idem, N7209/550/56.

15. FO to Shepherd, 5 July 1945; ibid.

16. Shepherd from Helsinki, 16 July 1945; FO 371/47399 N9119/550/56. The articles in *Vapaa Sana* on 6 June, in *Kontakt* on 18 May, and *Folktidningen* on 27 May 1945 particularly irritated the British. Not until the beginning of 1946 did Shepherd again have cause to complain about "unfounded and unfriendly" assertions. Cf. UM 12 L Englanti 1946.

17. According to this principle (and without revealing the real reason to the Finns), the ACC had discontinued at the beginning of March 1945 the scheduled flights allowed earlier between

Stockholm and Helsinki. Individual flights were still possible by the special license granted in each case by the ACC and cleared by Moscow. This practice, which also applied to the courier service of the British Section of the ACC, was maintained until the conclusion of the Paris Peace Treaty. The airfield at Malmi was returned to the Finns at the end of 1946. UM 110 E 11.

18. Howie from Helsinki, 17 and 25 July 1945, FO 371/47400 N8760/979/56; idem, N900/979/56. Cf. WO 32/14558.

19. See the discussion in chapter 8.

20. Correspondence between Zhdanov and Paasikivi, 25 July 1945; UM 110 E 11. Cf. also Shepherd from Helsinki, 26 July 1945, FO 371/47400 N9912/979/56; and Hamilton from Helsinki, 28 July 1945, State Department 740.00119 Control (Finland) /7-2845.

21. FO to Howie, 29 July 1945; FO 371/47400 N9375/979/G. WO 32/14558.

22. Howie from Helsinki, 2 August 1945; FO 371/47400 N9775/979/56.

23. FO to Howie, 31 August 1945; FO 371/47400 N11057/979/56.

24. FO to Clark Kerr, 12 August 1945; FO ibid. Cf. also Harriman from Moscow, 13 August 1945; State Department 740.00119 European War/8-1345.

25. FO 371/47401 N11439/979/56.

26. Howie from Helsinki, 21 September 1945; FO 371/47401 N12727/979/56. WO 32/14558.

27. Exchange of telegrams between Howie and FO on 22-28 September 1945; FO 371/47401 N12678/979/56. Zhdanov to Paasikivi, 8 October 1945, and P. K. Tarjanne's memorandum, 9 October 1945; UM 110 E 11.

28. Admiralty memorandum, 23 September 1945; FO 371/47401 N12732/979/56.

29. FO 371/47408 N13462/1131/G56. Cf. Grew's memorandum, 6 August 1945; FRUS IV 1945, pp. 619-20. Hyvämäki (1977), p. 281. The Soviet Union established diplomatic relations with Hungary on 25 September 1945, slightly later, just as Stalin had mentioned in May.

30. Appendix to Thompson's memorandum to Dunn, 15 July 1945; State Department 711.60d./7-1545. The memorandum itself is printed in FRUS Potsdam I, p. 418. The memorandum of the British embassy in Washington, 20 August 1945; State Department 741.60d./8-2045. Bevin to Walsh (in Helsinki), 18 August 1945; FO 371/47399 N10827/550/56.

31. As no credentials were presented, no accreditation was necessary. The Finns could thus in principle only notify the British who had been chosen. Cf. Walsh from Helsinki, 22 August 1945; FO 371/47399 N10827/550/56 and the attached remarks by the Northern Department. Walsh from Helsinki, 3 September 1945; FO 371/47399 N11382/550/56; and FO to Walsh, 4 September 1945, ibid.

32. Walsh from Helsinki, 3 September 1945; FO 371/47399 N12022/550/56. Diplomatic relations between the Soviet Union and Finland were restored on 6 August 1945. The Finnish minister to Moscow was appointed on 21 August 1945, and the Soviet minister to Helsinki (who was appointed at the same time) presented his credentials to the president on 26 August 1945.

33. Byrnes's memorandum, 17 August 1945. At the bottom of the memorandum in President Truman's own handwriting: "Approved, Harry S. Truman, August 18, 1945." FRUS IV 1945, pp. 630-31. Byrnes to Hamilton, 17 August 1945; FRUS ibid. p. 631.

34. Hamilton from Helsinki, 21 August 1945; FRUS IV 1945, p. 631. The United States and Great Britain notified the Finnish government of the recognition on 20 August 1945.

35. FRUS IV 1945, p. 632. It was probably because of President Mannerheim's illness and leave of absence that the presentation of credentials was postponed until 4 March 1946.

36. Gripenberg's diary entry for 30 August 1945. The description is based on information given by Mannerheim. Cf. T. Heikkilä (1965), pp. 130-32.

37. Hulley from Helsinki, 31 August 1945; State Department 701.60d.11/8-3145. Gripenberg's diary entry about Jutila's "almost total lack of English" may have been sour grapes.

38. Walsh from Helsinki, 3 September 1945; FO 371/47399 N12022/550/56. According to Walsh, "Dr. Söderhjelm had intimated that the only real reason for Jutila's appointment to Washington

was that the other members of the Government were utterly fed up and could not tolerate him any longer." Cf. FO 511/115.

39. Walsh from Helsinki, 3 September 1945; FO 371/47399 N11382/550/56 and attached remarks. Wuori's portfolio was inherited by his fellow party member Onni Peltonen, whereas Jutila was succeeded by the Agrarian Vihtori Vesterinen.

40. Howie from Helsinki, 5 September 1945; FO 371/47401 N11439/979/56 and ibid, N12058/ 979/56. WO 32/14558.

41. Communiqué of the ACC and the favorable replies of the Finnish Foreign Ministry, UM 110 E 11.

42. FO 371/47399 N11535/550/56.

Chapter 10. From Potsdam to Moscow

1. Minutes of the discussions on Italian war reparations; FRUS II 1945, pp. 212-16.

2. FRUS II 1945, pp. 116-17.

3. See the Appendix.

4. The Soviet proposals on 12 September 1945 for the peace treaties with Hungary, Bulgaria, Finland, and Rumania; FRUS II 1945, pp. 147-50.

5. Remarks by the British delegation, 17-18 September 1945, concerning the Soviet drafts of peace treaties with Rumania, Bulgaria, Hungary, and Finland; FRUS II 1945, pp. 219/29. An understanding in principle had already been reached at the Moscow meeting of foreign ministers in 1943 on the civil liberty clause to be included in the Italian agreement.

6. Minutes of the Council of Foreign Ministers on 20 September 1945; FRUS II 1945, pp. 269-75.

7. FRUS II 1945, pp. 263-67. Lundestad (1978), pp.127-28.

8. Charles E. Bohlen's memorandum, 20 September 1945; FRUS II 1945, pp. 267-69. The diary of Walter Brown (Byrnes's aide), 20 September 1945; James F. Byrnes Papers folder entitled "602 Conference 2-1 Potsdam," Clemson University Library, Clemson, South Carolina.

9. For the London conference see Yergin (1978), pp. 122-32. Gaddis (1972), pp. 263-73. Wheeler-Bennet and Nicholls (1972), pp. 419-24. Curry (1965), pp. 147-56. Harriman and Abel (1976), pp. 506-10. The minutes of the conference and the supporting American documentation are found in FRUS II 1945, pp. 99-559. On the "bathroom discussion" of Dulles and Byrnes, see the interview of Theodore C. Achilles, the secretary of the American delegation, "Oral History Interview with Theodore Achilles," pp. 6-9, Harry S. Truman Library, Independence, Missouri. Knight (1978). For the Soviet version, see Istoriya diplomatii (1974), pp. 30-35,

10. Yergin (1978), pp. 131-32, 146-47. Cf. Ward (1979), pp. 18-49.

11. Truman's letter of 12 October 1945; Perepiska Predsedatelya Soveta Ministrov SSSR, vol. II, pp. 271-73; FRUS II 1945, pp. 562-63. Memoranda of Harriman's discussions with Stalin in Garga on 24 and 25 October 1945; FRUS II 1945, pp. 567-76. Harriman and Abel (1976), pp. 511-16. Molotov's remark to Byrnes concerning Norway; FRUS II 1945, p. 646.

12. After Yalta, the Foreign Ministers had met (besides Potsdam) in San Francisco and London; it would now be the turn of Moscow. At the back of Byrnes's mind there was also an idea of talking to Stalin in Moscow, if the discussions with the "inflexible" Molotov were to draw a blank.

13. The Great Powers agreed among themselves that these names would not be mentioned in the communiqué issued by the Moscow conference. To guard against subterfuge, they decided instead that they would be mentioned in the instructions given to the Soviet-American-British commission going to Bucharest. The Soviet Union took charge of supervising the government formation in Bulgaria.

14. On the Moscow conference, see Yergin (1978), pp. 143-51; Gaddis (1972), pp. 276-81; Wheeler-Bennet and Nicholls (1972), pp. 424-29; Curry (1965), pp. 156-83; Harriman and Abel

(1976), pp. 523-27; Kennan (1967), pp. 283-90; Ward (1979), pp. 50-77. For the minutes of the conference and supporting American documentation, see FRUS II 1945, pp. 560-826. For the Russian version, cf. *Istoriya diplomatii* (1974), pp. 35-36 and *Istoriya vneshney politiki SSSR* (1980-81), vol. 2, pp. 31-33.

Chapter 11. A Delayed Peace

1. "The report of the discussion between the delegation of Karelian members of Parliament and the Prime Minister." Juho Niukkanen Papers, VA, file 10:II e.

2. A copy of the note is in the archives of the Finnish Foreign Ministry; UM 7 B Pariisi 1946 II A 2. The cabinet was aware of the undertaking because of advance information about it given by Paavolainen and Wahlforss. When Enckell brought the matter up for discussion with General Zhdanov on 16 September, the latter replied that his task was only to supervise the fulfillment of the terms of the armistice agreement. Enckell's *Anteckningar*, 16 and 21 September 1945; Carl Enckell Papers, VA, file 79.

3. The head of chancery of the Finnish Foreign Ministry, P. J. Hynninen, instructions to Wuori on 21 September 1945; UM 7 B Pariisi 1946 A 1-2.

4. Enckell's *Anteckningar*, 22 September 1945; Carl Enckell Papers, VA, file 79.

5. Shepherd from Helsinki, 26 September 1945; FO 371/47370 N13353/33/56.

6. Shepherd's report to FO on his press conference; FO 371/47370 N13669/33/56. Cf. (for example) *Hufvudstadsbladet* and *Helsingin Sanomat*, 26 September 1945.

7. Bevin to Shepherd, 25 September 1945; FO 371/47370 N13421/33/56.

8. Ibid. Cf. Wuori from London, 26 September 1945; UM 7 B Pariisi 1946 II A 1-2.

9. Wuori from London, 9 October 1945; UM 7 B Pariisi 1945 IIA 1-2.

10. Sundström from Moscow, 16 September 1945; UM 7 B Pariisi 1946 II A 1-2. Cf. Sundström to Svento, 25 September 1945; UM 5 B Moskova.

11. Sundström from Moscow, 7 October 1945; UM 12 L Neuvostoliitto 1945. Hulley's account of his discussion with Tuomioja: Hulley from Helsinki, 16 October 1945; FRUS IV/1945, pp. 656-57.

12. Minister Jutila did not arrive in Washington until November, presenting his credentials to President Truman on 21 November 1945; UM 5 C 8 1945.

13. Wuori from London, 2 and 8 October 1945; UM 5 C 7 1945. Cf. the confidential reports of the Finnish Foreign Ministry 21/1945, 5 October 1945, UM 7 B Pariisi 1946 II A 1-2.

14. Hynninen to Wuori, 17 October 1945; UM 7 B II Pariisi 1946 A 1-2.

15. Shepherd from Helsinki, 6 and 10 October 1945; FO 371/47408 N13462/1131/G56 and FO 371/47370 N14043/33/56.

16. Minute by G. Warr, FO 371/47408 N13462/1131/G56.

17. Shepherd from Helsinki, 31 October 1945; FO 371/47415 N15192/2392/56.

18. Eero A. Wuori's interviews on 25 February and 4 March 1963; Eero A. Wuori Papers, VA, file 10.

19. Other members of the delegation, besides Minister and Mrs. Helo, were the head of the Finnish State Radio, Hella Wuolijoki; Professor G. Hjelmman; the Director of the National Theatre, Eino Kalima; the writer Lauri Viljanen; a teacher, Klaus U. Suomela; two factory workers, Fanni Ylänne and E. Saarinen; and three Communist members of Parliament, Mauri Ryömä, Ville Pessi, and Hertta Kuusinen. Three other members of the delegation—Minister of Justice Urho Kekkonen, Professor Selim Palmgren, and the artist Orest Bodalew—had returned to Finland before the meeting with Stalin.

20. Shepherd's account of the discussion with Hella Wuolijoki on 29 October 1945; FO 371/47408 N15193/1131/56 and the comment made by G. Warr of the Northern Department of the FO; FO 371/47408 N14193/1131/56.

21. Hertta Kuusinen, "Suomalainen kulttuurivaltuuskunta generalissimus Stalinin ja ulkoasiain-

komissaari Molotovin puheilla." *Vapaa Sana*, 16 October 1945. Lauri Viljanen, "Keskustelu Stalinin työhuoneessa." *Helsingin Sanomat*, 16 October 1945. Helo (1965), pp. 106-16. Helo's speech in extenso, ibid. pp. 110-13.

22. Shepherd from Helsinki, 29 October 1945; FO 371/47408 N15193/1131/56. Cf. Hulley from Helsinki, 12 October 1945; State Department 740.00119 European War/10-1245.

23. Cf. H. Heikkilä (1983), pp. 105-6.

24. War Office directives to the British officers of the ACC and Warner's memorandum based on these directives; FO 371/47399 N14455/550/56 and FO 371/47401 N13643/979/56.

25. Wuori from London, 5 and 9 December 1945; UM 5 C 7 1945. Cf. "Ulkomaanedustuksen tiedotuksia" 100 and 104/1945; UM 5 C 1.

26. Wuori from London, 11 December 1945; UM 12 L Englanti 1945. Cf. Eero A. Wuori's interviews, 25 February and 4 March 1963; Eero A. Wuori Papers, VA, file 10.

27. Sundström to Svento, 21 December 1945; UM 5 B Moskova 1945.

28. Sundström from Moscow, 14 January 1946; UM 5 C 18 1946.

29. G. Warr's report of his discussions with Wuori on 31 December 1945; FO 371/56183 N303/303/56. Cf. Wuori from London, 31 December 1945; UM 5 C 7 1945.

30. For a general review, cf. *Helsingin Sanomat*, 29 December 1945.

Chapter 12. Domestic Tensions

1. Gripenberg's diary entry for 6 January 1945.

2. See Tarkka (1977), pp. 82-88, and sources cited. See also *Pravda*, 12 March 1945, and *Izvestiya*, 16 March 1945. George Kennan, then serving in the U.S. embassy in Moscow, believed that the Russians would consciously avoid going too far in Finland, since there was no pro-Soviet sentiment in that country. Kennan from Moscow, 4 February 1945; State Department 860d.00/2-445.

3. Tarkka (1977), 88-95, 127-31.

4. Skyttä (1969), p. 265.

5. Tarkka (1977), pp. 122-26.

6. Tarkka (1977), p. 133.

7. Gripenberg's diary entry for 8 August 1945.

8. See the account, based on the minutes of the cabinet meeting in T. Heikkilä, (1965), pp. 171-74, and Gripenberg's diary, 8 August 1945.

9. Tarkka, (1977), pp. 133-38. T. Heikkila, (1965), pp. 174-82.

10. Tarkka, (1977), p. 139.

11. Tarkka (1977), p. 143.

12. Tarkka (1977), pp. 145-49.

13. Hulley from Helsinki, 13 September 1945; FRUS IV 1945, p. 620.

14. Howie from Helsinki, 11 September 1945, and Warner's instructions to Shepherd, 25 September 1945; FO 371/47404 N12072/1043/56. Magill (1981), pp. 132-33. WO 32/14558.

15. See Hamilton from Helsinki, 23 March 1945; FRUS IV 1945, pp. 609-11. Ibid., 5 April 1945 (conversation with Cay Sundström), State Department 860d 00/4-545. According to Sundström, "foreign influences" would if necessary compel Parliament to make adequate concessions in the war guilt question. Ibid., 25 April 1945, FRUS IV 1945, pp. 612-13. Ibid., 13 July 1945, FRUS IV 1945, pp. 615-17. Ibid., 26 July 1945, State Department 860d.00/7-1645. Hulley from Helsinki, 13 September 1945, FRUS IV 1945, p. 620. Ibid., 7 November 1945, FRUS IV 1945, p. 621.

16. Tarkka (1977), pp. 157-81.

17. Carl Enckell's *Anteckningar*, 16 November 1945; Carl Enckell Papers, VA, file 103.

18. Tarkka (1977), pp. 181-86. Skyttä (1969), pp. 186-87. See also Shepherd from Helsinki, 28 November 1945; FO 371/47404 N16791/1043/56.

19. Sundström from Moscow, 17 December 1945; UM 110 G 12. See also Sundström's general conclusions in his report of the activities of the Finnish legation, and of Soviet policy, in 1945:

Sundström from Moscow, 14 January 1946; UM 5 C 18 1946. For Soviet press comment, see *Pravda* (3,5,6,12,14,16,19, and 21 December 1945; 14 January and 7, 21, and 24 February 1946); and *Izvestiya* (11, 12, and 21 December 1945; 10, 13, and 16 January; 7 and 13 February 1946).

20. Wuori from London, Jutila from Washington, 29 November 1945; UM 110 G 12.

21. Egger from Helsinki, 28 December 1945; Politisches Departement E 2300 Helsinki. Bundesarchiv Bern.

22. Hulley from Helsinki, 27 December 1945; FRUS IV 1945, p. 624. Shepherd from Helsinki, 22 December 1945; FO 371/47404 N17439/1043/56.

23. Tarkka (1977), pp. 187-88. T. Heikkilä (1965), pp. 188-91. Savonenkov did not inform the British section of the ACC beforehand of his demand. For this reason, Howie presented a protest, with the consent of the Foreign Office; FO 371/47404 N17372/1043/56.

24. Tarkka (1977), pp. 186-87, 192-96.

25. Tarkka (1977), pp. 213-14.

26. Tarkka (1977), p. 214, 222-23.

27. Shepherd from Helsinki, 18 February 1946; FO 371/56182 N2208/271/56. See also the memorandum of Shepherd's visit to Enckell on 18 February 1946; UM 110 G 12 and Tarkka (1977), pp. 214-15. Colonel Magill also warned Enckell separately about the sentences to be handed down by the tribunal, which should not be too light. Enckell's *Anteckningar*, 22 January 1946; Carl Enckell Papers, VA, file 103. Magill, p. 137.

28. Wuori from London, 19 February 1946; UM 110 G 12.

29. Tarkka (1977), pp. 216-23.

30. FO 371/56182 N2340/241/56 and N2990/271/56. In his report of 26 February 1946, Shepherd thought his warning had decisively influenced the Finns' change of mind.

31. Tarkka (1977), pp. 257-58.

32. Hulley from Helsinki, 24 February 1946; State Department 860d.00/2-2446.

33. Polvinen (1980), pp. 191-93.

34. Ahtokari (1971), pp. 167-71 et seq. Käkönen (1970), pp. 201-3.

35. Zhdanov to Paasikivi, 3 June 1945, and Savonenkov (for Zhdanov) to Paasikivi, 25 June 1945; Gustaf Mannerheim Papers, VA, file 615. Savonenkov informed Howie of the warning sent to Paasikivi on 5 June 1946; FO 371/47408 N6795/1131/56.

36. For a resumé, see *Pravda*, 20 May 1947.

37. Pohlebkin (1969), p. 327, 329-30. Ingulskaya (1972), pp. 157-63.

38. Shepherd from Helsinki, 13 July 1945; FO 371/47408 N8597/1131/56.

39. Hamilton from Helsinki, 26 July 1945; State Department 860d.00/7-2645.

40. Gripenberg's diary entry for 18 August 1945. The memorandum is based on discussions between Harriman and Undén, in the presence of the secretary-general of the Swedish Foreign Ministry, Assarsson. See also Magill (1981), pp. 127-28.

41. Gripenberg's diary entries for 27 February and 17 September 1945.

42. Svento (1960), p. 55. For Mannerheim's pessimism, see Hamilton from Helsinki, 9 April 1945. State Department 860d.00/5-945, and Ravndal from Stockholm, 18 October 1945 State Department 860d.00/10-1845.

43. Paasikivi to Gripenberg; Gripenberg's diary entry for 24 February 1945. Urho Kekkonen claimed that the same phenomenon was repeated in April 1945 with the formation of the new Paasikivi government. Kekkonen (1962), p. 392.

44. Gripenberg's diary entries for 6 January, 27 February and 24 May 1945. See also interviews with Eero Wuori, 25 February and 4 March 1963; Eero A. Wuori Papers, VA, file 10.

45. Gripenberg's diary entries for 6 and 24 January, 5 and 24 February, 24 May, and 5 August 1945. Mannerheim's state of health decisively weakened in the autumn of 1945, when it was confirmed that he was suffering from a stomach ulcer. See also Henrichs (1959), pp. 430-31.

46. Heinrichs (1959), p. 438-39.

47. FO 371/47403 N8839/1043/56. Jägerskiöld (1981), pp. 170-83.
48. Hulley from Helsinki, 27 October 1945; State Department 860d.00/10-2745. See also Gripenberg's diary entry for 6 March 1945.
49. Hulley from Helsinki, 6 November 1945, State Department 860d.001/11-645; and Johnson from Stockholm in the same file, 6 November 1945. Gripenberg's diary entry for 7 November 1945.
50. Shepherd from Helsinki, 7 November 1945; FO 371/47415 N15286/2392/56. See also FO 511/119. Orlov was following the ACC line, after Moscow (obviously Stalin in person) had given consent for the president's journey. Cf. Heinrichs (1959), pp. 429-30.
51. Fagerholm (1977), p. 208.
52. Fagerholm (1977), p. 209. Hyvämäki (1977), p. 283.
53. Gripenberg's diary entries for 15 and 17 February and 4 March 1946.
54. See (for example) Stalin's statement to Prime Minister Mauno Pekkala in connection with the signing of the Friendship and Mutual Assistance Treaty in Moscow, 1948. Wirtanen (1972), p. 175, and Oinonen (1971), passim.
55. Sundström to Svento, 13 February 1946; UM 5 B Moscow 1946.
56. Carl Enckell's *Anteckningar*, 27 January 1946; Carl Enckell Papers, VA, file 103. Paasikivi knew of the visit through Mannerheim. Later, having already resigned from the presidency, Mannerheim told Gripenberg of Savonenkov's visit; Gripenberg diary, 18 October 1946.
57. Boheman (1964), p. 251.

Chapter 13. Hardening Attitudes

1. Truman (1965), vol. 1, pp. 598-606.
2. For the reaction of the Soviet Union to the Fulton speech, see Trukhanovsky and Kapitonova (1979), pp. 27-32.
3. For a good general presentation of hardening American attitudes toward the Soviet Union, see Gaddis (1972), pp. 282-315 and Gaddis (1978), pp. 180-84. See also Yergin (1978), pp. 163-92, and Ward (1979), pp. 78-84. The "Long Telegram" is reproduced in extenso in Etzold and Gaddis (1978), pp. 50-63.

Chapter 14. The Deputy Foreign Ministers in London

1. FRUS II 1946, pp. 1-87. Byrnes (1947), pp. 123-24. Wheeler-Bennett and Nicholls (1972), p. 423, 430. Ward (1979), pp. 84-90. In the autumn of 1945 in London, the foreign ministers had agreed in principle to include the human rights article in the peace treaties.
2. Council of Foreign Ministers, United Kingdom Delegation Circular No. 100. Minutes of Meeting at Lancaster House on 5 April 1946. Draft Peace Treaty with Finland. FO 371/57208. The Soviet draft is in FO 371/57156 U3717/69/79.
3. For the attitude of the War Office toward the treaties with Italy, the Balkan countries, and Finland, see WO 193/770. The War Office regarded the Åland question as the only "live issue" concerning Finland.
4. United Kingdom Delegation Circular No. 104. Minutes of Meeting held at Lancaster House on 10 April. Treaty of Peace with Finland. FO 371/57209. See also CFM, Conference of Deputies, Second Session. Record of Decisions taken at Lancaster House, London, on Wednesday, 10 April 1946 at 11 a.m. State Department. RG 43. Records of International Conferences, box 21.
5. United Kingdom Delegation Circular No. 107. Minutes of Meeting held at Lancaster House on 16 April. Treaty of Peace with Finland. FO 371/57209. Peace Treaty with Finland. Proposed Redraft by U.K. Delegation of Articles 3, 4, 5, and 6 of Soviet Draft Treaty. State Department. RG 43. Records of International Conferences, box 21. CFM, Conference of Deputies, Second Session. Records of Decisions taken at 3rd, 4th, and 5th Meetings held at Lancaster House on 16th, 18th, and 20th April 1946; ibid. The results of the Deputy Foreign Ministers' deliberations on Finland

were presented in a memorandum dated 20 April 1946 to the Council of Foreign Ministers. CFM (D) (F) (46)8. FO 371/56183 N6098/303/56.

Chapter 15. The Foreign Ministers in Paris

1. Dixon (1968), pp. 212-13.
2. Sundström to Svento, 5 June 1946; UM 5 B Moskova 1946.
3. FRUS II 1946, p. 266.
4. The report of the deputy foreign ministers was based upon the decisions made at the meeting on 6 May 1946. Summary Minutes of the 17th Meeting of the Deputies, 6 May 1946. State Department. RG 43. Records of International Conferences, box 66. CFM, Report submitted by the Deputies to the Council of Foreign Ministers on the Treaty with Finland, 9 May 1946; ibid., box 15. Minutes concerning Finland, taken at the meeting of the Council of Foreign Ministers on 8 May 1946, FO 371/56183 N6095/303/56, and FRUS II 1946, pp. 300-301.
5. For the initial stage of the conference, see FRUS II 1946, pp. 88-440. Ward (1979), pp. 90-102. Pick (1950), pp. 38-58. Curry (1965), pp. 210-22. Byrnes (1947), pp. 124-30. See also Vandenberg (1952), pp. 262-88. Connally (1954), pp. 296-99. For a Soviet view, *Istoriya diplomatii* (1974), pp. 36-42.
6. The ACC in Helsinki had earlier reported that the Finnish Air Force after the war was made up of about 2,200 men; FO 371/57157 U4020/69/40.
7. UK Delegation Brief No. 40, 6 May 1946; FO 371/56183 N5991/303/56.
8. The military articles of the almost identical Finnish and Rumanian treaties were approved at the meeting of the deputy foreign ministers on 5 June 1946. Meeting of the Deputies, 5 June 1946. State Department. RG 43. Records of International Conferences, box 66. The British minutes are in FO 371/56184 N7473/303/56. For the report on Finland by the military commission and a list of the decisions of the meeting of 4 June 1946, see State Department. RG 43. Records of International Conferences, boxes 21 and 92. Ibid., boxes 15 and 60, for the Soviet and British summary of the state of affairs concerning the Finnish draft at the commencement of the second stage of the Council of Foreign Ministers' deliberations.
9. FRUS II 1946, pp. 630-31. Dixon (1968), pp. 216-17.
10. Treaty of Peace with Finland. Meeting of the Deputies, 28 June 1946. RG 43. Records of International Conferences, box 66. FO 371/56184 N8492/303/56 and N8560/303/56.
11. Ibid. See also FRUS II 1946, pp. 648-49, 668-73, 683-84. State Department. Meetings of the Deputies, 27 and 29 June, 1 and 16 July 1946. RG 43.Records of International Conferences, box 66. The British minutes are in files FO 371/56184 N8492/303/56 and FO 371/56184 N8560/303/56.
12. Bohlen (1973), pp. 254-55.
13. For the latter stages of the Paris conference, see FRUS II 1946, pp. 441-940. Ward (1979), pp. 103-26. Pick (1950), pp. 59-76. Curry (1965), pp. 222-38. Byrnes (1947), pp. 130-37. (1952), pp. 285-303. The draft peace treaties for all five former satellite countries are given in extenso in FRUS IV 1946. For a Soviet view, *Istoriya diplomatii* (1974), pp. 42-46.

Chapter 16. Finland Expectant

1. Cf. FRUS II 1945, pp. 815-24.
2. G. Warr's account of his discussion with Wuori, 31 December 1945; FO 371/56183 N303/303/56. Wuori from London, 2 January 1946; UM 5C7 1945.
3. FRUS II 1946, pp. 1-7 and sources. For Byrnes's note to the French Government on 13 January 1946 cf. also UM 7 B Pariisi 1946 II:A2.
4. Jutila from Washington, 24 January 1946; UM 7 B Pariis; 1946 II:A2.
5. Wuori from London, 17 January 1946; UM 7 B Pariisi 1946 II:A2.

6. Gripenberg's diary entry for 25 January 1946.

7. Wuori from London, 6 February 1946; UM 7 B Pariisi 1946 II:A2.

8. Sundström from Moscow, 25 January 1946; UM tulleet sähkeet, Moskova, 1946. Cf. Sundström to Svento, 13 February 1946; UM 5 B Moskova 1946.

9. Wuori from London, 4 February 1946, UM 7 B Pariisi 1946 II:A2.

10. Without mentioning him by name on this occasion, Paasikivi spoke of Heinrichs as ''a very clever man.'' *Paasikiven linja* (1966), pp. 52-53.

11. Erik Heinrichs's memorandum of 25 January 1946 UM 7 B Pariisi 1946 II:A2.

12. Minutes of the meeting on 19 February 1946 at 5:30 p.m. compiled by K. G. Idman; UM 7 B Pariisi 1946 II:A2. Cf. Gripenberg's diary entry for 19 February 1946. The discussion was based upon Enckell's memorandum of 8 February 1946, which emphasized that the Finnish peace treaty primarily concerned the Soviet Union; therefore Helsinki had to make its wishes known to Moscow in good time. Enckell's memorandum of 8 February 1946; Carl Enckell Papers, VA, file 103.

13. Minutes of the meeting on 1 March 1946 compiled by K. G. Idman; UM 7 B Pariisi 1946: II:A2.

14. On Pekkala's government and its formation, see Hyvämäki (1977), pp. 285-88. The British also considered that the balance in the cabinet had moved to the left; Walsh from Helsinki, 29 March 1946, FO 371/56176 N4257/226/56.

15. Hamilton from Helsinki, 2 April 1946; State Department 860d.00/4-246.

16. Hulley's summary report from Helsinki, 12 March 1946; State Department 760d.61/3-1246. Cf. Krosby (1978), pp. 60-61.

17. Hamilton's discussion memorandum of 21 March 1946; Appendix to the report from Helsinki, 2 April 1946, State Department 860d.00/4-246.

18. UM 7 B Pariisi 1946 II:A2.

19. Wuori from London, 5 April 1946; UM 7 B Pariisi 1946 II:A2. Cf. Wuori from London, 9 and 11 April 1946, ibid., and Hankey's memorandum of 5 April 1946, FO 371/56183.

20. Minutes of the meeting of the foreign affairs committee of the government on 9 April 1946, compiled by P. J. Hynninen; UM 7 B Pariisi 1946 II:A2. Besides the president and the prime minister, those present included ministers Enckell, Heljas, Kilpi, and Leino.

21. Minutes of the meeting of the foreign affairs committee of the government on 13 April 1946, compiled by P. J. Hynninen; UM, 7 B Pariisi 1946 II:A2.

22. For Pekkala's speech, see *Helsingin Sanomat*, 17 April 1946. Hyvämäki (1977), p. 291.

23. For the reactions of the FO see FO 371/56179 N5061/232/56, N5144/232/56, and N5275/232/56. Walsh from Helsinki, 26 April 1946; FO 371/56179 N5467/232/56. Wuori informed the FO for the first time as early as 29 March 1946; FO 371/56183 N4815/303/56. When he met Wuori two days later, Warner stressed that His Majesty's Government would not create any obstacles if the Soviet Union were to agree to relax the conditions of the armistice; Warner's memorandum of 1 April 1946, ibid.

24. Hamilton from Helsinki, 16 and 17 April 1946; State Department 760d.61/4-1646 and 760d.61/4-1746.

25. Sundström from Moscow, 18 April 1946; UM tulleet sähkeet, Moskova, 1946.

26. Memorandum on Finland's economic situation and its wishes for the final peace treaty; UM 12 L Neuvostoliitto 1946.

27. The delegation of ministers from Moscow to the Finnish Foreign Ministry, 23 April 1946; UM 12 L Neuvostoliitto 1946. Memorandum of the discussion between the delegation of the Finnish Government and Generalissimus Stalin; Carl Enckell Papers, VA, file 81. Hyvämäki (1977), p. 292. Svento (1960), pp. 28-30. Leino (1958), pp. 139-41. For the communiqué and Pekkala's radio speech on 25 April 1946, cf. *Helsingin Sanomat*, 26 April 1946. See also Pekkala's and Leino's statements given at a meeting by the Finnish-Soviet Society in Helsinki on 29 April 1946; *Helsingin Sanomat*, 30 April 1946.

28. Walsh from Helsinki, 30 April 1946 and attached comments by the FO; FO 371/56179 N5740/232/56.

29. Shepherd from Helsinki, 4 and 21 May 1946; FO 371/56179 N6144/232/56 and FO 371/56180 N6750/232/56. On the public disorders on the First of May, cf. Blinnikka (1969), pp. 136-37; Voionmaa (1971), pp. 442-43; *Izvestiya*, 26 May 1946. On the disquiet created by the revived activity of the communists, which Colonel Magill believed was affecting even President Paasikivi and Foreign Minister Enckell, see Magill from Helsinki, 18 June 1946; FO 371/56173 N8268/144/56. For the shifts in internal politics, see Hyvämäki (1954), pp. 106-15; Voionmaa (1971), pp. 443-47. Maxwell Hamilton, however, presumed that the communists endeavored to function as best they could as long as the exceptional circumstances that obtained until the coming into force of the peace treaty continued. On the other hand, Paasikivi had similarly to maintain caution in his internal politics. Hamilton from Helsinki, 5 June 1946; State Department 860d.00/6-546.

30. Jutila from Washington, 26 April 1946; UM 12 L Neuvostoliitto 1946 (The visit to Moscow by the delegation of ministers in April 1946). Directives of the Finnish Foreign Ministry to foreign representatives on 25 April 1946; ibid. Cf. Ravndal from Stockholm, 29 April 1946; State Department 760d.61/4-2946.

31. Hamilton from Helsinki, 2 May and 3 June 1946; State Department 760d.61/5-246 and 760d.61/6-346.

32. Hamilton from Helsinki, 3 June 1946; ibid.

33. Hamilton from Helsinki, 8 May 1946; American Legation in Helsinki, Secret Correspondence 1946, box 886. National Records Center, Suitland, Maryland.

34. UM 7 B Pariisi 1946. II:A2.

35. Helo from Paris, 1 and 14 May 1946; UM 7 B Pariisi 1946. II:E1. Cf. Helo (1965), pp. 130-32.

36. UM to Helo, 7 May 1946, and Helo from Paris, 7 and 8 May 1946; UM 7 B Pariisi 1946. II:A2.

37. UM to Wuori, 13 June, and Wuori from London, 20 June 1946; ibid.

38. Bevin to Shepherd, 27 June 1946; FO 371/56184 N8541/303/56.

39. Wuori from London, 26 July 1946, and Helo from Paris, 8 July 1946; UM 7 B Pariisi 1946. II:A2.

40. Jutila from Washington, 23 July 1946; UM 7 B Pariisi 1946. II:C.

41. Wuori from London, 20 July 1946; UM 5 C 7 1946.

42. Enckell's statement, 11 July 1946; UM 7 B Pariisi 1946. II:A2.

43. Helo (1965), pp. 136-37.

Chapter 17. Talks Get Under Way

1. Minutes of the initial meetings of the Paris Peace Conference and the procedural committee; FRUS III 1946, pp. 26-172. Cf. Ward (1979), pp. 127-35; Pick (1950), pp. 77-80.

2. For the comments concerning Finland, see Hankey to Shepherd, 26 July 1946; FO 371/56184 N9528/303/56.

3. Shepherd from Helsinki, 3 August 1946; FO 371/56185 N10037/303/56. Cf. also Enckell's comments to Shepherd, 8 August 1946. Shepherd from Helsinki, 9 and 12 August 1946, FO 371/56185 N8817/303/56; idem, N10364/303/56.

4. Comments of the Northern Department of FO. FO 371/56185 N10364/303/56. Cf. Lord Hood from Paris, 12 August 1946, and the reply of FO, 16 August 1946; FO 371/56185 N10088/303/56.

5. Shepherd's telegrams from Helsinki, 6 August 1946, FO 371/56185 N10088/303/56; idem, N10245/303/56; idem, N10364/303/56. In their report on 24 July 1946 concerning the draft peace treaties of the Balkan countries and Finland, the British chiefs of staff made it clear that they had no comments regarding Finland.

6. FO directives to Lord Hood in Paris, 16 August 1946, and to Shepherd in Helsinki; FO 371/56185 N10088/303/56, FO 371/56186 N11041/303/56.

7. Shepherd from Helsinki, 2 August 1946; FO 371/56185 N10039/303/56.

8. Hamilton from Helsinki, 19 July 1946; FRUS III 1946, pp. 6-8.

9. Gripenberg's diary entry for 29 June 1946. Former President K. J. Ståhlberg had particularly emphasized the importance of the territorial question to Paasikivi; Enckell's *Anteckningar* of 1 and 7 May 1946, Carl Enckell Papers, VA, file 103. In their letter to Paasikivi, representatives of the Karelian evacuees had asked him to travel to Moscow to achieve a revision of the frontiers. The president did not, however, at that stage consider such a trip expedient; Lennart Heljas's memorandum on the Paris Peace Conference, Lennart Heljas Papers.

10. Carl Enckell's *Anteckningar* of 17 to 19 July 1946; Carl Enckell Papers, VA, file 103. Cf. Gripenberg's diary entry for 22 October 1946. Memorandum on the activity of the peace delegation; Juho Niukkanen Papers, VA, file 10:IIC.

11. Leino (1958), p. 153. T. Heikkilä (1965), p. 281.

12. Hyvämäki (1977), pp. 292-93. The composition of the delegation was finally decided at the meeting of the foreign affairs committee of the government on 2 August 1946.

13. Shepherd from Helsinki, 9 August 1946; FO 371/56185 N8817/303/56.

14. Directives to the peace negotiators; UM 7 B Pariisi 1946 II:A2. Cf. the minutes of the meeting of the peace delegation on 9 August 1946 at 2:30 p.m., compiled by Tauno Suontausta; Tauno Suontausta Papers, VA. Gripenberg's diary entry for 13 August 1946. Hyvämäki (1977), p. 293.

15. Cf. Lennart Heljas's memorandum on the Paris Peace Conference; Lennart Heljas Papers, in the possession of Prof. Eino Murtorinne, Helsinki.

16. Voionmaa (1971), p. 452.

17. Paasikivi's comment in the foreign affairs committee of the government on 15 June 1946. Lennart Heljas's memorandum on the Paris Peace Conference; Lennart Heljas Papers.

18. T. Heikkilä (1965), p. 289.

19. Jakobson (1968), pp. 46-47.

20. Helo from Paris, 9 August 1946; UM 7 B Pariisi 1946 II:A2. Gripenberg's diary entry for 13 August 1946.

Chapter 18. The Finnish "Peace Crisis"

1. On the discussion concerning Italy, Rumania, and Hungary, cf. FRUS III 1946, pp. 175-236; Ward (1979), pp. 135-36; Wheeler-Bennett and Nicholls (1972), pp. 434-35; Curry (1965), pp. 243-46; Byrnes (1947), pp. 141-43. On the American displeasure toward Czechoslovakia, see Lundestad (1978), pp. 169-73.

2. Minutes of the delegation of 14 August 1946; UM 7 B Pariisi 1946 II:B1.

3. Minutes of the delegation of 15 August 1946; UM 7 B Pariisi 1946 II:B1. Cf. Hyvämäki (1977), pp. 293-95, and Voionmaa (1971), pp. 452-56. For the text of Enckell's speech, cf. *Helsingin Sanomat*, 16 August 1946, and FRUS III 1946, pp. 237-40. For the original version concerning the territorial concessions, see Voionmaa (1971), pp. 471-72. On the report to Helsinki, cf. T. O. Vahervuori's memorandum of 19 August 1946; UM 7 B Pariisi 1946 II:B6. See also Enckell's *Anteckningar* for 14-17 August 1946; Carl Enckell Papers, VA, file 103. Heljas's "Muistiinpanoja"; Lennart Heljas Papers.

4. On the general discussion and Molotov's speech on 15 August 1946, see FRUS III 1946, pp. 240-43. For Molotov's speech in extenso, cf. Molotov (1949), pp. 121-25.

5. Voionmaa (1971), p. 459.

6. FO 371/56186 N10679/303/56.

7. Minutes of the delegation of 17 August 1946 and the attached telegram to Helsinki; UM 7 B Pariisi 1946 II:B1. T. O. Vahervuori's memorandum of 19 August 1946; UM 7 B Pariisi 1946 II:B6.

8. Memorandum of the visit by Prime Minister Pekkala and Foreign Minister Enckell to the Soviet embassy in Paris on 19 August 1946 at 7 p.m.; UM 7 B Pariisi 1946 II:B1.

9. T. O. Vahervuori's memorandum of 26 August 1946; UM 7 B Pariisi 1946 II:B6. The

telegram of the Finnish Foreign Office to the peace delegation in Paris on 20 August 1946 at 6:30 p.m. Ibid. On the composition of the expanded committee for foreign affairs and the discussion conducted there, see T. Heikkilä (1965), pp. 287-90.

10. Hyvämäki (1977), p. 298 and sources. Cf. Bevin to Shepherd, 10 September 1946; FO 371/56187 N11519/303/56.

11. Dunn to State Department, 23 October 1946; FRUS IV 1946, p. 887. Hamilton could send fairly detailed reports on the development of the Finnish peace initiative from Helsinki. According to his information, Leino was said to have visited Moscow at the end of July or the beginning of August to "receive instructions" for conducting the peace negotiations. Hamilton from Helsinki, 27 September 1946 (Finnish Political Notes, August 1946) State Department 860.00/9-2746.

12. Enckell from Paris, 2 September 1946; UM 7 B Pariisi 1946 II:B1.

13. *Vapaa Sana*, 17 August 1946. Upton (1970), pp. 196-97.

14. *Työkansan Sanomat*, 17 August 1946.

15. On the peace crisis see Upton (1970), pp. 196-98; Leino (1958), pp. 155-57; Hyvämäki (1954), pp. 117-19; T. Heikkilä (1965), pp. 287-92. For the American diplomatic reports on the peace crisis, see Hamilton from Helsinki, 27 August and 27 September 1946; State Department 860d.00/8-2746 and 860d.00/9-2746. Cf. Hamilton from Helsinki, 12 September 1946; FRUS IV 1946, pp. 857-58. For similar British reports, see Ledward from Helsinki, 26 and 28 August 1946; FO 371/56186 N10902/303/56 and N10943/303/56. Cf. Ledward's telegrams from Helsinki, 31 August 1946; ibid., N11189/303/56 and N11190/303/56. Svento confirmed to Shepherd on 6 September 1946 that Kuusinen had acted in accordance with instructions received from Moscow. Shepherd from Helsinki, 7 September 1946; FO 371/56187 N11451/303/56.

16. Minutes of the delegation of 20 and 22 August 1946; UM 7 B Pariisi 1946 II:B1.

17. Minutes of the Finnish peace delegation, 19-22 August 1946; UM 7 B Pariisi 1946 II:B1. Comments on the draft peace treaty made by the delegation in extenso, FRUS IV 1946, pp. 282-97.

18. Minutes of the delegation of 29 August 1946; UM 7 B Pariisi 1946 II:B1. Hyvämäki (1977), p. 297. At first, Pekkala and Leino intended to leave for Finland alone. On the insistence of the delegation, fearful of one-sided information being broadcast, Heljas and Voionmaa accompanied them. Cf. Lennart Heljas's memorandum on the Paris peace conference; Lennart Heljas Papers.

19. Heljas's memorandum mentioned in the previous note. On another occasion (the meeting of the foreign affairs committee on 2 August 1946), the president's irritation was directed at the newspapers *Työkansan Sanomat* and *Vapaa Sana*, which had described "the moderation and justness" of the conditions of the peace treaty. In his opinion, "one must not forget that we had the Winter War, when we were not the aggressor. The Balkans did not have a similar situation." Paasikivi maintained that the communist policies would alienate Finns from the Soviet Union. "Finns cannot be punched into friendliness with the Soviet Union." Heljas, ibid.

20. Prime Minister Pekkala's account to the parliamentary foreign affairs committee about the activities of the peace delegation on 5 September 1946; UM 7 B Pariisi 1946 II:B3. For the radio speech in extenso, see (for instance) *Helsingin Sanomat*, September 7 1946. Hyvämäki (1977), p. 297. Cf. Hamilton from Helsinki, 7 October 1946; State Department 860d.00/10-746.

Chapter 19. The Commissions and the Final Decision

1. Officially, only the conclusions of the commission meetings were recorded. However, the British delegation recorded more extensive minutes for its own purposes that give the main contents of the speeches made by the delegation members. Minutes of the political and territorial commission for Finland, 16 August 1946; FO 371/56186 N10681/303/56.

2. Minutes of the commission, 19 August 1946; FO 371/56186 N10733/303/56. The Soviet proposal to discuss the draft treaty was rejected straight away by six votes to four, with France abstaining. On the "expulsion" of the Finns, see T. O. Vahervuori's memorandum of 26 August 1946; UM 7 B Pariisi 1946 II:B6 and Voionmaa (1971), p. 459.

3. Minutes of the commission of 29 August 1946; FO 371/56186 N11234/303/56. Cf. Enckell

from Paris, 30 August 1946; "Suomen rauhansopimuksen käsittely Pariisin konferenssissa," I, UM 7 B Pariisi 1946 II:B1.

4. *New York Times*, 30 August 1946.

5. Enckell from Paris, 30 August 1946; "Suomen rauhansopimuksen käsittely Pariisin konferenssissa," I, UM 7 B Pariisi 1946 II:B1. Cf. Enckell from Paris, 7 September 1946, ibid.

6. FO 371/56188 N12364/303/56; FO 371/56187 N11404/303/56. According to the State Department, "great self-confidence and decisiveness" were characteristics of Foreign Minister Evatt representing the Australian Labour Party. "He is eager to put his finger in every pie and slow to show confidence. Quick to make decisions, even if sometimes forgetful in concluding important matters, he is highly regarded because of his intelligence and political courage." State Department memorandum to Truman on 7 October 1947 in preparation for Evatt's visit; President's Secretary's file, box 159, Harry S. Truman Papers.

7. Minutes of the commission, 3 September 1946; FO 371/56188 N12364/303/56.

8. Minutes of the meeting of the deputy foreign ministers of 4 September 1946; FO 371/56187 N11571/303/56. Cf. Gladwyn Jebb's account in the internal meeting of the British delegation of the same day; FO 371/56187 N1105/303/56. In the meeting of the Italian commission on 27 August 1946, the Soviet Union accused Australia in strong terms of holding up the conference. In Vyshinsky's opinion, Hodgson was like a newly arrived country boy who wanted to do everything himself and did not have confidence in others; FRUS III 1946, p. 288.

9. Minutes of the commission on 5 and 7 September 1946, FO 371/56187 N11567/303/56; idem, N11569/303/56.

10. Ibid. In the final peace treaty, the number of the article is 35.

11. FRUS III 1946, pp. 392-93.

12. Minutes of the juridical commission of 11 September 1946, and minutes of the political and territorial commission for Finland of 12 September 1946; FO 371/56187 N11692/303/56. The commission was convened once more on 1 October 1946 to accept (with minor technical changes) the final report drafted by Lord Hood. Minutes of 1 October 1946, State Department, RG 43, Records of International Conferences, box 29. For the report in extenso, see FRUS IV 1946, pp. 568ff.

13. On the negotiations between the Great Powers in Paris, see Ward (1979), pp. 144-46 and cited sources.

14. Y. Leino (1958), pp. 162-63. O. Leino (1973), pp. 196-97. Heikkilä (1983), pp. 292-93.

15. Y. Leino (1958), p. 163.

16. Svento to Pekkala, 24 September 1946; UM 7 B Pariisi 1946 II:B1. Enckell from Paris, 28 September 1946; ibid. Cf. also minutes of the Finnish peace delegation, 26-28 September 1946; Tauno Suontausta Papers, VA.

17. Enckell from Paris, 28 September 1946; UM 7 B Pariisi 1946 II:B1.

18. Y. Leino (1958), p. 163.

19. Minutes of the meetings of the military commission on 30 September and 1 October 1946; FRUS III 1946, pp. 600-601, 613-14. FO 371/56188 N12660/303/56 and idem, N12718/303/56. Cf. minutes of the Finnish delegation on 26 and 27 September 1946; Tauno Suontausta Papers, VA.

20. FRUS IV 1946, p. 681. FO 371/56187 N11688/303/56.

21. Cf. the memorandum of the British delegation on the motor torpedo boat question; FO 371/56189 N13015/303/56.

22. The report of the commission of 5 October 1946; FRUS IV 1946, pp. 589-91. Cf. Vahervuori's memorandum of 5 October 1946; UM 7 B Pariisi 1946 II:B1.

23. Minutes of the commission of 4-5 October 1946; FRUS III 1946, pp. 677-79. Cf. the account of the meeting, "Balkanin maiden ja Suomen taloudellinen komissio," of 4 October 1946; UM 7 B Pariisi 1946 II:B6. For the final report of the commission, see FRUS IV 1946, pp. 573-89.

24. Vandenberg (1952), pp. 304-5.

25. Tompkins (1970), p. 176. On the expression of opinions sent to President Truman where a just peace for Finland was presupposed, see Official File 434, Harry S. Truman Papers.

26. Dunn from Paris to State Department, 23 October 1946; FRUS IV 1946, pp. 887-88. Cf. FRUS VI 1946, pp. 242-49.

27. Minutes of the general meeting on 14 October 1946; FRUS III 1946, pp. 840-56. The complete minutes in shorthand of the meeting translated into Finnish are in the archives of the Finnish Foreign Ministry, UM 7 B Pariisi 1946 II:C.

28. Ward (1979), pp. 147-48. For the Soviet versions, see *Istoriya diplomatii* (1974), pp. 47-58; *Mezhdunarodnye otnosheniya* . . . I (1962), pp. 508-22; Kiselev (1974), pp. 197-258.

29. Ward (1979), pp. 150-51.

30. Shepherd from Helsinki, 30 October 1946; FO 371/56178 N14457/226/56.

31. Shepherd from Helsinki, 22 October 1946; FO 371/56178 N13678/226/56. Cf. Pekkala's account of 16 October 1946 to the parliamentary committee for foreign affairs; UM 7 B Pariisi 1946 II:B3. Helo from Paris, 7 October 1946; UM 7 B Pariisi 1946 II:B2. "Yleisselostus Suomen rauhansopimusluonnoksen käsittelystä Pariisin konferenssissa," compiled by Tauno Suontausta for the Finnish representatives abroad on 19 November 1946; UM 7 B Pariisi 1946 II:C.

Chapter 20. Preparation and Signing

1. U.S. Delegation Minutes, Council of Foreign Ministers, New York, 11 November 1946; FRUS II 1946, p. 1,104, 1,108. Corresponding British minutes, FO 371/56190 N14782/303/56.

2. FRUS II 1946, p. 1,259.

3. FRUS II 1946, pp. 1,384-85, 1,426-27, 1,533, 1536-37. FO 371/56190 N15779/303/56.

4. For the New York conference see FRUS II 1946, pp. 941-1,563. Ward (1979), pp. 152-71. *Istoriya diplomatii* (1979), pp. 58-60.

5. Byrnes's last official duty as secretary of state was to sign the peace treaties in Washington on 20 January 1947. The documents were then flown to Moscow, where Molotov signed them on 29 January 1947. The last to sign was Bevin, in London, on 4 February 1947. The ambassadors to Paris of the three Great Powers also signed the peace treaties, as well as French Foreign Minister Bidault, during the ceremony on 10 February. Cf. Wheeler-Bennett and Nicholls (1972), p. 438.

6. Cf. UM 7 B Pariisi 1946 III:A.

7. Jutila from Washington, 11 December 1946; ibid.

8. Jutila from Washington, 13 and 18 December 1946 and 1 January 1947; ibid.

9. Kelchner to Jutila, 16 January 1947; ibid. On 20 January 1947, the Finnish embassy in Paris received a verbal invitation from the Quai d'Orsay to attend the signing ceremony. An invitation of similar content was also delivered directly to Foreign Minister Enckell by the French minister to Helsinki; ibid.

10. Enckell's *Anteckningar*, 12 January 1947; Carl Enckell Papers, VA, file 103. Minutes of the committee for foreign affairs of the cabinet on 20 January 1947; idem, file 87. Hallituksen esitys n:o 129, *Eduskunnan pöytäkirjat ja asiakirjat* III (1946). For Paasikivi's initiative, see Lennart Heljas's notes on 14 January 1947; Lennart Heljas Papers.

11. Cf. *Paasikiven linja* (1966), pp. 88, 91-92, 102-4, 106.

12. Parliamentary minutes of 27 January 1947, pp. 3,208-24. See also Jääskeläinen (1980), pp. 182-85, 354-55.

13. Tauno Suontausta's memorandum "Rauhansopimuksen allekirjoittaminen," 16 February 1947; UM 7 B Pariisi 1946 III:C.

14. Cf. FRUS III 1947, pp. 515-24; Wuori from London on 23 January and 17 February 1947, UM 5 C 7 1947. The protests of the Balkan countries were not directed against the Soviet Union but concerned their mutual disagreements.

15. Caffery from Paris, 12 February 1947; FRUS III 1947, pp. 524-25.

16. Helo from Paris, 12 February 1947; UM 7 B Pariisi 1946I III:C. Cf. also Suontausta's memorandum of 16 February 1947, "Rauhansopimuksen allekirjoittaminen," ibid.

17. Sulzberger (1969), pp. 339-40.

18. Helo from Paris, 12 February 1947; UM 7 B Pariisi 1946 III:C.

19. Sundström from Moscow, 28 February 1947; UM 7 B Pariisi 1946 III:B. The document arrived by courier post on 11 March 1947; ibid.

Chapter 21. Ratification

1. The general rhetoric of Truman's speech gave rise to criticism even at its preparation stage. According to Clark Clifford, Navy Secretary Forrestal posed the question whether the intention really was to support "free peoples" everywhere—for instance, in Finland and China. If not, the formulation of the speech would have to be checked. In an interview given to Feis twenty years later, Clifford could not, however, any longer remember what answer was given to Forrestal. The problem then was primarily one of finding general phrases that could be expected to have some effect on the decision of Congress concerning economic aid. To be too exact might only be detrimental. Feis (1970), pp. 192, 203-4.

2. On the origins and publication of Kennan's "containment theory," see Kennan (1967), pp. 313-67. On the Truman doctrine and the Marshall Plan, see Yergin (1978), pp. 275-329; Gaddis (1972), pp. 316-52; Truman (1965), pp. 134-41; Istoriya diplomatii (1974), pp. 249-56; Istoriya vneshney politiki SSSR (1980-81), vol. II, pp. 129-37. For a general Finnish version, cf. Apunen (1977), pp. 37-48.

3. Acheson to Marshall, 8 March 1947, and Marshall to Acheson, 9 March and 20 April 1947; FRUS III 1947, pp. 534, 542-43.

4. On the pleas, see FRUS III 1947, pp. 527-33, 535-37.

5. FRUS III 1947, pp. 541-43, 544-45.

6. The British memorandum, 11 April 1947; FRUS III 1947, pp. 538-40.

7. Acheson's memorandum, 11 April 1947, and State Department to the British embassy, 24 April 1947; FRUS III 1947, pp. 537-38.

8. The memorandum of the British embassy in Washington on 8 May 1947 and the reply of the State Department on 28 May 1947; FRUS III 1947, pp. 546-47.

9. FRUS III 1947, pp. 545, 547-50.

10. Sundström from Moscow, 23 March 1947; UM 7B Pariisi 1946 III:D. On Prime Minister Pekkala's recommendation, President Paasikivi had decided to postpone ratification at the meeting of the State Council on 21 March 1947 until a reply had been received to Sundström's inquiry. Enckell's Anteckningar, 21 March 1947; Carl Enckell Papers, VA, file 103.

11. With the Americans delaying ratification, the British followed suit in the manner described above. Voionmaa's memorandum, 11 April 1947; Muistiosarja 1947, UM.

12. Wuori from London, 3 and 17 April and 2 May 1947; UM 7 B Pariisi 1946 III:D. Cf. also the Finnish Foreign Ministry's political bulletins; UM:n poliittisia tiedotuksia 9/1947, UM 5 C 1.

13. The decision to ratify was made public in Finland on 27 April 1947. On Finland's ratification, see Enckell to Sundström, 18 and 26 April 1947; UM 7 B Pariisi 1946 III:B, UM:n poliittisia tiedotuksia 9/1947, UM 5 C 1. Minister Sundström's subsequent inquiries also did not produce any results. Sundström to Enckell, 29 June and 20 July 1947; UM 5 B Moskova 1947.

14. See Jääskeläinen (1980), pp. 177-79.

15. Higgs from Stockholm, 16 December 1946; American legation in Helsinki, RG 84, box 886, Secret Correspondence 1946. National Records Center, Suitland, Maryland.

16. Hamilton from Helsinki, 7 February 1947; idem, box 886, Confidential Correspondence 1947. Ylitalo (1978), p. 74. The date given by Ylitalo (19 March) does not correspond to the one in the original document.

17. On Zhdanov's visit, cf. Hamilton from Helsinki, 12 February 1947, State Department 760d. 61/2-1247; idem, 19 February 1947, 860d.00/2-1947; idem, 20 February 1947, 860d.00/2047; idem, 5 March 1947, 860d.00/3-547; idem, 19 March 1947, 860d.00/3-3-1947; Sorvali (1975), pp. 239-42; Ylitalo (1978), pp. 50-51, 55-56. On Soviet concern see Sundström's account, 18 June 1947; UM 12 L Neuvostoliitto 1947.

18. Shepherd from Helsinki, 19 February 1947; FO 371/65919 N2331/159/56.

19. On internal political developments, see (for instance) Hyvämäki (1977), pp. 312-14; Rautkallio (1979), pp. 96-107; Ylitalo (1978), pp. 76-81.

20. Acheson to Hamilton, 16 April 1947; State Department 860d.00/4-1647.

21. Hamilton from Helsinki, 17 April 1947; idem, 860d.00/4-1747. Cf. Shepherd from Helsinki, 18 March 1947; FO 371/65919 N3529/159/56 and N4238/159/56.

22. Hamilton from Helsinki, 13 May 1947; idem, 860.00/5-1347; Lundestad (1978), pp. 294-95.

23. FO 371/65919 N3529/159/56. FO 371/65920 N4238/159/56 and N4987/159/56. Wuori from London, 2 May 1947; UM 5 C 7. For articles in the Soviet press, see Izvestiya on 26 April 1947. Negotiations being held at the same time about the Saimaa canal also came to a halt. Cf. Hamilton from Helsinki, 12 and 16 May 1947; State Department 860d.00/5-1247; idem, 860d.00/5-1647.

24. Ylitalo (1978), pp. 80-81.

25. Shepherd's account on 19 March 1947 of his discussion with President Paasikivi the day before; FO 371/65919 N3530/159/56.

26. Warner's comment; ibid.

27. On Marshall Aid and Finland, see the minutes of the committee for foreign affairs of the State Council on 7, 8, and 10 July 1947. The last two meetings were also attended by President Paasikivi; Valtioneuvoston ulkoasiainvaliokunnan pöytäkirjat 1947, UM. Minutes of the parliamentary committee for foreign affairs of 10 July 1947; Eduskunnan arkisto. A copy of the minutes can also be found in the Carl Enckell Papers, VA, file 86. Cf. also Enckell's Anteckningar for 5-11 July 1947; Carl Enckell Papers, VA, file 103. Gripenberg's diary entry for 6 August 1947. Jutila from Washington, 6 August 1947; UM 12 L Yhdysvallat 1947. Hamilton's report (compiled by Ylitalo) of 12 August 1947; State Department 860d.00/8-1247. Ylitalo (1978), pp. 109-22. Rautkallio (1979), pp. 113-22. The proposition to demonstrate Finland's willingness to give information about its economy was made in the parliamentary committee for foreign affairs in accordance with the government's official line by J. O. Söderhjelm of the Swedish People's Party, who had voted together with the Communist members. See also Söderhjelm (1970), pp. 107-10.

28. Healey to Leskinen, 29 August 1947; FO 371/65910 N10315/3/56. For a similar American view, see the report by Hamilton (n. 27 above). In his reply, Leskinen informed Healey that he considered British concern to be exaggerated. Leskinen to Healey, 12 September 1947; FO 371/65923 N11086/159/56.

29. Shepherd from Helsinki, 1 July 1947; FO 371/65910 N2330/3/56. Douglas from London, 25 July 1947; State Department 741.60d./7-1747.

30. Cf. FRUS III 1947, pp. 552-68.

31. Sundström from Moscow, 19 September 1947; UM 5 C 18 1947. Members of the delegation led by Foreign Minister Molotov and consisting of ministerial officials included Deputy Foreign Minister Malik and Chef de Protocol Molotshkov. Finland was represented by (besides Minister Sundström) Secretary of Legation Vanamo, Attaché Bergman, and Press Attaché Pasuri.

Conclusion: Finland and the Great Powers, 1944-1947

1. Meretskov (1968), p. 366.

2. Tarkka (1977), pp. 71-72.

3. Upton (1970), pp. 161-63.

4. Ward (1979), pp. 174-75.

5. Ludlow (1979), pp. 160-62.

6. Eden's memorandum, "Soviet Policy in Europe outside the Balkans," 9 August 1944; WP (44) 436, CAB 66153.

7. H. Heikkilä (1983), pp. 147-48 and sources.

8. Shepherd from Helsinki, 15 February 1947; FO 371/65910 N2330/3/56.

9. Department of State, Policy and Information Statement, Finland, 8 August 1946; James F. Byrnes Papers, Clemson University Library, Clemson, South Carolina.

10. Bohlen's memorandum, 18 October 1945; State Department, Records of Charles E. Bohlen, 1942-1952, Memoranda, box 4.

11. H. Freeman Matthews's memorandum, 15 July 1947; State Department, Matthews-Hickerson file, box 9.

Bibliography

Abbreviations

AA	Auswärtiges Amt, Bonn
CAB	Cabinet Office. Public Record Office, London.
FO	Foreign Office. Public Record Office, London.
FRUS	*Foreign Relations of the United States. Deiplomatic Papers, 1944-1947.* Washington, D.C.
MF	Militärgeschichtliches Forschungsamt, Freiburg/Br.
OKW	Oberkommando der Wehrmacht.
SA	Sota-arkisto, Helsinki.
UD	Utrikes departementet, Stockholm.
UM	Ulkoasiainministeriö, Helsinki.
VA	Valtionarkisto, Helsinki.

Bibliography

Manuscript Sources

United States

National Archives, Washington, D.C.
    Department of State.
        740.0011 European War 1939
        740.00119 European War 1939
        740.0011 Moscow
        740.00119 Control (Finland)
        711.60d Political Relations between the United States and Finland
        741.60d Political Relations between the United Kingdom and Finland
        760d Political Relations between Finland and other States
        860d Internal Affairs of Finland
        Record Group 43 Records of International Conferences
        Records of Charles E. Bohlen
        Matthews-Hickerson file
        Harley Notter file
National Records Center, Suitland, Maryland
    American Legation in Helsinki
Franklin D. Roosevelt Library, Hyde Park, New York.
    Franklin D. Roosevelt Papers
        Official File
        President's Secretary's File
Harry S. Truman Library, Independence, Missouri
    Harry S. Truman Papers
        Official File
        President's Secretary's File
    Theodore C. Achilles (Oral History Interview)
Clemson University Library, Clemson, South Carolina
    James F. Byrnes Papers

Britain

Public Record Office, London
  Foreign Office
    371 General Correspondence
    181 British Embassy in Moscow
    511 British Legation in Helsinki
  War Office
    Record Group 32
    Record Group 193
  Cabinet Office
    CAB 66/53

Finland

Ulkoasiainministeriö (Ministry for Foreign Affairs), Helsinki
  5 B Moskova 1945-47
  5 C 1 Poliittiset tiedotukset 1944-47
  5 C 2 Tukholma Raporttisarja 1944-47
  5 C 7 Lontoo Raporttisarja 1945-47
  5 C 8 Washington Raporttisarja 1945-47
  5 C 18 Moskova Raporttisarja 1945-47
  7 B Pariisin konferenssi 1946
  7 K Toinen maailmansota
  12 L Neuvostoliitto 1945-47
  12 L Englanti 1945-47
  12 L Yhdysvallat 1945-47
  110 A-G Jatkosota
  Sähkesarja 1944-47
  Muistiosarja 1945-47
  Valtioneuvoston ulkoasiainvaliokunnan ptk. 1945-47
  Tukholman sotilasasiamiehen salaisten kirjeiden konseptit 1943-45
Valtionarkisto (National Archives), Helsinki
  Carl Enckell Papers
  Waldemar Erfurth, Kriegstagebuch 1941-44 (Copy)
  G. A. Gripenberg Papers
  Gustaf Mannerheim Papers
  Juho Niukkanen Papers
  Tauno Suontausta Papers
  Eero A. Wuori Papers
Sota-arkisto (Military Archives), Helsinki
  Ye Pääll/PM Salainen kirjeistö (Chief of General Staff: Secret correspondence)
  Op 1/PM Salainen kirjeistö (Operations: Secret correspondence)
  Puolustusrevisio (Defense Review Committee)
  Päämajan yhteysosasto (Archives of the Liaison Section of GHQ)
  Erik Heinrichs Papers
  O. J. Willamo Papers
Eduskunnan arkisto, Helsinki. Archives of the Finnish Parliament. Minutes of the Parliamentary
    Committee for Foreign Affairs
Lennart Heljas Papers, in the possession of Prof. Eino Murtorinne, Helsinki

Germany

Auswärtiges Amt (Foreign Ministry), Bonn
  Büro des Staatssekretärs. Finnland 1944
  Botschafter Ritter. Finnland 1944
  Deutsche Gesandtschaft Helsinki 1944
Militärgeschichtliches Forschungsamt (Archives for Military History Research), Freiburg/Br.
  Oberkommando der Wehrmacht. Akten 1944-45
  (Geb) AOK 20. KTB und Akten 1944-45

Sweden

Utrikesdepartementet (Foreign Ministry), Stockholm
  HP 1 Af 1944

Switzerland

Bundesarchiv (Federal Archives), Bern
  Politisches Departement. E2300. Helsinki.

Printed Sources

Ahto, Sampo. 1980. *Aseveljet vastakkain: Lapin sota 1944-1945*. Hämeenlinna.
Ahtokari, Reijo. 1971 *Asekätkentäjuttu*. Porvoo.
Alava, Ali. 1974. *Gestapo Suomessa*. Hämeenlinna.
Apunen, Osmo. 1977. *Paasikiven-Kekkosen Linja*. Helsinki.
Baltiyskiy, N. (Kuusinen, O. W.) 1945. "Finlyandiya pered vyborami v seym." *Voyna i rabochy klass* 7:7-10.
Bartenyev, T., and J. Komissarov. 1977. *Kolmekymmentä vuotta hyvää naapuruutta*. Keuruu.
Beletsky, V. N. 1980. *Vstrecha v Potsdame*. Moscow.
Berezhkov, V. N. 1972. *Gody diplomaticheskoy sluzhby*. Moscow.
Blinnikka, Aulis. 1969. *Valvontakomission aika*. Porvoo.
Blücher, Wipert von. 1951. *Gesandter zwischen Diktatur und Demokratie*. Wiesbaden.
Boheman, Erik. 1964. *På vakt: Kabinettssekreterare under andra världskriget*. Stockholm.
Bohlen, Charles E. 1973. *Witness to History, 1929-1969*. New York.
Byrnes, James F. 1947. *Speaking Frankly*. London.
Cadogan, Alexander. 1971. *The Diaries of Sir Alexander Cadogan, 1938-1945*. Edited by David Dilks. London.
Carlgren, Wilhelm. 1973. *Svensk utrikespolitik, 1939-1945*. Stockholm.
Ciechanowski, Jan. 1948. *Vergeblicher Sieg*. Zürich.
Connally, Tom. 1954. *My Name Is Tom Connally*. New York.
Curry, George. 1965. "James F. Byrnes." In vol. 14 of *The American Secretaries of State*. Edited by Robert H. Ferrell and Samuel Flagg Bemis. New York.
Davis, Lynn Etheridge. 1974. *The Cold War Begins*. Princeton.
Dixon, Pierson. 1968. *Double Diploma: The Life of Sir Pierson Dixon*. London.
Eduskunnan pöytäkirjat ja asiakirjat 1944-1947.
Erfurth, Waldemar. 1950. *Der finnische Krieg, 1941-1944*. Wiesbaden.
Etzold, Thomas, and John Lewis Gaddis. 1978. *Containment: Documents on American Policy and Strategy, 1945-1950*. New York.
Fagerholm, K. A. 1977. *Puhemiehen ääni*. Helsinki.
Feis, Herbert. 1960. *Between War and Peace: The Potsdam Conference*. Princeton.
Feis, Herbert. 1970. *From Trust to Terror*. London.

Foreign Relations of the United States. 1955-72. Diplomatic Papers, 1944-1947. Washington D.C.

Gaddis, John Lewis. 1972. *The United States and the Origins of the Cold War, 1941-1947.* New York.

Gaddis, John Lewis, 1978. *Russia, the Soviet Union, and the United States: An Interpretative History.* New York.

Grimnes, Ole Kristian. 1969. *Et flyktningesamfunn vokser fram. Nordmenn i Sverige, 1940-45.* Oslo.

Gripenberg, G. A. 1961. *London-Vatikanen-Stockholm.* Helsingfors.

Gromyko, A. A. and B. N. Ponomarev, eds. 1980-81. *Istoriya vneshney politiki SSSR.* Vols. 1-2. Moscow.

Haahti, U. S. 1979. "Varjosota: Lapin sodan 1944-1945 alkuvaihe." *Sotilasaikakauslehti* 10:694-705.

Halsti, Wolf H. 1972. *Lapin sodassa.* Keuruu.

Harriman, W. Averell, and Elie Abel. 1976. *Special Envoy to Churchill and Stalin, 1941-1946.* London.

Heikkilä, Hannu. 1983. *Liittoutuneet ja kysymys Suomen sotakorvauksista 1943-1947.* Helsinki.

Heikkilä, Toivo. 1965. *Paasikivi peräsimessä: Paaministerin sihteerin muistelmat 1944-1948.* Keuruu.

Heinrichs, Erik. 1954. "Kun sota päättyi." *Suomen Kuvalehti* 36:14-17.

Heinrichs, Erik, 1959. *Mannerheim-gestalten.* Vol. 2. Helsingfors.

Helo, Johan. 1965. *Vaiennettuja ihmisiä.* Helsinki.

Hyvämäki, Lauri. 1954. *Vaaran vuodet 1944-1948.* Helsinki.

Hyvämäki, Lauri. 1977. *Valtioneuvosto toisen maailmansodan jälkeen vuoteen 1957.* Vol. 2 of *Valtioneuvoston historia 1917-1966.* Helsinki.

Ingulskaya, L. A. 1972. *V bor'be za demokratizatsiyu Finlyandii.* Moscow.

Israelyan, V. L. 1964. *Antigitlerovskaya koalitsiya, 1941-1945 gg.* Moscow.

Istoriya diplomatii. 1974. Vol. 5/1. Moscow.

Istoriya vtoroy mirovoy voyny 1939-1945. 1977-79. Vols. 8-9. Moscow.

Jääskeläinen, Mauno. 1980. *Sodanjälkeinen eduskunta, 1945-1963.* Vol. 8 in *Suomen kansanedustuslaitoksen historia.* Helsinki.

Jägerskiöld, Stig. 1981. *Från krig till fred: Gustaf Mannerheim, 1944-1951.* Keuruu.

Jakobson, Max. 1968. *Kuumalla linjalla: Suomen ulkopolitiikan ydinkysymyksiä, 1944-1968.* Porvoo.

Juva, Mikko, Niitemaa Vilho, and Tommila Päiviö, eds. 1970. *Suomen historian dokumentteja.* Keuruu.

Käkönen, U. A. 1970. *Miehityksen varalta: Päämajan tiedustelua, 1943-1945.* Helsinki.

Kekkonen, Urho. 1962. "J. K. Paasikivi." *Oma Maa* 11:381-96.

Kennan, George F. 1967. *Memoirs, 1925-1950.* Boston.

Kiselev, K. V. 1974. *Zapiski sovetskogo diplomata.* Moscow.

Knight, Jonathan. 1978. "Russia's Search for Peace: The London Council of Foreign Ministers, 1945." *Journal of Contemporary History* 1: 137-63.

Krosby, H. Peter. 1978. *Kekkosen Linja.* Helsinki.

Kulha, Keijo K. 1980. *Aseveljien aika.* Porvoo.

Kuosa, Tauno. 1979. *A. F. Airo.* Porvoo.

Kuusinen, Hertta. 1945. "Suomalainen kulttuurivaltuuskunta generalissimus Stalinin ja ulkoasiainministeri Molotovin puheilla." *Vapaa Sana,* 16 October.

Leino, Olle. 1973. *Kuka oli Yrjö Leino?* Helsinki.

Leino, Yrjö. 1958. *Kommunisti sisäministerinä.* Helsinki.

Lie, Trygve. 1958. *Hjemover.* Oslo.

Linkomies, Edwin. 1970. *Vaikea aika: Suomen pääministerinä sotavuosina, 1943-1944.* Helsinki.

Loewenheim, Francis L., Harold D. Langley, and Manfred Jones, eds. 1975. *Roosevelt and Churchill: Their Secret Wartime Correspondence.* London.

Ludlow, Peter. 1979. "Britain and Northern Europe, 1940-1945." *Scandinavian Journal of History* 4:123-62.

Lundestad, Geir. 1978. *The American Non-Policy towards Eastern Europe, 1943-1947.* Oslo.

Magill, J. H. 1981. *Tasavalta tulikokeessa.* Mikkeli.

Mannerheim, G. 1952. *Minnen.* Vol. 2. Helsingfors.

Martola, A. E. 1973. *Sodassa ja rauhassa: Muistelmia.* Keuruu.

Mattila, Tapani. 1968. *Merivoimiemme sodanjälkeinen miinanraivaustyö:* Vol. 2 in *Suomen Laivasto.* Helsinki.

Meister, Jürg. 1958. *Der Seekrieg in den osteuropäischen Gewässern, 1941-1945.* Munich.

Menger, Manfred. 1979. "Das militärpolitische Verhältnis zwischen Deutschland und Finnland im Herbst 1944." *Militärgeschichte* 3:297-309.

Meretskov, K. A. 1968. *Na sluzhbe narodu.* Moscow.

Mezhdunarodnye otnosheniya posle vtoroy mirovoi voyny. 1962. Vol. 1. Moscow.

Molotov, V. M. 1949. *Problems of Foreign Policy: Speeches and Statements, April 1945-November 1948.* Moscow.

Nevakivi, Jukka. 1976. *Ystävistä vihollisiksi.* Helsinki.

Novikov, N. V. 1976. *Puti i pereputya diplomata.* Moscow.

Nykopp, Johan. 1975. *Paasikiven mukana Moskovassa.* Helsinki.

Oinonen, Väinö. 1971. "Generalissimus Stalin kohotti maljan Suomen armeijalle." *Sotilasaikakauslehti* 11:561-62.

Paasikiven linja. Puheita vuosilta 1944-1945. 1966. Helsinki.

Palm, Thede. 1971. *The Finnish-Soviet Armistice Negotiations of 1944.* Uppsala.

Palm, Thede. 1972. *Vägen till vapenvilan.* Ekenäs.

Perepiska Predsedatelya Soveta Ministrov SSSR s presidentami SSA i Premier-Ministrami Velikobritanii vo vremya Velikoy Otechestvennoy Voyny 1941-1945 gg. 1957. Vols. 1-2. Moscow.

Pick, F. W. 1950. *Peacemaking in Perspective.* Oxford.

Pohlebkin, V. V. 1969. *Suomi vihollisena ja ystävänä.* Porvoo.

Pohlebkin, V. V. 1980. *J. K. Paasikivi ja Neuvostoliitto.* Espoo.

Polvinen, Tuomo. 1978. "Franklin D. Roosevelt ja sodanjälkeinen maailma." *Kanava* 7:405-8.

Polvinen, Tuomo. 1979. *Barbarossasta Teheraniin.* Vol. 1 of *Suomi kansainvälisessä politiikassa, 1941-1943.* Juva.

Polvinen, Tuomo. 1980. *Teheranista Jaltaan, 1944.* Vol. 2 of *Suomi kansainvälisessä politiikassa, 1941-1943.* Juva.

Puntila, L. A. 1972. *Kenttäpostia 1944.* Helsinki.

Puroma, A., and Hj. L. Sonck. 1958. *Sotatoimet saksalaisia vastaan Pohjois-Suomessa, 1944-1945.* Vol. 8 of *Suomen Sota 1941-1945.* Kuopio.

Raikkala, Hannes. 1966. *Suojeluskuntain historia.* Vol. 3. Vaasa.

Rautkallio, Hannu. 1979. *Suomen suunta, 1945-1948.* Savonlinna.

Raysky, N. S. 1979. "Bor'ba SSSR za vyipolnenie reshenii Krymskoi konferentsii 1945 g. o Pol'she." *Voprosy istorii* 7:22-36.

Rendulic, Lothar. 1952. *Gekämpft, gesiegt, geschlagen.* Heidelberg.

Resis, Albert. 1978. "The Churchill-Stalin Secret 'Percentages' Agreement on the Balkans. Moscow, October 1944." *American Historical Review* 2: 368-87.

Riste, Olav. 1979. *London Regjeringa: Norge i krigsalliansen, 1940-1945.* Vol. 2. Oslo.

Russell, Ruth B. and Jeannette E. Muther. 1958. *A History of the United Nations Charter.* Wisconsin.

Rystad, Göran. 1968. "Porkkala-Hanko-Åland." *Scandia,* pp. 1-23.

Salewski, Michael. 1945. *Die deutsche Seekriegsleitung, 1935-1945.* Vol. 2. Munich.

Sarva, K. 1952. *Suomen puolustusvoimien kotiuttaminen v. 1944.* Finnish Military Academy, Helsinki.

Seppälä, Helge. 1974. *Itsenäisen Suomen puolustuspolitiikka ja strategia*. Porvoo.

Schramm, Percy Ernst, ed. 1963. *Kriegstagebuch des Oberkommandos der Wehrmacht, 1940-45*. Vol. 4/1. Frankfurt am Main.

Shtemenko, S. M. 1973. *General'nyi shtab v gody voyny*. Vol. 2. Moscow.

Skyttä, Kyösti. 1969. *Presidentin muotokuva*. Vol. 1. Helsinki.

Söderhjelm, J. O. 1970. *Kolme matkaa Moskovaan*. Tampere.

Soikkanen, Hannu. 1980. *Eduskunnan toiminta sota-aikana*. Vol. 8 of *Suomen kansanedustuslaitoksen historia*. Helsinki.

Sorvali, Pentti. 1975. *Niukkasesta Kekkoseen*. Jyväskylä.

Sovetskiy Soyuz na mezhdunarodnykh konferentsiyakh perioda Velikoy Otechestvennoy Voyny 1941-1945 gg. 1978-80. Vol. 3, *Dumbarton Oaks*. Vol 4, *Yalta*. Vol. 5, *San Francisco*. Vol. 6, *Potsdam*. Moscow.

Sulzberger, Cyrus. 1969. *A Long Row of Candles*. New York.

Svento, Reinhold. 1960. *Ystäväni Juho Kusti Paasikivi*. Porvoo.

Tanner, Väinö. 1952. *Suomen tie rauhaan, 1943-1944*. Helsinki.

Tarkka, Jukka. 1977. *13. artikla*. Porvoo.

Tompkins, C. David. 1970. *Senator Arthur H. Vandenberg: the Evolution of a Modern Republican*. Michigan.

Trukhanovsky, V. G., and N. K. Kapitonova. 1979. *Sovetsko-angliyskiye otnosheniya, 1943-1978*. Moscow.

Truman, Harry S. 1965. *Memoirs*. Vols. 1-2. New York.

Tuompo, W. E. 1968. *Päiväkirjani päämajasta, 1941-1944*. Edited by Tauno Kuosa. Porvoo.

Upton, A. F. 1970. *Kommunismi Suomessa*. Rauma.

Ursin, Martti. 1980. *Pohjois-Suomen tuhot ja jälleenrakennus saksalaissodan 1944-45 jälkeen*. Rovaniemi.

Vandenberg, Arthur H. 1952. *The Private Papers of Senator Vandenberg*. Edited by Arthur H. Vandenberg, Jr. Boston.

Viljanen, Lauri. 1945. "Keskustelu Stalinin työhuoneessa." *Helsingin Sanomat*, 16 October.

Voionmaa, Väinö. 1971. *Kuriiripostia 1941-1946*. Edited by Markku Reimaa. Helsinki.

Vuolento, P. 1973. *Suomalais-saksalaiset sotilaalliset neuvottelut syksyllä 1944*. Finnish Military Academy, Helsinki.

Walker, Richard L. 1965 "E. R. Stettinius." In vol. 14 of *The American Secretaries of State*. Edited by Robert H. Ferrell and Samuel Flagg Bemis. New York.

Wallace, Henry A. 1975. *The Price of Vision: The Diary of Henry A. Wallace, 1942-1946*. Edited by John Morton Blum. Boston.

Ward, Patricia Dawson. 1979. *The Threat of Peace: James F. Byrnes and the Council of Foreign Ministers, 1945-1946*. Kent.

Wheeler-Bennett, John, and Anthony Nicholls. 1972. *The Semblance of Peace*. London.

Wirtanen, Atos. 1972. *Poliittiset muistelmat*. Keuruu.

Woodward, E. L. 1972-74. *British Foreign Policy in the Second World War*. Vols. 3-5. London.

Yegorov, P. Y. 1974. *Marshal Meretskov*. Moscow.

Yergin, Daniel. 1978. *Shattered Peace: The Origins of the Cold War and the National Security State*. Boston.

Ylitalo, J. Raymond. 1978. *Salasanomia Helsingistä Washingtoniin*. Keuruu.

Ziemke, Earl F. 1960. *The German Northern Theater of Operations, 1940-1945*. Washington, D.C.

Index

Index

Austria, 202, 208, 258
"Autumn maneuvers," 44, 45, 46, 278. See also
    Germany; Lapland; Soviet Union

Balchen, Bernt, 76
Balkan countries. See Bulgaria; Hungary;
    Rumania
Beasley, John, 244, 245
Beck-Friis, Swedish minister to Helsinki, 109
Belgium, 250
Berg, Norwegian envoy to Finland, 186
Bevin, Ernest, 99, 125, 156, 162, 164, 167: and
    Foreign Ministers, Council of — London
    conference, 145-53 passim, — Moscow
    conference (1944), 156, 157, 158, — New
    York conference, 258, — Paris conference,
    203, 206, 208; and Marshall Plan, 271; and
    Paris Peace Conference (1946), 239; and
    Potsdam Conference, 99
Bidault, Georges, 99, 227: and European
    Economic Recovery, Conference on, 271;
    and Foreign Ministers, Council of — London
    conference, 147, — Paris conference, 205;
    and Paris Peace Conference (1946), 235, 237
Big Three Summit Conferences. See Potsdam
    Conference; Teheran Conference; Yalta
    Conference
"Bill of Rights," and peace treaties, 146-48, 150
Birke, 38, 39, 45, 49-50
Blücher, Wipert von, 39-40
Bogomolov, Soviet representative to peace
    treaty signing, 261
Boheman, Erik, 18-22 passim, 35, 36, 187: and
    war guilt issue, 102-3
Bohlen, Charles, 151, 208, 285
Bonnet, Georges, 209
Border question: and Karelia, 230; and Paris
    Peace Conference (1946), 240-41; and peace
    treaty, 210-13, 215-19 passim
Born, von, acting Finnish prime minister, 35
Bothnia, Gulf of. See Gulf of Bothnia
Bratianu, Dinu, 158
Britain: and Allied Control Commission, 58-60,
    131, 278; and armistice agreement, 134-36;
    diplomatic relations of, 78, 79, 94, 133, 136,
    137; and Deputy Foreign Ministers,
    Conference of — in London, 196-200
    passim, — in Paris, 204-5; and draft treaty
    (1944), 27-30; and foreign aid, 263; and
    Foreign Ministers, Council of — London
    conference, 145-53 passim, — Moscow

conference (1945), 156, 157, 158, — New
    York conference, 257, 258, — Paris
    conference, 201-8 passim; and Iran crisis,
    194-95; and nonintervention policy, 6, 9,
    108, 111, 174, 278, 283; and Paris Peace
    Conference (1946), 227-30 passim, 237,
    244-50 passim, 253; and peace treaties, 131,
    210, 213, 222, 253, 266-73 passim; press
    attacks on, 132; and war guilt issue, 174,
    182; and Western European Union, 282-83
Brotherus, K. R., 108
"B-section," 57. See also Allied Control
    Commission
Bulgaria: and Deputy Foreign Ministers,
    Conference of — in London, 196-97, — in
    Paris, 204-5; diplomatic relations with, 78,
    94, 100, 136, 157-58, 193; and Foreign
    Ministers, Council of — London conference,
    143-50 passim, — Moscow conference
    (1945), 158, — New York conference,
    258, — Paris conference, 203, 204-5; and
    Moscow negotiations (1944), 86; and Paris
    Peace Conference (1946), 234, 235, 237,
    251; peace treaty with, 143-50 passim, 258,
    265, 267, 273, 274; reparations of, 251, 252,
    258. See also Hungary; Rumania; Soviet
    Union
Burmistrov, Major General, ACC representative,
    65, 66
Buttlar, von, General, German Armed Forces
    High Command, 49
Byelorussia, 87, 227, 244, 252-53
Byrnes, James F., 155, 167: and diplomatic
    relations with Finland, 137; as "eternal
    compromiser," 191-95 passim; and Finnish
    parliamentary elections (1945), 98, 137; and
    Foreign Ministers, Council of — London
    conference, 143-54 passim, 281, 282, —
    Moscow conference (1945), 156, 157, 158,
    191, — New York conference, 257, 258,
    259, — Paris conference, 201-6 passim; and
    Paris Peace Conference (1946), 227, 228,
    234, 235, 253-54; and peace treaties,
    ratification of, 267; and Potsdam Conference,
    100, 101; resignation of, 259; and Stettinius,
    replacement of, 96, 97

Canada, 244
Caplan, Daniel, 113, 138
Castrén, Erik, 23, 120, 179
Castrén, Urho: and Allied Control Commission,

Kekkonen, Urho, 75, 105, 128, 214, 219: and war guilt issue, 104, 170, 171, 177-81 *passim*
Kelchner, Warren, 259
Kelly, P. D., 59, 111
Kemi, Battle of, 48, 51, 52. *See also* Germany; Lapland; Soviet Union
Kennan, George F., 131, 158: and diplomatic relations with Finland, 79-82 *passim*; "long cable" of, 193-94
Kerr, Archibald Clark. *See* Clark Kerr, Archibald
Kesäranta talks, 230-33. *See also* Paris Peace Conference (*1946*)
Kilpi, Eino, 128
Kirk, Alexander, 191-92
Kiselev, K. V., 252-53
Kivimäki, T. M., 174-81 *passim*
Kivinen, Lauri, 216
Koivisto, Juho, 175
Koivisto Islands, 211, 217
Kollontay, Aleksandra, 17-23 *passim*, 32, 80-81, 203
Kommunisti, 280
Kontakt, 132
Kopola, I., 40
Korea, 157, 195, 264
Kotka, airfield at, 132
Kozlov, G. K., 46
Kruus, Hans, 237-38
Kukkonen, Antti, 174-81 *passim*
Kuusamo, Battle of, 33. *See also* Continuation War; Soviet Union
Kuusinen, Hertta, 175, 239, 240: and "peace crisis," 242; and Stalin, talks with, 165, 166
Kuusinen, O. W., 112
Kymi, airfield at, 63. *See also* Armistice agreement

Ladoga, Lake, 211. *See also* Border question
Lagus, Major General, involved in Lapland War, 51, 52
Lapland: and border question, 212, 216, 218; German troop disarmament in, 18-23 *passim*, 33, 34; war in, 37-54, 64-65
League of Nations, 199
Leahy, William, 90, 191
Ledward, British chargé d'affaires, 268, 273
Leino, Yrjö, 75, 128, 173, 175, 215, 219-20: and Kesäranta talks, 230, 231; and Paris Peace Conference (*1946*), 231, 236, 240, 241
Lend-lease plan, 92. *See also* United States

Leskinen, Väinö, 272
Liberal party (of Finland), 20
Liberated Europe, Declaration on, 88, 89, 95, 96, 128
Lie, Trygve, 75, 76, 125, 248
Linkomies, Edwin, 17: war guilt trial of, 174, 178, 179, 181
"List of 61," 64, 103, 241. *See also* War guilt issue
Litvinov, M. M., 25, 58
"Long cable," 193-94
Lotta Svärd. *See* Women's Auxiliary Corps
Lublin government, 88, 89, 93. *See also* Poland
Lupu, Nicolae, 158
Luukka, Emil, 128
Lyngen Line, 49-50, 53. *See also* Germany; Lapland; Soviet Union

MacArthur, Douglas, 151, 154, 156
McNeil, Hector, 222
Magill, J. H., 59, 111, 112, 125-26, 213
Malinovsky, Rodion, 15
Mallet, Victor, 102
Malmberg, Lieutenant General, head of Suojeluskunta, 67-68
Malmi, airfield at, 63, 132. *See also* Armistice agreement
Manchuria, 193
Maniu, Juliu, 158
Mannerheim, Gustaf: and arms dump plan, 183; and coastal defense, 119-20; and demobilization, 66, 68, 115-16, 117; and Germany, breaking of relations with, 16-21 *passim*; "isolation" of, 76, 163-64, 184-87; and Lapland War, 38-53 *passim*; and Military Cooperation, Treaty of with Soviet Union, 117, 118, 123; and Moscow negotiations (*1944*), 33, 34, 35; and parliamentary elections (*1945*), 127-28; resignation of, 187; and war guilt issue, 104, 109, 174, 183-87 *passim*
Marshall, George C., 259, 267
Marshall Plan, 264, 271-72, 285. *See also* Truman Doctrine
Martola, A. E., 57, 60, 72, 73, 75
Matthews, H. Freeman "Doc," 94, 285
Meretskov, K. A., 22, 46, 50, 51, 54
Michael (king of Rumania), 15, 87
Miehikkälä, Prisoners of. *See* "List of 61"
Möller, Oskar, 178, 179
Molotov, V. M., 89, 91: and Foreign Ministers,

Tuomo Polvinen is professor of history at the University of Helsinki and Finland's leading diplomatic historian. He is the author of *Suomi kansainvälisessä politiikassa (Finland in International Politics)*. *Between East and West* is a translation of the latter half of this work.

D. G. Kirby teaches Baltic history in the School of Slavonic Studies at the University of London and is author of *Finland in the Twentieth Century* (Minnesota, 1979).

11 5/95